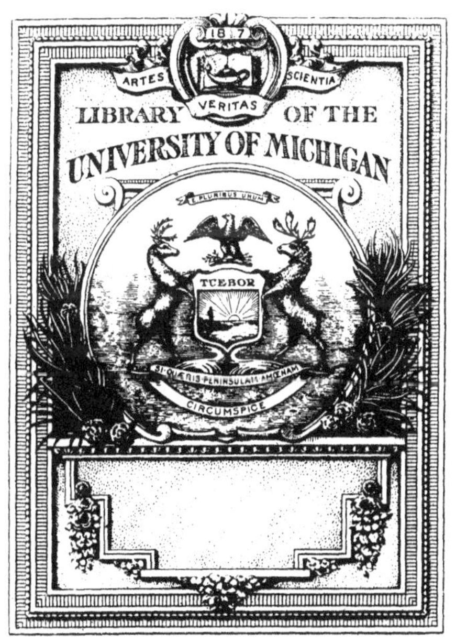
ARTES
VERITAS
SCIENTIA
LIBRARY OF THE
UNIVERSITY OF MICHIGAN
CIRCUMSPICE

I0754350

THE

EARL'S DAUGHTER.

BY

THE AUTHOR OF "AMY HERBERT," "GERTRUDE," "THE CHILD'S FIRST HISTORY OF ROME," ETC.

EDITED BY

THE REV. W. SEWELL, B.D.

FELLOW OF EXETER COLLEGE, OXFORD.

Life, ... is energy of Love,
Divine or human; exercised in pain,
In strife, and tribulation; and ordained,
If so approved and sanctified, to pass,
Through shades and silent rest, to endless joy.
The Excursion.

VOL. I.

LONDON:
LONGMAN, BROWN, GREEN, AND LONGMANS,
PATERNOSTER ROW.
1850.

LONDON:
STEVENS AND CO., PRINTERS, BELL YARD,
TEMPLE BAR.

THE EARL'S DAUGHTER.

CHAPTER I.

THERE was an unusual stir in the old cathedral town of ———. It was neither a market-day, nor the anniversary of a public fête; neither the season of the annual visitation, nor of any public meeting; yet the narrow footways were thronged, and knots of idlers stood inconveniently at the corners of the streets, making their remarks upon the few carriages which enlivened the generally dull town, or noticing with interest the occasional approach of the rows of neatly dressed school children, who, with orderly steps and serious looks, were bending their way to the open square in which stood the great entrance to the cathedral. Gravity, indeed, was the pervading deportment of all the assembling crowd; but a deeper, more reverent, and anxious feeling might be traced upon the features of some, who, fully aware of the difficulties of a Christian life, were about to witness the renewal of those vows by which the ignorant and untried, the weak and the erring, in the midst of a sinful world, and about to enter upon the scene of its temptations, pledge themselves in the sight of an All Holy God, to be His in spirit, in truth, and for ever. It was the day appointed for the Confirmation of all within the diocese of ——- who had attained the age required by the Bishop, and on few occasions had a more careful preparation been made for the due observance of this important rite. The time had gone by when the verbal repetition of the Church Catechism was alone deemed necessary for the candidates. A more zealous spirit had arisen, and many, who had themselves been allowed to renew their baptismal vows without thought or prayer, now, warned by past experience, endeavoured most earnestly to urge upon others the importance of the period which they had reached, and the real meaning of the words, which from childhood, had been familiar to their lips!

The Confirmation of that day was felt to be a most solemn act of self-dedication; and as the knights of old, when preparing to assume the insignia and encounter the perils of their order, were accustomed to fast, and watch and pray, that they might be enabled to struggle and conquer in the unknown dangers before them; so the young aspirants to the full privileges of Christianity were taught to humble themselves by repentance, and prepare their hearts by prayer, that in the hour of temptation they might not be forgetful of their high calling, and fall short of their eternal reward. The spectacle which the cathedral church of St. Mark exhibited when the choir was filled, before the service of the church began, was one of no common interest. The broad light of the sun, as its rays streamed through the stained windows, fell upon fair young faces chastened by holy thoughts, and boyish features subdued into stillness by the pressure of a strange and hitherto unfelt awe. There were countenances which told of fear and wonder, and some, it might be, of indifference; there were eyes bent upon the page in which the vow to be renewed was recorded; and lips moving in silent prayer that strength might be granted for its fulfilment;

whilst, at times, over those youthful faces there passed the shadow of a dark cloud, the cloud of the memory of sin: the vision of cherished offences, of indulged tempers,—vanity and pride, selfishness and irreverence,—the bitter fruits of an evil nature, now a second time to be publicly renounced for ever. Was it to be marvelled at, if in some then present the weakness of humanity for a moment shrank from the warfare imposed upon it, and would fain have returned to the bondage of Egypt, the indulgence of earthly inclination, rather than brave the battle with those stern enemies—the world, the flesh, and the devil—which throng the borders of the land of promise?

But the wish, if it arose, was founded on error. The candidates for Confirmation were no longer free to choose. Once baptized, once admitted into the fellowship of the Catholic Church, and there could be no drawing back. The members of Christ, the children of God, the inheritors of the kingdom of heaven, could never again "be as the heathen." They might despise their privileges, and break their vows; but the privileges had still been granted, and they must be answerable for them; the vows were still upon their heads, and so would also be the punishment for neglect. For them it could never be a question, whether they would accept Christianity: but whether, having accepted, they would renounce it; and even the most indifferent amongst the professed followers of Christ would surely have trembled to risk the woe which must inevitably follow an open, deliberate apostacy.

But although no second promise could in reality increase the binding responsibility of the first, yet the public ratification of a covenant with God must ever be regarded with awe. The baptismal vow was now for the first time fully impressed upon the consciences of many by whom it had scarcely before been remembered, and they trembled as the moment approached when they were to seal it with the consent of their own lips.

The peaceful soothing words of the daily service were said, and when they were ended there stood before the altar of God, the high-born inheritors of honour and wealth, and the gentle children nursed in affluence and retirement, and the humble offspring of poverty, united by one creed, one hope, one danger, and summoned to join in one common act of self-dedication.

Together they listened to the earnest supplication which was to bring down upon them from on high the "sevenfold gifts of grace;" and then side by side they knelt, and each in turn bowed beneath a hand of blessing—the blessing of their spiritual Father in Christ.

Once more they were seated as before, to receive from the Bishop's mouth the words of advice, and warning, and consolation, which were to guide them amidst the temptations of life; and when the final benediction was given, and the full tones of the organ pealed through the long aisles, they parted even as they had met, for the greater part unknowing and unregarding, to many a distant home, never to meet together again in one place till they should stand before the judgment-seat of God, to answer for the fulfilment of the vow which had that hour been registered in heaven.

CHAPTER II.

It was the evening of the same day, a day of unwonted brilliancy and warmth. The sounds of busy life were fading upon the listening ear, the cattle were returning from the pastures, the birds were seeking their nests, the tired workman was slowly wending his way towards his home, and the deep tones of the cathedral clock as it struck the hour of eight fell with a warning voice upon the few who were still engrossed in their round of daily occupation.

The peacefulness of such an hour was felt even amidst the bustle of a crowded town, and the jar of folly and vice; but in the quiet garden of the old grey manor-house of St. Ebbe's there was nothing to disturb the hallowing effect of its influence. The low ivy-covered walls which enclosed it seemed built for the very purpose of excluding all thoughts of the busy world; the long green walks invited to regular exercise and meditation; the neatly-trimmed borders, gay with flowers, spoke of carefulness and simplicity, and appreciation of the loveliness of nature; and the quaint sun-dial, raised upon a circle of rough stone steps in the centre, gave a silent call to the unthinking to note the flight of time, whilst it bade them, in the words of Holy Writ, which were graven upon its pedestal, "watch and pray, that they might not enter into temptation." The building itself, with its weather-stained walls, and mullioned windows and deep porch, accorded perfectly with the quaint style of the garden. It was not large, and boasted few architectural ornaments; but it was the existing symbol of bygone years, and insensibly carried back the mind to times far removed from the present, when if mankind were not wiser and better they were at least less restless, and when the lords of the manor of St. Ebbe's were willing to "dwell amongst their own people," and knew no higher interest in life than that of providing for their welfare. So it was not now; the house, and the garden, and the lands, which once were deemed indissolubly attached, had been divided into separate lots: the manor-house had become a farm-house, the farm-house had been neglected; and, ruined and dilapidated, would have fallen into almost hopeless decay, but for a succession of fortunate events which placed it in the hands of those who were willing to expend some money and much taste in restoring it, though not to its original beauty, yet to a condition in which it might be inhabited with comfort.

The inmates of the manor-house, in its present state, were widely different from its early occupants; and if the first Sir Ralph de Bretonville, whom tradition asserted to have been the founder of the family, could have looked upon the youthful figures standing upon the dial-steps, and watching the gradual fading of the gorgeous sunset, he might have deemed them beings of another race, so little could they have resembled the uncouth train of revellers, huntsmen, and serving men, with whom his own halls must have been filled.

They were two girls, who appeared to have scarcely passed the age of sixteen—unlike in dress, height, and figure; but showing, by an unrestrained ease of manner, that the tie between them, if not of blood, was one of familiar intimacy.

The taller—and, seemingly, the elder—of the two was finely formed, and dignified, almost commanding in manner. Her dark hair was braided, with studied neatness, across a high forehead, and one long ringlet fell on either side upon the well-turned neck, over which a shawl had been hastily thrown to protect her from the evening air. Her complexion was clear, and brilliant with the hues of youth and health; and none, probably, could have turned an indifferent gaze upon the perfect contour of her features;—the deep-set hazel eye—the Grecian nose—the full expressive mouth, which bespoke intellect and energy, and natural elevation of character;—and as she stood, with one hand pointing to the glowing sky, and the other resting upon the dial-plate, whilst the dazzling hues of sunset fell upon her graceful figure, she might have been fitly deemed the representative of the Sibyl, or the Pythoness, exulting in the first enthusiasm of inspiration.

Her companion it will be less easy to pourtray; for Lady Blanche Evelyn was not regularly beautiful. She was slight in figure, and rather below the usual height;—her complexion was naturally pale, though, at that moment, tinged by the faint crimson-flush of interest and agitation;—her eyes, dark and exquisitely soft, were not striking in their brilliancy, like those of her friend. There was less of a marked outline in the contour of her face, even of the long-chiselled nose and peculiarly sweet mouth; and the clustering ringlets of glossy chestnut hair, which shaded her features, gave an air of greater youthfulness to her general appearance. The forehead—high, open, and intellectual—bore, indeed, some resemblance to her companion's, but the expression of the whole countenance was but little affected by it.

It was not intellect which could have been uppermost in the thoughts of any person, looking, for the first time, upon Lady Blanche Evelyn. The sparkle in her eye, the smile upon her lips, the light eager animation of manner, chastened by refinement and simplicity, were the tokens of a heart delighting in the first freshness of life;—remembering the past without regret, and painting visions of the future with innocent enjoyment; and if, for a moment, a transient shade of thought passed over the sunshine of her fair young features, it was the thought, not of foreboding or discontent, but of a mind to which the mysterious realities of the unseen world were presenting themselves with all their overwhelming power.

Graceful, gentle, and childlike as she was, she might have been deemed by many unfitted to cope with the trials of the world; but, whether it were from the natural dignity of one upon whom the honours of a long line of ancestry were destined to descend, or from a strength of character unknown only because untried,—an under current of firmness ran through her words and actions; scarcely indeed perceived, except by minute observation, but then displaying itself even in the intonations of her musical voice, and the increasing earnestness of her gestures, as she pursued her conversation.

"To-morrow," she said, as she threw her arm affectionately around her companion, "to-morrow, Eleanor, by this time I may have seen him, and you may have seen him too; our plans will not seem dreamy then."

"They will to me," was the reply; "till I can see how they may be carried out: and I dread to-morrow, lest it should make me forget to-day."

"Sometimes, it seems impossible to forget," replied Blanche, as she gazed intently upon the golden sky. "Now, it seems so; and then again,—oh! Eleanor, I feel it will be very hard:—when my thoughts are given to earthly things my heart will follow: and yet at this time how can I help it?"

"Then, it cannot be wrong," said Eleanor, soothingly.

"If I could but think so! But, after this morning, no one who had really fixed principles would be as changeable as I am."

"No one thinks you changeable, except yourself," answered Eleanor.

"I know myself better than others know me, then," said Blanche. "Even, after all I have promised—all those prayers, and the charge, and all my resolutions, I cannot keep my mind fixed as I ought. I have such dreams of home, and of papa; and when I shut myself up this afternoon, and tried to do what Mr. Howard advised, I was wandering to things gone by,—all that has happened since we have been here. I wonder whether others have the same difficulties."

Eleanor thought for a few moments, and then said, rather abruptly, "Did you notice that sickly girl who sat to the right of us, at the head of the charity-school?"

"Yes," exclaimed Blanche; "her eyes never seemed to move except when the chanting began, and then she looked up amongst the arches of the cathedral with such intense awe. I was vexed with myself for thinking about her, and yet it did me good."

"She was blind," continued Eleanor; "one of her companions led her up to the altar as we left it. Mr. Howard says she comes from Rutherford; and I mean to ask papa if he knows her."

"I think I could bear to be blind," observed Blanche, "if I could only feel, as I am sure she did. But the world is so beautiful, and it is so pleasant to live and to be loved!"

"Yes," said Eleanor; "for you, especially, who have everything else that the world can give."

"Why should I have so much?" exclaimed Blanche. "It is very strange; and when I looked at that poor girl it frightened me. And yet, Eleanor," she continued, and a shade, almost of sadness, passed over her face, "it may all be marred. I shall be like a stranger in my home, and papa may have lost his English tastes, and be vexed that I am not what he pictured."

"You are fanciful," replied Eleanor, with an air of authority; "you should remember what Mrs. Howard says about not creating evils."

"But he will be my all," said Blanche, humbly; "If his love fails me, what shall I have to look to?" Eleanor's countenance expressed surprise, and Blanche instantly corrected herself; "on earth, I mean," she said; "but that is an instance of what I mentioned just now about forgetting. I know that I ought to be calm and trusting, thinking of to-day instead of to-morrow. Do you remember the Bishop's saying it was part of our duty?"

"Yes," replied Eleanor; "I was looking at the blind girl at the instant, and her face brightened when she heard it, as little Clara's does when she first gains a new idea."

Blanche was silent for several minutes. "I must not think," she exclaimed, at length; "the time is coming so near. When the sun goes down again, I may be watching it from the terrace at Rutherford."

"And I from the rectory," said Eleanor. "We shall be separated then."

The words sounded reproachfully; and Blanche eagerly exclaimed, "Only for a few hours; our homes will be almost the same. You do not think, Eleanor, that I could be happy if it were not so."

"Not now. But, Blanche, the path of your life

will lead you away from me into the world, and, amongst gay friends; you will have many other ties."

"But *the* one," said Blanche; "where can I find that? The blessing which was given us to-day together will never be repeated again;—ours can never be a common love."

Eleanor grew very thoughtful. "Promise to love me always," she said. "Doubt comes over me sadly at times."

Blanche did not promise; but she looked at Eleanor with wonder, as if not comprehending the meaning of her words, and before she could reply, some one was heard to repeat her name; and a little girl, about ten years of age, ran up to them, exclaiming, "You must come directly,—this moment; you must not wait a minute: Mrs. Howard wants you in her room. Pray, Eleanor, don't keep her."

"Is it for me? Did Mrs. Howard send for me, Clara?" and the colour faded from Blanche's cheek.

"Yes, Mrs. Howard; and"—the child stopped, put her finger upon her lip, and smiled archly.

"Who? What? Who is here?" asked Eleanor.

"Never mind; don't ask questions. Mrs. Howard told me I was to make haste."

Lady Blanche said nothing; she leant against the sun-dial, and every limb trembled.

"You are ill, dearest," said Eleanor, affectionately; "and this suspense is dreadful for you. Clara, you must tell us—Is Lord Rutherford arrived?"

Clara was delighted at her own power, and turning away, exclaimed, "For once Eleanor Wentworth cannot have her will."

"But Blanche Evelyn can;" and Blanche drew the little girl towards her, and said in a faint voice, "If you love me, Clara—"

The appeal was successful. Clara's arm was put within hers; and, looking up in Blanche's face to watch the effect of her information, she whispered, "I have not seen him; but Mary and Agnes have."

Blanche scarcely waited to hear the last word, before she had flown towards the house; but as she reached the porch she stopped—her courage had failed.

Eleanor was at her side immediately. "He must love you—dote upon you, Blanche; and his letters—you do him injustice by being afraid."

Blanche put her hand before her eyes; and holier thoughts came to her aid. One Father, she had, who knew the weakness of His child, and could strengthen her as well against the infirmity of nature, as against the temptations of sin. She placed her icy fingers within Eleanor's, and clasped them with the energy of nervous resolution; and then, with a firm step, turned away to seek for the first time, since she had been conscious of existence, the presence of her father.

CHAPTER III.

The Earl of Rutherford was a man, the ruling principle of whose character was generally supposed to be easily discovered from his expressive countenance: conscious nobility, a love of command, an impetuous temper, and a powerful intellect, were plainly inscribed upon it. He was born to honour, accustomed from infancy to rule, and the world had decided that pride was the governing motive of his actions. So at least it was said, when, fifteen years before, he had suddenly left his ancestral home, upon the death of a wife, whom, if he had not loved, he had at least treated with the outward marks of respect; and confiding his infant daughter to the care of a lady, the personal friend of the countess, left England with the avowed determination of remaining abroad for some years. The step, strange though it appeared, was declared not incompatible with his character. The grief preying upon his heart was said to be less the death of his wife, than the failure of a male heir; and the Lady Blanche Evelyn, although born to inherit both the title and its annexed estates, was considered to be an object of compassion rather than of love to her haughty father, from the feeling that it was impossible for a woman fitly to support the dignity of the family, and the dread lest the event of her marriage with some yet more distinguished individual should sink his own noble house into comparative insignificance. All this the world said. The Earl of Rutherford was pitied, but censured; his sorrow it was imagined would be transitory, and his journey was considered merely the impulse of a hasty moment. That he would return again, it might be with a foreign bride, or at least to seek another in England, was considered a matter of certainty; and yet, year after year went by, and the Castle of Rutherford was still left unoccupied. Political engagements it was known were in a great measure the cause of the earl's absence, but they would not account for an exile of such length; and the rumours which were at first circulated regarding a second marriage at length ceased. Tidings of him were heard—sometimes at Rome, sometimes at Vienna, once at Constantinople; but all gave the same impression. If Lord Rutherford had been considered proud at home, he was thought to be yet more so in the careless ease of continental society. The noblest and fairest ornaments of European courts passed before him, but all were alike unnoticed; and, at the expiration of fifteen years, he was returning to his native land, with the same impenetrable manner, the same cold reserve of tone, for which he had been remarkable on leaving it. And in the mean time his child grew up in retirement, under the care of a lady every way calculated for such a charge. Mrs. Howard was a widow, who, at the age of thirty, found herself suddenly reduced from a situation of affluence and happiness, as the wife of a beneficed clergyman, to one of almost hopeless poverty. The death of her husband, which had been so sudden as to prevent him from making any satisfactory arrangement of his property, joined with other circumstances perfectly unforeseen, had combined to produce this great misfortune; and, but for the long-tried friendship of the Countess of Rutherford, Mrs. Howard's prospects would indeed have been dark. Through her exertions, however, the manor-house of St. Ebbe's was purchased, and fitted up so as to accommodate Mrs. Howard and the few pupils whose education she was able to undertake; and when, in the prospect of approaching death, the countess gazed in sadness upon her child, her chief earthly consolation was derived from the hope that the earl would consent to place the infant Lady Blanche under the care of the only person in whose affection and principle she was able implicitly to confide. Lord Rutherford was not present to receive the dying injunction of his wife, but her wishes were received with an attention nearly amounting to superstition. Lady Blanche was removed to St. Ebbe's, and the sole charge of her education trusted to Mrs. Howard, with but one stipulation—that she should have no companion. For a few years this agreement was easily kept. During the child's infancy she was perfectly satisfied with Mrs. Howard as her nurse, instructress, and playfellow; but new wants were discovered with increasing years, and Mrs. Howard, believing that such a solitary education might operate unfavourably upon her character, at length prevailed upon the earl to allow her to receive into her family Eleanor Wentworth, the daughter of the rector of Rutherford. Blanche was at this time about seven years of age, and fully able to appreciate the charms of companionship. Eleanor was clever, generous, and affectionate; and the progress made by both the children from the period of their being placed together convinced Mrs. Howard that she had judged wisely in the advice which she had given: and when, in the course of events, the care of three little orphan nieces devolved upon her, she had no difficulty in persuading Lord Rutherford to allow them also to share her attention at St. Ebbe's.

The charm of society was felt chiefly by Blanche. Eleanor returned to her home at stated times, and mixed with other friends, and enjoyed the novelty of other scenes; but to Blanche the occupations of the manor house, the interest of the village of St. Ebbe's, and the dull liveliness of the old cathedral town, were the only excitements of life. Even the Castle of Rutherford, her destined home, was but like a beautiful dream, associated with visions of the mother who had been described as the most lovely and perfect of earthly beings, and the father, whose supposed virtues and talents formed the great romance of her childhood.

And the Earl of Rutherford, if judged by his letters, was indeed formed to excite admiration, if not respect. They were the letters of a refined, highly cultivated, affectionate mind;—keenly alive to the charms of grace and luxury, yet mourning over the unreality of all earthly enjoyments;—joining in the pursuits of the world, yet sighing for the sympathy of the few who were alone deemed worthy of friendship; and seeing too deeply into life to be satisfied with aught that earth could give. One thing alone seemed to give him real pleasure, the hope of returning to England and devoting himself to his child;—and yet year after year went by, and still he lingered in a foreign land. Blanche learnt by degrees to attach but little meaning to his expressions of dissatisfaction with continental habits, and of desire to revisit his own country. He might be—no doubt he was—sincere; but the circumstances or the feelings which detained him abroad appeared as binding as ever; and a shade of discontent was just beginning to dim the brightness of her hitherto happy life, when the intelligence that her father was actually on his way to England, and would probably arrive in the course of a few weeks, brought back all her early enthusiasm and delight. Yet the satisfaction, after the first moment, was by no means unalloyed. Her own departure from St. Ebbe's would be the inevitable consequence of the earl's return, and with this was involved separation from the friend who had supplied a mother's place, and claimed all but a mother's affection; and as Blanche recalled the fondness which had been lavished upon her from infancy, she wept in bitterness of heart for the ingratitude which could for an instant rejoice in such a prospect.

As regarded Eleanor, the case would be very different. She was to return to her parents at the same time, and the near vicinity of the rectory and the castle formed, at least in the simple mind of Lady Blanche, a reason for believing that the change of life would be merely nominal;—that they would share the same interests, and partake of the same pleasures, and be to each other, what they had hitherto called themselves,—sisters in affection, if not in relationship.

She could not contemplate the possibility of change,—and the fears which Eleanor sometimes expressed, were to her merely the fancies of an excitable, over-anxious mind.

But, as the season approached for the earl's arrival, the struggle in the mind of Blanche between hope and regret—the future and the past—became mixed with other thoughts, which served to calm her spirits by diverting her feelings into a different channel. The period of her Confirmation had been unavoidably fixed for the time when Lord Rutherford was expected;—and though Mrs. Howard would at first willingly have either hastened or deferred it, so as to give a more favourable opportunity for due preparation, she soon saw reason to be thankful that events had been so ordered as to leave no possibility of choice. The gay, gentle, confiding spirit of Lady Blanche, open to every impression, and apparently incapable of the possibility of concealment, yet retained within it a depth of reflection and principle which Mrs. Howard had never penetrated. Unknown to herself, Blanche was timid, and reserved. She could speak openly upon all ordinary subjects,—confess her faults, and laugh at her mistakes, and lament her ignorance, till even a very keen observer of human nature—and such Mrs. Howard was—might imagine that she had told all that was in her mind. But there were occasions when the deepening colour of her cheek, or the hesitation of her voice, gave indications that in the hidden world within there lay feelings far loftier and purer than any which she ventured to express. Her words were the words of a humble, candid, light-hearted, simple child; but her thoughts—who may tell the earnestness, and reverence, and trustfulness, with which the young heart devotes itself to its Maker before the evil influence of the world has chilled the warmth of its early affections? What Lady Blanche really was, Mrs. Howard never knew, till in the intimacy of serious intercourse which preceded her Confirmation, the anguish of repentance for youthful sins overcame her natural reserve; and hopes, and fears, and doubts, and the bitter conflict of the soul, which all—even the most outwardly innocent—must endure, in the work of bringing back the heart to God, were confessed without a thought of concealment. From that moment the tie between them was one which earth has no power to break.

To Blanche this newly-acquired sympathy was an unspeakable blessing; it soothed her in the moments of self-reproach, when the delight of her father's anticipated return distracted her thoughts from the solemn subject of her approaching Confirmation; and enabled her to view clearly the life which was opening before her, and to arrange definite plans for her future conduct, instead of doubling and vacillating in the desire of doing everything, and the dread of succeeding in nothing. If Mrs. Howard had been dear to her before, as her truest and wisest friend, her mother's chosen representative, much more was she dear now ; and, even when trembling before the door which was to admit her into her father's presence, a sudden pang of sorrow shot through her heart as she caught the tones of Mrs. Howard's voice, and thought how soon she might listen for them in vain. Mrs. Howard herself opened the door as Blanche placed her hand upon the lock. She did not speak ; but her silent kiss told more than the most eloquent words ; and, as she walked slowly away, Blanche allowed herself to hesitate no longer, and entered the room. The earl was standing by the window—his eye fixed upon the travelling-carriage which had brought him that evening from London ; but his thoughts wandering to years, now so long passed away, that they seemed but as indistinct, yet painful, visions. He was recalling the day when, in the company of his wife, he had paid his first visit to St. Ebbe's ; and the associations awakened by the remembrance were so absorbing, that the sound of his daughter's footsteps was unheeded. Blanche remained irresolute—afraid to intrude herself upon him, yet faint from the effort to restrain her agitation. A few moments elapsed, but to her they seemed like hours ; and then the carriage drove off, and the earl, heaving a deep sigh, turned suddenly round, and became aware that he was not alone.

It was a strange meeting ! He did not move or smile ; but the colour forsook his cheeks, and his lips quivered ; and as Blanche drew near, he gazed upon her steadfastly, and sinking into a chair, the name of his wife escaped his lips. Blanche stood before him motionless. The earl's head was averted as if he dreaded to look again ; but, when at length the simple word, "Papa," fell upon his ear, he started, passed his hand across his forehead like one awakening from a dream, and, clasping his child to his heart, he blessed her fervently, and poured forth the fulness of his contentment; and, at that moment, the fondest hope of affection which Blanche had ever ventured to indulge appeared about to be fully realized.

"My visit, to-night, must be but short, my child," said the earl, when the excitement of feeling had in a measure subsided, and Blanche ventured to inquire how long he could stay with her. "I have business in the town, and must leave you almost immediately; but to-morrow we will start early, and reach Rutherford in time for you to see it in its beauty."

"And for the first time," said Blanche: "it seemed hard, papa, never to have been allowed to go there before; but I am glad of it now. I would much rather see it first with you."

The earl smiled.

"And with Miss Wentworth? We are to take her with us, I believe."

"Will you really?" and Blanche's eye sparkled with delight. "We hoped it might be so; but Dr. Wentworth was afraid you might not like it."

"Shall you like it?—that is the question, Blanche."

Lord Rutherford spoke shortly, and Blanche was a little awed.

"I shall like everything that you like, dear papa," she said; "and Eleanor and I have not set our hearts upon it."

"But you would prefer it, my love; only say so, and it shall be."

Blanche had penetration enough to see that her father really wished her to choose; and, as she warmly expressed her pleasure at the proposal, the earl's gentleness of manner returned.

"My engagement is pressing," he said, as he rose

to depart, whilst Blanche hung upon his arm, "and a night's rest will be desirable for us both; but we will meet at eight to-morrow, if, as Mrs. Howard assures me, you are quite prepared for such a sudden move."

The mention of Mrs. Howard brought back Blanche's sad thoughts.

"You will let her come and see me sometimes, dear papa, won't you?" she said, timidly.

"Let her come!" replied the earl; "rather, ask her if she will be kind enough to take the trouble: she may not think as little of a long journey as you do."

Blanche looked grave; for she could not bear, even in jest, the idea of any obstacle to a continued intercourse with her best friend. The earl no sooner perceived it, than he began to assure her that if the distance were ten times as great, it should not interfere. She need not have a thought upon the subject; and if Blanche had not herself stopped him, he would have insisted upon seeing Mrs. Howard again at once, and inducing her to name a certain time for a visit to Rutherford.

Blanche scarcely understood this instantaneous attention to her wishes. Mrs. Howard's object had been to guard her against the peculiar dangers of her position in life, by accustoming her to yield her own will even on the most trifling occasions. She often saw others preferred before her, and her natural disposition led her to obey rather than to command; and this, added to the influence of Eleanor Wentworth's apparent decision of character, made her insensible to her own powers. Perhaps too much so; Mrs. Howard at least began to fear lest, in fostering gentleness and consideration, she had kept her too much in ignorance of the influence which her rank and fortune would naturally give her; and lest the sudden consciousness of superiority might prove more injurious to her character than if she had been accustomed to it from childhood. But it was too late to remedy the mistake. Blanche was about to enter upon the world, unknowing of its snares, and guarded only by the simple piety of a humble spirit, which has learned to distrust itself, and to lean only upon God. As she was then, there was nothing to fear; but how long her simplicity would remain untainted, her heart uncorrupted by the flattering homage which awaited her, was a question which only the most unhesitating faith could have borne to ask.

CHAPTER IV.

Mrs. Howard sat in her dressing-room that evening long after her usual hour of rest. She was too anxious, her mind was too preoccupied, to hope for sleep. She could only think over the past, and pray for the future; whilst she dwelt upon the dispositions of her two young charges, and the trials to which they might be exposed in their journey through life.

It would have been difficult to tell which excited the greater interest; perhaps the one for whom she feared the most seemed then the nearer to her heart; yet Eleanor Wentworth's character was, in itself, much more open to temptation than that of Lady Blanche. Nothing but the certainty that, at the rectory of Rutherford, Eleanor would be as carefully guarded from evil as at the manor-house of St. Ebbe's, would have relieved the load of apprehension which pressed upon Mrs. Howard's spirits as she thought upon the fickleness of purpose, the pride and jealousy, the hasty, though generous temper, which were continually marring the influence of her talents and high principles.

But Eleanor was not, like Blanche, to return to a home where she would be the cherished idol of every heart. She would be loved, indeed, deeply and tenderly; but it would be with a Christian love, which would watch over her faults, and tell her truth without reserve. She would have quiet occupations; duties to her parents and her sister; duties in her father's parish; amusements in her garden and her books; and society in the castle and its neighbourhood.

Mrs. Howard almost smiled at the feeling of dread which she had allowed to disturb her, as she owned to herself that Eleanor's situation in life seemed peculiarly free from temptation; whilst, again, she sadly reverted to Blanche—noble, beautiful, and rich, but deprived of a mother's care, and with no one to be her daily guide and counsellor, but the father, whom there was reason to fear might be little fitted for such an office.

The position was undoubtedly one of peril, and self-accusations mingled with Mrs. Howard's forebodings. Memory went back to the hour when, as an innocent, unconscious infant, the child of her early friend had been committed to her care; when, after the lapse of but a few weeks from the death of the Countess of Rutherford, the earl had placed his daughter in her arms, and bade her love and guard her for her mother's sake. To love her was indeed easy; but to guard, to teach, to educate her—how had the task been performed? It was a sad array of errors and neglects, which conscience brought before the mind of one whom the world rightly judged to have discharged her duty faithfully and unshrinkingly; so much seemed to have been left unsaid, undone; so much higher an example might have been set; so many warnings and instructions given. As the painful reflections crowded upon her mind, a gentle tap at the door was heard, and Blanche entered the room. She was looking pale and ill, and her eyes were dimmed with tears; and Mrs. Howard, startled at her sudden appearance, inquired, in alarm, the cause. Blanche tried to smile, whilst she assured her that it was merely a whim—a freak;—she was restless, and could not sleep, and the light was shining underneath the dressing-room door; and—but her voice failed her, and hiding her face upon Mrs. Howard's neck, she said, "To-morrow!— I cannot leave you."

"It will not be leaving me, my dearest child," replied Mrs. Howard. "We shall still be one in affection, and your father promises that we shall meet frequently."

"But that will not make things as they have been," replied Blanche. "I shall only have you for a short time, and I shall want you every hour in the day."

"Perhaps that is the very reason why it is good for me not to be with you," said Mrs. Howard; "we must not depend too much upon our fellow-creatures, however we may love them."

"If I were not so ignorant," said Blanche, "and if I knew what sort of life I was going to lead, it would not seem so bad; but seeing papa has upset all my ideas. I don't mean that he is different exactly in appearance from what I thought, but his manner is. He put me forward when I talked to him, and seemed to make me settle things; and I would much rather he would not."

"You will be used to that in time, my love," replied Mrs. Howard, smiling; "and you must recollect you are no longer a child."

"No, indeed," exclaimed Blanche, "after to-day I could not be; but that, again, makes me unhappy. How shall I know what is right or wrong in trifles? I cannot ask papa;—at least I think I cannot;—and I may decide badly, and do what I ought not; and perhaps all my resolutions may fail. You know it is so sometimes, when people have felt a great deal more than I have."

"You can apply to me always," replied Mrs. Howard, "in cases in which you really have no one else to consult; but it is not advice which can keep you right."

D

"No," said Blanche; "but if—if I should grow careless, and not pray properly—"

"Fear for yourself, my love," replied Mrs. Howard, "and then no other friend need fear for you; but if you can attend carefully to the few rules I gave you the other day, I think you will find your duties less difficult than you imagine."

"I always now have some time to myself in the middle of the day," said Blanche; "but here I can do as I choose."

"And you will do as you choose at home, my dear," replied Mrs. Howard. "I have no doubt of it. The best thing, however, to say to yourself, is: not that you will, if you can, but that you *must;*—that everything must, to a certain degree, give way to it; that if you cannot be alone at one hour, you will be at another. We require not long prayers but frequent ones, to keep up our watchfulness."

"And then self-examination," said Blanche; "it is so difficult."

"Yes, most difficult; and the only way to make it easy is to practise it frequently; to carry it on from one part of the day to another, at the times we fix for our private devotions."

"The difficulty to me," said Blanche, "is, that all this makes one think so constantly of oneself!"

"So it may, at first; but the mind must be educated like the body. How is it, for instance, that you are able to walk without stumbling? If you are in a dangerous road, you observe where you are going; but, generally speaking, you are kept in safety, not by thinking of yourself, but of the objects around you."

"That is what I want to do with my mind," said Blanche.

"And it will come by-and-by, my love; but you must be contented to walk carefully in the dangerous road first; and, after a time, you will find yourself instinctively shrinking from evil, and able to pursue the right path—not so much by watching yourself as by keeping your heart fixed upon God."

"It will be very long before that time comes," said Blanche.

"Yes, because it is the perfection of a Christian life; but we must be patient. In your case, I confess it is likely to be particularly difficult, because you will have so many temptations."

"Not more than others, I suppose," said Blanche; "and yet it seems that I shall never be as good as some whom I have read of."

"But I am afraid you will have many more temptations than people in general," continued Mrs. Howard; "and I should be happier if I felt that you ununderstood this. God has given you rank and wealth, and no one in your home to share the attention which will be paid you; and your papa is very likely to be over-indulgent and blind to your faults."

Blanche leant her head upon the mantelpiece, and in a low voice said, "You will pray for me."

"Pray for you daily and hourly," replied Mrs. Howard, earnestly. "God only knows how precious you are to me. Perhaps I am over-anxious; but luxury and flattery are very insidious."

"I need not indulge myself in luxuries, even if I possess them," said Blanche.

"No; though I am afraid the temptation will be greater than you are aware of. If your mind is corrupted, dearest Blanche, the commencement will almost inevitably be self-indulgence in trifles."

"I don't think I quite know what you would call trifles," said Blanche.

"Such as a little indolence in rising," replied Mrs. Howard; "a little waste of time in light reading; a slight carelessness in conversation, saying things which are not strictly right for the sake of amusement; or spending money thoughtlessly; or even consulting your own ease by making yourself too comfortable, and so rendering yourself indisposed to exertion for other people. All these things are considered allowable by the world: you may do them, and no one will notice them; and your conscience may, perhaps, scarcely reproach you for them; but they are the beginnings of evil—the first steps towards that love of self-gratification which is the peculiar snare of the rich."

"I like ease and comfort now," said Blanche.

"I think you do, my love," replied Mrs. Howard; "and I am not saying that the liking them is wrong, but dangerous; and against the danger I know only one safeguard, as far as our own endeavours are concerned. There are times, you know, when we are bound to deny ourselves the use even of lawful pleasures;—one day at least in every week we should do so. If we check our inclinations then, we may hope they will not gain the mastery over us at other times."

"I shall not know what to do when I am at home," said Blanche.

"And I cannot tell you exactly," replied Mrs. Howard; "because, of course, you must be governed in a great degree by the habits of your father's house. Only when we have determined to do something, half our difficulty is over. A sincere will must soon find out the way, without being singular or acting in any way to attract notice."

"But I wish so much—so very, very much—that I could have some rules," said Blanche.

Mrs. Howard half-smiled as she kissed her, and said,—"And I wish so very much that I could give them, because I know it would make you happier; but I can only repeat in a general way what I have said to you before; little details must be left to yourself: it is impossible to shake off the burden of responsibility, Blanche, though I know you would willingly do it if you could."

"But if I make my rules and keep to them," said Blanche, "still I may attend to them only as a matter of form, and then they will be of no use."

Mrs. Howard was silent for a few moments; the most earnest-minded often feel bitterly the contrast between the advice which they give to others, and the practice which they are conscious of in themselves.

"It is very hard," she said, at length, "to feel, even in a remote degree, as we ought; but, dearest Blanche, if you follow the plan you have had marked out for these days;—begin them, for instance, earlier than usual, if possible, and give up your first thoughts to self-examination and meditation upon those chapters in the Gospels which describe our Lord's sufferings; using special solemn confessions, and also arranging your prayers for the rest of the day, with a particular view to these subjects of meditation;—I think you will scarcely fail to have some deeper gratitude—some more sincere penitence; you will at least feel that the day is not like other days."

"I will try," said Blanche; but she sighed as if distrusting herself.

"And you must hope, too," continued Mrs. Howard; "hope is a great instrument of good with us all. The work of a Christian is the work of a whole life, and we must not despair because we are not perfect at once; especially when we have such aid promised and given. In a very short time, my love, you will, I trust, be fully admitted into the communion of the Church."

Blanche looked distressed, and for a few moments did not attempt to speak: at last she said, "I thought you would have been with me."

"And I thought so too, and hoped more earnestly than I can say; but it has been otherwise ordered, and it may—it must be better for us both. Yet we cannot really be separated; my prayers and my heart will follow you, and we shall surely be united in one spirit as members of the body of Christ—more closely even than at this moment."

Again, there was a pause; the struggle of over-excited feelings overcame Blanche's efforts to restrain them, and bursting into tears, she exclaimed, "I am not worthy."

"No," replied Mrs. Howard, and she placed her hand fondly on Blanche's head, "you are not worthy; no one can be, not even an angel from heaven. But if the blessing is greater than words can tell, so also is the love. Blanche, it is a Father's voice which calls you; perhaps now, for the first time, you can understand what a father's affection must mean." The allusion had the effect which Mrs. Howard desired.

Blanche raised her head, and a smile gleamed through her tears as she said, "I will try to think of it, and not be afraid."

"And you will be assisted and accepted, dearest; you must not doubt it. There is much that I could say to you even now upon the subject, though we have so often talked of it before; but I do not think you will allow anything to interfere with such a duty. I do not think you will ever make false excuses, or turn away with coldness, whatever examples may be set you. In time," and Mrs. Howard's voice involuntarily became more subdued in its earnestness, "you will cease to look upon it as a *duty*—it will be your *all* in religion."

"Papa will be with me to help me, and teach me," said Blanche; "that is one great comfort."

Mrs. Howard sighed, and made no direct answer; but, rising from her seat, unlocked a cabinet, and taking from it a locket attached to a hair chain, she hung it round Blanche's neck, saying, "Will you wear it, not only in remembrance of me, but of the day on which it was given you? The date has been engraved on it, that when you look at it you may be reminded of the vow by which you have bound yourself.—And now, dear child, we must part."

Mrs. Howard's usually calm voice became low and tremulous. Blanche held the locket in her hand, and gazed on it long and tearfully; and then, placing it within the folds of her dress, she once more received Mrs. Howard's fervent blessing, and glided silently from the room.

CHAPTER V.

THE sun was still high in the horizon, when on the following day a travelling carriage was seen standing at the bottom of the steep ascent on the summit of which was built the old baronial castle of Rutherford. There was apparently some discussion as to its movements, for a servant was engaged in carrying messages from his master to the postilions, and the eager tones of a young girl's voice were heard endeavouring to win some compliance with her wishes contrary to the will of her companions.

"It will be a pleasure to me to walk, I assure you," she said; "the distance is but a few hundred yards, and really I deserve some trouble for having been so foolish as not to watch which way the carriage turned. It will make a considerable difference now to go by the road."

Lord Rutherford listened politely, and quietly remarking that Miss Wentworth was under his protection, and that he could on no account leave her till he had seen her safely under her father's care, sent an angry reproof to the postilions for their stupidity, and ordered them to drive round to the rectory. Eleanor looked annoyed, and Blanche raised her eyes to her father's face, to see if it would do to interfere; but there was an expression in it which was not encouraging. The cheerful smile which had brightened it during the first part of their journey was gone, and, leaning out of the window, he kept his eyes riveted upon the old grey walls appearing in the distance above the trees.

"My father!" exclaimed Eleanor, as the carriage turned.

Lord Rutherford withdrew his head, and sank back upon his seat. His mouth grew more stern, his brow was more gloomy than before; yet it might have been only from the effort to repress some rising agitation, for, as Dr. Wentworth approached, a smile of recognition again lighted up his features, and with a cordial voice, and a warm pressure of the hand, he returned a greeting which might have been termed affectionate.

"I have much to thank you for," he said; "but you shall not be detained now: we have a fellow-feeling for our children."

Dr. Wentworth's mild but strikingly sensible countenance betrayed some painful thoughts, even as he assisted his daughter to alight, and welcomed her eagerly; but they were momentary only, and again drawing near the carriage, he said, "Lady Blanche is almost a stranger; we have not met I think for two years."

Blanche bent forward and gave him her hand. Lord Rutherford was evidently interested in watching the meeting, yet he looked annoyed rather than pleased with Dr. Wentworth's kind expressions of satisfaction.

"I am not parting from Eleanor," said Blanche, in answer to Dr. Wentworth's regret that his daughter's return home should be necessarily alloyed by a separation from her friend. "I wish you would not talk of it: we shall meet, as we have done, every day."

Dr. Wentworth smiled doubtfully.

"To-morrow Eleanor will be with me the first moment she can be spared," continued Blanche, gaily; "and if that should not be early, I must be with her, and then we will arrange for the future."

There was a silent assent, and Eleanor, who had been standing apart, went round to the other side of the carriage to say good-b'ye.

"It is good-b'ye, really,—for long, for ever in some ways, Blanche," she whispered.

Blanche was distressed.

"Eleanor, it is cruel to say so; but time will show."

"Yes, time will show;" and, trying to appear indifferent, Eleanor once more said, "good-b'ye," and, putting her arm within her father's, turned away.

Blanche watched them, as they stayed to give some directions to a man who was to follow with the luggage; and, when at last they were lost to her sight, felt as if Eleanor's words were prophetic.

But the painful foreboding was soon forgotten. The earl's voice recalled her to happiness; for, delighted at being freed from all restraint, he now gave free vent to his affection, and pointing to the range of richly-wooded hills, the green meadows, and neat clustering cottages, he told her that all she could see was her own; that earth for him had but one treasure; and that, whilst she was spared to him, nothing would add to his enjoyment, except by ministering to hers.

"Now," he said, when the winding road brought them full in front of the castle, "look, once more; there is no view of it like this."

Blanche looked, and her heart throbbed within her as she realized for the first time the grandeur of her future home. Rutherford Castle stood upon a high promontory, which rose almost perpendicularly from the banks of a deep-flowing stream. The most ancient part of what had once been a fortress of considerable strength was built upon the solid rock, and the huge blocks of masonry could scarcely be distinguished from the impregnable walls of nature's formation: but the advance of civilization had induced the Lords of Rutherford, from time to time, to add to the original stronghold, at first a lower tower and massive wings, then gateways, and turrets, and quadrangles, till the castle, stretching over the crest of the hill, formed a pile of building which, although irregular in outline, was still as a whole singularly imposing. Immediately in front of the castle was a broad space of smooth turf, and from this the ground to the left fell in a bank thickly planted with trees, which, as it neared the river, was broken by grey moss-grown rocks. But the most striking points of scenery were not discoverable from below; and when Blanche clasped her hands in ecstasy, and declared that she had never imagined any thing half so beautiful, the earl smiled contentedly, and, bidding the postilions hasten, he sat in silence listening to her exclamations, as every step in advance brought them some fresh object of beauty.

The high battlemented gateway was passed, and the carriage entered the park; and, after a drive of about half a mile, slowly ascended the hill. As they approached nearer and nearer to the castle, Lord Rutherford roused himself from his leaning posture, and, gazing from the window, seemed endeavouring to recall the long-past scenes which were associated with nearly every object that met his eye. Blanche, with an instinctive delicacy of sympathy, did not attempt to interrupt him: her pleasure was no longer openly expressed, and it was not till the carriage stopped before the heavy portal, and a glorious landscape, with a foreground of rock and river, and a distance of far-spreading woods and pastures, and fields ripening with the golden corn, was disclosed before her, that she exclaimed, "Papa, it does not seem like earth!"

At the sound of her sweet voice, the earl awoke

from his reverie. "It shall be paradise to you," he said "if mortal power can make it so;" and, alighting from the carriage, he hurried her forward into the hall.

The servants were assembled to receive them; and the earl presented Lady Blanche to them as their mistress. "Your mistress now," he said emphatically, "as much as she must be in years to come;" and as he spoke many eyes of admiration and respect were turned to the gentle girl, who so gracefully and meekly returned the reverential salutations of her dependants.

Lord Rutherford's impatience scarcely waited till the necessary introduction was over. Proudly and firmly he passed on through the splendid apartments; yet, if Blanche had watched his countenance, she might have seen that all was not equally firm within. It was but the outline of a marble bust which caught his attention, but he quickened his steps, and compressed his lips, whilst he turned to see whether the bright fair features of his child did indeed resemble the cold but matchless beauty which the hand of art had so exquisitely sculptured.

Blanche followed him, bewildered by the novelty of her situation and the strangeness of all she saw; so different from St. Ebbe's, with its few simple rooms and modern furniture. The dark oaken panellings and grotesque carvings, the rich yet cumbrous cabinets, the heavy gilded cornices, and faded tapestries, were of the fashions of centuries past; and Blanche, though delighted to behold what she had so often in imagination pictured, yet felt something of awe steal over her, as they traversed the empty chambers which for years had been disused; and which, even when the castle was filled with guests, had been considered more as a necessary incumbrance than as at all conducing to its convenience.

Lord Rutherford read what was passing in her mind.

"These are but the vestibules," he said; "the ante-rooms—endurable for appearance, but not habitable. You shall have something different for your own enjoyment;" and, pushing aside some massive folding doors, he led the way into a hall paved with marble, and partly filled with rare plants. "They have attended to my orders well," he observed, as he looked around him with a pleased air; "and here are your rooms, Blanche. Look at them, and tell me what more they require." As he said this, Lord Rutherford entered a small but lofty and very prettily shaped apartment, which though harmonizing with the rest of the castle in its general style, was fitted up with many of the refinements of modern luxury. The choice pictures, the piano and harp, the sofas, couches, work-table, and books; and, especially, the flowers with which the vases on the tables were filled, gave Blanche, in an instant, the idea of forethought, and care, and affection; though, when she tried to express her gratitude, she could find no words to satisfy her feelings.

The earl, however, did not need words; he looked at her for a moment with proud delight, whilst in her grace and beauty she stood in the centre of the room, the fitting mistress of all that wealth and love could bestow; and, after pointing to a small study opening from the outer room, he said, carelessly, "We will see the view from this side now, Blanche; it is different from the other."

Blanche followed him through the hall into the garden; but when she leant over the parapet, which bordered the terrace in front of the window, she started almost with alarm upon discovering the giddy height at which she stood above the deep river that flowed round the castle.

To the right, the walls of the keep shut out the view over the distant country; but immediately before her the ground sank almost perpendicularly, and far, far below gleamed the clear waters of the rapid stream, as it forced its way between the rocky foundations of the castle and the lofty wooded hill which formed its opposite bank. For about the space of a quarter of a mile it was inclosed in a narrow ravine; but a sharp projecting point of land then opposing its further progress, its course was suddenly diverted in a different direction; and the eye, no longer able to follow its windings, turned rather to the long vista of hills, locked into each other, and capped by the rugged outline of a mountain-peak, which formed the termination of the valley.

The scene was striking even to the earl, accustomed though he was to the varied beauties of other lands; but to Blanche, as she beheld it for the first time under the dark shadows and brilliant lights of a soft yet not cloudless sky, its effect was magical.

"It is your home, Blanche," said the earl, as he stood beside her, watching the feelings that were plainly working in her countenance.

"And yours, too, papa," said Blanche, striving at length to give her father some idea that she appreciated his affection. "It can never be my paradise without you."

"Then we will make our agreement to-night, my child," replied the earl; "our happiness shall be in each other,—and, whilst we are together, the world shall never intrude upon us with its cares."

Blanche smiled sweetly, yet the words so full of hope and happiness fell with something of a discordant sound upon her ear. The serpent had entered into Eden, and how could she dare to anticipate immunity from evil? The earl, however, seemed at that moment to have no forebodings;—every trace of sadness had passed from his brow, and his voice was more cheerful than Blanche had yet heard it. He would not however allow her to linger longer on the terrace, fearing lest she would be fatigued after the journey; and, summoning her maid, insisted that she should retire to her room for a short time to rest before she rejoined him for the evening. Blanche, however, did not rest: she retired indeed, but it was to kneel humbly before her God; to acknowledge his mercies, and pray that the blessings which He had vouchsafed to grant her might never lead her heart astray.

CHAPTER VI.

If the first waking to a sense of sorrow is bitter almost beyond any other moment of suffering, so the first dawning of happiness, at least upon the young, is bright beyond the power of description. Blanche dreamt that she was in the old manor-house of St. Ebbe's, grieving over a letter from her father, which, as had so often been the case, gave her no prospect of seeing him. She opened her eyes, and the sun was shining into a spacious, gorgeously furnished chamber, fitted rather it might seem for the palace of a queen than for her own simple tastes.

For an instant, she scarcely understood the reality of her senses; but, as she hastily rose and gazed from the window, a full consciousness of her happiness came over her. There were the old grey castle walls, the silvery stream, the woods and hills, now bathed in morning light, and the distant mountain-peak wreathed with a vapoury mist,—all which she had beheld the previous evening, and which she felt must be for ever associated with the thought of her father's love. It was then very early, but Blanche did not consider the hour, and had no remembrance of the preceding day's exertion; and, long before the earl had left his room, she was wandering through the garden and the park, exploring overgrown paths, and mounting hillocks, to gain a clearer idea of the beauties of her new home. Lord Rutherford gently found fault with her, when she appeared at breakfast, for having given herself so much unnecessary fatigue; but when Blanche gaily declared that she did not feel it, and that she could bear more than many who appeared much stronger, he seemed quite satisfied that she should follow her own fancy, and began to make arrangements for what was to be done during the day.

"You will find it but a short walk to the rectory," he said; "and I suppose you will wish to go there the first thing, unless Miss Wentworth should be here soon, which, from what I remember of the family habits, is not very likely. I never could induce Dr. Wentworth to leave his books till after luncheon."

"But Eleanor's habits are the habits of St. Ebbe's, not of the rectory," replied Blanche, "and she will do whatever she thinks will please me. I should like to go to her, though, extremely. I want so much to see more of her family—her sister and her brother—and especially her mother."

"Her sister must be a mere child," replied the earl; "and her brother, I suspect, is away; and as for Mrs. Wentworth, she is not a person to get on with, as it is called. She is very good, and all that ladies always are; but I never could understand that she was anything more."

"Eleanor is very fond of her mother," said Blanche.

"Yes, my love, very likely she may be; but I don't want you to be disappointed, and I have no idea that you will be fond of Mrs. Wentworth."

Blanche however was disappointed. She had set her heart upon finding in Mrs. Wentworth a second Mrs. Howard.

"Eleanor used to show me some of her letters," she said; "and they made me think she must be almost perfect."

Something like a contemptuous smile crossed the earl's face.

"You will have different notions of perfection,

Blanche," he said, "as you grow older. It is not so often to be met with as some people think."

Blanche made no reply. That peculiar smile was one to which she was unaccustomed, and Lord Rutherford not continuing the subject, nothing more was said about Mrs. Wentworth.

"I shall make Eleanor come back with me, and assist in all I have to do," said Blanche, as her father suggested that there would be ample employment for her in choosing how she would have everything placed in her rooms, and making herself at home in them. "She promised me she would; so I had better go to her at once."

"Then we will walk together," said the earl. "I must see Wentworth myself, and thank him for the care he has taken in seeing your apartments prepared for your reception."

The path to the rectory was much shorter than Blanche had anticipated, leading down the steep hill upon which the castle stood, and then following the course of the river for a little distance, till it terminated at a wicket-gate, which opened into the shrubbery adjoining the house. Blanche was delighted with the neatness and beauty of the small pleasure-ground through which they passed, and the comfortable appearance of the parsonage, with its trelliced verandah covered with creepers. She would not have exchanged her own magnificent home for it; but she felt that there was nothing to give rise in Eleanor's mind to any feelings of envy or discontent. It was the home of affluence, if not of riches.

The drawing-room was empty when they were shown into it, and Blanche had time to recognise many things which Eleanor had described before; and to study with much interest a likeness which she was certain must be that of Mrs. Wentworth, before any one appeared.

The first interruption was from a huge Newfoundland dog, which sprang through the open window in bold defiance of the warning voice of his master, who immediately followed. He was a young man, apparently about three or four-and-twenty, tall and rather striking in his appearance, and with a countenance which would have been termed extremely handsome; but Blanche, as startled by the intrusion she turned from the examination of Mrs. Wentworth's picture, was less aware that his features were regular, and his manners polished, than that he was not entirely the person she had expected to meet in Eleanor's brother. Such it was evident, from the strong resemblance, he must be. There was cleverness certainly in his bright blue eye, and the high forehead round which his dark hair was carefully arranged; and his mouth was good-tempered, though perhaps a little sarcastic; but a self-satisfaction betrayed itself in his look and general deportment, which almost from the first glance Blanche felt to be repugnant to her taste. Yet there was little said that could show anything of his disposition. A few apologies were made for his sudden entrance, and a little regret expressed that they should have been kept waiting; and then Mr. Wentworth bowed, and retired, with the intention of seeking his mother and sister, whom he believed were to be found in the garden.

"I should have known him anywhere," exclaimed the earl, when he was gone; "and you would, too, I am sure, Blanche. Did you ever see such a likeness?"

"It is striking, certainly," replied Blanche, with some hesitation; "but——"

"Well," said the earl, laughing, "what is your but? I should have thought it impossible to criticise anything so regularly handsome."

"I did not mean tc criticise, papa," said Blanche,

blushing; "but I don't think it would please me if Eleanor were exactly——"

The sentence was not concluded, for Eleanor at that instant appeared, her face bright with pleasure and excitement.

"It is so kind, so very kind in you, Blanche," she said. "I did not in the least expect you; for I am sure you must have as much to do as I have."

"I have left it all," replied Blanche, "till you were with me. You know I am never able to please myself; and you must go back to the castle presently, and help me to arrange my rooms, and then we will settle all sorts of things. But I wanted so much, first, to see your mother and little Susan."

"And Charles!" exclaimed Eleanor, eagerly. "He told us you were here: he came only last night, and he is going away again to-morrow."

"So soon!" observed the earl; "we shall scarcely have time to make his acquaintance."

"I don't know why he should go," replied Eleanor; "but I don't think he finds as much amusement here as he does elsewhere. Home is rather dull for a young man."

Blanche believed this because she was told it, but it seemed strange. She could not imagine what society any one could want beyond such a sister as Eleanor, such parents as she believed Dr. and Mrs. Wentworth to be, and such a home as Rutherford Rectory.

"Mamma will be here instantly; she is longing to see you, Blanche," continued Eleanor.

"I think I hear Mrs. Wentworth's voice," said Lord Rutherford; and he went a few paces into the garden to meet her; but though his words were cordial and easy, his tone was not; and but for Mrs. Wentworth's perfect calmness of manner, there might have been something awkward in the meeting.

Blanche did feel as her father had expected, when Mrs. Wentworth advanced towards her, and simply took her hand as she would have done that of an indifferent person. She had expected some show of feeling, at least for Eleanor's sake; but Mrs. Wentworth's soft, quiet voice underwent no change in its intonation, even when she looked at the earl, and said, "Lord Rutherford's return will now be doubly welcome to us all."

A few trifling observations passed, and Lord Rutherford, with a slight accent of impatience, inquired if there was no hope of seeing Dr. Wentworth.

"He has been called into the village unexpectedly," replied Mrs. Wentworth: "but we expect him to return immediately. Can I deliver any message for him?"

"Perhaps I might be allowed to leave a note in his study," replied the earl. "I think I know where to find it," and he left the room.

Blanche in the meantime had been interested in observing Mrs. Wentworth more minutely. She resembled Eleanor's description, in her tall, slight figure, and delicate, though rather harassed-looking countenance; but there were no traces of the feelings which had been so vividly portrayed in her letters. That she was Eleanor's mother, Blanche could scarcely believe, as she watched the eager impetuosity of the one, and the marble frigidity of the other; still less could she believe that Eleanor could ever dare to unburden her heart to such a mother. And yet the love which she had been told existed between them had been her "beau ideal" of what the tie between a parent and a child might and ought to be. When Lord Rutherford was gone, however, there was a little change in Mrs. Wentworth's manner. The questions which she asked were marked by consideration, and a desire to understand something of

Blanche's feelings, at this her first visit to her home; and though the tone in which they were put was cold, it still betrayed something more of real sympathy than before; and when Blanche began to express her pleasure in the taste and care which had been shown in furnishing her rooms, a quiet smile even stole over Mrs. Wentworth's features, and her eye brightened, though she immediately afterwards turned from the subject. But Blanche had not much time for any further remarks. Eleanor insisted upon taking her to the school-room, and the garden and shrubbery, and, as she said, making her at home at once; and Blanche, only too glad of an excuse to be alone with her, readily followed. It did not require much time to see the whole, but Blanche lingered with pleasure to listen to all that Eleanor had to say of past enjoyments and future hopes associated with the place in which she had been born, as well as to make acquaintance with her sister Susan, an intelligent-looking child, about eight years of age, who was now to be Eleanor's pupil.

"I think you must be happy, Eleanor," she exclaimed, as they seated themselves at length on a garden-seat, in a retired part of the shrubbery. "I do not see one thing that is wanting. And you will lead such a useful life."

"I have been talking to papa already about what I am to do," replied Eleanor. "I am to teach Susan in the mornings, and to go in the afternoons to see some of the poor people; and sometimes I am to ride with him, and he is going to read with me some part of the day."

"And your music and drawing?" said Blanche.

"Oh! I must contrive to have some time before breakfast. You know I cannot arrange for every hour exactly till I have tried; but that will be the sort of life."

"And what is to become of me?" said Blanche.

"That is what I wished to talk to you about. We must manage to go to the poor people together; and, when Susan has a holiday, I can come up to you in the morning, and we can ride together; and then, these nice summer evenings, there will be no difficulty in meeting."

Eleanor spoke eagerly and confidently, and Blanche did not stop to analyse possibilities; nor did she remark how much her friend had changed since they had parted the preceding evening. She was too much accustomed to Eleanor's varying moods to inquire their cause.

"I am longing to begin," continued Eleanor; "but to-day you know is no day, and Charles being here makes such a difference. It is impossible to do anything but idle away one's time with him."

Blanche smiled, but she did not wish the subject to be pursued; for she was afraid lest Eleanor might discover that Mr. Wentworth, notwithstanding his handsome face and his agreeable manners, did not entirely answer her preconceived expectations.

"And now I have talked all about myself," said Eleanor, "I should like to hear something about yourself:—the castle, and your father, and your own rooms. They must be exquisite, I am sure. Mamma had the whole choosing of the furniture, and everything, and she has such taste!"

"Yes, indeed she has," exclaimed Blanche; but I wish I had known it, I should have thanked her so much more."

"Oh! mamma is not a person to require thanks; she only requires to know that you like it: and I saw by her smile just now that she was satisfied. That is her unselfish smile. I believe she would have it if she was in the greatest suffering, if she thought another person was happy."

"I did not know what it meant," said Blanche; "but I suppose I shall understand you all by-and-by, when I don't feel so shy."

Eleanor laughed.

"As to that, Blanche," she said, "you have no right to complain. The joint wisdom and gravity of my whole family—uncles, aunts, and cousins included, and I have an interminable number, could never be half as awful as Lord Rutherford's politeness, I don't know what I shall do at the castle."

"I think I rather like being afraid of him," said Blanche. "Do you remember, Eleanor, how we used to walk up and down the garden at St. Ebbe's, and discuss the different kinds of affection?"

"And how we always differed," said Eleanor. "You with your fondness for looking up; and I with my perverse inclination to look down; no, not down exactly, but quite on a level."

"And then our appeals to Mrs. Howard," said Blanche. "That will be the one great thing wanting to my happiness. If she were but here!"

"Yes," replied Eleanor, "but she will be with us soon, and then it will be such great, such very great pleasure; and now, without her, I have more hope of making you think as I do in all sorts of ways; for she always supported you."

"But," said Blanche, "before Mrs. Howard talked to us, I never could see anything in your arguments to convince me that love is greatest when persons are on an equality; and there is one thing, you know entirely against it, devotion—which is the highest and purest love."

"I can't follow you in an argument, Blanche, to-day," exclaimed Eleanor; "my mind is not up to it, as it is sometimes."

Blanche looked disappointed. "I thought," she said, "that you would let me talk of these things always."

"Yes, so you shall; but I don't think I am in that sort of sober mood to-day; I am too happy."

"I am happy, too," said Blanche; "but my extacies went away with my walk this morning, and I don't wish them to last."

"Mine never do," replied Eleanor, laughing; "so I am in no fear. I shall pay dearly for all my enjoyment before night comes, I dare say. It would be much better to be like you, Blanche; your extacies never go quite away, I am sure, though you say they do."

"I don't know," said Blanche; "certainly, I don't feel much of them at this moment; and some feelings you have which are much more lasting than mine."

Blanche spoke as she thought, truly; yet it was only her own humility, and a natural respect for Eleanor's talents and decided opinions, which could have blinded her to the fact, that Eleanor was in reality swayed by every passing impulse; that she expressed herself strongly, but that she acted weakly. And, if Blanche had been quicker in discerning, Eleanor would have felt greater hesitation in owning her faults. But it required no effort to lament changeableness and hastiness, and the defects of an enthusiastic temperament, when she was sure to be met with a quick refutation of her self accusations, and to hear instances adduced which apparently proved her to be the very reverse of what she acknowledged. It was one of the weaknesses of Blanche's character that where she loved she could not or would not see anything amiss. "I must try and be regular in my habits," she said, "pursuing the conversation; "but I am afraid it will be very difficult. I should like especially to know something of the poor people, if your papa will put me in the way."

"Papa hopes you will take a great interest in

them," said Eleanor; "he told me this morning that it was of immense consequence to you and to them; and he talked a great deal about the vast power, either for good or evil, which had been placed in your hands."

"In mine!" exclaimed Blanche; "now when I am so young."

"But you are not going to remain young always," replied Eleanor; "and, besides, whether young or old, you are still Lady Blanche Evelyn, the heiress of Rutherford."

"Yes," answered Blanche, with a deep sigh, which made Eleanor laugh heartily.

"You are the very strangest person, Blanche! Just think how many thousands there are in the world who would envy you."

"And I am to be envied," exclaimed Blanche, "for my friends,—for papa, and Mrs. Howard, and you;—and for my health too, and my education, and innumerable things; but not because I was born to have power."

"Yes, if you exercise it properly," said Eleanor. "If! but there is a doubt. Mrs. Howard is afraid of me; she thinks I shall be spoilt, and that papa will not tell me of my faults. Oh! Eleanor, it might be very different if I had a mother."

"You may have one, if you choose," replied Eleanor, "Mamma is already inclined to feel for you as her child."

Blanche did not receive the comfort which was expected from this assurance: her notion of a mother's affection was of something widely different from Mrs. Wentworth's cold shake of the hand. "Your mamma is very kind," she said; "I am sure she will do everything she can to help me. But still I must be left very much to myself; and, even during the few hours I have been at home, I have understood more of what Mrs. Howard meant. The castle is so grand, and the servants seem almost to bow before me; and as for papa, he watches my every look, that I may not have a wish ungratified; and when I awoke this morning, and saw my beautiful room, I did not feel as I used to do at St. Ebbe's; I thought that I could order more and have my own will; and then I remembered what Mrs. Howard said, and I was frightened."

Eleanor was touched by this simple confession. That which caused alarm to Blanche, would, she well knew, have passed unnoticed by herself. "You will be used to it all, dear Blanche, by-and-by," she said; "and then you will not think so much about it, and worry yourself; and I dare say we shall both be able to go on steadily; and, if you want to know the poor people, we can go to them together. The first person we must find out is the blind girl who was confirmed with us. Papa says he knows who she is very well; it was her aunt, who is the mistress of the Charity School, that she was staying with; but she is coming back directly. We will go and see her the first day we can, won't we?"

"Even this shadow of a duty was some relief to poor Blanche, whose conscience had a natural tendency to become morbidly sensitive, and Eleanor saw that she had struck upon the right chord. Anxious to make Blanche feel as light-hearted as herself, she continued to plan a scheme of duties and occupations, so cleverly and earnestly, that before the conversation was interrupted both were equally satisfied. Eleanor having talked herself into the belief that she was certainly devoted to a useful life; and Blanche, having listened, till she was persuaded that with such a friend, constantly at hand to remind her of neglects, she could never go far astray.

The afternoon was spent at the castle, where Blanche

found sufficient to occupy and interest both herself and Eleanor in the arrangement of her rooms; and when they parted it was with the agreement that, if the earl had no other plan for the ensuing day, they were to walk together into the village. "And if he wishes me to ride with him, instead," said Blanche; "I must ask him to let me come to you for an hour in the evening."

Eleanor willingly agreed, delighted to find that as yet there was no cause for jealousy, since even the society of Lord Rutherford did not make Blanche forget her.

CHAPTER VII.

And so passed the first day of Blanche's residence at Rutherford Castle; and so passed several days; varied, indeed, by drives, and rides, and books, and visits, both to rich and poor; but all, equally bright and unalloyed, for the petty disappointments and trifling vexations from which no care and no affection can guard us, were little felt by one who carried in her own breast a shield against them. Each morning, long before the Earl was awake, Blanche knelt in the solitude of her own chamber to pray for guidance during the day; and then, with her Bible in her hand, paced the broad terrace overhanging the river, that she might study the will of her Maker, amid the scenes which brought His power and goodness most clearly to her view. Each day she planned her occupations with a view to her own improvement, her father's happiness, and the comfort of those who were in a measure entrusted to her care; and not the most busy hour nor the most absorbing pursuit could lead her to forget that it was needful to withdraw some moments from this world to devote to the contemplation of another. Mrs. Howard had early implanted in her mind habits of order and punctuality; and, duly as the time came, which she had fixed upon as the most free from interruption, Blanche retired to her own chamber to consider what she had done since last engaged in the same duty; or, if prevented at the exact minute, the first leisure opportunity was eagerly seized upon, without any regard to the plausible excuses, which might easily have been made from weariness or a pre-occupied mind. Blanche never forgot Mrs. Howard's words, "Not, I will if I can, but I must." And one especial reason she now had for allowing nothing to interfere with her religious duties, in the hope of being so soon admitted to the full communion of the Church, and the anxiety fitly to prepare herself.

On the second Sunday after Blanche appeared in the old village church of Rutherford, the accustomed invitation was given to all "such as should be religiously and devoutly disposed," and as Blanche listened to the words a feeling of loneliness stole over her. Eleanor was near, with the mother, who could share every thought and feeling; and the father, whose voice faltered, as his eye rested upon the countenance of the child he so dearly loved, and to whom for the first time the exhortation was addressed. And Blanche stood in that sacred building, with but one exception, the noblest and wealthiest of all; and with her was the proud earl whose sternest will would have yielded to her wishes, as the humblest of his servants would have submitted to his; but the one great blessing which she then desired, a parent's sympathy and advice on the subject most deeply concerning her happiness, was denied her.

Upon this topic alone no word had passed between them—they met in the morning and the world was the theme of their conversation; they parted at night and no words of prayer were uttered to call for a blessing upon the midnight hour. Poetry, and painting, and music, and literature, and even the deeper subjects of science and philosophy, were all at times introduced, and Blanche with her natural refinement and superiority of mind was fascinated by the earl's eloquent language and exquisite taste. His words were as the words of enchantment; for, as he spoke of Italy and Greece, and the sunny islands of the south, even Blanche forgot for the moment that earth was but the stepping stone to heaven; its beauty, but a type of that which shall be hereafter; its genius and its learning, but the faint and misused relics of that perfect creation which only when it issued taintless from the hands of its Creator, was pronounced to be "very good." But the earl ceased, and Blanche was left to her own meditations, and then as she retraced the conversation and sought for something which should be treasured in her memory, a vague sense of unsatisfactoriness filled her mind. A glittering pageant seemed to have passed before her; but it was gone. And of what avail was it to her to have vividly realised the solemn beauty of Genoa, and the dazzling lustre of Naples; to have wandered in fancy beneath the vast dome of St. Peter's; or stood amidst the giant ruins of the Coliseum; to have floated in the dark gondolas of Venice, or gazed upon the blue waters of the Mediterranean; or how could it content her to hear of Raphael, and Michael Angelo, and Guido;—of Dante and Ariosto, and Tasso and Petrarch, and the names which associate Italy with all that is most precious in poetry and art, if all were but for the amusement of the hour, bearing no voice of warning from the past, no lesson of instruction for the future? But Blanche did not yet understand all she had to fear. She marvelled indeed at her father's apparent neglect of the subject most interesting to herself; she thought it strange that not even an allusion was made to it: but she was captivated by the brilliancy of his conversation, and accounted for his silence by remembering her own reluctance to converse upon serious subjects, except at peculiar times and under certain circumstances. She had been told that her own manner gave no true impression of her mind, and so she supposed it must be with him. A faint cloud was stealing over the sunlight of her joy, but she saw it not.

And the day drew near to which Blanche so earnestly looked forward with mingled hope and awe. It was the evening before, and having returned from a long ride with her father over one of the most beautiful portions of his property, she sat down on a bank which overlooked the windings of the river, and the opening into the country beyond.

There was nothing to disturb the repose of the scene, except the distant lowing of cattle in the pastures, and the dashing of a mountain torrent, which, escaping from a woody dell on the opposite side, fell sparkling and frothing over a steep broken cliff, and wound its way amidst stones and mosses till it was lost in the deep current of the larger stream.

Blanche rested her head against the trunk of a tree, and gave way to one of those delicious reveries of feeling rather than of thought; which, when the fancy is free, and the heart unburdened by care, are amongst the most perfect enjoyments of our early years.

The loveliness of the landscape was in accordance with the tone of mind which she had been endeavouring to attain during the day; and when, at length yielding to fatigue, she fell asleep, the images which haunted her dreams were pure and holy as her waking thoughts.

A few minutes afterwards there was the sound of an approaching footstep; and, advancing from the shade of the shrubbery, the earl stood by her side.

What could he have seen in a countenance so fair in its youthful purity, to make him start and sigh—and then gaze long and steadfastly with a frowning brow, and a mouth quivering with agitation? Was it that in those features he saw a resemblance which recalled the tale of his by-gone life; or did he read the visions which were passing before the eye of his sleeping child, and shrink from the conviction that the hopes which to her were all in all, were to him scarcely more than the superstitions of an age of darkness?

Yet, Lord Rutherford was no sceptic. He was but what thousands have been before him; in name, the follower of Christ—in heart, the slave of the world. Whatever might be his own indifference to religion he had no desire that it should be shared by his daughter, and the character of Lady Blanche often derived a peculiar though painful interest from the simple ardent piety which occasionally broke forth through her natural reserve; and which, to the earl's refined but hackneyed taste, gave her the appearance rather of a being from another sphere than of one born to participate in the vain heartlessness of fashionable society. He could admire, though he could not imitate; and now, as he watched her, so calm, and peaceful, and tranquilly happy, a pang of envy crossed his mind. Such peace as hers, even were it delusive, would be cheaply purchased at the sacrifice of all that he had hitherto valued. Yet, it was envy, not self-reproach; and the next moment he pictured her such as he intended she should be—the star of a glittering assemblage—flattered, courted, idolized; gathering around her all that was most attractive in grace and intellect; herself, the centre to which every eye would be directed in homage.

But the earl's countenance changed. In imagination there rose up before him the still, shrouded form of one, who in by-gone years had realized much that he desired to see in Blanche, but upon whose brow the sorrow of unrequited affection had set its indelible stamp; and when his eye again dwelt upon the living image of the wife whose love he had despised, he shuddered, and stooped to kiss his daughter's forehead with superstitious awe; and a passing dread, lest the features which bore the impress of life might but chill him with the mocking beauty of death. The kiss awoke Blanche from her short sleep; and the earl, hastily recovering himself, began to blame her imprudence. Blanche endeavoured to laugh away his fears, but proposed to return to the castle, as she had an engagement to keep.

"And not spare me a few minutes?" said the earl, with a slight tone of pique; "the sun will have set soon, and then we shall have no temptation to stay."

Blanche gathered up the folds of her riding habit, and taking her father's arm they pursued their walk by the path which led along the side of the hill. For some time both were silent. Blanche could never thoroughly overcome a certain sense of restraint in her father's presence; and Lord Rutherford, wrapt in his own thoughts, was contented to know that she was with him without seeking for conversation. Blanche was the first to speak.

"I never knew, till now," she said, "what it was, thoroughly to enjoy beautiful scenery. At St. Ebbe's, there was so little to see; but, even then, I used to fancy there must be an exquisite charm in it."

"You are young," replied the earl; "you have no painful associations. When you have reached my age you will feel very differently about all beauty."

"Yet some feelings of pleasure must increase," replied Blanche, more gravely than usual; "the best and highest."

"From being able to appreciate beauty better, you mean; from learning to look at it with an artist's eye? But that is a mistake; our greatest enjoyments are those which we never pause to analyse."

"I was not thinking of that exactly," said Blanche, with hesitation.

"Of what then, my love? What do you call the best and highest pleasure?"

Blanche hesitated, and then replied, timidly, as if doubtful of the manner in which the observation would be received, "I suppose, if we were very good, we should be grateful for beauty, as people are for favours and presents."

Lord Rutherford became suddenly thoughtful. "You are a metaphysician, Blanche," he said, after a pause; "that was not one of the accomplishments I expected from Mrs. Howard."

"If I am," replied Blanche, laughing; "it is certainly without knowing it."

"You are one, though. I have discovered a lurking taste in you before; and if you really have a fancy for the subject, we will study a few books together on the subject. I should be sorry for you to have prejudiced notions. Though you are a woman, a little deep reading will do you no harm."

Blanche promised to read anything he wished; though she still disclaimed any love for metaphysics; and the earl began to enumerate a list of authors, ending with—

"But, my dear Blanche, until you have read a little, I advise you not to trouble yourself with too much thinking. You will only be puzzled, and it can lead to no good. Take up your music and drawing, study history if you will, and we will have Italian and German lessons together; but don't attempt to dwell upon subjects beyond human comprehension."

Poor Blanche could not at all understand the reason of this speech; and began to fancy that she had done or said something wrong.

The earl instantly remarked her change of manner, and said kindly, "I would not for the world find fault with you, my dear; you must not imagine it; but I have seen the mischief of too much thought with some minds, and you have been unusually silent the last two days!"

"It was not that kind of thought which made me silent," exclaimed Blanche, eagerly; "I was thinking of—"

"Of what?—there can be no thought, which you would not wish me to know."

Blanche blushed deeply; she would willingly have sheltered herself under her former reserve, though at the same time longing to break down the barrier, and receive the sympathy which even then she could not doubt of obtaining. The earl evidently expected a reply.

Blanche felt herself forced to speak, and began; "I have been thinking; that is, I have been trying to think;—one ought to prepare oneself for to-morrow. My first Communion," she added, in a tone which scarcely caught the earl's ear.

He stopped suddenly in his walk. "Ah! yes; quite right. But you are very young, my dear."

"Not too young; am I?" said Blanche, anxiously; "I have been confirmed."

"No, not if you wish it; still, it is not right to force any one. Mrs. Howard was always rather over-strained in her ideas."

"Indeed, indeed, it was not Mrs. Howard only; but the rector, and the bishop, and every one said it. I thought it was always so," replied Blanche. "Is there really any reason against it?"

The earl smiled. "No possible reason, my dear child; but you know very little of the world, and I don't want you to tie yourself down; and in fact, my love, these things are best left to every one's own feelings. If you like it, do it by all means; only don't let me see your bright face clouded again; it makes me uneasy."

Poor Blanche felt chilled to the very heart.

But her father had no idea of the effect of his speech, and continued, "It might have been more pleasant for you to have waited a little. I am expecting your aunt, Lady Charlton, shortly; and Sir Hugh and your two cousins. You will like to become acquainted with them, as they are some of your nearest connections."

"Yes, indeed," exclaimed Blanche, relieved at finding something to say. "Dear mamma's sister! I am sure I must be fond of her."

Lord Rutherford's tone was constrained, as he answered, "Only her half-sister; there is no resemblance;" and then he stopped suddenly, and there was a long pause.

The thoughts of Blanche reverted to the former subject. The visit of one person or of hundreds—of relations or of strangers—seemed equally indifferent to her at that moment.

They had reached the termination of the path; and the earl, leaning over a fence, which protected the edge of the precipice, riveted his eyes upon the stream, and appeared lost in a reverie.

"It is like the current of human life, is it not, Blanche?" he said, at length. "See how it whirls its rapid course; and how the light froth, and the fragments of the bank, are borne along by it; like the frothy hopes and the fleeting pleasures of the world. And think, too, how little we know of the end to which it is hastening."

"Is it not travelling towards the ocean," said Blanche, timidly; "as we are all travelling towards eternity?"

Lord Rutherford raised himself, and put his hand suddenly upon her shoulder—"What is eternity, Blanche?" he said. "We use words without meaning, when we speak of it."

"But," replied Blanche, and notwithstanding the softness of her voice, it sounded tremulous in its earnestness; "we are told to think of it, and it must be for our happiness; for this world, they say, is full of disappointment."

"They say!" repeated the earl; "then you have never found it so yourself."

"I have been very happy," said Blanche, whilst she looked at her father with a smile of affection; but it was followed by a sigh. She could not say, "I am happy."

"Yes," continued the earl, thoughtfully, "you are standing, as I once stood, upon a spot from which you can view the past without regret, and the future without fear. For you it may be a resting-place for years; though for me it was but a point, quitted as soon as reached, and to which I could never return. Value your peace, my child, whilst you have it; for it is vain to hope that any thoughts of eternity will restore it to you when it is once gone."

"But, papa," answered Blanche, firmly, whilst something within her own mind seemed urging her to overcome her reserve and speak more directly, "even now I can feel comfort from such thoughts. I have been happy, because I have always had some one to love; but though I know that the happiness cannot last, I can bear to think so, and even to look forward to a time when I may be left quite alone; because true love does not seem to belong to earth, but to eternity. Is it not true, then, that these ideas do help us to bear trials?"

Lord Rutherford made no answer; he withdrew his arm, threw himself upon a bench, and relapsed into silence. Blanche was frightened at her own temerity, and a sense of indescribable wretchedness oppressed her. Her father's principles, she thought, could not be the principles of a Christian. The earl perceived he had distressed her, and starting up and again drawing her arm within his, said, as he pursued his walk:—

"I have vexed you, my dear child. Heaven knows how unwillingly! But you have been educated in retirement, and your life has been made up of dreams. It is impossible that you should understand the view which a stern, worn man, who has borne the struggle of years, takes of those subjects, which to you are everything. When you have heard them discussed and argued upon, and when you have known something of men's actions as well as of their creeds, you will see the value of your favourite notions more truly. They may be important to you, but they will not bear contact with the world."

"And must I know the world, papa?" inquired Blanche, with difficulty summoning courage to answer. "I would much rather live here alone with you."

Lord Rutherford laughed.

"Mrs. Howard has certainly performed her duty strictly," he said. "She promised to educate you in seclusion, and she has kept her word. But have you no wish for gaiety, Blanche; for such an introduction into the world as your station in life offers you?"

"I should like it, dear papa," replied Blanche; "and I think of it very often. But I would rather stay here and keep my own notions, because I believe they will make me better than any others."

"Well!" exclaimed the earl, carelessly, "cherish them as long as you can; they will do no one any harm but yourself; only, when your aunt and cousins come, I prophesy that you will think less about them."

Poor Blanche was not comforted by this prospect.

"Then I shall be happier, to-morrow, with you, alone, papa," she said pointedly; anxious, if possible, to solve, by some allusion to the first topic of the conversation, the painful doubt whether her father intended to join with her in the service of the next day. Lord Rutherford did not, at first, see that she had any particular meaning in her words; for the subject referred to was not one likely long to remain in his thoughts. When however it occurred to him, he answered hastily:—

"You must talk to Mrs. Wentworth, my dear; she will understand you in all these things better than I do."

"I don't know Mrs. Wentworth well," replied Blanche, whilst tears rushed to her eyes; "and there is no one I love like you."

Lord Rutherford played with his stick, but said nothing more; and, at length, when he saw that Blanche was again about to speak, he turned suddenly into another walk and left her. And then Blanche was indeed miserable. The sky and the woods, the rocks and the river, the beauties which had before entranced her with delight—all were changed. Their brightness was gone; the spell by which they had charmed her was destroyed. She was alone; and there lived not the being upon earth who could fill the void which that one conversation had caused in her heart. Who could recall the reverence and holy affection which had, till then, formed her dream of happiness in her splendid home? Who could restore the delusion which hitherto she had cherished, even against her own secret convictions?

But the spirit of youth is too buoyant to sink at once under any disappointment, however severe. It is the succession of griefs, the wearisome days, and the restless nights and the bitterness of long deferred hope, which at length will bow us to the dust; and Blanche had, as yet, known nothing of these. Her elastic, sanguine spirit again suggested the thought from which she had before found comfort. Her father's manner, and even his words, might be no true index to his mind. He had not said that he should not be with her; he had fully allowed that it would be right for her to attend the service, though he seemed to fear that she was too young. Persons had different opinions upon these subjects; perhaps, after all, she had misunderstood him; and, soothed by the idea, Blanche's countenance resumed, in some degree its former serenity. The suspense, however, still rested as a weight upon her heart. She met her father at dinner, and found herself almost unconsciously watching his looks, and weighing his words in the faint hope of learning from them something more of that inner world of principles and motives upon which all her happiness seemed to depend. But she learnt nothing. The earl was silent and pre-occupied, and she dared not ask him the cause. When the castle clock struck ten, Blanche, as was her custom, rose to retire to rest. Then, more than ever, she missed the prayers which had closed the evenings at St. Ebbe's. Hitherto she had accounted for the omission by supposing, either that her father had some reason for delay until they had been longer settled at home; or that it was not a foreign custom, and therefore he might not think of it till some other person suggested it: but now it appeared too truly an indication of the neglect of all religious forms, except that which the world has thought fit to honour with respect, the outward observance of the day of rest.

Blanche leant over her father's chair, and kissed his forehead again and again, as was her wont. Her love was not chilled, but it was altered. Doubt was mingled with it, and dread, and the fond clinging of the heart to happiness, which seems about to pass away. The earl looked up from his book, and as he took her trembling hand in his, he said,—

"We have been bad companions, to-night, Blanche: are you tired of me?"

A fear of losing self-command, made Blanche pause before answering. Lord Rutherford moved his chair, that he might discover the reason; but she had turned her head aside.

"You shall have other amusements soon," continued the earl, and an accent of annoyance marked his words.

"Oh, no, papa! I want nothing—no amusements."

"But what then? What do you want?"

Blanche was pained at her own weakness; she could only distress her father by showing her feelings, since to explain them was impossible.

"I wish for one thing, papa," she said, in a light, gay tone, whilst her lip quivered with agitation, "that you should kiss me and say good-night."

The earl pressed her to his heart, and whispered, "God bless you now and ever, my own precious child;" and Blanche retreated to her room, once more happy. Her father did then consider the blessing of God the one first object of desire. Surely, therefore, he must intend to seek it where especially it is bestowed.

CHAPTER VIII.

We close our eyes in peace, and we re-open them to sorrow and care. It is the lot, sooner or later, of all; the fulfilment of the earthly curse denounced upon our first parents, and from it there is no escape. We may, perhaps, have felt, upon lying down to rest, —the anxieties of the day at an end, the weariness of exhausted nature inviting us to repose, and the heart calmed by repentance, and the blessed trust in forgiveness and protection,—that if it were then permitted for the Angel of Death to call us to our long, last sleep; the summons, awful though it must ever be, would be hailed rather as a visitation of mercy, than as an event to be shrunk from in alarm. But God "seeth not as man seeth." He views the sins dormant but not destroyed; the passions lulled but not extinguished. He beholds us unfit for the kingdom of His holiness, and knows the warfare which must be endured, before the powers of a regenerate nature can fully triumph over the temptations of Satan. And if, at times, He does in mercy make us "to lie down in green pastures, and lead us beside the still waters," it is only that by such seasons of refreshment we may gather strength for the battle, which is to "bring every thought into captivity to the obedience of Christ."

When Blanche entered Rutherford church, the ensuing day, she felt but little of the peace which had been with her when she lay down to rest at night. A breakfast *tête-à-tête* with the earl, and a few remarks during their short walk from the castle to the village, had again aroused her distrust. Many such remarks had been made before, but they had fallen on an unheeding ear, or rather on one which did not understand, because it would not suspect evil. Now, the petty indications of motives and feeling, which it is not in the power of the most practised art to conceal, were as daggers to her heart, for they struck upon the points on which alone her earthly happiness was then vulnerable.

At any time a doubt which affected her father's principles must have been poignantly felt; but on no other occasion could it have caused so much suffering. For Blanche had striven humbly and earnestly to realise the awfulness of that most holy service in which she was then, for the first time, to be permitted to join. She had prayed and watched against the entrance of every unhallowed or worldly thought, and had dedicated herself to her Saviour with all the warmth and sincerity of youthful devotedness. At such a moment, even the purest of earthly affections might have been deemed intrusive; and yet, when she knelt in the temple of God, and bowed her head in reverence, and opened her lips in prayer, there arose in her heart, not feelings of faith and hope, but of sadness and fear. The words of confession were repeated, but the earl's voice at her side pronounced the same language in a tone of proud indifference, and Blanche forgot the repentance necessary for her own sins, in anguish lest he should be insensible to his. And praises, and thanksgivings, and intercessions, were uttered with a wandering mind; and the solemn declarations of Scripture received but a half attention; whilst she caught, as if by fascination, her father's restless eye and listless posture, and then turned in wretchedness to herself, to discover that she also, though not in like manner, was sinning against God. There was a painful struggle in her heart whilst going through the usual service. To be distracted then, seemed a miserable evidence of weakness and insincerity; and to present herself before God with thoughts clinging to earth, a fearful presumption. Once it seemed easier and better to delay,—to wait for another opportunity,—to risk anything rather than offer a divided heart; but at that moment the voice of the preacher spoke of Him, who "in that He Himself hath suffered, being tempted, is able to succour them that are tempted;" and, instead of giving way to despondency, Blanche prayed the more fervently to be pardoned and assisted, whilst she strove again to recall her scattered thoughts. The last words of the sermon were ended; the concluding prayers were said; there was a solemn stillness in the church, followed by the rush of movement and departing footsteps. No tones of joy or praise were heard whilst one by one they, who were unwilling or unable to remain, left the congregation; but silently and hastily they poured forth into the open air,—some, it might be, to grieve for the blessing of which they felt themselves unfitted to partake; but too many to stifle the reproaches of conscience in the cares and follies of the world.

Blanche looked at her father, as he seated himself by her side, and her heart bounded with joy; but, as the church became more empty, the earl rose, and stood for a few instants with his hat in his hand, and when the way of retreat was at last opened without fear of mixing himself with the crowd, he, too, followed the common example.

And the door was closed.

It was a moment of bitter, most bitter sorrow; —beyond it we may not look; but when Blanche left the church she no longer felt that she was alone.

CHAPTER IX.

"Lady Blanche is late in coming to you this morning; is she not, Eleanor?" said Mrs. Wentworth, as the luncheon-bell rang, and little Susan ran away to prepare for what was to be her dinner.

"Rather, I think," was the reply; "but Blanche is never quite mistress of her own time. Her father is so uncertain, and will make her do the very things she has determined not to do. He may have taken her for a ride, as likely as not."

"Strange, certainly," said Mrs. Wentworth, musingly, "that when a man like Lord Rutherford devotes himself to the happiness of his daughter, he should manage to do just the very things she does not like."

"Oh! indeed, mamma!" exclaimed Eleanor; "I do think you are wrong there. Blanche does like most things which her father proposes; the only worry is, that they come at the wrong time."

"And does she like, then, the prospect of having the castle filled with visitors, and of gaieties going on continually?" inquired Mrs. Wentworth, with a slight tone of asperity, which suited but little with her usual gentleness.

"Yes, very much," replied Eleanor. "Lady Charlton is a delightful person, so every one declares. And it will be very nice for me, too."

Mrs. Wentworth seemed rather discomposed. "You must remember, my dear," she said, "that what suits Lady Blanche will not suit you. Your line of duties will be totally different."

"Oh! yes, of course, mamma," and Eleanor coloured, and endeavoured to assume an indifferent air: "but you know there is no one whom Blanche loves as she does me; and she never will enjoy anything if I am not with her."

"Then I am afraid she will pass a very unhappy life; for you can be with her but seldom at the best."

"It is not exactly the being together, but the feeling that we are near, and understand each other, and can compare opinions, which is the pleasure;—and—"

"Well," interrupted Mrs. Wentworth," compare opinions if you like it, and sympathise with and love each other; I should be very sorry if you did not: but that does not imply the necessity of meeting every day, especially now."

"You are afraid for me, mamma," said Eleanor, laughing. "You think I shall become dissipated, and forget Susan, and the school, and old Nanny Marshall, and the almshouse women."

"I have no cause to doubt you, my love," replied Mrs. Wentworth affectionately; "but it is scarcely strange that I should have some misgivings about every society of which Lord Rutherford is the head."

Mrs. Wentworth spoke quickly, and Eleanor looked up in surprise. But her mother's face betrayed no particular feeling; it was even more placid than before, as she added, "You can scarcely have failed to discover that he is not the most fitting person for the guardianship of a young, enthusiastic, interesting girl like Lady Blanche."

"He would spoil her, if she could be spoilt," said Eleanor carelessly.

"Yes; he would spoil her," repeated Mrs. Wentworth. "He would infuse into her mind low worldly notions; and make her think much of fashion and ultra-refinement, and the admiration of his own peculiar circle; and if she pleases him he will idolise her, and if not—"

"He can never cease to love her," said Eleanor.

Mrs. Wentworth was silent. The sudden burst of feeling was over, and she had relapsed into her former indifference.

"Blanche is very like her mother's picture," observed Eleanor.

"Yes, very," replied Mrs. Wentworth; "but it is not of her that I am thinking now, Eleanor. No one can see her indeed without feeling most deeply for her; but it is you who are my charge, my delight."

Eleanor smiled, and as she drew near her mother's chair, and bent over it to kiss her, she said, "And I shall be so always."

Mrs. Wentworth shook her head. "Ah! Eleanor, that is your stumbling-block; confidence in yourself."

"But I have begun well; have I not, mamma? Just remember how steady and regular I have been ever since I came home; and how much you say yourself that Susan is improved. And the old almshouse women, you should have heard yesterday all the civil things they said! You must not distrust me more than anyone else. Please, don't look so grave, and conjure up such a castle spectre."

"Ah! if it were only a spectre! But, Eleanor, I can look back many years. I know what the tone of society used to be at Rutherford, and I see no possible reason for supposing that it will be different now."

"You were not injured by it, mamma," said Eleanor; "and why should I be?"

Mrs. Wentworth sighed. "I had many safeguards," she said; "yet, I will not say that I was not injured.

There was only one over whom evil seemed to have no power."

"The countess," said Eleanor, inquiringly.

"Yes; she was indeed too heavenly-minded to be approached by any ordinary influence; and"—but Mrs. Wentworth stopped, as if unwilling to continue the subject.

"Mamma," said Eleanor, "Lord Rutherford is very fond of Blanche; was he very fond of his wife?"

The consciousness that luncheon was ready appeared suddenly to have crossed Mrs. Wentworth's mind, for she did not give a direct reply; but merely saying, that Susan would be tired of waiting for her dinner, she went away, and Eleanor was left to answer for herself as best she might the question which had lately become one of considerable interest. Before, however, she had satisfied herself, her meditations were broken in upon by the entrance of her father and Lady Blanche.

"Reposing from the fatigues of instruction, I suspect, Eleanor," exclaimed Blanche, gaily. "Has Susan been a very naughty child?"

"Reposing from the weariness of disappointment rather," replied Eleanor. "You were to have been here an hour ago."

"So I was; but it is papa's fault. He would come and sit with me; and he read to me part of the time, and then we talked, and at last the post came in, and I had to write in a great hurry to my aunt, who is to be here the day after to-morrow."

"Indeed! Is Lady Charlton coming so soon?" inquired Dr. Wentworth.

"Yes," so she says, "if Sir Hugh feels himself equal to the journey; but she writes as if he was very much out of health. But do you know my aunt?"

"I can't tell," said Dr. Wentworth, rather bluntly.

Blanche and Eleanor laughed, and begged for an explanation.

"Why, it is rather the case of the Irishman and his tin-kettle; which he declared could not be lost, because he knew where it was,—at the bottom of the sea. My knowledge of Lady Charlton is about as valuable. Know her I do; inasmuch as I have spoken to her often, and even dined in company with her some sixteen or eighteen years ago; but time is very like the sea; you can see through it, but you cannot grasp what you are looking at. After all, it may only be Lady Charlton's shadow, which I think I know."

"I know exactly what she is like in appearance," said Blanche; "tall and thin, dark hair and eyes, very elegant and —"

"Fascinating," added Dr. Wentworth.

"Yes, fascinating; that is precisely the word papa used."

"And your cousins, I suppose, are fascinating too?" said Eleanor, in a constrained voice.

"No one knows anything about them, except that poor Maude is an invalid, and that they have been educated abroad."

"Oh! I remember," exclaimed Eleanor; "Charles knew them, I am sure; he said he had made acquaintance with some relations of yours at Florence. It was at a ball, I think, they met, and then they were at a great many gay parties together."

"A great many too many," muttered Dr. Wentworth in an under-tone.

"That was a twelvemonth ago, papa," said Eleanor. "It is not quite fair upon Charles, is it Blanche; to quarrel with him for last year's follies?"

"I quarrel with no one, Eleanor," replied Dr. Wentworth, very gravely; "but we will not keep Lady Blanche waiting;" and he led the way to the dining-room. Blanche followed, with the feeling that her original distaste to Mr. Wentworth had received some increase ; yet she blamed herself for it, and in order to conquer her prejudice, paid particular attention when other allusions were made to him in the course of her visit, in the hope of receiving more satisfactory answers. But to her surprise, she found that Dr. Wentworth, who, even in his most courteous moods was short and straight-forward in manner, was when this subject was approached, so abrupt as instantly to stop the conversation. It was clear that his son was not at that moment perfectly in his favour.

This afternoon was to be devoted to the village, for Lord Rutherford was obliged to be absent the greater part of the day, and Blanche generally arranged her duties in such a way as to give him always the first place in her attention. Under Dr. Wentworth's guidance she had taken into her special charge a certain number of the poor, principally the aged and infirm, to whom her presence was almost as an angel's visit; so new and strange did it seem that one so young and so far removed from themselves, should take a personal interest in their comfort. A few there were, indeed, who remembered the time when the countess had occupied herself in a similar manner, and who regarded Lady Blanche with a degree of compassionate affection, which mingled with their respect as they noticed the resemblance to her mother. From them it was that Blanche heard many little traits of the countess's character, which she could have learnt from no other source ; and they were treasured in her memory, and fondly dwelt upon as the touches which were to mark more vividly the outline of her mother's image. Yet, when all had been repeated, and she believed that she had gained a clear knowledge of what the countess must have been, there still remained an undefined doubt of something untold. Reverence and love were ever associated with her name by all who spoke of her; but pity was added also; and why, Blanche could not understand. For it was not the pity which is bestowed so lavishly and unthinkingly, by the living who are toiling through this weary world upon the dead who have entered upon their rest, but rather that which must ever be felt for those whom neither high station nor wealth, nor even goodness, have shielded from severe trial. Blanche was sure that her mother ought to have been happy, but she could not believe that she had been so. As she listened to the cottagers' oft-told tales, she fancied that it was only a natural interest which made her listen so intently for all they could tell; but, if she had been as careful an anatomist of her feelings as she was of her faults, she might have perceived that this longing desire to know more of the history of the countess's daily life was almost always aroused after conversations with her father, which were now very frequent.

It is the gift of a superior mind to bring out the latent powers of others; and Lord Rutherford's constant intercourse with his daughter had done more than the most unwearied study towards maturing her judgment, and enlarging her ideas upon all worldly subjects. Blanche had lived in reality months instead of weeks at the castle, and every day brought some fresh evidence to the earl's mind of her quick intellect and refined taste. He delighted in engaging her in an argument, and seeing the ease with which she would pursue her own train of thought, whilst fully comprehending his; and the graceful candour with which, when once convinced of error, she yielded her point and begged for further instruction. He was more and more satisfied, more and more convinced that Mrs. Howard had educated her well. And Blanche? Alas! how little can we read of the secrets of the heart! How selfish and blind are we, even in our love!

If Lord Rutherford had been asked whether he had succeeded in rendering his daughter happy, he would have answered, without a moment's hesitation, perfectly. She had employments, amusements, interests, luxuries, friends; and, to crown the whole, himself: and though free from the petty conceit of an inferior intellect, which believes that it is all which it desires to be, Lord Rutherford could not but be conscious that the powers of entertainment which had excited the admiration of the first circles, both in England and on the continent, must be more than equal to the task of whiling away the leisure hours of a young girl, whose knowledge of the world was confined to the immediate neighbourhood of the place of her education. And he thought correctly. Blanche was amused, excited, interested still—but the arrow had entered into her heart; and when she left her father's presence, her smiles too often vanished, whilst she sought the solitude of her own chamber, to grieve over the bitterness of her disappointment.

It was then that she most thought of her mother. Had it been the same with her? Had she also loved, and reverenced, and dreamt a dream of perfection; and awoke to find it but delusion? Or had she, like the earl, been gifted with the highest of earthly gifts, while destitute of that "pearl of great price," which alone could be her ornament in Heaven? This, Blanche could not think. All that she heard and saw—the letters, the favourite books, the kind acts which were so thankfully remembered, showed plainly that the Countess of Rutherford had been in her inmost heart a Christian; and then, how great must have been the pang at finding herself united to one whose heart was centred in the world!

Blanche thought upon the subject till it haunted her as a spectral form, mixing with her imaginations by day and night; and, if forgotten for a time, recalled by some accidental occurrence as painfully as if it had never passed away. Yet the fear could not be named,—certainly not to Eleanor, and scarcely even to Mrs. Howard, who had been much separated from the countess both before and after her marriage, and had never hinted a doubt of her happiness. The mention of it would have involved an acknowledgment of disappointment in her father, which Blanche shrank from allowing to herself, and could not have borne to embody in words; though she often reproached herself for a want of sincerity in withholding the confidence which she knew was expected. There was one person, indeed, from whom much might be learnt; but how was the inquiry to be made? Mrs. Wentworth, she had reason to believe, knew all the circumstances of her mother's history; but Blanche had already asked all the questions which she dared, and had learnt the principal events, and many additional traits of habit and character; and Mrs. Wentworth was not a person from whom to seek further confidence. There was a great deal of sincerity, but no openness in her disposition: she seldom encouraged conversation, and when she did, it was confined to facts,—serious and important, and often placed in a new and striking light,—but still merely facts. Her own feelings she left to be discovered by inference; and Blanche, accustomed to Mrs. Howard's warmth of expression, felt chilled even by her kindness, and would frequently have preferred silence to a succession of details, which might have aroused the intensest interest, but for the cold way in which they were narrated. There was one hope, however, still to rest upon; Lady Charlton was described by every one to be a most charming person, something like the countess in appearance, and with a manner so winning that no one could withstand it. Even Mrs. Wentworth had once been roused into a momentary enthusiasm when speaking of her qualifications as an agreeable companion, and Blanche already clung to the idea, that in her aunt she might find a friend who would throw light upon the subject which distressed her mind, without requiring her to state the fears which she would willingly have hidden from her own heart.

CHAPTER X.

Lord Rutherford perceived, with great satisfaction, the pleasure with which Blanche looked forward to her aunt's visit. He had resolved that his sister-in-law should be surprised and charmed by his daughter's elegance and beauty; and he well knew the effect which Blanche's simple, eager cordiality would have upon one who had so long been accustomed to the sparkling frigidity of the fashionable world. Blanche was always courteous, always attentive; but, when her feelings were interested, she was attractive far beyond any person whom he had ever seen. He remained at home the whole of the day on which Lady Charlton was expected, under the pretence—perhaps even the belief—that it would be a great mark of neglect if he were to run the least risk of not being ready to receive his guests. "Sir Hugh was so unwell, and they had not met since they parted last year in Italy; and Blanche would feel awkward in probably having to receive her cousins alone. True, they could not possibly arrive before five o'clock, and he had an engagement, at two, in a neighbouring village; but there might be some mistake; they might come before,— at any rate it was safe, and he would send an excuse; and then the earl's eye wandered to Blanche, who was seated at her drawing-frame, and he begged her to give him one air upon the harp—his favourite. Blanche's face lit up with a smile of pleasure,—and the earl felt the time only too short, as he leant back upon the sofa, his eye delighting in his child's grace, and his ear drinking in the sweet sounds which her talent was producing. It was perfect human enjoyment; for at that moment no memories awoke to mar it.

"We will walk down the carriage drive, if you like it, my love," he said, as the timepiece struck the quarter before five: "these spare minutes are always very tedious."

Blanche disappeared as soon as the suggestion was made; her father's marked attention to her wishes, had made her scrupulously mindful of his. Lord Rutherford's careful inspection when she returned, was not perceived; but it was bestowed with the wish to decide whether she would be less likely to appear to advantage in her walking than in her morning dress. Lady Charlton's eye was fastidiously correct in dress, and it was possible that she might be struck by some deficiency of which Blanche was unconscious. But the straw bonnet and shawl disarmed criticism, and Lord Rutherford smiled at his own doubts. The afternoon was very still, but the atmosphere was clear, and the sky blue and cloudless. Blanche felt the softening, soothing influence of nature's purity and beauty; and the over interest, and even agitation, which she had experienced in the expectation of the meeting, were calmed. But she was silent, and so was the earl.

"We shall see them from this point," he said, at length, as he led his daughter to a bench upon the summit of a steep knoll. "It was an old boyish habit of mine, to stand here and watch for arrivals."

Blanche looked towards the winding road which passed over the village green. "There is something,—a carriage;—yes, a carriage, I am sure. Don't you see it, papa?"

"Eyes of sixteen against eyes of fifty, Blanche," said the earl, smiling. "Are you certain that you don't hear the rumbling of the wheels?"

"Oh! papa, you won't believe; but I do see it, though. It is coming nearer; it has just passed the first turning, and it is very quick too. There must be four horses; so it must be them."

"Well, then, we will return; but look once more: are you sure?"

"Yes, quite; it is by the blacksmith's shop. I can see the horses now distinctly."

Lord Rutherford quickened his pace towards the house. He looked thoughtful and uneasy.

They stood upon the steps together. The earl leant moodily against the castle wall; he saw no external objects. His eye was turned inwards to his own heart, and the images of the years that were past away. He started, however, as the sound of wheels became more distinct; and, when the leaders appeared on the crest of the hill, he drew Blanche forward to meet the carriage. Blanche thought that it was the impulse of hospitality and affection; but it was merely restlessness: he felt himself compelled to move.

Lady Charlton was the first to perceive them, and the carriage was instantly stopped.

"Kind!—like yourself, always," was her salutation, as she extended her hand, which the earl took with something of trembling cordiality. "And my dear Blanche, too! but I must walk."

The carriage-door was opened, and Lady Charlton alighted.

"We are not in public," she said, as she kissed Blanche's forehead, and again gave her hand to the earl.

Blanche's smile was very sweet, and her few words—few from repressed feeling—were all that her aunt could desire.

"You don't want introductions," continued Lady Charlton. "Maude, Adelaide; you know your cousin, of course."

There was another warm greeting, and Blanche was recovering her momentary shyness and agitation. She remained at the carriage-door, bending forwards and speaking eagerly, whilst her eye sparkled with pleasure, and a bright colour flushed her usually pale cheek. Lady Charlton watched her for a few moments, and the seemingly involuntary exclamation escaped her,—"Yes, she is just what I could have imagined; I must have known her in any place."

The earl turned away.

"Don't distress yourself, my dear," continued Lady Charlton, as Blanche was about to address some person, or apparently thing, which bore a resemblance rather to a bundle of shawls than a human being. "Poor Sir Hugh! he is miserably tired—half dead with opiates;—he has been suffering fearfully the last week, but he would come: he will be himself by-and-by: they had better drive on" and the carriage proceeded.

Blanche walked leisurely to the castle with her father and aunt. She was confused; there had scarcely been time to recognise any one, but the general impression was agreeable. Lady Charlton was undoubtedly an elegant, distinguished looking person; her voice too was musical, and her manner very winning from its ease and kindness. And her cousins—she thought she knew them apart: one had a sallow complexion and light hair, a plain but very clever face, rather severe and grave in its expression—that must be Maude, the invalid: and the other was a brunette, with dark hair, braided; dressed handsomely and carefully, lively in manner, and altogether pleasing from youth and gaiety, and the quickness of a pair of very bright eyes, rather than from any regular beauty. The earl said little; but Lady Charlton had words upon every subject at command. No one could be in the least restrained with her. Even in those few minutes, she seemed to take exactly that position which Blanche had felt must be filled before she could be quite at ease with her father. Lady Charlton was affectionate and interested, but she was not timid. Blanche could scarcely understand the boldness with which she rallied the earl upon his long absence, his present love of seclusion; and prophesied that he was yet to prove himself as distinguished a person in England as he had been abroad. Lord Rutherford was at first grave, but not annoyed; and, after a few minutes, he appeared to have caught himself something of Lady Charlton's vivacity, and answered her remarks in a tone almost as full of cheerfulness as her own. It was a new phase of character which Blanche had not before perceived.

"And Sir Hugh has been very ill, then," said Lord Rutherford, as he saw the carriage stop at the castle, and two servants assist in helping a seemingly decrepit old man to alight.

"Yes," and Lady Charlton sighed; "it is very sad: one can never be prepared for these attacks. He was at a great dinner only a fortnight ago, and quite the life of the party; made a speech, and proposed toasts, and kept up the whole thing till after twelve o'clock; was quite himself, in fact: and now, you see what he is."

"I suppose the dinner was the root of the evil," observed the earl.

"Well! yes; I suppose it might have been so: but the complaint is constitutional, hereditary. Blanche, my dear, you may think yourself happy in being descended from another family. The Evelyns never were a gouty race."

"I should hope not," said the earl, quietly.

Lady Charlton laughed. "Now, my dear Rutherford, that is one of your old exclusive fancies. I really flattered myself that fifteen years' experience of continental liberalism would have done something towards destroying them; but you are just the same, I see: just the same spirit of the Spanish hidalgo in you—'This comes of walking on the earth.'"

"And the Spanish hidalgo was right," said Blanche, archly.

Lady Charlton smiled, and answered, "Quite right, my dear; but I don't know how it is—the older one grows, the less inclined one is to hang, like Mahomet's coffin, between heaven and earth: there is something very solitary and uncongenial in the position; and therefore, since one cannot yet have the higher, I am willing to rest satisfied with the lower, and to be very happy upon earth, in spite of the Spanish hidalgo."

"And the gout," said Lord Rutherford. "Sir Hugh, I suspect, would tell a different tale."

"Oh! poor Sir Hugh! you will see him very unlike himself, Blanche; or rather you will not see him at all. He and Pearson go their own way when he is in this state. A first-rate servant Pearson is; and such a nurse!"

By this time they had reached the castle. As they entered it, Blanche again repeated her welcome to her aunt, and Lady Charlton's manner in an instant changed. She was no longer the cheerful, amusing woman of the world; but the thoughtful, warm-hearted, sympathising friend. She took Blanche's hand in both hers, and thanked her with a warmth of affection which Blanche fully appreciated. Dr. Wentworth's description recurred to her mind. Fascinating!—Yes, that was the right word.

Blanche was alone till nearly dinner-time. Her cousins were engaged in dressing for dinner, or perhaps in resting after their journey. She did not see anything of them after showing them to their rooms. Her aunt she supposed was with Sir Hugh; her father, she knew, had business to transact. The solitude was very precious to her; it gave her leisure for thought, for examining her own impressions. Blanche trusted very much to first impressions, for as yet she had never known deception. All seemed bright and hopeful—not from any particular cause that she could fix upon—the sensation of relief and satisfaction was indefinable; the castle was the castle still — her own position was the same — her one great grief was as real as it had ever been; but her heart was lighter.

The earl was waiting for her as she left her room. He had come on purpose to take her himself to the drawing-room, that she might not be shy; so he said: but his survey of Blanche's dress and general appearance betrayed his true motive. A smile of intense pleasure passed over his face as he looked at her: the simple white dress was the symbol of the pure, spotless mind.

CHAPTER XI.

"ELEANOR," said Mr. Wentworth to his sister, as he entered the school-room the day after the arrival of Lady Charlton at the castle, "you must leave those never-ending lessons, and come out; I want you."

"I beg your pardon, Charles, you must wait: if you have returned to stay here for several months, you must learn to amuse yourself."

"More easily said than done," was the reply; and the young man threw himself into the first arm-chair which presented itself, and continued: "Four months! it is a terribly long time. What on earth shall I do with myself?"

"Read," replied Eleanor, still occupying herself with an exercise, which she was correcting.

"Read!" my dear Eleanor," replied her brother, with a sigh of languid weariness. "But I have read; I do read. It is nothing else but reading from morning till night."

"But it will only last a little longer," said Eleanor, soothingly; "and then——"

"And then comes ordination," added Charles.

There was an accent of bitterness in his voice. Eleanor looked up, and put her finger to her lips, as she glanced at her little sister.

"Susan, child, run into the garden, and find Brown," exclaimed Charles impatiently. "Tell him he must have my horse ready for me by three o'clock."

Susan ran away, only too glad of the excuse to change her employment.

"You forget Susan's age," said Eleanor, in a reproachful tone, when she found herself alone with her brother.

"Yes, I did at the moment; but there would have been no harm done."

"Only that she is very likely to repeat to papa all that you say to me, and you would not like that."

"I don't know; he must hear it some day or other."

"Oh! no, Charles: you intend to change your views, and look at the matter differently."

"My dear Eleanor," was the answer, spoken coolly and rather satirically, "it is exceedingly easy for you to talk; but, begging your pardon, you know nothing whatever of the subject. Ordained I must be—I intend to be; but not to be my father's curate; not to vegetate upon a hundred a year in a country village, with no one but my own family to speak to. I was not born for such a life, and I can never endure it."

"Would you not be just as badly off in any other place?" inquired Eleanor. "You will have the castle, and the society there, for a change."

"Lord Rutherford and Lady Blanche?" said Charles, doubtfully.

"Yes; and I think you will scarcely require more. You will go far before you meet any one the equal of Blanche, at least."

"Equal! no; to watch her is like looking up at a star; but confess, Eleanor, notwithstanding all your romance, it is awfully out of one's reach."

"Yet Blanche is the most warm-hearted, enthusiastic, poetical person imaginable," exclaimed Eleanor.

"Very likely; you young ladies are extremely warm-hearted to each other, and no doubt very poetical in your private journals; but that does not help us poor men. Lady Blanche makes a most lovely picture; but pictures are not society."

"Then you will have others besides Blanche," continued Eleanor. "Lady Charlton, and"—

"The Charltons? Are they here? When did they come? You never told me anything about them."

Mr. Wentworth grew evidently excited at the information.

Eleanor could not forbear laughing. "Why, my dear Charles, I was not quite prepared for such a burst. They are here—Lady Charlton, and Sir Hugh."

"And Adelaide?" interrupted Charles.

"Christian names!" exclaimed Eleanor. 'Really Charles, that is rather surprising. Do papa and mamma know of this great intimacy?"

"My dear Eleanor, you are a mere baby. Christian names are nothing at all; it entirely depends upon the people. I should never think of calling Lady Blanche Evelyn, Blanche."

"No, because she is Lady Blanche."

"But if she were Miss; I could not. Don't you understand? Some persons are to be regarded at a distance. They never give one the opportunity of approaching nearer; they are never off their guard."

"Which, I presume then, that the Miss Charltons are," observed Eleanor, in a tone of amusement.

"They are very quick—very agreeable. I should not exactly choose to see you like them; but they will be great acquisitions. When I say them, however, I really only mean Adelaide. The other is clever enough—a very phœnix in learning and accomplishments; but she is anything but agreeable, if you happen to take her in the wrong mood."

"She is an invalid, I believe," said Eleanor.

"Yes, she thinks herself so, and she looks hideously ugly; people say, from ill health. It was the fashion abroad, to admire her forehead and eyes, and call them intellectual; but I never could get over the complexion."

"I don't see that she is likely to be much of an acquisition," continued Eleanor.

"Yes; in her way, she will be: she plays marvellously, and sings! I never heard any amateur voice in the least equal to hers. Upon the whole, I am immensely glad they are here."

"I must ask you to go, now," said Eleanor, gravely. "Susan must come to her lessons; don't you hear her in the passage?"

"Run away, child, we are not ready for you yet," exclaimed Charles, rising from his chair with some effort; and going to the door, in spite of his sister's evident annoyance, he sent Susan on another message, and then returning said, "These four months! —they will be a great trial."

"I should not find them so, if I were in your place," observed Eleanor, whilst the colour mounted to her cheeks. "I should be glad to be with you anywhere, especially at home."

"Charles seemed a little surprised at her manner. "I don't understand," he replied. "Of course, I am glad to be with you; but just think for a minute;" and his voice became quite energetic; "I have passed through the university, and made rather a noise there; since then I have been travelling for two years, seeing most enchanting places, enjoying first-rate society—and now I am told that I am to sit down for life—it is the life which frightens me!—in an old country parsonage, with not a single person to speak to beyond my own family, and the chance visitors at Rutherford Castle. Doubtless, there are persons for whom such prospects might do very well; good, quiet, humdrum men, who, exactly the reverse of Charles the Second, may be warranted never to do a foolish thing, and never say a wise one;—but I am not one of them. If my father wishes me to do anything he must give me a sphere: he ought to do so; for I have never caused him any trouble. I have never been wild, or extravagant; and yet he looks as grave as if I was a complete scapegrace."

"The notion of your ordination makes him do that," said Eleanor.

"And whose fault is the ordination?" exclaimed Mr. Wentworth. "He has dinned into my ears, ever since I was a baby in arms, that I was to be a clergyman, and what possible right has he to find fault with me now because I intend to be one?"

"Papa looks at the profession more seriously than you do," observed Eleanor.

"Serious; it is serious enough, no one doubts that; but all the more reason why I should have a little life and enjoyment beforehand."

"Papa thinks that is not the right sort of preparation," said Eleanor, in a tone of mild suggestion, rather than of reproof.

"I don't mean it as preparation—and yet call it so, if you will. When I am ordained, things will be different. I shall be a clergyman; and I shall conduct myself like one. My father cannot suppose I mean to disgrace myself by being a vulgar, fox-hunting, drinking, negligent, country parson."

"The race is happily becoming extinct," said Eleanor; "but my father will not be satisfied with your merely escaping disgrace."

"He wishes to see me honoured; and he shall do so. Once let me have the opportunity; place me in London; give me, as I said before, a sphere; and, before he dies, he shall see me a bishop."

Eleanor shook her head, and said more courageously "That is not the tone to please papa, Charles.

He does not understand it. He does not know what it is to wish to be a bishop."

"Neither do I wish it, Eleanor; if I could be any thing else. But I am all but shut out from every other profession. I am not educated, and not inclined for the army; I am not at all fitted for a physician; and utterly without interest at the bar—if I could bring myself to submit to the drudgery of studying for it. I know I must take orders; and all I ask is, that my father should try to place me where my talents—for you know, Eleanor, it is impossible to deny that I have some talents," and Mr. Wentworth laughed faintly, and settling his cravat, glanced at himself in the looking-glass—"should have scope."

Eleanor's reply showed an evident wish to put an end to a disagreeable subject. She was quite sure, she said, that her father would do everything in his power to promote her brother's views, by-and-by; but that she could not herself see what steps were to be taken at once.

"One, very simple," exclaimed Charles, eagerly. "Let him consent that I should have a curacy in London; or, at least, that I should try for one; instead of insisting upon my drudging on a weary existence here, with nothing to rouse energy."

"You had better resign yourself, my dear Charles," and Eleanor tried to laugh. "When papa once has made a decision, he is very resolute."

"And he will find that his son can be resolute too," exclaimed Mr. Wentworth. "I have made up my mind what I will do, I will be off—off to Australia; no power on earth shall stop me, if I am thwarted."

"You, in Australia! a settler!" and Eleanor laughed: no, papa feels he is perfectly safe there. But, my dear Charles · there is a much surer way of bringing him round to look at things in your own way. Stay here quietly, and do as he wishes; study, and visit the poor people, and then he will be satisfied; and will see himself, by degrees, that you are not likely to gain any harm by ultimately settling in London. You must own," she added, with some hesitation, "that papa's anxiety is natural enough, considering the way you talk."

"But I don't talk so to him," exclaimed Mr. Wentworth. "Neither he nor my mother know half I really feel."

"Poor mamma!" said Eleanor, speaking seriously, yet not without some satisfaction at her brother's implied confidence in herself; "with her high views, her very exalted notions of a clergyman's office, I certainly should not like her to hear you rattle on in this random way. I don't approve of it, you know, myself; only I am sure you don't mean it."

"I do mean it, though," exclaimed Charles, petulantly; "and what is more, I am convinced that there are not half a dozen men in England who would not say precisely the same. Of course, I shall do my duty; but it must be in the right place—not here."

"Not even with Lady Charlton and her family, at the castle?" said Eleanor, pointedly.

"Oh! nonsense, they would make a difference; but it would only be for a time; they can't stay."

"Blanche expects them for a very long visit," replied Eleanor.

"Lord Rutherford and Adelaide Charlton!" said Charles, musingly. "A very incongruous mixture. Adelaide's high spirits will never stand the castle proprieties."

"Charles, dear; promise me one thing, please," said Eleanor, laying her hand upon his arm. "Don't speak of Miss Charlton in that way before mamma; it is just the sort of thing to annoy her."

Mr. Wentworth laughed. "My dear Eleanor, you really are more childish than I imagined; but anything you like: only, when you know Adelaide, you will see that it is impossible to call her anything else. And, remember, if I am to stay here and be well behaved, I must have full leave to go to the castle as often as I choose."

"Leave from me as much as you wish," replied Eleanor; "if you will only be cautious. I could not bear you to vex mamma, and she is rather suspicious of you already."

Mr. Wentworth put on an air of mock gravity; and folding his hands, and casting his eyes to the ground, promised to be as demure as Susan, if only his sister would help to provide him with amusement. "And suggest to my father that I shall not be fitted for his curate," were his last words, as he went out of the room, leaving Eleanor in a state of mind by no means to be envied.

He was scarcely gone, when Mrs. Wentworth came through the garden to the school-room window. She held a note in her hand, which she put into Eleanor's silently, and then stood by apparently engaged in twisting the straggling tendrils of the clematis which darkened the apartment. Eleanor returned the note with thanks; her colour was heightened, and her eyes sparkled with pleasure. "Shall I write an answer, mamma; or will you?"

Mrs. Wentworth paused for a moment before she said, in a tone of annoyance, "I was afraid it would be so. I was sure you would be vexed, my love."

"Vexed! dear mamma."

"Yes. It is nothing very grievous; but your father and I think it best to decline. He wished me not to show you the invitation; but I could not agree. I have too much confidence in your good sense, and your love for me."

"Oh, mamma! the first day! and an express invitation to us all; and Blanche so extremely urgent!"

"The very reason, my love, why it may be more desirable to decline." Eleanor bit her lip, and made no reply.

"You will understand some of our objections," continued Mrs. Wentworth. "As an acquaintance begins, so it may be supposed to continue. We do not wish to be dining at the castle perpetually, now."

"Because of Lady Charlton and her party, I suppose," replied Eleanor, trying to be good humoured. "But, dear mamma, she is a very charming person."

"I don't know what she is," was Mrs. Wentworth's reply, spoken more quickly than was her wont: "only you will be contented at home, my child."

"Contented with you, mamma? oh! yes, always; but"—

"But you must try and think as I think; try, and not dream of the castle by night and by day." Eleanor smiled, though without cheerfulness. "Consider what it would be to me," continued Mrs. Wentworth, "to see you restless and excited; or to find you longing for different society, and know that you were neglecting your own simple duties."

"I should never neglect my duties by being with Blanche," exclaimed Eleanor eagerly; "she would always keep me right."

"My love, indeed you are mistaken. Lady Blanche is a very sweet girl, most amiable and winning; but, when you are together, her spirit cannot be the ruling one."

Eleanor's head was raised proudly, as she replied, "It should be, if I were Blanche. Rank, wealth, beauty, talent! Mamma, Blanche ought to rule a kingdom."

"Let her learn to rule the kingdom of her own heart," replied Mrs. Wentworth; "that will be the most needful lesson. Poor child! hers is a position of great temptation."

"Mamma," said Eleanor thoughtfully, "you might help her."

Mrs. Wentworth paused. "I might possibly, if circumstances were different; if the opportunity should occur; but your affection, I think, a little deceives you, Eleanor. Lady Blanche is not likely to give me the opportunity; she is too gentle and yielding to profit by the sort of help I should give. She would require something less severe. Mrs. Howard is more likely to be of use to her than I am."

"Mrs. Howard is so far off," replied Eleanor.

"Yes; but they can write. Though, of course, my love," continued Mrs. Wentworth, assuming a tone of greater unconstraint, "I do not mean that I would not do everything for her that I possibly could; only there are some dispositions so easily moulded that they take impressions from everything; and, if it should be so with Lady Blanche, you will find that the daily life at the castle with her relations will really form her character. And, besides," and Mrs. Wentworth's voice sank, as it sometimes did, into a tone so low that it scarcely seemed intended for conversation, "there are different atmospheres, different circles—the castle and the rectory—no, never again."

Eleanor made no comment upon this speech; yet the thought crossed her mind, with wonder, why, if the circles were so different, and the atmospheres so uncongenial, she should have been allowed to grow up from childhood in unrestrained intimacy with Blanche.

"And you will be satisfied then, my dear, not to dine at the castle to-day," said Mrs. Wentworth in her natural manner; "we have an engagement which will do very well as an excuse for us all. Your father talked, this morning, of asking Mr. Moulton, of Enfield to stay; as he is going to ride with him to see the workhouse; and though we might leave them at home, it will be better not."

Eleanor sighed at the prospect of exchanging a cheerful evening at the castle for the society of an elderly gentleman, whose only interest in life seemed to be the faults of the poor-laws. The sigh was not utterly selfish; it was as much for her brother as herself; and she ventured to add a petition for him: but Mrs. Wentworth negatived the idea instantly.

"Charles! oh dear! no. He was much too great a stranger to go by himself; he would be quite a burden to Lord Rutherford; and, moreover"—but this time Mrs. Wentworth's thoughts were not betrayed by an undertone; and Eleanor could only conjecture that the "moreover" might have some reference to Miss Charlton. She was not forbidden, however, to go to the castle in the morning—that was some satisfaction; and she might see Blanche; she might just have a glimpse of Adelaide Charlton; and, without hesitation, she expressed her intention to her mother.

They had not meet the preceding day, she said; and Blanche would think it unkind if she were not to go near her.

"Lady Blanche will call upon you, my dear; if she is anxious about it," said Mrs. Wentworth, quietly and coldly.

Eleanor changed colour. "Anxious about it, dear mamma; what can you mean?"

"Nothing, my dear; only I think you might as well leave the castle for to-day."

A torrent of eager words seemed about to rush forth, for Eleanor's eyes flashed with anger and vexation. Mrs. Wentworth stopped her before the first word was spoken. "My love, you have trusted me always; do you doubt now that I would make you happy in your own way if it were right?"

The haughty spirit was subdued in an instant, and Eleanor's arm was thrown round her mother's neck.

"Mamma, you are always right; yet you cannot love Blanche as I do."

"I loved her mother," was Mrs. Wentworth's calm reply; and, as she walked slowly away, Eleanor threw herself upon a chair, and burst into tears.

CHAPTER XII.

"Here, Pearson! stop a minute, can't you? What in the world are you going away for, Idiot?" growled Sir Hugh Charlton, helplessly stretching out his hand to reach a small hand-bell, which had unfortunately been placed just beyond his reach.

"I beg your pardon, sir; very sorry, quite forgot," muttered the stout, obsequious, black-haired, black-whiskered, and most shrewd-looking individual, whose character was constantly summed-up by Lady Charlton, in the emphatic description of "the best creature in the world."

"The medicine, the drops! where are they? why don't you fetch them?" continued Sir Hugh, as Pearson remained by his side, pretending to adjust the pillows at his head, and eyeing with great apparent solicitude the arrangements of the gouty stool, which supported his master's feet. Pearson did not say, that he had been on the point of departure when he was brought back; he placed the hand-bell more conveniently than before, gave an additional touch to the pillows, brought the newspaper within reach, and then, as he was leaving the room, remarked, that the earl had invited some friends to dinner, so he had been told by Mr. Hilyard, the butler.

"People to dinner, did you say? Here, Pearson, where are you going? why, in the name of wonder, don't you speak out?"

"Dr. Wentworth's family from the rectory are coming, so Mr. Hilyard informed me, Sir Hugh; but, perhaps, you would wish me to inquire. When you have taken the medicine, if I might be allowed, I would ask." Pearson returned almost in an instant. The drops were properly measured and administered, and Sir Hugh's next order was, not to fidget about the room like a mouse, but to go and hear who was coming; an order fully expected by the ingenious Pearson, who immediately departed to gossip, for at least a quarter of an hour, in the housekeeper's room.

He was gone, but Sir Hugh murmured still, "Wentworths! who were the Wentworths? People he had never heard of! Wentworth!" He stopped and rubbed his chin, and thought, and muttered again, "Wentworth! yes, he did know the name, he remembered it. That intolerable fool, Pearson, where was he gone? he knew every one. Heaps of Wentworths there were everywhere—England—France—Italy." He seized the hand-bell, but, without ringing it, called for Pearson at the highest pitch of his voice.

The call was answered by Lady Charlton. "My dear, Sir Hugh, such a noise! it quite frightens one."

"Well! madam, and I intended it should. Here am I—Pearson gone—you away—left by my daughters—it is too bad."

"Oh! but my dear Sir Hugh, you must not be exacting. Poor children! they are only having a little music with Blanche."

"No; not with me," said a very sweet voice; and Blanche, who had just entered the room, came up to Sir Hugh's chair. "You know, Aunt Charlton, you promised I should be of use. Can I do anything for Sir Hugh? Might I not sit a little while with him?"

"Oh! my dear Blanche, this is too good of you," and Sir Hugh grew calm directly. "Really you must excuse me—a gouty man must make a great many apologies; but that fool—my man, I mean,—a very good servant—a capital servant, Pearson—but forgetful. Lady Charlton, pray place a chair; it distresses me quite." Blanche brought a chair for herself, and placed it by Sir Hugh; her work-basket was in her hand, and again she hoped that she was not intruding.

Lady Charlton smiled, and said, "Sir Hugh would be only too happy; and, for herself, she had letters to write, very important ones; but Blanche must not fatigue herself. You can read, if you like it, my love, for a little while. Sir Hugh is a great reader, and a writer too sometimes, only I shall be in disgrace if I mention it." She looked meaningly at Sir Hugh.

"My dear Lady Charlton—Frances—you are really too bad. Blanche will be shocked; it is nothing; nothing at all, I assure you. Just a pamphlet, nothing at all to speak of. There is one—Frances, my dear—on the side table; I think you will find one. But, never mind;" seeing that Lady Charlton cast an unsearching, and unseeing eye round the room. "Never mind, Pearson will find it. I can ring."

"Pearson is going to dinner," replied Lady Charlton, rather quickly, "but Blanche, I dare say, will read to you. Let me see, that book on geology I think it was you began. My dear Blanche, I really am ashamed of myself for allowing you to have such a task. I dare say, if the truth were told, you know no more of the 'ologies' than I do; but you will learn something—names, at least. I quite marvel at myself for not being wiser, considering Sir Hugh's tastes. We had not very much science in Italy; and a great drawback it was for him. Good-b'ye, my love. Maude and Ady will be in despair when they hear you are not coming back."

"As much in despair as I shall be in delight," said Sir Hugh, twisting his sallow and worn features into what he believed to be an irresistible smile.

"But I shall have mercy upon you, Blanche," said Lady Charlton, returning to look into the room again. "Remember we are to have a riding party this afternoon; and your friends, the Wentworths, I hear, are to dine with us."

Lady Charlton was gone before she heard, or at least, before she appeared to hear Sir Hugh's impatient exclamation of "Wentworth! that was the very thing! that fool Pearson! why did he not come back? Who are the Wentworths?"

"Friends of ours at the rectory," said Blanche; and her voice acted with a magical effect upon the irritable Sir Hugh, who immediately composed himself to the semblance of a deferential listener. "Eleanor Wentworth and I were educated together," continued Blanche. "She is my very great friend."

"Ah, yes, very true—very nice; no doubt she is charming. But I thought—you must excuse a little impatience, my dear—the gout is trying, especially trying,—for a man of active habits, in the prime of life. I spoke rather eagerly, just now; but I thought I remembered the name of Wentworth abroad."

"It might have been Dr. Wentworth's son; he has been travelling," said Blanche.

Sir Hugh put his finger to his lip, and presently, with a sudden start of recollection, exclaimed:—

"Yes, I have it. I remember. Pearson knows;—idiot!" and the voice sank again into an angry growl, "what a time he is at dinner!"

Before Blanche could answer, a furious peal summoned Pearson from his repast. Blanche could scarcely help smiling at the insinuating tone of the servant, when compared with the gesticulation of the master. Sir Hugh burst forth without preparation, requiring Pearson to recollect all he had ever heard or known of any one of the name of Wentworth ; and Pearson, with the utmost composure, began a quiet and rather interesting account of Sir Hugh's first acquaintance with Mr. Wentworth ; how they had met in Italy, and he believed Sir Hugh had told him that Lady Charlton had been acquainted with his family ; and,—no doubt, Sir Hugh would recollect him perfectly—a tall gentleman, very handsome ; he used to sing with Miss Adelaide ; and, as Pearson glanced doubtingly at Sir Hugh, and saw a pleased smile on his face, he ventured to add, "People had remarked—at least he had heard it said—how well Mr. Wentworth and Miss Adelaide danced."

"Yes, yes, I know. You may go now ; you won't be wanted yet. Lady Blanche will do me the honour of sitting with me. Go ; can't you?" and Pearson hastened to escape Sir Hugh's lightning glance. "Such gossips these people are, my dear," continued Sir Hugh in his mildest voice. "Such intolerable gossips! One would think I was an old man with no memory ; telling me all those facts! Of course, I recollect! Mr. Wentworth was a handsome young man, certainly ; he danced attendance upon Adelaide. Lady Charlton grew frightened ; but it was all nonsense ; Adelaide is a great deal too sensible—a shrewd girl you will find out—not equal to Maude. Maude is a genius—plays, sings, draws—there was a copy of hers, of a Guido, as good as the original. I should not have known the difference ; and I am a very good judge, as good as the earl, I flatter myself ; and he has the reputation of being a first-rate connoisseur. Had, that is, some years ago ;—years you can't remember, my dear Blanche, for a very good reason—there was no Lady Blanche then; no such bright star in the dark firmament;" and he bowed with the most studied politeness; "except, if there must be an exception,—you will not quarrel with mine—the countess, your mother. A charming woman—a very charming woman." Sir Hugh paused to take breath; he saw that Blanche had laid down her work at his last words, and was listening eagerly for the rest. "Poor thing! Ah! years gone by! poor thing! Yes, I remember perfectly. Mrs. Wentworth was here a good deal in those days; she must have been this young man's mother."

"Mrs. Wentworth was a great friend of dear mamma's," said Blanche, speaking with an effort; yet determined, if possible, to keep him for a few minutes to the point.

"Yes, my dear—yes, I remember. Mrs. Wentworth and the countess, poor thing!" and the sigh which accompanied the words evidently came from the heart. Blanche's fingers moved quickly at her work; but it was from nervousness, not industry. Was the sigh for her mother's death or for her life? "Poor thing!" again began Sir Hugh. "Your father is altered, my dear; a great blow that was—sudden to him. She was a lovely creature! I had a great regard for her."

"It must have been so sad for papa, being away when she was ill," observed Blanche.

"Yes, I suppose so; one can't tell. One can never say! it was a very lonely life. But people were mistaken. A proud man, Lord Rutherford;—very natural pride, my dear; don't think I find fault with it. A very proud man! Nobody knows him thoroughly that has not lived with him for years. Lady Charlton and I, of course, are intimately acquainted with his character; but other people talked great nonsense. However, I always understood him.

We had tastes in common. He was devoted to geology. I gave him introductions when he went abroad, and they were of great use to him. I wanted him to take notes, and write. I told him I would assist. If he would have given the facts, I would have dressed them—adopted them and clothed them; they should have been my 'enfans trouvès;'" and Sir Hugh laughed so long and heartily at his own wit, that he did not perceive how little his companion sympathised with his mirth.

"That is the luncheon-bell, I think," said Blanche, rising, and collecting her work.

"Luncheon! so late is it? But time passes so rapidly 'With thee conversing'—you know the rest."

"I am afraid it is easier to forget times and seasons than luncheon," said Blanche; "but I cannot leave you alone. May I ring for Pearson?"

"Ah! thoughtful as you are! it is quite reversing the natural order. A sad enemy is the gout; very sad, indeed, to an active man in the prime of life;—a sad enemy!"

Sir Hugh shook his head long and dolefully, but would not allow Blanche to do anything for him. "It would distress him too much," he said; "it was unnatural, improper—her society, that was all he required—he had been so flattered, so honoured;" and, with the words still ringing in her ears, Blanche at last contrived to escape to the drawing-room.

CHAPTER XIII.

"And so the Wentworths will not come, Blanche," said Lord Rutherford, as his daughter seated herself at the luncheon-table. "Dr. Wentworth has a prior engagement."

"Not come! How very disappointing! May I see the note?"

It was from Mrs. Wentworth, polite and chilling. Blanche said nothing, but looked very vexed.

"I grieve for the failure of my first attempts for society, Adelaide," said the earl, addressing his niece. "Only, remember, it really is not my fault."

Blanche took up the note again to examine it. "A prior engagement is so odd. Eleanor must have known that I should want her; and they are not going out I am nearly sure, unless it may be Mr. Wentworth. He returned yesterday, I believe."

Adelaide Charlton looked up eagerly; but her mother's eye was fixed upon her, and the eagerness vented itself in a quick demand for some bread.

"That must be our Mr. Wentworth," said Maude, speaking in a deep, but peculiarly mellow voice, which was yet disagreeably abrupt. "He said he came from Rutherford."

"I thought he was living away," observed Lady Charlton.

Her tone struck Blanche directly: it was new to her; there was more gravity and sternness in it than she was prepared for.

"Young Wentworth is a handsome man," said

the earl, carelessly; "but he is too much of a coxcomb to be a gentleman."

"Those travelled young men very often are," observed Lady Charlton. "It is 'We and the world' with them; and really, at last, one is disgusted in spite of oneself."

"But Mr. Wentworth must be superior to that class, I think," said Blanche; "his sister is so fond of him."

"And you swear by his sister then?" asked Maude, sharply.

Blanche was rather startled, and did not know what to reply.

"Maude, my dear; you really must be careful in your expressions. Lord Rutherford will think you a complete Goth," said Lady Charlton.

"Give me a better word," answered Maude, "and I will use it."

"Maude's favourite theory," said Lady Charlton, addressing the earl. "I must tell you of it, to prepare you for anything strange you may hear. She says—what is it, my dear Maude? Explain your own notions; you will do it much better than I shall."

Lord Rutherford assumed a listening attitude; but it was clear that he was perfectly indifferent, and Maude raised her piercing grey eyes to his face, and said:

"My notions are, that I should like a piece of cake; if my uncle will be good enough to cut it."

Lord Rutherford complied with the request, and did not trouble himself to ask for any further explanation of Maude's notions. Blanche was still silent, pondering upon Eleanor Wentworth's refusal, and a sudden check seemed to have been put to Adelaide's usual vivacity. The party was becoming dull; and Lady Charlton, who dreaded dulness as an enemy, endeavoured to infuse a little spirit into it by inquiring what were the afternoon plans. Blanche observed that the refusal had rather disturbed them; for Eleanor Wentworth, she had hoped, would have formed one of a riding party with them: at least, with Adelaide and herself. Maude, she understood, very seldom rode.

"No, never; except by myself," was Maude's ungracious answer.

"Papa talked of taking you and my aunt for a drive," continued Blanche, with a slight air of restraint, caused insensibly by her cousin's manner; "and Sir Hugh"—

"Oh! never mind Sir Hugh, my love," exclaimed Lady Charlton. "Pearson will take care of him. He will not be in a condition to move for the next week. But he is quite happy; don't distress yourself about him: he wants nothing except his new book on geology. A great blessing it is," she added more gravely, "that he can occupy himself: he is devoted to science."

"Blanche," said the earl, rising suddenly, "can you come with me and look at the shrubs they have been planting this morning on the bank? We will prepare for the driving and riding afterwards, if your aunt and your cousins will arrange together what they wish to do."

He threw open the window, and walked out upon the terrace. Blanche followed him with a sensation of freedom and pleasure. The earl drew her arm within his: he did not take her to see the shrubs; but, when they reached the end of the terrace, he turned again, and continued to walk without speaking; though once he passed his hand caressingly over hers, and looked in her face and smiled: and Blanche had learnt to value such a look. Lord Rutherford's laugh was for the world; his smiles were almost exclusively for her. He stopped at length and drew a long breath, and in a light tone exclaimed, "Well, Blanche! we are alone again: shall we remain so?"

Blanche hesitated. "I have not made up my mind, papa:—it is such a very early day. I like them."

"Like them,—yes, I suppose you do. But it is not duty, is it? I never wish you to like any one from duty."

Blanche laughed faintly; she had already learnt that duty was not in her father's catalogue of allowable motives. "No: I suppose it is not from duty; but feelings are such mixed things, it is hard to analyze them. I am not sure that I shall love them," she added, more boldly; "except, that is, my aunt."

"Lady Charlton is a very sensible woman," said the earl. "I never knew her do but one foolish thing in her life. That scatter-brained piece of pomposity, Sir Hugh! how could she marry him?"

"Yes; it is strange, very strange," said Blanche, thoughtfully; "she is so superior,—she could never have loved him."

"Blanche, my child, you must learn to put aside your romance," said the earl gently, but seriously. "There are more marriages in the world without love than you, in your simplicity, can imagine. I do not wonder at Lady Charlton's marrying without love —no one who has had any experience of life could do so—but it is marvellous that, when she was resolved upon a sacrifice, she should have devoted herself for nothing,—absolutely nothing," he added, angrily.

"Yet she must have loved him, too, I suppose," said Blanche, musingly. "If there was nothing else, it must have been love; I should not like to think it was not."

"Not like it!" said the earl. "Why, what could it signify to you?"

"Because," replied Blanche, and the colour deepened on her cheek, and she spoke hurriedly—"because it seems a false thing to do to marry without it; it is an untruth; it cannot really bring a blessing: at least, I think not,—it seems so to me," she added, timidly, as if ashamed of her own eagerness.

The earl paused; his voice was altered when he spoke again; it was low and tremulous. "And you believe that love must bring a blessing; that it must be happiness?" he said.

"Yes, real, true, holy love," replied Blanche: "surely it must be so."

"It may be,—one cannot tell," answered the earl; and then, in an under tone, he added, "Yet it is a dream,—an unreality."

"That is not what people generally think it; is it?" said Blanche, quickly, for she was struck by the peculiarity of his manner.

"They call it happiness," said the earl; "but they do not know their own meaning. Happiness!" he repeated, bitterly; "no, happiness is for the cold and calculating; for those who can trust themselves, who know their own weakness, and can foresee the consequences of their own actions. Love is impulse, feeling, excitement."

"But there is something in it besides, calmer and deeper," replied Blanche; "or it could never last: and marriage would be miserable, most miserable," she added, earnestly.

Lord Rutherford stopped suddenly in his walk. "Did you ever hear of a miserable marriage, Blanche?" he said, quickly.

"In books, people have said it;—there are such things," replied Blanche, almost frightened by his manner.

He laughed sarcastically. "Yes, in another sphere,—in the world, the dreamy world: not in the real Utopia of St. Ebbe's." He was going to turn again on the terrace; but, checking himself, added, in his usual tone, "This is but idle talking. Go to your aunt, Blanche, and settle what you will. I will ride with you, if you wish it." He did not wait for question or reply, but strode down the walk which led to the river's bank, and was soon lost to sight amongst the thick trees.

"You are not going out with Adelaide, merely to please her, my love?" said Lady Charlton, as Blanche, about half an hour afterwards, came into the room dressed in her riding-habit, and looking rather grave.

Blanche brightened in an instant, and said that riding was her favourite exercise: but her aunt did not seem satisfied.

"We shall not stay with you, my dear, if you allow us to interrupt your usual habits. You are very busy, I am sure. No one could have been educated by Mrs. Howard without being so."

"Mrs. Howard is so good with her business," exclaimed Blanche; "she is so really useful: what I have to do is very little. I am sure, if she could be here, she would put me in the way of doing a great deal more."

"But she is coming to you, is she not?" inquired Lady Charlton. "I am sure I heard your father say something about it."

"She was to have come; but she has been obliged to delay: one of her nieces is ill," said Blanche. "I am longing for her, to help me in every thing; to make me methodical and energetic, and like herself, if she could," she added, laughing.

Lady Charlton began the first words of a compliment, but stopped. "I won't say what I was going to say, my dear; I don't think it would be in your way, though it would be true; and I will not offer to take Mrs. Howard's place,—that would be out of the question; but you must let me know if I can ever be of any use to you. I dare say you go about amongst the poor people. Your dear mother always did," she said, with a change of tone which made Blanche's heart thrill, though she could not trust herself at that moment to answer the allusion.

"I go sometimes," was all she replied,

Lady Charlton drew near and kissed her tenderly. "You shall let me go with you; I shall like it. It will seem that the old times are come back—quite—when I look at you," she added, gazing in Blanche's face with a sad smile.

Blanche returned the kiss, and, unfastening a brooch which she always wore, showed a miniature, exquisitely painted. "Will you tell me if it is like?" she said. "I have been afraid to ask papa."

Lady Charlton took the brooch in her hand, and turned to the light. She was looking at it attentively, and Blanche, leaning over her, was waiting with great interest for her opinion. Lord Rutherford came to the window. Blanche, by a kind of instinct, took the brooch hastily from her aunt; but not before the earl had remarked it.

"A new trinket, Blanche?" he exclaimed, cheerfully. "Let me see."

Blanche's hand shook, and the brooch fell to the ground. The earl stooped to pick it up. There was a silence of some moments.

Lady Charlton said, "It is very like," and held out her hand for it.

"The carriage is waiting," was all Lord Rutherford's reply.

He walked away, and Lady Charlton, as she returned the brooch to Blanche, said, "You shall talk to me, my love: it is not a subject for him."

CHAPTER XIV.

THE first determination which Blanche formed the next day was that she would go to the parsonage early. The disappointment of the preceding afternoon had vexed her considerably, and she was resolved not to run the risk of another refusal. She would go herself and make the request, and then it could not, she hoped, be denied.

The subject was mentioned casually at breakfast. Blanche began to feel herself sufficiently at home with her aunt and cousins to leave them to themselves, and said she should go to the rectory the first thing, and engage Eleanor for the day; "and we will walk, if you like it, in the afternoon," she added, addressing Lady Charlton. "I must go into the village."

"Must! my love," exclaimed the earl quickly. "Who says must to you?"

"I say it to myself," replied Blanche, smiling: "it is not an imperative must; only my aunt said she would like to go with me sometimes; and——"

"Yes, my dear, certainly," interposed Lady Charlton; "of all things I shall like to accompany you; but to-day, I rather think, I have an engagement. A great friend of mine, Mrs. Cuthbert Grey, is staying in this neighbourhood, and I promised to go and see her when I came here. She is on a visit to the Donningtons. I think I had better take advantage of the fair weather. Ady, what do you say?"

Adelaide answered carelessly that, if it must be, she supposed it had better be; but that Maude would do just as well as herself. "I shall go with Blanche this morning, if I may," she continued. "Blanche, you will take me to the rectory; I delight in walking the first thing after breakfast."

"Immensely intimate," said Maude, in her cold sepulchral tone; "the civility must be for Mr. Wentworth: you don't know any one else."

"You will stay at home, Ady," interrupted Lady Charlton, glancing quickly at the earl; but he was now engrossed in the newspaper, and knew nothing that was passing.

Blanche was puzzled for an instant, but took the matter simply, and assured them that ceremony with the Wentworths would be quite unnecessary. They met every day. If Adelaide liked to go, she might do so easily.

"She will stay at home, my dear," repeated Lady Charlton, decidedly; and of course the question was supposed to be settled.

But Blanche stood at the green gate of the rectory, and was trying to open it, when she heard some one behind her say, laughingly, "Where there is a will there is a way, Blanche. Did you never hear that before? An exceedingly romantic spot this for a parsonage, I must say."

Blanche was silent from surprise.

"I can open the gate, I dare say," continued Adelaide; "or—look, there is Mr. Wentworth."

Blanche was excessively annoyed, and answered coolly, that she would not trouble Mr. Wentworth; she should leave a message for Eleanor, and go back.

"When you have come on purpose to see her? I am sure you will not do anything of the kind: you could not be so capricious. Mr. Wentworth——" and as the gentleman drew near, Adelaide held out her hand with the ease of an old acquaintance. "How very strange! Where did you drop from?"

Mr. Wentworth reciprocated the surprise, expressed a due amount of pleasure, and threw open the gate.

Adelaide waited for her cousin to go forward; but Blanche paused resolutely. "Thank you," she said, addressing Mr. Wentworth, "but I am afraid I must return now. Since we have met you, perhaps you will do me the favour to deliver a message to Eleanor. I want her very much to spend the day with me, and to come as early as possible. Mrs. Wentworth is quite well, I hope?"

"Quite, thank you; but surely,—indeed, Lady Blanche, you must not go back without seeing my mother; she will be vexed if you don't; you have given yourself so much trouble."

"Only a pleasant walk," replied Blanche. "Pray say to Mrs. Wentworth how sorry we were she could not dine with us yesterday. Good morning." She bowed, and turned away; but Adelaide was already within the gate. Such a bewitching rose she had seen!—amongst the briers,—nearly hidden it was,—Mr. Wentworth must give it her.

Mr. Wentworth plunged into the thicket, and Adelaide still advanced. Blanche could not let her go on alone, for the next moment she would be in front of the house: and so she was; and not only before the house, but before the whole family party, who were talking together on the lawn. Blanche had nothing to do but to go up to them, and introduce her cousin and apologize; though the apology was a difficulty, for her gentle spirit was very considerably roused.

Setting aside the neglect of Lady Charlton's wishes, Adelaide was unquestionably rude to herself, and Blanche had never experienced rudeness before. Mrs. Wentworth received the excuse for the intrusion politely, but without any cordiality; and even Eleanor's warm kiss and exclamation of delight, could not take away the general awkwardness. Adelaide alone was quite at her ease, and admired the house and garden in a tone of easy familiarity, not unmixed with patronage, which made Mrs. Wentworth's civility freeze into a stiffness nearly amounting to haughtiness.

The restraint however was at an end, when both Dr. and Mrs. Wentworth were called away. Then Eleanor and Blanche strolled to a distance by themselves; and Adelaide, declaring that the walk had tired her, and therefore she would wait till they returned, threw herself upon a garden-bench, and began a quick, laughing conversation of reminiscences with Mr. Wentworth.

"You are worried, Blanche," was Eleanor's first observation, when they were beyond hearing. "You have never looked as you do now since the days when we used to puzzle over Dante together."

"I wish it was a Dante worry now," replied Blanche: "I could understand that; but really to be angry and uncomfortable without knowing why, is rather trying."

"Are things going wrong at the castle?" inquired Eleanor.

"Oh, no! not in the least,—that is, I suppose they are not; but new people fret me and puzzle me. I don't know what they mean; and Adelaide Charlton is so persevering,—so wilful, I suppose Mrs. Howard would say; and her manner is—I can't tell what to call it—but excessively disagreeable."

Eleanor laughed heartily. "Now, that really is delightful, Blanche, to find that you can be severe like the rest of the world."

"It is not for myself," continued Blanche; "really I should not care what she did or said with me; we are cousins, and it does not signify: but it must look very strange to your mother. By Adelaide's tone, I should have fancied her to have been your intimate friend for years."

"Knowing Charles well, makes her at home with us, I suppose," replied Eleanor: "he said to me yesterday that he knew her in Italy. But do forget her oddity, Blanche, if you can, and tell me how you are going on altogether."

Blanche sighed, and then laughed. "I can't tell, and I don't know anything; I believe I am quite cross this morning. The castle seems in a complete bustle. My aunt has brought such innumerable servants, I stumble upon a new face in every corner. And it is so noisy to what it was: even when I am alone, the atmosphere of bustle seems to be around me. Moreover, I suspect I shall see exceedingly little of papa; for you know it is not really seeing him, talking in a common way, when other people are present: and Sir Hugh has taken possession of the library, so that I can't get the books I want; and Adelaide sings snatches of songs to the piano, and will not practise a single thing steadily with me; and Maude reads and says nothing, but looks as if she was not at all happy. In fact, Eleanor, I suspect I am immensely selfish;—I mean it in earnest!"

Again Eleanor laughed, and expressed herself charmed to find that Blanche could descend to the level of humanity, and be tormented by trifles. "Put out; actually put out," she exclaimed; "as I am when Susan says her lessons badly."

Blanche was silent for a few moments. She was full of thought. "There is a way of taking things, I am sure," she said; "a right way and a wrong. Just as when one begins to wind a skein of silk; if one can find the right end, it all runs smoothly; and if one begins with the wrong, it must be entangled. When I can understand them all better, perhaps I may be able to find the right end. Just now there seems an entanglement;—wills and ways mixing. They never mixed at St. Ebbe's."

"My dear Blanche, how exceedingly amusing!" exclaimed Eleanor; "but you never were in a home before,—I forgot. You don't understand what it is for grown-up people to live together. Why that sort of mixing of wills and ways, as you call it, goes on perpetually here."

"Does it?" said Blanche. "But how do you manage?"

"I go my own way, and let other people go theirs," said Eleanor lightly; "and things come round again."

"But I don't see exactly how it can be here," observed Blanche. "Your father and mother are so good, and your brother —"

"Ah!" interrupted Eleanor, "that is the point. Charles is delightful, exceedingly clever, and he can talk amusingly, and sketch, and sing duets, and rave about Italy; there is no one like him. But it does not quite do; it does not suit papa and mamma: they think a clergyman ought to be graver, and they don't know what Charles is really like; and so they are vexed with him; and he is provoked, and complains to me, and takes up my time in listening to him: and then Susan is idle because I don't attend to her, and mamma is angry with me because she says I neglect my duties; and there is a history of my home, Blanche; so now choose between the two." Blanche did not attempt to choose. A shadow of the deeper anxiety which was for ever corroding her peace, crossed her mind: and the lighter evils of which they had both been complaining, melted into nothing. Adelaide Charlton's laugh just then reached them. Eleanor stopped and listened.

"She is happy," said Blanche, gravely.

Eleanor looked round in wonder. "That from

you, Blanche! One would suppose you envied her."

"Oh! no, never; but I suppose it is natural to some people not to think. However, I did not come here to moralize; we must settle what we will do to-day. You will come to the castle as soon as you possibly can; and then we will walk, if you like it, in the afternoon. My aunt is going to pay visits, and I thought you and I might go together to see poor Susannah Dyer."

Eleanor hesitated for an instant. "You are going to walk?" she repeated in a musing tone.

"Yes; do you see any objection; would you rather not? I thought, as it was our settled day, we had better not put it off."

"Is it our day? I had forgotten," said Eleanor.

"Yes, on Thursdays we agreed to go; and as my aunt will probably be here a long time, it seemed desirable not to give up one's usual duties, if it could be helped. My aunt does not wish it; she told me so yesterday; and she half offered to go with me herself."

"Lady Charlton!" exclaimed Eleanor.

"Yes; she is not at all what I know you fancied her; she is not in the least a fine lady. I put her out of my catalogue of worries, for she is delightful."

"But she will not go with us," observed Eleanor.

"No, because of the visit; we shall have the afternoon to ourselves. Dear Eleanor! I shall enjoy it so very much."

Eleanor could not help being pleased. The tone of Blanche's voice was in itself sufficiently animating to dispel the feeling of distrust which was continually lurking, though unperceived, in her mind. She agreed that it would be very pleasant, and very right; and began to discover decided reasons why it was necessary they should go—the chief being, that as they had promised it would be necessary to keep the engagement, and that poor Susannah Dyer being blind, and helpless, and ill, had a particular claim upon them.

"And now I must go back," said Blanche, when the point was settled. "Back to my duties. Such strange ones they are, Eleanor; so unfitted for me; at least, so unlike all that I should have formed for myself."

"To stay in the drawing-room, and play the agreeable, and be referred to as the lady of the house," said Eleanor. "I shall like to come and see how you behave."

"No, you would not like it," exclaimed Blanche, energetically. "One never does like to see people out of their sphere; mine most decidedly is not to rule. You must see my aunt, Eleanor; she is the person to be at the head of affairs; you would say at once, that she could decide every question brought before her, and could tell precisely how, and why, and when, everything should be done. Papa says she has immense tact, and I think I can see it. There is an indescribable something about her which is very charming; her walk, the turn of her head, her smile—and very handsome she is too! handsome for her age; she must have been beautiful."

"I shall be afraid of her," said Eleanor, coldly and proudly.

"Oh! indeed, I don't think you will; though one or two things make me think she might be alarming if she chose it. I doubt whether Maude or Adelaide get on with her; she seems very short with them; and Maude shuts herself up the moment her mother comes into the room. As for Adelaide, she rattles on always; but there is a difference even in her."

"And Sir Hugh," inquired Eleanor; "what is he like?"

Blanche appeared uncertain how to reply, and after

waiting some seconds, laughed and said, "I don't think it is fair to question me in this manner about my relations; you shall come and judge for yourself. But I must go now, I have been very rude in leaving Adelaide such a time."

"I don't imagine Miss Charlton thinks you rude," said Eleanor, looking towards her brother and Adelaide. "I doubt whether she is tired of her companion."

Blanche stood still, and watched them. Adelaide, sitting upright, was speaking quickly; and Mr. Wentworth, standing before her and playing with a walking-stick, was listening with an expression—which, to Blanche, seemed that of attentive deference.

"He is very handsome, Blanche; is he not?" said Eleanor.

Blanche smiled thoughtfully. "Yes, very; extremely handsome. I am glad Adelaide has some one to talk to that she likes." She walked on quickly. Eleanor would not make another observation, for she was disappointed. They heard Mr. Wentworth say, as they drew near, "The charm is not in the place, but in the people." He spoke with feeling; but Adelaide only laughed, and, rallied him for his old-fashioned sentimentality; and as Blanche approached, thanked her for having interrupted their tête-à-tête, which she declared was becoming tiresome as they had said all they could think of. Mr. Wentworth turned from her, and addressed a few words to Blanche; but, after a short interval, Adelaide again dexterously engaged his attention, and kept up a series of bantering repartees till they reached the shrubbery-gate.

CHAPTER XV.

BLANCHE returned home dissatisfied. It was provoking to have spent half her morning without pleasure or profit; for her conversation with Eleanor had brought her neither. It was unconnected, desultory, and not free from petulance and irritation. She found Lady Charlton and Maude in the morning-room; one working, the other reading. Blanche took out her drawing materials. She was determined to employ herself in something which would tone her mind, and the drawing was one which her father particularly wished her to copy. Lady Charlton no sooner observed what she was doing than she left her worsted frame, and stood by watching her, and called to Maude to come and admire; but Maude only turned round languidly, and contriving to peep at the drawing without giving herself trouble said nothing, and returned to her reading. Lady Charlton laughed at her as sadly uncouth in manner, but assured Blanche that it was always her way; she was such a first-rate connoisseur; she would admire nothing, except Raphael and Guido and the old Italian masters: and then, saying that she must inquire if Sir Hugh was dressed, she left the room.

Blanche went on drawing and thinking, in a tranquil undisturbed state, which was very soothing. She was copying a Holy Family from an engraving, colouring it according to her own taste; and, as the first soft hue brought out the beautiful outline of the group, her attention was more and more fixed upon it. She had no wish for conversation; silence was natural to her, especially since she had lately spent many hours alone; and Maude, leaning back in her easy-chair, turned the leaves of her book so quietly that Blanche soon lost all consciousness of her presence. She finished the first tint, and, laying down her brush, took up the print to examine it more closely. The expression of the different faces was wonderful; pure, simple, almost severe, in their high spiritual beauty. Blanche forgot that she was an artist; she forgot to criticise or admire, and, resting her head upon her hand, she bent over it wrapt in thought.

"Are you dreaming?" was the question which woke her from her reverie; spoken in Maude's deep voice of melody. She was standing at a little distance with a closed book in her hand; a smile was upon her lips, but it had nothing of gentleness in it. Blanche started as she was addressed.

"You were dreaming," repeated Maude. "Was it of the colour of Joseph's robe?" and she laughed.

Blanche took up her pencil and replied, "It is difficult not to dream a little with such a beautiful subject before one."

"It is beautiful, is it?" continued Maude, in the same careless way. She drew nearer to the table.

Blanche moved her own drawing, and placed the engraving in a good light, and then was going away.

"Don't go," said Maude, putting her hand upon her shoulder; "tell me why you like it?"

"Why?" and Blanche's eye flashed with enthusiasm; "because it is unearthly, pure;—because it raises one's mind to look at it;—because," she added, her voice unconsciously sinking; "it brings before one the only reality."

She was again going, but Maude a second time detained her. "Then you don't like it because it is a good drawing?" she said, abruptly.

"In a measure I do; but that is a different kind of admiration—it is an artist's, and I am no artist."

Maude took the engraving in her hand, and turned to the light. "That finger is out of proportion," she said, pointing to the extended hand of the Virgin. She laid the print on the table, and gazing from the window, allowed Blanche to resume her drawing without further comment.

Blanche began her work in a different spirit. She was no longer unconscious that Maude was in the room, her presence oppressed her, and she could not succeed. Maude came behind her, and hummed a light French air; and Blanche, in despair, laid down her pencil, and looking round, said simply, "If you don't mind very much—if you would not think me odd—I should be so glad if you would go away."

Maude did not move. "Which do you like least," she said: "my presence, or my song?"

"I like neither," replied Blanche, laughing.

"Don't you? But listen! I will try something else."

She leant against Blanche's chair and paused for a second; and then, as if a voice sounded in the far distance, the melody of a German hymn fell upon Blanche's ear, soft at first, and liquid in its sweetness, but gradually swelling and deepening, till the full burst of praise seemed to fill the spacious room. It ceased suddenly as it had begun, and there was silence.

A tear rolled down Blanche's cheek.

Maude pretended not to notice it, but in her natural quick manner exclaimed, "You have not told me a word about your visit this morning. Did Adelaide carry on her flirtation successfully? I knew she would go."

"I should like to hear it again," said Blanche, unheeding the question; and looking up at her cousin with a peculiar smile—half of melancholy, and half of eager delight.

"You like music, do you?" said Maude. She seated herself at the piano, and touched a few chords, whilst Blanche returned to her drawing. Maude suffered her fingers to wander over the keys, slowly at the commencement, and as it were thoughtfully; but increasing in power and force till they moved with a rapidity which was electrifying. But again they sank into a low prelude, and the same clear flute-like notes, which before had seemed to Blanche as scarcely belonging to a human voice, were blended with them. The words were distinct as the music.

"Il passato non è
Ma se lo pinge
La viva remembranza.
Il futuro non è,
Ma se lo finge
La credula speranza.
Il presente sol è,
Che in un baleno
Passa del nulla in seno.
Dunque la vita è appunto
Una memoria, una speranza, un punto."

As the song proceeded, Blanche's pencil dropped from her hand. So surpassingly sweet it was; so thrilling in its mournful melody; so real in its expression: it seemed the true language in which the vanity of human life should be told. Maude repeated the last lines to herself, whilst she carelessly turned the leaves of a music-book which was open before her.

Blanche left her seat, and stood beside her.

"'Una memoria, una speranza, un punto;'

and that is all!" exclaimed Maude, looking round.

Blanche's colour deepened, and then it faded quite away, as she said, whilst her voice faltered; "Oh! Maude! Could you bear to think so?"

"It is truth," answered Maude. "There needs no ghost come from the grave to tell us of it." And she sang the two last lines again, with an intensity of feeling which she did not attempt to check.

Blanche stood with her eyes riveted upon her,—drinking in the sounds which at each repetition seemed more and more perfect.

"Tell me," exclaimed Maude, with an air of triumph, as she ended, "What is it, if it is not so? Where is the past? In what part of the world will you dig till you can find it?"

"But how can that which has been cease to be?" said Blanche, raising her eyes timidly to her cousin's face.

Maude paused; and regarding her steadily, said, "Are you a child, Blanche, or a woman?"

"A child, I believe," replied Blanche, laughing. "Papa tells me so."

"Yet you have notions; what are they?" The question was put with such an air of command, that Blanche, for a moment, felt herself bound to obey it; but it was only for a moment, and she answered with reserve, that it was hard to explain them: perhaps when they had been together longer, it would be less difficult.

"But I like notions; I like theories;" persisted Maude; her large grey eyes lighted up with what might almost have been termed a fierce eagerness. "I must know," she added, laying her hand upon Blanche's wrist.

Blanche drew back. A very slight accent of hauteur might have been perceptible in the tone in which she said, "Another time; not now."

Maude's brow was clouded; she rose from the piano, threw herself into a chair, took a book from the table, and tossed it down with an air of contempt; and, after some time, began walking about the room.

Blanche was annoyed with herself for being annoyed. She scarcely knew why she had been; and she sat at her drawing-table, busied in discovering the state of her own mind, and wishing that Maude would speak again and give her the opportunity of making something like an apology.

The silence was long and awkward, and disturbed at length by the dull, slow, heavy sound of crutches.

"Sir Hugh is drest, I suppose," said Blanche, glad to find something to say.

Maude did not reply.

The sound grew louder, and the complaining voice of Sir Hugh was heard, telling Pearson, as usual, that he was a desperate idiot.

Maude laughed sarcastically at the mild, deprecatory intonation which followed. She took up her book and disappeared through the window, whilst Blanche went to the door.

"Ah! my dear Blanche! I thought I should find you here; my first walk, you see. I was determined to pay my respects to you. A delightful room this!—infinitely improved!—What in the name of wonder are you doing, Pearson? Why don't you keep behind me?—Infinitely improved, my dear. That window I remember quite well. It was a plan of my own; I saw how things ought to be long ago; but your father—a very first-rate man is the earl; don't imagine that I have not the highest appreciation of his talents. Excuse me, will you? may I be allowed to rest?" And Sir Hugh was assisted into an arm-chair; and, to the consternation of Blanche, wheeled to a comfortable convenient position, which he evidently intended should, at least for the present, be a permanent one. "I was telling you," began Sir Hugh again; but he was interrupted by an exclamation—

"Sir Hugh! this really is too bad! It is far too great an exertion for him, Blanche; but he would come; he was so charmed with your half-hour's conversation yesterday. It won't do though.—Pearson, you must help your master back to the study."

"Lady Charlton! Frances, my dear! I insist; —you must not interfere. I was telling you, my dear Blanche—"

Lady Charlton broke in again. "My dear Sir Hugh;—indeed, I must have my own way. Hark! really there are visitors; and the earl—that is his footstep, I am certain. I assure you, Sir Hugh, you make me quite anxious. It is too much, a great deal too much for you," she added, her tone becoming gradually but perceptibly irritable; and taking the crutch from Pearson's hand she put it near her husband.

"Pshaw! Lady Charlton," and with an impatient jerk, the crutch was thrown to the ground, to the imminent peril of Pearson's toes. "My dear Blanche, I was telling you—"

The sparkle of Lady Charlton's eye alone told what was passing in her thoughts. When the door immediately afterwards opened, and the earl introduced Mr. and Miss Wentworth, her manner was that of the most bland goodhumour.

"So distressed, I am! so exceedingly distressed!" began Sir Hugh, attempting to rise as Eleanor came up to him.

Lady Charlton stood close beside him. "Poor Sir Hugh! He has been suffering fearfully: he is not fit to be here; but his spirits carry him beyond his strength. Your brother is an old acquaintance, Miss Wentworth. We met last year at Florence."

Mr. Wentworth was upon the point of holding out his hand to receive a cordial greeting; but the extreme civility of Lady Charlton's reception made him exchange the proposed shake of the hand for a bow, and a hope that Lady Charlton had been well since he last had the honour of seeing her.

"Quite well, thank you. You were in Italy, I believe, long after us."

"Only a few weeks; Florence became very dull."

"Indeed! I was not aware of it. We saw little general society. Rumours reached us of gaieties, but as you know," appealing to the earl, "general society is not very inviting abroad."

Lord Rutherford carelessly assented.

"We had a splendid summer at Florence, Mr. Wentworth," said Sir Hugh; "I don't know whether you ever recollect such another. I don't, except the year ——. Lord Rutherford can tell the date, I dare say; we were travellers together, taking a scientific tour on the Rhine. If you remember," he continued, addressing the earl, "you were developing your sketching powers, and I flatter myself you made considerable progress, by the help of a few occasional hints; the few hints, Mr. Wentworth, which a man engrossed in a great object could afford to give. Geology was my study: I gave up everything for it."

"Twenty years ago," said the earl coolly.—"Blanche, my love, how has your drawing advanced this morning?"

Blanche brought it forward to be criticised.

Mr. Wentworth had recovered from the slight shock of Lady Charlton's reception, and now, with a very quiet and rather dignified air, joined in the remarks which the engraving and the copy called forth. Sir Hugh looked on from a distance, stretching his head, and constantly endeavouring to interpose observations of his own, which were as constantly taken up by Lady Charlton, and repeated in a new form, and, to judge from Mr. Wentworth's manner, an interesting one, for his marked attention was given to whatever she uttered; and, as Lord Rutherford was about to replace the drawing in its former position, he begged permission to bring it nearer for her inspection and Sir Hugh's.

Blanche liked him better as she watched what was passing; she had not thought before that he could be so easy and agreeable, and yet so respectful.

"A very pleasant thing it is to meet a travelled friend again, Mr. Wentworth," said Sir Hugh, quite excited by the patience with which a disquisition upon the comparative merits of two of the early Italian masters had been listened to; "quite a gratification, I assure you. Lady Charlton and myself shall have great pleasure in renewing past recollections; and my daughters—Maude! where is Maude? My dear Blanche, surely she has been with you this morning?"

"Maude is walking on the terrace," said Lady Charlton quickly, "and Adelaide is rambling over the grounds, I suppose; she went out directly after breakfast."

Blanche did not think it well to throw more light than was necessary upon the movements of either. There was a certain intonation in her aunt's voice which she was just beginning to interpret.

"Ah, well, you will meet at luncheon; but I forgot—really—Lord Rutherford—Lady Blanche, I ought to apologize." Lady Charlton bit her lip, and gave an apparently involuntary push to Sir Hugh's chair, which made him stop short, with an exclamation of pain.

Lord Rutherford was talking to Eleanor at the window, and did not hear what was said, and the burden of hospitality fell upon Blanche. Gracefully but timidly she repeated the request that Mr. Wentworth would remain, and the invitation was soon seconded by the earl, with that perfect though distant politeness which leaves no room for complaint. Mr. Wentworth was therefore established on a comparatively familiar footing; and Blanche, feeling herself no longer bound to entertain him, left the room with Eleanor.

CHAPTER XVI.

IMPORTANT consequences, it is well known, often follow from very slight beginnings. Mr. Wentworth's first introduction at Rutherford Castle was marked by no circumstances but those incidental to morning visits; yet it gave the tone to the intercourse which was to follow.

The earl's reserve and pride would have induced him to hesitate long before he allowed any persons in the neighbourhood, except his own peculiar friends, to be on such terms as to call early, and lounge away an hour and remain to luncheon, and perhaps join the riding and walking parties in the afternoon; but what had been done once came rather naturally a second time, and certainly Lord Rutherford had no cause to suppose that Mr. Wentworth's presence or absence had the slightest effect upon the only individual with whom he chose to concern himself. Even as Eleanor's brother, Blanche could only partially like Mr. Wentworth. His talents, his versatility of manner and ease of conversation, and the right principle and good sense which he always put forth when conversing with her could not blind her to his faults; and Blanche could only feel interest where she felt respect. It was perfectly indifferent to herself whether Mr. Wentworth formed one of the circle or not; but childlike though she was, and simple in many of her ideas, Blanche could not fail to perceive that it was not so to others. Yet, even when the fact was acknowledged, Blanche scarcely thought of it. She noticed that Adelaide Charlton liked to talk and laugh with Mr. Wentworth; and she observed that for some reason or other Lady Charlton frowned and looked vexed; and she discovered that Mr. Wentworth contrived to ingratiate himself with Sir Hugh, and was rather disliked by Maude. But the little incidents, which would have afforded matter for sarcasm and ridicule to a more experienced eye, passed before her as the scenes of a theatre before a preoccupied, abstracted spectator. For Blanche lived in a world of her own; or rather she lived in the world of her friends and relations, seeing the same sights, hearing the same sounds, and performing the same actions; yet often deriving impressions totally contrary to theirs, from all that was passing around.

So probably it must often be when religion becomes the predominant feeling of the heart very early in life: it is all-powerful then, for it has no master passion to oppose it. Adopted later in life, it must struggle with past evil recollections, and be frequently crushed and overborne by what we falsely term the realities of the world. We try to think that earth is nothing, that heaven is all; but when we have toiled for years in the pursuit of wealth, or pleasure, or fame, how shall we in a moment persuade ourselves, that they are worthless? Like the fisherman in the eastern tale, we have voluntarily opened the casket in which the mighty spirit of delusion was encased, and that which seemed at first but a faint mist of evil has gathered itself up into a giant form, and made itself our lord; and, when we would fain command it back to its original nothingness, we find that our will is powerless to enforce obedience. That Blanche retained her earnestness and sincerity of purpose was not owing to any particularly advantageous circumstances; life at Rutherford Castle was, in its exterior, what life is in almost all places where there is no one great business or occupation to mould it into some definite form: there were rather late breakfasts, mornings seemingly frittered away in light reading, music, letter-writing, and not very profitable conversation; afternoons devoted to some drive or ride; seven o'clock dinners and idle, talking, musical evenings. What was the purport of all that was said or done no one seemed to inquire. Lord Rutherford, indeed, spent much of his time in his study, and busied himself in managing his estates. His object was a definite one; yet he was the only person, except Blanche, who appeared dissatisfied with it. After the first excitement of his sister-in-law's arrival was over he seemed inclined to sink back into the reserved and even contemptuous mood, which had occasionally shown itself before when he was alone with Blanche. Lady Charlton's vivacity indeed often roused him, and brought out flashes of brilliant wit and quick observation; but he soon relapsed again into silence,—in Sir Hugh's presence especially; though, fortunately for his temper and his peace, the gout lingered much longer than was expected, and kept Sir Hugh in a great measure a prisoner to his room. When he was absent the earl would occasionally read aloud, or enter into conversations with Lady Charlton, which, as they seemed to possess a power to engage his attention and give him pleasure, were eagerly listened to by Blanche.

They were certainly very agreeable, full of anecdote and information. Blanche's opinion of her aunt's talents and power of mind, and even of her principles, increased daily. For Lady Charlton never gave way to the earl's implied doubts of goodness, or clever sarcasm upon things and people whom Blanche had learned to reverence. She spoke openly, and in a measure earnestly upon all serious topics; blamed what was wrong, and approved of what was right, and when left alone with Blanche sympathized with any indication of her deeper feelings, more particularly when they were in any way connected with her mother. Blanche was beginning to lean upon and trust her, at times even to think that she might partly supply Mrs. Howard's place as a guide in her daily actions. They were very different, different in a way which Blanche felt better than she could describe; but their ideas seemed the same. Lady Charlton was more cheerful, more full of life and hope; she had more interest in passing events than Mrs. Howard; but they liked the same people, approved of the same books, professed the same motives. Blanche could not have spoken to her aunt upon anything which immediately involved her own most sacred thoughts, for such confidence can scarcely be given except to one person, and Lady Charlton was too recent a friend, and too lively and lighthearted, to offer occasions for alluding to them; but in all minor points she seemed a safe counsellor, and one whom the earl was particularly pleased that Blanche should apply to.

"I wish you knew her," wrote Blanche to Mrs. Howard, in one of the weekly letters, which no occupation was ever allowed to stop. "I should feel more çertain then of my own opinion about her. Perhaps you will think it is not right to sit in judgment upon one who is so much my superior in age, and so nearly related to me; but I do not know how to help it. I think you can scarcely imagine how entirely I am forced to form my own decisions, and act upon my own will. The last few months, since we parted, have worked a marvellous change. I am mistress of the castle, and forced to order and arrange, and treated with a deference which at first completely puzzled me. Papa seems to delight that it should be so. He will never allow the least opposition; he calls me queen in jest, and when I beg him to tell me what he wishes for himself, a cloud comes over him, and he insists that he has no will but mine: and yet to others he is so different. This is not what ought to be, is it? It frightens me: I long for some one to remind me of my duties; to scold me, and tell me when I do wrong—which indeed is every hour in the day. I wish my aunt would do it. She has such very high principles, such good notions about everything. I am sure she must perpetually see that I am not acting rightly, but she never hints at its being possible. I do make her give me advice in common things, receiving visitors, arranging for dinner-parties, and so on; but it is all done laughingly, with a half apology, as if she had no reason to suppose I did not know all that she does. What I most wish just now is to have some plan for the arrangement of my time. I have thought a good deal about it lately; for the kind of life I lead at present is exceedingly unsatisfactory, and yet I cannot tell how to alter it. If we have visitors, I must attend to them; and really that takes up more time than any one not on the spot would imagine. My aunt constantly says that she will not interrupt me, if she thinks I have anything to do: but then she begins talking, and I am bound in courtesy to listen; and very willingly, I must own, for she is the most agreeable person I ever met with. Anecdotes she has to bring forward on every occasion, and they are never wearying, they are told so quickly, and with such spirit. She quite understands giving one resting-places, and entering into anything one says in reply. Really the hours pass by, and I have not the least idea that they are gone. Yet they are not satisfactory to look back upon. Then, if my aunt is not with me, Adelaide and Maude are; and Adelaide is like a butterfly, flying from one pursuit to another, and calling upon me to follow her and Maude—I meant to have written a great deal about her, but I must not to-day: if I once begin I shall certainly not leave off in time. She interests me though, that I must say; and frightens me too. We had a little quarrel the other day, a very tiny one, but still sufficient to make me feel what she might be if she were offended. I am afraid I am very proud: she rather ordered me, and my spirit rebelled, and I showed that I was annoyed. I thought perhaps she would have been angry with me a long time; but instead of that she came up to me afterwards, the first moment we were alone, and gave me a kiss, so kind! it made me ten times more vexed with myself than I was before. Yet the next moment she was just like her old self, and I do not feel I have advanced in the least with her. All this is sadly wandering from my first subject, but when I write to you I always do wander: so many things come to my mind which I long to say. You will understand though that I lead a very unsettled, idle life, and that Eleanor leads a very useful, busy one; and when we meet to compare notes I become discontented with myself, and long to do better, but do not know how to set about it. My aunt said she would go with me to visit the poor people, and I know she would, if she could find a leisure day; but there is always some engagement. Poor Susannah has been very much neglected in consequence. Eleanor has promised to go when she can, but Dr. Wentworth trusted her particularly to me. She sent me a message the other day, asking to see me. You see I tell you all my faults, as I used to do in the happy old times: sometimes—is it wrong to say so?—I fancy they were happier than these. At any rate, I know that I never went to bed then with the same burden of unfulfilled duties upon my conscience. Some rules however I can keep, and some things I hope I do not forget. I can never be sufficiently thankful that I was confirmed when I was. Preparation would have been so much more difficult here, and I think I might have gone on in an unsettled way, fancying that confirmation would be a new starting-point, and work some great change in itself. Whereas, now I feel that all has been done for me which I could expect, and that if I do not advance steadily, I must go back without any prospect of being roused and warned again. Still I am uncomfortable and anxious. The very fact of bringing my present mode of life into a definite form, by writing about it, makes it assume a more serious aspect. I am sure it must be very faulty in some way; and what will it be when I go to London?"

CHAPTER XVII.

The answer to this letter brought a sad disappointment to Blanche. The continued illness of Mrs. Howard's niece made her anticipate the probability of going abroad, and would at any rate interfere with the visit to Rutherford, which had so long been promised. Blanche had not realized before how much she had lived upon the thought of this visit,—how entirely she had looked forward to it as the means of making Mrs. Howard acquainted with the fears and uncertainties which she had never yet found courage to mention openly. A week spent together would have sufficed to show the loneliness of mind,—the absence of sympathy,—the uncongeniality between herself and her father upon the one most important point, which caused her daily grief. There would have been no need of words: Mrs. Howard would have felt and understood all. Now that sinking, decaying isolation of heart must still remain, unless she could explain. But what was there to explain? What had she to say?—the loved, petted, idolized daughter of a man in whom the world agreed to see no fault except pride,—why was she not happy?

"Read it, Eleanor," she said, putting the letter into her friend's hand, as they met that same afternoon at the parsonage, whilst tears, in spite of herself, rose to her eyes. "There is not a shadow of hope for months,—probably not before next year."

Eleanor glanced at the full sheet. "Am I to read it all?"

"If you will: it is in answer to mine. But I have scarcely thought of the advice in it yet."

Eleanor took the letter, and Blanche walked up and down the gravel path, and very soon afterwards Mrs. Wentworth joined her. Blanche could not conceal that she was out of spirits, and there was real kindness in the tone in which Mrs. Wentworth addressed her, with a regret for the unpleasant news which she had only just heard. Poor Blanche was always very alive to sympathy. The tears, which had only glistened before, fell fast, and Mrs. Wentworth was touched by her distress; and opening the French window of a small room, which fronted the flower-garden, begged her to go in, and seat herself, and be alone if she liked it. "It was her own little room," she said; "and no one would come near to disturb her."

Blanche was only too willing to hide herself from observation. She expected Mrs. Wentworth to follow her; but she did not; and Blanche leant back on the sofa, and for a time indulged her own sad, disappointed fancies. When she at last raised her eyes, it was to rest them upon an object which at once withdrew her thoughts from the present trial, and sent them far back into the past. On one side of the fireplace hung a small painting, the subject of which she recognised in an instant. It was her mother's likeness; but how different from the subdued, sorrow-stricken countenance which dwelt in her memory as the only true resemblance of the lovely Countess of Rutherford. The picture before her represented a young lady, who could scarcely, so it seemed, have passed the age of twenty, standing on the steps of the castle, dressed in a riding-habit, and caressing a splendid horse, which she was evidently prepared to mount. The face was bright, even mirthful; the eyes sparkling with expectation; the mouth joyous in its expression of happiness. There was no striving for effect in the picture; nothing but the simple representation of what must actually have been witnessed. Blanche felt, as she looked upon it, that the artist who could so have portrayed her mother must have drawn her as she actually stood, without forethought or design. Five years afterwards, that fair, young creature had become the pale, serious, care-worn woman, whose beauty was overshadowed by a fixed, it might almost have been called, a stern melancholy; and whose fascination was the influence of that purity of mind which grief has prepared for heaven.

The picture, and the thoughts that it called forth, struck a chord in the mind of Lady Blanche, which at that moment was peculiarly though painfully sensitive. If her mother had been spared, not even Mrs. Howard's friendship would have been needed. And again an undefined doubt, followed by a longing for a truer insight into that mother's history, arose within her. Her attention was so engrossed, that Mrs. Wentworth knocked at the door without being answered, and Blanche started when she came in, as if the privacy of her own apartment had been intruded upon. The attitude in which she was standing, leaning upon the mantelpiece and gazing upon the picture, told at once the subject of her thoughts.

"I did not know you had it," she said, in a tone of gentle reproach, as Mrs. Wentworth came up to her. Mrs. Wentworth appeared at a loss for a reply. "And it must be like her," continued Blanche, still with the same manner, as if she was vexed at having long been deprived of a great pleasure.

"It was like her once,—for a short time," said Mrs. Wentworth, her voice sinking at the last words, as it so often did when referring to persons and events connected with other days.

"I feel it must have been like," repeated Blanche; "more like than the bust at the castle; more like than this," and she unfastened her brooch.

"It is not the face by which she was most known," said Mrs. Wentworth, rather indifferently. "I am sorry you have seen it; it will only disturb your ideas."

"No, no!" exclaimed Blanche. "I should be so glad if I could know her as she was always; as a child,—as a woman,—as what I am now," she added, with a faint smile.

A slight contraction was visible in Mrs. Wentworth's forehead, the effect, perhaps, of some sudden pain; but she answered in her usual, undisturbed manner:—"There is no picture of Lady Rutherford as she was at your age, my dear Lady Blanche. This was taken three weeks after her marriage."

"And for you?—was it her gift to you?" inquired Blanche, with eagerness.

"No, not her gift. It was—" Mrs. Wentworth paused, coughed, and then added quickly, "it was the earl's once."

"And he parted with it?" exclaimed Blanche. "Oh, Mrs. Wentworth! even to you!"

"I loved her," was the reply, uttered sharply and bitterly; and Blanche in an instant reproached herself for her words.

"Yes, indeed, I know you did. I know you were her great friend. Forgive me: you had of course a claim. But is there no copy,—no other picture like it, taken at that time? Three weeks after her marriage! How happy she looks!—my own sweet mother!" and Blanche drew near with the impulse to press her lips to the cold, lifeless figure. She checked herself however. Mrs. Wentworth's calmness seemed a reproof for indulging anything like excited feeling. "Perhaps," she said, turning to Mrs. Wentworth, with a smile of singular attraction, so full it was of subdued eagerness, and softness, and hope,—"perhaps, some day, if I might be permitted, I would ask to have it copied. It would be a great treasure. You will understand," she added; and in her earnestness she took Mrs. Wentworth's hand, as if to entreat by action as well as by word.

To her surprise, Mrs. Wentworth hesitated. "She would, if it were possible;—anything which could be done should be, Lady Blanche might be certain of that. Artists were very rarely in the neighbourhood; but it might be possible, just possible."

Blanche drew back her hand,—she began her reply proudly, and it was an apology; she had not known that she was asking such a favour:—then conscience reproached her for pride shown to her mother's early friend, and she tried to alter her manner. Mrs. Wentworth stood passively by her, listening politely. An unpleasant silence followed what Blanche said,—a stiffness and restraint on both sides; but it was broken in upon by Mrs. Wentworth.

"The original is so invaluable to me," she began.

Blanche interrupted her:—"You do not think I could wish for that? No, I assure you, not for a moment."

"There are associations connected with it," pursued Mrs. Wentworth, quietly: "no copy would possess them. I was present when the picture was taken. I watched its progress from the commencement. The first sketch was made on the countess's birthday,—she was just twenty. It was done by an amateur, a friend of Lord Rutherford's, who was staying at the castle. The countess had no idea of his intention; but I was aware of it, and assisted him. I kept her, that is, in conversation."

"And it was my father's?" said Blanche, musingly.

"Yes:" and again Mrs. Wentworth's manner grew very constrained; and, after a short pause, she said, awkwardly, "I do not think the earl would like to see it; it might remind him—" Blanche waited some moments for the continuation of the sentence; when it came, it was so hurried that she could scarcely comprehend it:—"It might remind him," repeated Mrs. Wentworth, "that is, it would certainly bring to his recollection:—I think it might annoy him to be spoken to about it," were the concluding words.

Annoy! what a strange, cold expression! But Mrs. Wentworth was incomprehensible; and so different on this day to what she generally was, so frightened apparently out of her usual self-possession! Blanche felt quite bewildered. She turned from the picture, and saying that she was now quite rested, and would rejoin Eleanor, was preparing to go, when Mrs. Wentworth detained her.

"It is not pleasant to me to part in this way," she said, more freely; "to appear unkind, as I must do. Might I hope that you would excuse it; that you would make allowance for painful recollections? I think you will," she added, looking kindly at Blanche; "for your mother's sake I think you will excuse any unintentional awkwardness in one who loved her very dearly."

Blanche's displeasure vanished in an instant. "My mother's friend must always be privileged," she said, putting her hand into that of Mrs. Wentworth; "even if there were anything to excuse; but, indeed,—of course, I can understand." The mutual pressure of the hand was affectionate; but Blanche was relieved when she stepped into the open air: and she had not forgotten,—there had been no second offer of procuring a copy of the picture.

CHAPTER XVIII.

"VISITORS in the drawing-room, my lady," were the words which greeted Blanche, when she and Eleanor reached the castle, with the hope of making some arrangements for spending the afternoon more profitably than had seemed possible of late.

"Friends of my aunt's, I suppose," said Blanche, speaking to Eleanor in an under tone. "Is Lady Charlton there?" she inquired, aloud.

"Yes, my lady: Lady Charlton and Miss Adelaide. The carriage has been ordered away."

Blanche went into the house. "We need not appear, I imagine," she said to Eleanor. "I am supposed to be out; and if we once put ourselves in the way, there is an end to all our plans for poor Susannah." Eleanor agreed that there was no absolute necessity; but she stopped at the foot of the staircase, and wondered who the visitors could be.

"We shall be waylaid, undoubtedly," said Blanche, trying to hasten her.

"Hush! who is that speaking?" asked Eleanor, listening.

"Sir Hugh scolding Pearson, or Pearson scolding Sir Hugh," said Blanche laughing. "Really, Eleanor, you are determined to be caught." Blanche spoke in jest, but her words might possibly have been true, for just then the drawing-room door opened and a number of voices were heard.

"We shall be seen, if we attempt to go up-stairs now," said Eleanor decidedly; but she had no one to hear her observation, for Blanche had already escaped to her room. She sat there for some little time very patiently. Eleanor, of course, had waited the one moment too long and been detained; it was provoking, but there was no help for it, and Blanche took out Mrs. Howard's letter, in order to occupy the intervening time. It was curiously appropriate to that precise moment. So much of it was upon the subject of daily duties, daily interruptions, and the spirit in which they should be borne.

"I am not in the least surprised at your complaints of desultoriness, my dear child," began Mrs. Howard. "All persons situated as you are must in a certain way be desultory, or, more correctly, they must I suppose appear to be so; for it does not follow that you should be so really. When you laid down your strict rules, before you went away, I was convinced in my own mind that you would find a difficulty in carrying them out, but I did not like to dishearten you, since a plan of life is in itself good, even necessary, if we wish to discipline our minds properly. The great mischief of such plans is when the fulfilment of them is too rigidly insisted upon, and is raised into a virtue in itself, instead of being considered as merely a stepping-stone. However I need not descant upon the danger of too much regularity; your difficulty seems to lie quite in the other direction. Naturally it would be so, for you cannot possibly be entirely mistress of your own time, and you certainly are bound in duty to consider the comfort of your guests before your own. But there must be a limit to every duty, humanly speaking, or it will encroach upon another, and become a fault. And this limit, I think, is to be found by having a true sense of our position, not only in life but in our families. As a daughter, you are of course bound to obey; but, as the mistress of a household, you are equally bound to take the lead, and to set an example of order and strictness. I doubt if you are likely to remember this sufficiently. Your mode of life must in a great measure give the tone to your whole household, and one of the most important features in all families, especially in one which like your own possesses influence from rank and wealth, is that it should be under subservience to a law of duty and not of pleasure. I do not mean that it is possible to make laws for every hour, or every individual; but it should never be left in doubt that there are claims which *must* be attended to; employments which are *never* to be neglected except for some very obvious reason. If your mother had been spared, these responsibilities would not have been yours as yet; but you are peculiarly circumstanced, and there are duties incumbent upon you which seldom fall to the lot of persons of your age. I wish I could give you my ideas more in detail, for I am afraid I shall not satisfy you; but what I mean is something of this kind—I suppose you breakfast late, but that need not prevent you from rising early. If you set the example, the servants must in a measure follow it, so one great temptation in an easy life will be checked. I think you would find it useful not to shut yourself up entirely in your room, but to let your servants see what your habits are—as example is better than reproof, and indeed reproof can scarcely, I imagine, be in the catalogue of your duties at present. Then with regard to your mornings—you intended, I know, to study regularly; and certainly it seems to me that you ought to do so. Could you not manage to give a certain fixed time to your aunt and cousins, and any other guests, directly after breakfast, and then let it be understood that you wish to have an hour or two to yourself? I hardly think you would give offence, and your absence would by degrees be taken as a matter of course. Perhaps, also, you might be able to arrange to practise with your cousins, as you say they are both musical; but then, my dear Blanche, you must take the lead. If your cousin Adelaide likes, what you call, a butterfly life, it does not at all follow that you are to humour her: and though she may be some years older than yourself, that will not prevent your being of great use in keeping her steadily to one object, if you show you are determined to be steady yourself. So, again, I would beg of you if possible to decide upon seeing the poor people on fixed days; and, when these days come, say you have an engagement, and make any plans for drives, visits, &c., for your friends, independent of yourself. Your reading also may be a great help to you as regards system and regularity, if you can avoid the temptation of beginning every new book that is thrown in your way—a temptation which, I assure you, I can quite sympathise with. We cannot always be studying history and metaphysics, but when we do indulge ourselves in light reading it should be for some specified reason—at certain times, and under certain limitations. I really believe that half the mischief of novels, those I mean which are innocent, arises from their being so enticing that we are induced to read them at wrong times. It may seem a very slight fault to skim half a dozen pages more when duty calls us another way; but I am sure it injures the conscience and untones the mind. If we can read a very interesting book up to a certain moment, and then resolutely close it because we have something else to do, the relaxation can scarcely have done us harm. I am saying nothing about higher rules and motives, because we have talked of them so often before, and I am sure from your letter that you have not forgotten them.

"This constant self-discipline, no doubt, requires energy and watchfulness, but what is to be done without them? Especially what can be done by persons situated as you are, having scarcely any external restraints upon their inclinations? You must be a law to yourself if you wish to avoid that wretched frittering away of life which is the misery of hundreds of persons of your age at the present moment.

"All I have said is of course subject to one proviso—that your father should not object. If he were to insist, or even evidently to desire, that you should give yourself up entirely to your aunt and cousins, you can but submit: only here again you would find a law, and therefore a satisfaction. It is not *what* we do, but *why* we do it, that is of consequence. How often we say to ourselves, speaking of things of this world, 'It does not signify, it is all in the day's work?'—and so, neither, does it signify in the concerns of another world, whether we are called upon to rule a kingdom or pick up stones from the road, if only what we do is *work:* work that shall turn to account in the reckoning of the long day of life; work for Him to whom nothing is great and therefore nothing can be little."

Blanche refolded her letter and sat for sometime thinking over it. She could not at once fully enter into Mrs. Howard's views; or, at least, she could not at once see that they were practicable. Yet they had given her an idea, a principle which might materially assist her in the little difficulties that often perplexed her. Blanche's mind was resolute and decisive. This was not generally supposed; but those who were in the habit of interpreting her conduct, too often did so without the least knowledge of the real clue to it. Lady Charlton saw her amiable, agreeable, and attractive, and called her "a sweet girl;" and Mrs. Wentworth understood, from conversation with Eleanor, that she was very much fascinated by Lady Charlton, and accustomed to follow out her cousins' wishes, and, in consequence, was likely to lead a desultory objectless life; and supposed therefore that she was too gentle to be strong-minded. Lord Rutherford indeed understood her better; perhaps, if he had not done so; he never could have given her his full affection; for, like her, he required respect to bring out his feelings, though it was respect for the intellect, not for the heart; and one of the most satisfactory discoveries he had made in the progress of their intercourse was that she could have an opinion and a will of her own. But, even to him, it would have been a matter of surprise to witness the immediate effect of Mrs. Howard's advice. He could not have understood the working of a mind which obeyed conscience as it were instinctively, and to which the bare possibility of a duty suggested an instant endeavour for its performance. Blanche required only to perceive that Mrs. Howard was right in her views, and of this a very little consideration convinced her, and then her thoughts turned to the practical mode of carrying them out, quickly, sincerely, without delay, or reservation, or excuse, and in perfect simplicity: not at all considering it necessary to guard against observation, or to hide anything which she intended to do; but supposing other persons would regard her duties as she did herself, as matters of course. She had already solved several difficult questions, when Eleanor's quick step was heard in the gallery, and scarcely pausing to knock at the door she entered the room with the exclamation:—

"My dear Blanche! I am so—so sorry; I really am vexed to have kept you; but —"

"But if people will put themselves in the way they must expect to be caught," said Blanche laughing; "however, we can go now."

"No, I beg your pardon, that was what I came to

say," continued Eleanor, hurriedly. "I am afraid we can't go this afternoon. Lady Charlton wishes me so very much to stay: they are going out,—a large party: she quite pressed my joining them. I am to drive with your cousin Adelaide."

Blanche could not conceal her vexation. "And does my aunt expect me to go, too?" she inquired.

"Oh! no, I assure you, I was very careful. I did not mention your name. No one thinks you are in the house. They suppose I had come to the castle to look for you; and now I have left them with the excuse, that I must write a note to mamma to tell her what I intend doing."

"And shall you write?" asked Blanche.

"Why no, upon second thoughts, I don't see there is a necessity. I was to spend the afternoon with you, but whether I go for a walk or a drive must be a question of indifference." The latter part of the sentence was spoken in that tone of decision which is sometimes used to conceal a doubt. Blanche, without making any observation in reply, put aside the writing materials which she was placing for Eleanor's use.

"Why will you not go with us, Blanche?" continued Eleanor. "Why can you not wait till to-morrow?"

"Because to-morrow will be like to-day," said Blanche: "it will have its own duties."

"But I could walk with you then; I promise that I will not put myself in the way of temptation again."

"Then it was temptation," said Blanche, a little reproachfully.

"Perhaps so; it might have been: but I see no harm in it. Whether you go alone to Susannah, or whether I am with you, cannot make much difference to her."

"But it does to me," said Blanche, unable to repress a feeling of vexation that Eleanor should prefer a drive with a party of comparative strangers to a walk with herself.

Eleanor laughed, and declared that Blanche must be jealous of her cousin Adelaide; but there was self-dissatisfaction beneath her assumed indifference, and she brought forward a number of excuses for her determination. "Lady Charlton pressed it so much," she said, "it was almost impossible to refuse; in fact, I suspect she wants me as a chaperone. They had not settled how it was all to be arranged. Charles was there, striving hard for the honour of driving your cousin, himself; but Lady Charlton had evidently set her face against it. So, you see, I may be useful."

Blanche did her best to enter into Eleanor's gaiety, but she could not succeed very well; for, as she began to think of what was to be done, she saw that all her plans were disarranged; and Eleanor soon perceived it, also.

At the moment of accepting the invitation to join Lady Charlton's party, she had not remembered that Blanche could not well walk as far as Susannah's cottage alone. "However the next day would do just as well," she said, "and Blanche had better make up her mind to give up duty for that afternoon, and go with the rest."

This Blanche declined; since she was not wanted, she preferred having the time to herself. "I suppose you could not send an excuse to my aunt," she suggested.

But Eleanor negatived the idea instantly, and after again begging Blanche to forgive her, and promising to behave better for the future, hastened away.

CHAPTER XIX.

Blanche stood at the window, watching the party, which was collecting in front of the castle. She saw Eleanor join them, and converse a little with Adelaide; and, after some delay, they both seated themselves in the pony carriage, and drove off—closely followed by Mr. Wentworth on horseback. Blanche could almost have repented having refused to accompany them; since there was no apparent obstacle in the way. But she felt that she had done what was best for her own mind, and there was great pleasure in the quietness and solitude now so unusual; and when the rumbling of the wheels and the echo of the horses' hoofs died away in the distance, she lingered still by the open window to enjoy the unbroken silence within the house; and the low, soothing, mingled sounds of nature without. They are rare and precious moments, which are thus snatched from the whirl of life and spent in stillness and alone. Even when they are not devoted to direct meditation, and appear too fleeting to be productive of good, they yet tend to give us a knowledge of the realities which encompass us. By the depth of their solemnity and repose, they remind us that beneath the surface of this weary, working existence, there is another world — another, and an enduring life;— imaged in the unchanging sky and the returning sun, and the ever renewed beauty of the trees and flowers, and the steadfastness of the everlasting hills; and, if our hearts are open to the truth, they may sometimes teach us to remember, that as in far-off years the glorious temple rose silently in the city of Jerusalem, neither axe nor hammer nor tool giving warning or notice of the work, so the more glorious temple—the Church of the Living God,—is at this moment rising unperceived in the midst of a tumultuous world; each stone quarried and fashioned by the sharp edge of sorrow and the keen stroke of adversity, until perfected and prepared, it is fitted for that destined position which shall be the place of its rest for eternity.

Thoughts something like these filled the mind of Blanche as she sat alone, enjoying the unwonted quietness of the summer's afternoon. She had early learnt to look upon what is, not what seems to be; but, during the last few weeks, the truth had been at times overlooked. Notwithstanding the dissatisfaction expressed to Mrs. Howard, she had found much enjoyment in the society of Lady Charlton and her cousins; perhaps too much, for it had unconsciously relaxed the strict, watchful tone of her character. She perceived this now. Mrs. Howard's letter had given the first warning; and this short interval of reflection repeated it. Again she reverted to the question of duty, but less practically than before. There is a close connection between the mystery of what we see and the mystery of what we are; and when Blanche looked upon the glorious landscape beneath her, and the immensity of the sky above her, she was carried away far beyond the immediate consideration of daily pursuits into thoughts and speculations for which no answer could be found. Metaphysical difficulties suggested themselves; questions upon the origin of duty—its binding power—the irremediable consequences of its neglect—the very fact of its existence, involving the possibility of evil; and this again opening a new path for the reason to travel, till it stood upon the brink of a precipice, and recoiled shuddering from its own presumption. There are many amongst the young whom such thoughts harass when it is little suspected;—many, who are armed with no shield of faith for their protection. We may well pray for them, for their peril is great!

"Is that you, Blanche?" exclaimed a voice from below, as Blanche still stood at the window.

Blanche started. "Maude! alone! I thought I saw you with the rest."

"No, thank you; I am not a gregarious animal. And such a set too, as they were!—just fitted for Adelaide. But come down, I want you."

Blanche delayed. She had not settled what she was going to do; but, certainly, she had no intention of spending the afternoon with Maude.

"Come, you must come," repeated Maude, impatiently; "we will have a German lesson. I promised you one. We will sit upon the south terrace; it is deliciously warm."

Blanche went to another window, from which the terrace could be seen. It certainly was a most inviting spot, with the bright slanting rays of the sun upon it, and the flowers bordering it radiant in beauty; whilst, below, were contrasted the deep shadows of the trees on the bank, and the glittering lines of light which flickered on the sides of the distant hills. She paused for a moment to consider; and it seemed right to go;—right, since her afternoon was interrupted, to take advantage of Maude's offer.

"We will read," said Maude, holding up a book; "only make haste."

Blanche threw a shawl round her and ran down stairs. Maude met her at the hall-door. She looked quite satisfied,—an unusual thing for her,—and Blanche was glad that she had assented.

"I fancied I was quite alone," observed Maude,

as she sat down on a bench in the shade. "Why did you not go with the rest?"

"I was not asked," replied Blanche; "that is," observing Maude's look of surprise, "I did not put myself in the way of being asked. I meant to have gone out with Eleanor."

"Charity visiting, I suppose?" said Maude, with a slight sneer. "Well! you are very good, Blanche; but, depend upon it, it will be better for you to spend the afternoon in reading 'Egmont' with me."

"Egmont! Goethe's Egmont!" exclaimed Blanche hastily, and with doubt.

"Yes. Why not?"

"Goethe!" again repeated Blanche.

"Well!" and Maude looked up almost angrily. "What is the harm of Goethe?"

"I don't know, myself. I have never read anything of his."

"Only the name frightens you. Now, my dear Blanche, do for once have an opinion of your own. Don't be a Quixote and convert a windmill into a giant, and then set to work to fight it."

"But the world is the Quixote," said Blanche, laughing; "not I. I only go by what I hear."

"The world! that is some few bigoted individuals who condemn every creed which is not cut and squared after their own pattern. Your father does not say so, I am sure."

"No; he has often promised to read part of Goethe with me. Only part," she added, laying her hand upon the book, as Maude with a triumphant smile opened it. "Egmont is a part—a very grand part, perfectly unexceptionable."

"Are you sure?" said Blanche. "I think"—and she raised her eyes to her cousin's face with an expression of child-like confidence;—"I think I might trust you."

The sneer which still rested upon Maude's lips vanished directly. She turned to Blanche, and said eagerly, "Thank you; yes, of course you may trust. Whatever I might read myself, I could never ask you to listen to a word which might offend you."

"But Goethe," said Blanche, as if speaking aloud her own thoughts; "there is such a prejudice against him—there must be something wrong—something dangerous."

"Dangerous! absurd folly!" and Maude turned the leaves quickly in her irritation, exclaiming—as she went on, "The fear of weak, narrow-minded cowards—false to their own conviction—envious of a great mind. Blanche, you must not be one of them."

"I hope I should be always true to my own convictions," answered Blanche; "but it is very possible that you may call them narrow-minded. I think you would," she added, boldly.

Maude fixed upon her a steady, penetrating gaze, and said slowly, "I like that; better be narrow-minded and firm, than narrow-minded and weak. You shall read Egmont."

"Tell me its faults, first," said Blanche.

"Faults! it has none. It is the most wonderfully true, noble, inspiriting—but, you are a coward, after all;" and she threw down the book and stood gazing over the edge of the terrace.

Blanche went up to her. "I hope I am not a coward, Maude; but we all know the weak points of our own minds. Goethe's works must have something in them which does harm to some persons—I may possibly be one. Tell me if there is anything in Egmont which is generally objected too."

"By whom?" said Maude, sarcastically. "By Mrs. Smith—Brown—White—Green—Black?"

"By persons whose opinions I am bound to respect."

"By yourself, rather," exclaimed Maude, impatiently. "Do forget such folly, Blanche, and judge for yourself. As for the story, it is matter of history; though with Goethe, it is not history, but actual, breathing, reality. It is Egmont as he was, as he lived, and talked, and thought; with his gallant, chivalric bearing—his openness, generosity, disinterestedness, love of freedom, fearlessness of the world's censure. One must have loved him,—one must have been Clärchen, who died with him."

Blanche repeated quickly, "Died with him?"

"Yes; for him—with him; she loved him too well to survive him."

The next words were uttered by Blanche hurriedly, with an effort; "Who committed suicide, do you mean?"

"Pshaw! yet I might have known it,—it is all education. Suicide! Yes, what people call suicide. She kills herself. You are shocked. What a mistake to have told you! It is all spoilt now; but you shall read it still; and tell me whether Goethe cannot ennoble such a death."

Maude put her arm round her cousin to draw her back to the seat, but Blanche resisted. "I am not afraid to read it," she said; "but it will give me pain."

"Yes; that pain which is pleasure,—the pain of sympathy and admiration."

"That was not what I meant. I am sure I should admire it, but I could not sympathize with it."

"Not with Egmont?—not with Clärchen?

"Not with suicide," said Blanche, quietly.

"Pooh!—nonsense! Why will you harp upon the same subject? Of course, I do not admire suicide. I allow that it is a crime, *per se;* a great crime if you will; but I do say, and I will always say, that Goethe sanctifies it by the power of his genius; that such love as Clärchen's, is the love of a noble, self-devoting spirit; that it is beautiful, and true love."

"No; no!" exclaimed Blanche, eagerly.

"Not beautiful! Not true! Then what is so?" and Maude's eyes flashed with irritation.

"Love which lives through sorrow," said Blanche, her voice slightly trembling. "Not love which dies to escape it."

Maude laid down the book which she held in her hand, whilst waiting for a further explanation of her cousin's ideas, and fixed upon her a cool, patient gaze, which was peculiarly repelling.

Blanche turned away her eyes and went on; "You asked me once about my notions and theories," she said, "and I did not like to tell you; I am afraid I was wrong, but you must forgive me. I don't think I have what you would call theories; but I have principles. And, since you are kind enough to read with me, and talk to me, I should like you to know them, because then we shall understand each other better. And, another reason—they are true principles to me; and when you talk, it seems as if you were trying to uproot them. But it would be unkind to do so," she added, very earnestly, as she remembered the maze of perplexities in which but a short time before she had been involved, when suffering her thoughts to wander without check or guidance. "Even, if you could succeed, you would only be making me wretched, for they are my hope and comfort—my happiness." And, in her energy, Blanche clasped her hands, and drew up her slender, graceful figure in an attitude of strength and power, which made the half sneer upon Maude's face melt into a smile of admiration.

"And these thoughts and principles are what?" asked Maude, patronizingly.

Blanche pressed her hands more closely together, and still averting her eyes from her cousin, answered,

"They are what you may call narrow-minded prejudices—they are religion."

"Religion!—yes; certainly;—extremely right," said Maude, still in the same manner. "I hope I am religious too."

Blanche was for an instant distressed and perplexed.

"My dear child!" said Maude, speaking in a light playful way, which made Blanche shrink at the recollection of her own enthusiasm; "my poor Blanche! what an excitement you have worked yourself into! I declare you look quite ill."

Blanche with difficulty resisted the temptation to run away. "Thank you," she said, "I am not ill. I did not mean to be excited. I merely wished to say to you why I never could agree in your admiration of Egmont."

"Because of that naughty Clärchen," observed Maude; "but we will forget her; we will choose Schiller, if you like it, and give up Goethe for the present. By-and-by, when you have seen a little of the world besides St. Ebbe's, and this grim old castle, you will not be so much shocked at him."

Blanche drew back from the caress with which these words were about to be accompanied. "I never can wish that time to come," she said. "If it did, I should have learnt to bear with that which my reason, as well as my faith, tells me is utterly false."

There was a silence of some moments.

Maude appeared struck with the firmness of her cousin's tone. She dropped the patronizing air which she had assumed, and said, "Goethe's principles cannot be false, for they will find an echo in the heart of every one who can admire generosity and devotedness, and an undying, unchanging affection."

"I have not read his works," was all the answer

which Blanche made. She seemed weary of the argument.

Maude again had recourse to the volume by her side. Opening it towards the end, she read a few sentences to herself. "I cannot let you have such notions, Blanche," she exclaimed, after a short pause; "they are beneath you. You must read,—you must admire."

"As I should admire a dream or a fairy tale," said Blanche, smiling.

"That is what I don't understand; it is the only thing I can't understand in you," said Maude. "What do you mean by a dream? Patriotism, the love of liberty, generosity, love, are realities: you can feel them yourself; I know, I am sure you can."

"I hope I can," replied Blanche. "I think them very real, very lovely, and admirable."

"And therefore true," continued Maude; "true, that is the point,—that is the object to be sought after, desired, striven, prayed for!" She spoke earnestly, her dark grey eyes kindling, and her colour heightened.

"Yes, truth; it is the one thing needful," replied Blanche: "but Mrs. Howard says that a half truth must be the greatest of falsehoods."

"What? say it again," exclaimed Maude.

Blanche repeated the words.

"Goethe's truths are half truths, you mean," continued Maude.

"I think they must be; like the half truths of heathenism, which led men to idolatry."

"But a whole truth, who can find it?—who can be certain of it?" said Maude, in a musing tone.

"God is truth," replied Blanche, timidly and reverently.

"Yes," and Maude's manner became reverent

also; "but men also are divine—in their noblest feelings, their highest desires."

"We were made in the image of God," observed Blanche; "but the image is defaced."

"Granted, of course. Defaced; but not utterly ruined—not lost."

"No, indeed not," exclaimed Blanche, enthusiastically; "not lost,—still to be restored, renewed again; but it must be after the perfect original."

"I am tired of symbols," said Maude, hastily.

"Still, may I tell you, will you not think me very presumptuous if I say what such notions as I believe Goethe's to be appear to me to resemble?" continued Blanche: "those I mean which make persons interesting, and in a certain way good, without being Christians. I must use an illustration; I cannot explain myself else. It is as if he had accidentally met with separate fragments of what had once been the copy of a perfect statue; and because he admired each portion separately, supposed that by uniting them all together the whole would be beautiful."

"Of course, of course," interrupted Maude; "they could not be less beautiful when put together than they were before, supposing they were all the work of the same hand."

"But if parts were wanting," continued Blanche: "or if Goethe had never seen the perfect original, and therefore, instead of combining them according to the first design, formed a figure after the imagination of his own heart—distorted and deficient,—there would be no beauty in the whole, though every separate member might be perfect."

"Well!" was all Maude would say.

"I think,—it seems to me," continued Blanche, hesitating, "that this is something like such principles as you tell me are to be found in Egmont. The feelings described may be good and true separately; but they can scarcely be so when they are put together, because love and obedience to God are wanting."

"No," exclaimed Maude; "Goethe, in Egmont at least, would make men obedient to the principles implanted in them by nature and conscience. You would not wish for a better guide than conscience."

"It must be the conscience of the Bible, then," said Blanche; "not the conscience of a fallen nature. This is setting myself up as being able to decide very weighty questions," she added, blushing; "but I have gained all my ideas from Mrs. Howard. Thoughts used to come into my head and puzzle me, and I used to talk to her about them; and she made them clearer."

"I should like to argue her into admiring Goethe," said Maude, "that would be a triumph."

"Impossible!" exclaimed Blanche; "that is, to make her approve would be impossible; or admire either, in one sense; because she never admires what is not true."

"True! true!" repeated Maude to herself. "If one could only find what is true!"

"We are not true ourselves," said Blanche, "because of our evil nature; so that if there is truth anywhere, it must be in something distinct from ourselves."

"Yes; I suppose it may be so," replied Maude, doubtfully.

"In the Bible, then?" continued Blanche; and finding that Maude did not contradict her, she added, "Goethe and the Bible would not agree; therefore Goethe's principles must be untrue. Am I very obstinate?"

"You are very provoking," replied Maude, tossing the book from her. "I will never ask you to read Egmont again; you may be quite certain of that."

She spoke with irritation, but Blanche fancied that some portion of it was assumed. "I did not say that I would not read it, and admire it too," she said; "but you must let me try and think that Clärchen was a heathen."

Maude looked sullen. She went forward, picked up the book, and turned towards the house. Just then Lord Rutherford came upon the terrace; he had been riding, and had returned earlier than he expected. Maude's countenance struck him as he passed her, and, when he joined Blanche, he began to inquire what was the matter.

Blanche did not venture to tell him the whole. She had an intuitive perception of the points upon which they might differ, and avoided them carefully. Difference with him was very unlike difference with her cousin; it involved so much more. And then she was afraid of him; afraid of his cool, keen sarcasm; especially afraid, because she could not feel, as she did when conversing with Maude, that however at variance their sentiments might be, both were earnestly seeking after truth.

CHAPTER XX.

"AND you were not inclined to be of your aunt's party, then?" began the earl, after Blanche had briefly told him that she had just finished an argument with Maude, which left them apparently both where they had begun.

"The party was formed before I came back from the parsonage," replied Blanche; "and I meant to have gone for a walk with Eleanor."

"You are wonderfully fond of the parsonage, Blanche. Are you in love with Mrs. Wentworth yet?"

A remembrance of the morning interview came to Blanche's mind, and she answered quickly, "Oh, no! not at all in love." Adding, to soften her words, "she requires, I think, to be known well."

"Better than I ever knew her," observed the earl, with asperity. "She is one of those chill pieces of propriety whose very presence freezes one's blood. Marvellous it is to me that she should have such children. Miss Wentworth is superior in every way; and her brother is a very handsome, agreeable man."

"They are a handsome family," observed Blanche. "Dr. Wentworth——"

The earl interrupted her: "My dear, you were going out; into the village, I suppose."

"Yes, some distance; but I could not go alone, and the pony-carriage was given up for my aunt."

"Well! I will go with you; you are not tired, I suppose?"

Blanche thought of Maude. She fancied that it was unkind to leave her.

Her father drew near the steps which led down the bank. "You are going,—which way? Can I help you?"

Blanche mentioned her cousin's name; but the earl quickly negatived the idea of asking her to join them, ending however with, "unless you particularly wish it, my love. I would have you do whatever you like."

Blanche did not make a second proposal. She ran lightly down the steps, and taking her father's arm, they followed the path which led them through the underwood, and amongst the scattered trees, down to the edge of the stream. A rough bridge was thrown over it, and Blanche, leading the way, without thinking it necessary to explain where she was going, crossed it, and pursued the path over a green field to the foot of the steep, broken ground which bordered it. Lord Rutherford walked on in silence, till Blanche began to ascend the bank, when he stopped, and rallying her upon her forgetfulness of his age, asked where she intended to carry him.

"Only a little way—quite a little way by this bad road," replied Blanche: "we shall be in a straightforward lane, when we are at the top of the bank. But, papa, I will not go on if you had rather not. I was going to see Susannah Dyer."

"Susannah who? Oh! a poor woman, I suppose."

"A blind girl," said Blanche.

"Blind! poor thing!—extremely sad. Blanche, my darling, you will sit down, and rest first."

The afternoon was passing rapidly, and Blanche's hopes of visiting Susannah Dyer were becoming very slight; but she sat down obediently.

"Susannah was confirmed when I was," she commenced again.

"Oh, yes; I recollect you told me before. There is no harm in your going to see her: you like it, I suppose; and you have not much amusement."

Blanche smiled to herself at the word amusement, for it was not what she generally associated with her visits to the poor.

"Your aunt has been talking to me," continued the earl, following, as he always did, the train of his own ideas. "She says I bury you here: it is not the season for London, or she would make me take you there directly."

"Me! London! Oh! papa, I am quite happy where I am."

"Happy in your ignorance, my love! I am glad you are: but ignorance will not do all one's life; and you must be condemned to London, by-and-by, I am afraid. Condemned to a gay life,—balls, fêtes, concerts."

"They sound pleasant," said Blanche. "I suppose I shall like them; but Mrs. Wentworth tells Eleanor that she should not like her to be placed within reach of them."

"Mrs. Wentworth is not your guide, my love. I mean, you are not at all called upon to take her views. I don't wish you to do so. I like you to form your own."

Blanche was checked, and afraid to say how much she was inclined to respect Mrs. Wentworth's views. It was always the case when conversing with her father. With all his partiality—his devotion, it might be called—his eagerness to gain her confidence—insensibly, he repelled her. She was always choosing subjects for conversation, thinking whether he would be pleased. There is no real freedom where this feeling exists.

"Your aunt," again began the earl, "is very different from Mrs. Wentworth. She is a person of large, comprehensive mind, and very unprejudiced. You must find the difference in talking to them."

"My aunt is much the more agreeable," said Blanche.

"And her opinions are much the more valuable," continued the earl. "You could not find a safer friend to introduce you into the world. She understands the thing so well; you cannot possibly make mistakes if you follow her advice. She has an intuitive perception of right and wrong in all cases."

"I think she has very good, high notions," said Blanche.

"Yes; very good, very high: what all persons should have," said the earl quickly. "But I was thinking of society. I have perfect confidence in your good taste, my child; yet you might, in ignorance, offend against the customs of the world, if you had no one to direct you. And it is a woman's direction which is required: no man could understand what is wanted. I should be quite satisfied if I thought your first introduction into society would be under your aunt's chaperonage."

"And will it not be?" inquired Blanche, in a tone of surprise.

"There is a doubt. Sir Hugh has odd whims, and sometimes fancies he can only live abroad. I think it possible he will not remain in England more than a twelvemonth; if so, it would be my great wish to give you a little insight into life soon. You will be more than seventeen in the spring."

"Yes: but that seems a long time off," said Blanche.

"You might enjoy a season in town, then," continued the earl, and your aunt might be with us; "and, in the mean time, I think it would be desirable to show you something more than the routine of our present life. Your cousins would like it, so would your aunt, and it might induce her to remain with us longer. She had an idea the other day of persuading Sir Hugh to go down to his own place: and I had some difficulty in talking her out of it. It would be an absurdity. Sir Hugh never rests there: he no sooner feels himself tied down to a place, than he is in an agony to leave it."

"But is it not right for persons to live on their own property," inquired Blanche; "and take care of it and of the people, as you do?"

"Right, if they like it, my dear: but Sir Hugh's steward does infinitely more good at Senilhurst than Sir Hugh himself. However, the question now is not about him. What shall you say, Blanche, to an importation of visitors?"

Blanche laughed and blushed, and thought it might be pleasant, quite pleasant, if only her aunt could be the lady of the castle instead of herself.

"There we must differ," replied the earl, turning upon her a look of fond admiration. "There is but one who can fitly fill that station,—only one," he repeated, in a lower tone. Then, after a short pause, he resumed, "And will you like it, Blanche? that was my doubt. Tell me,—let me know," he continued, seeing that she was uncertain what to reply.

Blanche was obliged to speak; she never dared to delay an answer when her father's manner was impetuous; but she could only repeat that it might be pleasant. This she saw did not satisfy him, and making an effort to be candid, she added, "I cannot be sure till I have tried; and I do not like to say that I wish it, because I think it might do me harm."

"Harm?" the earl turned to her hastily.

"I might like it too well," continued Blanche,

her voice faltering a little, as, with an instinctive feeling that it would be better not to provoke any discussion upon duty; she added, "To-day I do not seem to care about it, because I have been disappointed about Mrs. Howard. I looked forward to her visit so much, that now I do not seem to have an interest in other people. I dare say I shall enjoy it though, dear papa," she said, perceiving that he looked disappointed; "and you will not scold me for being fond of Mrs. Howard." She looked up into his face with a smile, though a tear glistened in her eye. It was a smile of bright, heavenly beauty; but it brought proud visions of earth to the worldly mind of the Earl of Rutherford.

"No," he exclaimed; "I would have you love, venerate, delight in her. Whatever my Blanche loves must be most worthy. But there are affections—feelings to be brought forth under other circumstances. Scenes more fitted for you. You do not think, Blanche, that I could consent to see you wear out the best years of your existence here; when I have but to speak the word, and you may be the centre of attraction, the star, the guiding light of hundreds. No," he added, as Blanche's colour deepened, till her forehead was dyed of a crimson hue; "I would not pain you, my child, with your own praises. I speak selfishly, for my own happiness. To see you wasted at Rutherford would be wretchedness. For my sake, you must forget the dreams of your childhood, and look forward to the prospect opening before you."

"It will not be very difficult, I dare say," said Blanche, trying to throw her own mind into harmony with her father's. "I dare say I have a taste for gaiety, only I have never had any opportunity of indulging it."

"Then you shall have it now," exclaimed the

earl, his face brightening. "I have been remiss, certainly, in my attentions to the people about us; but we will have a few persons in the house to help us to entertain them, and then we can collect them *en masse*, and make it agreeable."

"Soon?" inquired Blanche, with a timidity which she could not hide.

Lord Rutherford laughed. "The execution-day is not fixed: but, my love,"—and his lightness of manner in a moment changed into seriousness—"you must not deceive me as to your wishes. Neither for your aunt, nor for myself, nor for any human being, will I consent to do what you do not like. You have only to say the word, and Rutherford shall be as quiet and monotonous for the next six months as it has been up to this moment."

The word monotonous gave Blanche a quick insight into her father's feelings. Though he would not own it, the desire for society was as much for his own sake as for hers. She could not disappoint him; and, besides, she was not in her heart inclined to do so. Blanche was young and naturally cheerful. She enjoyed change, and amusement, and excitement; and, though she dreaded them as possible evils, she had never experienced any harm from them. Eleanor, too, she knew would enjoy the novelty, and Adelaide Charlton would be delighted; and, with all these mingled inducements to bias her inclinations, she at length answered, as heartily as the earl desired, that "she should certainly like it, provided only that her aunt would undertake the management of every thing;" and then, hoping that her father would be satisfied, she stood up and proposed to continue their walk.

CHAPTER XXI.

WHEN Blanche reached the blind girl's cottage, she was not quite in the mood for such a visit. Her fancy had been wandering,—yielding to the gay ideas which her father had suggested. Lord Rutherford went with her till they were within sight of the house, and then he took out his watch and said that it was late, and hoped that Blanche would not stay too long. "It was a strange fancy to like coming to such an ugly place." Blanche was vexed that she had brought him; and blamed herself for not understanding him better, at least for not consulting his wishes more. This was one of the many trifling incidents which were continually reminding her of the little true sympathy there was between them. He did not really care for the things for which she cared, notwithstanding his desire of making her happy. She opened a wicket-gate, and walked up a narrow slip of garden to a square, red brick house, the only ornament of which was a straggling monthly rose. She was almost resolved not to go in: there was a sound of voices in the house, and she said to herself that perhaps it was another visitor, and she should be in the way. Good reasons, or such as are apparently good, always rise up to the aid of inclination. Her father was leaning over the palings, and she feared he was growing impatient, and her knock at the door was hasty in consequence. In answer to her first inquiry, she was told that Susannah was not well, and was only just dressed and coming out of her bedroom. Blanche was about to find an excuse, and say that she would call another day; but conscience reproached her, and she never turned away from that warning. After Mrs. Howard's advice, she certainly ought not to postpone any duty which presented itself, and, conquering the disinclination, she said that she could wait till Susannah was ready.

A delay of some minutes took place before she was admitted. Susannah was to be brought into the room, and seated in her proper chair; and a bustling neighbour was to be dismissed at a back door; and two children sent out in a hurry, with some broken playthings, which made the room look untidy: but the smile that brightened up the blind girl's intelligent face, when at last Blanche entered, quite rewarded her for her patience.

"And you are not well, Susannah, I hear?" said Blanche, sitting down by her side, and taking her hand; whilst Susannah turned to her with a look of gratitude, which did not need the light of the eyes to give it expression.

"I have not been very well this week, my lady; I believe I go out rather too much. But I have had a little nephew staying here till yesterday, my sister's child, who lives near your ladyship's aunt, at Senilhurst. That tempted me to go about with him and the other children; for he is a sweet little fellow, and I never liked to have him out of the way. We went over the hill to the village one day, and it was too far; but there is not much the matter."

"I wish I had known you were not well," said Blanche: "I certainly would have managed to see you before; but the days pass by, and there are so many things to do. I should have liked, too, to see your little nephew. How old is he?"

Blanche had touched the right chord to show her sympathy. The blind girl forgot her trials, whilst in the pride and delight which she felt in her sister's child, she expatiated upon his goodness, and affection, and his beauty too; for he was beautiful, she declared. She quite knew what he was like; but a heavy sigh followed.

"Poor Susannah!" said Blanche, kindly; "it must be a great trial."

The blind girl recovered herself in an instant. "I am not going to complain, my lady. It's all best, I know; and I am cheerful enough most times."

"Only out of spirits to-day, from not being well, I am afraid," said Blanche. "I wish I could stay with you and read to you."

"Ah! if you could! some of the hymns out of the book Miss Wentworth brought, I should like. They seem to be work for me afterwards; because when I sit knitting, I can remember them. It must be a glorious thing to make verses!"

Blanche smiled and said, "You told me one day you had tried to make verses yourself, Susannah. I dare say it amuses you."

"Yes, sometimes, in my poor way; it makes the time pass to see how the words fit."

"And verses suit some thoughts better than plain words, do;" continued Blanche.

"Yes, than some plain words; but not the Bible words."

"Many of them are really verses also, though not quite like ours," replied Blanche. "Just listen to these," and taking up a Bible, she turned to the passage in Isaiah which bears us, in thought, from this evil world to behold "the land which is very far off."

Susannah listened in the attitude of fixed attention, and when Blanche's voice ceased, she entreated for more. "It was so lovely," she said; "it was like rest—not rest though, quite; but moving on without feeling it."

Blanche could not refuse, and was beginning to read the fifty-fifth chapter, when the earl, unperceived, came within sight of the door. "That first verse is a verse for illness, Susannah; is it not?" said Blanche, pausing; "for the hot, weary days, when our lips are parched and dry; and a verse also for our sad days, when it seems that we have no pleasure; when we sit for hours still and lonely, and seem not to have any friends, or comforts, and long and thirst for them?"

"But that can never be your case, my lady," said Susannah.

Blanche answered quietly: "The lonely feeling comes to us all alike, at times, and so does the comfort. But I know it must be worse for you than for me; God has given me a great many blessings."

"Yes, so many to love you," continued Susannah. "I can fancy that better than all the grandeur."

Blanche could not repress a sigh as she replied, "I hope there are some in the world who love me, certainly—love me very dearly; but that love is not enough alone."

"No, not alone; I know it is not. I can feel it is not sometimes;" and the expression of the poor girl's face spoke deep awe and devotion; "but it comes for a time; and then it goes, and it is all dark—quite dark," she repeated, in a voice of melancholy, as if the privation from which she suffered had given her a keener insight into the meaning of the darkness of the soul.

Blanche paused for a few instants before she replied. She turned the pages of the Bible, and as she did so repeated, in an under tone, the first words of the evening prayer, beginning, "Lighten our darkness, we beseech Thee."

Susannah caught the words and said eagerly, "Does it mean darkness in our hearts?"

"Yes, in one sense it must," answered Blanche; "and night must mean the night of this life. It is a beautiful prayer."

"Lighten our darkness," repeated Susannah, thoughtfully. "Ah! my lady; that can never be for me."

"Not in this world perhaps," continued Blanche; "but the night will pass, Susannah, and the day will come—the glorious day. It is worth waiting for, worth suffering and striving for, worth patience."

Susannah's face lighted up with interest, as she folded her hands together with an air of devotion, and suffered a flower which she had been picking to pieces to fall from her grasp.

"Just think," pursued Blanche, "what it will be like; it will be light with no shadow, no cloud, no power of fading away—perfect light both for the body and the soul. And it must come; though the hours seem ever so long, ever so dreary, it must come. Oh! Susannah, it will be light for us both, and we both promised together to strive for it."

Susannah did not reply; the sympathy was beyond her comprehension. Since that one day which had united them in the same act of self-dedication, their paths had parted to the world's sight far asunder; and, whilst poverty and privation were her lot, it seemed that both life and death must be light to the envied heiress of Rutherford.

Blanche read her thoughts with wonderful quickness, and as her voice sank and faltered, she added, "You will not think it; but I have my moments of darkness too—sadness, loneliness, and disappointment. Even for me earth would be often dreary if it were my all."

The earl's cough at that instant warned her that

he was within hearing. She looked up and caught his eye. His look startled her. It was stern; but the sternness of suffering rather than of anger. He asked only if she was ready, took no notice of Susannah, and scarcely allowing Blanche to bid a hearty good-b'ye, led her from the cottage.

They walked on in silence for some distance. Blanche was nervous and uncomfortable. She dreaded she knew not what. As they stood again upon the brow of the steep bank they had ascended after crossing the river, and which commanded a splendid view of the castle and park of Rutherford, the earl stopped her suddenly, and whilst he pointed to the domain which was one day to be her own, said in a calm tone, the more bitter from its effort to be indifferent: "Then I have failed, Blanche, to make you happy. I give you all and you are disappointed."

For a moment Blanche was quite unable to answer. The restraint which she always felt when with her father now amounted to dread; yet she summoned resolution, and replied, "We must all be disappointed sometimes, I suppose, dear papa; but I have a great deal to make me happy; and I am very happy generally. I would not vex you for the world," she added, laying her hand affectionately upon his arm.

The earl took no notice of the caress, and after continuing his walk for some little distance, exclaimed, as if giving vent to a train of secret reflections, "You are right, Blanche; it must be so. I was a fool to think it might be otherwise. But a last hope, a last wish," he added, in a lower tone. "Folly though it may be to cherish it, it is hard to give it up."

"If it is a wish for me, papa," said Blanche, gaining courage as she spoke, "I think you may be satisfied; for I desire no change outwardly."

"Then what would you have? Why do you speak of disappointment?" he inquired, quickly.

Blanche evaded a direct reply, and replied, "Our sad feelings generally come from our own minds. There would be none, I suppose, if we were perfect."

A cloud gathered upon Lord Rutherford's face. "You must be careful," he said. "That morbid tenderness of conscience may lead you, you know not where."

"I hope it is not morbid," exclaimed Blanche; "for Mrs. Howard did not call it so: she understood it, and gave me sympathy."

"Sympathy!" said the earl, in an under tone; and Blanche repeated the word with an unconscious earnestness, for it expressed the true extent of her needs. They had crossed the bridge, which was divided by a little gate from the castle grounds. The earl opened the gate for Blanche to pass, but he did not follow her, and when she turned to look for him, she saw him leaning over it with his face buried in his hands. She walked on slowly; her heart was full of anxious, unhappy thoughts, and the sound of voices on the terrace above jarred painfully upon her. The idea of possibly meeting strangers made her hesitate to ascend the bank, and whilst waiting undecidedly, the earl rejoined her.

"Not that way," he said, as he heard Adelaide's laugh; and he went on before her, so that she had only a momentary glimpse of his countenance; yet, even in that instant, she fancied it looked paler than usual. They turned into a walk at the foot of the bank and reached the castle by a more circuitous path, which led to one of the side wings. A low door at the foot of a turret presented itself at the termination. The earl stopped before it.

"You know this way, of course," he said.

"Yes; I have explored it once or twice," replied Blanche.

"You think you know it," he continued, and a ghastly smile overspread his features. "But. I doubt if you do. It is a private entrance to your mother's apartments." They passed on and ascended a winding staircase, which Blanche had only noticed before as leading, she supposed, to the servants' rooms; and in a few seconds reached a small lobby, into which several doors opened. The earl took a key from his pocket, unlocked the nearest door, and putting another key into Blanche's hand, said, "This room opens behind the bed-room which you have seen. You will find letters and papers in the cabinet. Read them at your leisure, if you will." He did not wait for a reply, but turned into a passage communicating with the other part of the castle.

Blanche scarcely noticed that he was gone. She stood in her mother's apartment, her place of solitude and retirement, and all consciousness of the present was absorbed in feeling for her who slumbered with the dead. The room was small, and furnished very simply; the chairs were without carving or ornament; the curtains of the plainest pattern; the carpet worn and colourless from age. But a reading-stand was placed in the oriel window, and upon it lay a large open Bible; and a low hassock, bearing the marks of long use, was before it; and near, upon a little table, was a Prayer Book blotted with tears, and open at the service for the Burial of the Dead; and Blanche, with but one thought in her mind, cast a hasty glance around, and clasping her hands together, threw herself upon her knees to pray, where her mother must have prayed, for pardon, and strength, and acceptance at the Last Great Day.

A few moments calmed her mind, and she was able to examine the room more closely. It had evidently been left untouched since her mother's death, for the walls were discoloured and the paper was damp; and a sense of desolation came over Blanche as she tried to unlock a large inlaid cabinet filling a recess at the lower end, which at first resisted her strongest efforts from the length of time it had remained unopened. It was the only mark of peculiar refinement or expense in the room, with the exception of two small pictures upon sacred subjects, exquisite in design, but fast losing their beauty from the damp that had gathered over them. Blanche succeeded in unlocking the cabinet after some further efforts, and began a hurried inspection of its contents. Stray articles of various kinds were collected in it, of little value in themselves, yet put aside carefully and marked. Remembrances they were of absent friends; ornaments associated with happy days; things which once must have had a voice and language for the heart; now, like their possessor, silent in spirit and association. And there were other trifles, more painful perhaps to look upon as recalling the daily life which had since become but a dream: pens, sealing wax, scraps of paper, and memoranda, the items which form part of our ordinary existence, and which could tell a truer tale of life than the most valued relics. Blanche lingered over these unconsciously. They brought her very near her mother. It was as if but a few hours had passed since she had been seated at her desk, using the pen encrusted with ink, sealing, perhaps, the last letter which she ever wrote; or—the fancy flashed across Blanche's mind, with an overpowering rush of regret, as she caught sight of an infant's coral and rattle—amusing herself with the child who was destined only to learn the value of her care by its loss. But time was passing rapidly. Blanche had but a few minutes more to spare, and, shutting the drawer quickly, she opened another division of the cabinet. Manuscript books, letters, and papers filled it, and days would be required in order to examine them thoroughly. Blanche took the book which lay nearest. It was full of old accounts; she threw it aside, and opened another, it was the same; another, and still another, and the gong sounded for dinner; but Blanche could not go. Paper after paper, book after book, was examined; but nothing was found which could throw any light upon her mother's personal history; until, quite underneath the pile, she laid her hand upon a packet of letters and a journal book, marked "Not to be opened till after my death." The second gong sounded as she hastily unfastened the string which bound them; and, closing the cabinet, she took up the packet, locked the door of the chamber, and hurried to her own room to dress as quickly as she might, and appear at the dinner table, if possible, as gay and light-hearted as was her wont.

CHAPTER XXII.

"You were a complete truant this afternoon, my love," said Lady Charlton, addressing Blanche, as she threw herself into an arm-chair after dinner, professing to be too tired either to read, write, or work. "We had a charming drive, and I should have liked to introduce you to my friends the Cuthbert Greys. Very nice people they are in their way; a little too fashionable, perhaps, for your taste; but kind-hearted and extremely clever. I quite thought, when Miss Wentworth joined us, that you would be found somewhere."

Blanche did not exactly like to own that she had absented herself on purpose, and endeavoured to change the subject, by asking where they had been and what they had seen.

"The carriage party went round by Staplehurst Common, and over the hill to the old monument in Lord Hervey's grounds," said Eleanor; but Miss Adelaide Charlton and I drove through the copse."

"Miss Adelaide did not go with you anywhere by her own consent," exclaimed Adelaide, coming forward from the window where she had been standing.

Eleanor laughed, and promised to be less formal another time; "Though it is an error on the right side," she added.

"You must come with me to my room. I want to show you that sketch we were speaking of," continued Adelaide.

"What sketch?" asked Maude, haughtily and quickly.

Adelaide's blush was not perceived in the twilight; but she did blush as she answered, in a tone of affected indifference, "Oh! only one that was taken for me abroad,—I dare say you don't remember."

"There was one which I took," said Maude: "is that it?"

"No, no, Maude! What can it signify to you?" and, calling to Eleanor, Adelaide hastened out of the room.

Blanche watched this little scene with surprise, and a feeling of annoyance which she could not account for. She stood in silence for some moments, when Maude's hand was laid upon her shoulder, and Maude's deep voice of satire whispered in her ear, "Jealous, Blanche?" Blanche started; but, before she could reply, Maude had glided past her, and she was left alone with her aunt. She could not go then, although she longed to do so; but it would have been unkind, when they had scarcely met all day; and as Lady Charlton drew a chair towards her, and beckoning to Blanche to seat herself in it, said, in her most winning tone, "Now, my child, we will have a few minutes of pleasure," Blanche would have been well contented, but for one reason, to remain.

"You were grave at dinner, my love, and you are grave now," began Lady Charlton. "What is there to make you so? must I not know?"

"I did not mean to show that I was grave," replied Blanche.

"But you cannot hide it, dear child,—not, at least, from me. You are graver than you ought to be, Blanche, for your years."

"It is my disposition, I suppose," said Blanche.

"Nò, my love, I assure you it is not your disposition. You are naturally light-hearted; but you suffer yourself to brood too much upon serious subjects."

"That cannot be, surely?" exclaimed Blanche.

"Yes, indeed, it can. You would say so, if you had had my experience. You are very like your mother, Blanche."

"You would not wish to see me different, then, would you?" asked Blanche, almost reproachfully.

"Not in many things; but, in that one, perhaps I might. Much more of your happiness may depend upon it than you are at all aware of."

Lady Charlton spoke so energetically, that Blanche looked at her with astonishment. "Was not my mother happy?" was the question which trembled on her lips; but then, as often before, she dreaded to ask it.

"I should like to have my own way with you," continued Lady Charlton, in a lighter tone. "You should not be buried at Rutherford much longer if I had."

"Papa means to make Rutherford very gay," said Blanche.

"Ah! my love, he means—I quite give him credit for his meaning. But can he do it? I know him better than you do, Blanche. There is not a man of greater natural talent, or greater powers of pleasing, in England, than your father,—but not at Rutherford; there is a weight upon him here."

"What! how?" asked Blanche, quickly.

Lady Charlton hesitated, "A weight I called it,—well! it is one: the weight of the place; the old walls, and the old furniture; it even makes me melancholy. Now at Senilhurst, where I would take you if I could, you would find everything different; a cheerful house, lovely grounds, open and bright, a very pretty pasture country, not overpowering in beauty: you know; or, at least you will know by-and-by, that nothing is more fatiguing than being always on the mental tiptoe of admiration; —everything in fact to enliven you. It would be a new phase of existence, and a good introduction to a season in London."

Blanche liked the description, and said so; and Lady Charlton was excited too, and gave a yet more glowing picture of the enjoyments she would find at Senilhurst.

"I should recommend it far more than remaining here," she said. "There is nothing to be done in a place like Rutherford. Entertainments—young people's entertainments I mean—are out of character. And you would not have the change—I see that is what you want—complete change of scene."

"When I have been here only a few months?"

"That does not signify, my love," replied Lady Charlton; "it is the effect of the place which is pressing you down. If your father had consulted me, he never would have brought you here. There is nothing so desirable for young persons as cheerfulness. Grave thoughts and anxieties come quite soon enough," she added, with that sudden transition to a tone of sorrowful feeling, which always gave a peculiar interest to her conversation.

"I should have no village at Senilhurst; no poor people, or school," said Blanche: "that I should regret."

"Yes; but, my dear, you would have them. You should see what we are doing there, and help us. Sir Hugh is a great man for education, and gives me carte blanche to do as I like when we are at home; and you shall help me. My own girls, unfortunately, have never taken to that sort of thing, and it has been a great vexation to me. Ady is too giddy, and Maude is so wrapt up in German metaphysics. I assure you, Blanche, you could be of the greatest possible use to me."

"And poor Eleanor," said Blanche, unconsciously giving utterance to her own train of thought.

"Yes, she would miss you; but, my dear, you cannot be always together."

"We have been so till now," said Blanche. "I could not bear to think of our being really separated."

"No, indeed, I can quite understand that; you must be just like sisters: but the being parted for a time will only make you enjoy being together the more afterwards."

"It will be such a very long parting," observed Blanche, "if I am to go to London in the spring; unless—I wonder whether Mrs. Wentworth would let her go with me there."

"We had better not look forward, my dear child; take the day as it comes. Go to Senilhurst with me now, and leave the spring to itself."

"Mrs. Wentworth would not allow it, I am afraid," said Blanche, unheeding the warning; "and I could never make up my mind to ask her, if I thought she would say No."

"Mrs. Wentworth's strictness would come in the way, I suppose," said Lady Charlton: "but never mind, my love; leave it, as I said, and remember you will get on better in London than you would elsewhere, without Miss Wentworth. There will be so much to amuse and interest you. It pleases me immensely, Blanche," she added, bending forward to kiss her niece's forehead, "to find you take to the idea so kindly, as the poor people say; and I shall tell your father we have settled it."

"Oh! no, no," began Blanche; but Lady Charlton stopped her—"My dear, you don't know your own power, and you must be taught it. Believe me, you have but to say the word, and horses would be ordered for Senilhurst to-night. And now you have quite cheered me, and I must exert myself, and go and see after Sir Hugh. Shall we have tea soon? I am tired, and must go to bed early to-night; so, if you can, don't let that Mr. Wentworth keep us till midnight singing glees and trios."

Blanche rang for tea, and thought it might be possible to snatch a few moments for solitude and a cursory inspection of her precious packet of papers, before it was brought in. Eleanor and Adelaide were crossing the gallery as she went up stairs. She heard Eleanor say, in a laughing voice, "I shall certainly tell how carefully you have kept your treasure;" whilst Adelaide replied, by a faint "Oh! no, no! indeed you must not!" which, of course, meant pray do. But Blanche did not stop to interpret words, or search into hidden meanings; only she thought it strange that Eleanor should have found so much to occupy her with Adelaide Charlton as to leave no time for her.

CHAPTER XXIII.

It was nearly midnight before Blanche went to her room for the night. Notwithstanding Lady Charlton's injunctions, music had been the order of the evening; and music is, perhaps, of all amusements the most enticing. Lord Rutherford was particularly silent, and seemed quite in the mood for enjoying a gratification which could be obtained without effort; and Sir Hugh, who generally joined the party for an hour or two before he went to bed, was charmed with the opportunity of displaying his scientific knowledge. Duets, trios, glees, and quartettes, succeeded each other rapidly; or rather the quartettes were the beginning, and the trios the finale: for, after a short time, Maude, whose voice was of the greatest consequence, professed her determination not to sing another note, and the piano was left to the possession of Adelaide, Eleanor, and Mr. Wentworth; Blanche only joining them occasionally. Blanche was much occupied with her own thoughts; but not sufficiently so to render her unobservant of what was going on around. Music was a delight to her, and in general such an evening would have been a great treat; but when at length the piano was closed, and Eleanor and her brother departed, she felt relieved; as if something which had annoyed and offended her was removed. Yet it was hard to say what that something was. There had been nothing to find fault with in the singing. Nothing in the manner or behaviour of any one of the party to herself. Eleanor had seemed anxious to make amends for any apparent neglect; and Maude, as if wishing to show that she had quite forgotten their difference of opinion, was particularly gentle, and pointed out a beautiful passage of Egmont, which she assured her she had marked because it was so entirely unobjectionable. Every one had been kind to her; yet Blanche was fretted. It was so strange, she said to herself, that she should be so; so odd that she could not bear to watch Adelaide; that she quite disliked hearing her speak to Mr. Wentworth. She was really very good-natured and sang nicely, and with a good deal of spirit and taste of a certain kind. But it must be the taste, Blanche thought, which jarred upon her. It was too marked—too personal—and there was a system of amiable quarrelling and bantering kept up between Adelaide and Mr. Wentworth in the intervals between the different songs, which was especially disagreeable to her. She could not help hoping that, if this style of intercourse was to go on, Mr. Wentworth would discontinue his visits.

Thoughts of Adelaide, however, were soon dispelled when the door of Blanche's apartment was closed against interruption, and she was at length left at liberty fully to examine her mother's papers. Late though it was, she could not rest satisfied with the slight glance which was all she had before given them, and seizing upon the journal, as being the most likely to afford her the information she desired, she began to read it.

But disappointment was destined to follow. There was no record of passing events to tell the secret history of the Countess of Rutherford, although there was sufficient to show that she had been singularly gifted with refined taste and powers of observation, chastened by deep piety. The journal was not exactly what its name implied. It was rather a book of remarks, thoughts, extracts, and prayers. To the writer it must have been full of memories and suggestions; for there were dates and private marks, bearing reference, apparently, to the seasons at which the observations had been made; and there was also a visible change in the style of writing from the commencement to the end. The first pages showed more imagination than reflection; more of hope than contentment. The last were almost entirely short extracts from devotional writers, expressive of great mental sufferings, and an endeavour to be resigned under affliction. They were unconnected, and sometimes abruptly terminated. The handwriting was often illegible, and a few sentences were introduced, apparently without meaning; but the concluding words, written several months before death had summoned the Countess of Rutherford to her rest, were the declaration of the Psalmist: "I will patiently abide alway, and will praise Thee more and more."

Blanche repeated the verse to herself again and again, for it seemed sent as her mother's legacy—her last accents of advice and encouragement. But there was nothing strictly personal in all this; and she turned to the letters. They also were, for the most part, unsatisfactory, being chiefly written by Lady Rutherford's friends, with the exception of a few from the earl, dated in the first year of his married life, and preserved most carefully in a little silk case. These were kind and considerate; but implied frequent long absences, and gave few indications of any wish to be at Rutherford. Engagements, it was said, kept him in London. He hoped to be in the country soon, but could not promise certainly; he trusted that the countess was amusing herself, begged her to deny herself no gratification; was glad to hear that Mrs. Wentworth was with her. These, and many similar wishes, came in every letter. But Blanche was chilled as she perused them; for it was not the love which would have been shown to herself.

Surely, she thought, there must have been something more. This could not have been the affection for the sake of which her mother had left home, and friends, and early ties, and pledged herself, by the most solemn and binding engagement, to love, and honour, and obey, until death. One letter of the packet was still unread, and, with a sickening feeling of doubt and disappointment, Blanche unfolded it. It was without a direction, and in her mother's handwriting, addressed to a dear friend.

The first sentence attracted her attention by a painful fascination. "You tell me I must struggle against my misery; but do you know what you require? You would not be willingly unkind; yet by such words you raise a barrier between us, which leaves me doubly desolate. Weary and heartsick I have been so long, that sorrow is my natural element, and hitherto I have borne it in silence. But if the captive sinks under the burden of captivity, who shall blame him? I wander, day after day, seeking for I know not what—longing for rest which never comes; listening for—I am listening now—but you will find fault with me. God hears me; I turn to Him. He will hear my child. I give her to Him. —If my husband comes—I am dreaming—too late." And those few sentences, the half-collected, half-unconscious outpourings of a broken heart, were the only indications granted to Blanche of the cause of that grief which had preyed upon her mother's health, and it seemed too evident, at length, crushed the powers of her mind.

The morning dawned brilliantly and cloudlessly upon Rutherford Castle, and as Blanche roused herself from a short slumber, the last words of her mother's letter flashed upon her memory before she could recall where she had heard them, or why they should be accompanied by a pang.

The recollection came but too soon, and with it the conviction that her most painful suspicions were verified—that her mother's life had been rendered miserable by neglect. For, in the clear thoughts of the morning, Blanche could put together words, and incidents, and trifling remarks, which had fixed themselves in her memory from the very pain they had caused, and by their aid find a clue to many circumstances hitherto mysterious. Long before the household had risen she sat up in her bed, gazing upon the straggling, nearly illegible, characters which showed the wretchedness of her mother's feelings, almost as much as the words themselves; whilst indignation and fear were succeeded by bitter self-reproach, as she allowed herself to pity one parent at the expense of her affection for another. Her mother had been lonely and heartsick, and no one had been near to comfort her. She had been left to breathe her anxious wishes, and no one had been at hand to gratify them. She was ill in body and in mind, and there was no one to administer to her needs or calm her distracted spirit. Whose fault could it have been? Blanche rested her forehead on her hand to still the beating, throbbing pain, which was settling there. It was no new thought that her father was proud and worldly, and had no sympathy with her highest hopes. Day by day the assurance had become "doubly sure;" and the gulf between them more widely marked. But could he also be cold and neglectful; he, who was so devoted to his child's happiness, whose every thought was centred in her gratification, whose eagerness to indulge, was even painful and burdensome? Alas! for that most bitter of all doubts, which bids us look with suspicion on those whom duty bids us reverence.

When the party assembled at the breakfast-table the pale face of Lady Blanche excited general notice. The earl looked at her with uneasy interest, but only asked if she had slept well; whilst Lady Charlton took occasion to remark that it was evident the place did not agree with her; she had thought so for a long time but did not like to say so. "Senilhurst would do her a great deal of good, if you would but think so," she added, addressing Lord Rutherford.

"Senilhurst will do very well, if Blanche likes it," he replied; "but I very much doubt if she does."

Blanche smiled faintly, and said she should miss many things at Rutherford extremely.

"But, my love," and Lady Charlton turned round with a sparkling eye; "it was only last night you entirely entered into my views, and quite enjoyed the idea: you really are very incomprehensible."

"I don't much care," began Blanche; but she stopped, for she knew that indifference would vex every one.

"You don't care, my dear? I wish I could understand you. I wish I knew what you were aiming at."

"She is not aiming at anything, " said the earl, coolly. "She likes staying at Rutherford; and, if so, at Rutherford we will stay."

Lady Charlton compressed her lips and went on with her breakfast. Soon after Adelaide came into the room. Lady Charlton looked up, and said, "You are very late. Is your father dressed?"

"I don't know," was Adelaide's careless reply, as if the question did not at all concern her.

"I must know. I wonder what Pearson has been about; pray inquire," continued Lady Charlton to one of the servants. "Pearson has grown extremely absurd of late," she added to herself; "he never can be in time; and Sir Hugh won't bear it."

Pearson made his appearance, and was immediately

accosted with, "Sir Hugh is not at breakfast, I suppose?"

"Yes, my lady; at breakfast, and quite enjoying it. He hopes to see your ladyship as soon as is convenient."

"Oh!" and as Pearson withdrew, Lady Charlton gave a slight push to her plate, and declared she had no appetite, and really felt quite unwell. As it was such a beautiful morning, she thought she should like a little stroll on the terrace for the sake of the air.

Blanche half rose to accompany her, or at least to ask if she could be of any assistance; but Lady Charlton motioned to her to remain, and murmuring a few thanks went away. Silence followed. Lord Rutherford took up a newspaper, and Adelaide began reading a letter; whilst Maude occupied herself in studying a large historical picture that hung opposite to her; and Blanche tried to finish a breakfast for which she had not any appetite. Maude looked at her from time to time with an expression of greater gentleness in her features than they seemed naturally formed to wear; and as Adelaide lingered, according to her custom, tasting first one thing and then another, sighing because the tea was cold, and ordering coffee which, when it came, she did not wish for, Maude declared herself ashamed of wasting so much time, and proposed to Blanche to leave her.

"Yes, do go; never mind me," exclaimed Adelaide, good naturedly; "I have quantities of amusement—the most charming letter you ever read, Maude, from Caroline Grey. She is so sorry not to be in the neighbourhood, with her mother and sister, now we are here." Maude's lip curled. "I leave you to your friend very willingly," she said, "so long as I am not required to undergo the penance of reading what she writes."

"Ah well! you don't like her; but that I can't help. Blanche, Caroline Grey would just suit you; you shall know her some day."

"And hate her, as I do," whispered Maude, putting her arm within that of Blanche, and drawing her out of the room. "Caroline Grey is Adelaide's dearest weakness," she added, laughing, as she led Blanche to the library. "Almost more silly than herself, if that were possible. But we wont talk about her. What have you done, Blanche, to put my mother in such a ferment?"

"I!" exclaimed Blanche. "Is my aunt vexed?"

"My dear child, what a perfect innocent you are! Vexed?—She is angry, furious."

"Oh! no, surely."

"Hark! Here she comes!" said Maude, and Lady Charlton walked into the room, inquired for some sealing-wax—asked Maude where Adelaide was, and, after a formal "Better, thank you," in reply to Blanche's inquiry of how she felt, again departed.

"I am afraid she is annoyed," said Blanche, much perplexed.

"Only annoyed!" said Maude. "Well, we must hope it may be nothing more. But what concerns me most, Blanche, is yourself. You look wofully pale this morning, and I must know the reason why?"

"I slept badly," said Blanche.

"But why? Sleeping badly is never an ultimate cause, and my mind cannot rest till it has reached one."

"I did sleep badly: but I cannot tell you the reason why," said Blanche, quietly.

"But I must know. I must insist upon knowing. Had it anything to do with our stupid afternoon, yesterday? Did I bore you by my German nonsense?"

"Oh! no, no; I scarcely thought about it."

"Not complimentary; one would rather be hated than forgotten. Still I forgive you. But the pale looks and the bad night,—I shall go backwards, like the wonderful history of the House that Jack built, till I find the cause."

Blanche's eyes filled with tears, and Maude's manner altered directly.

"There is something more in this than a little fever, or a fit of worry," she exclaimed. "Blanche! I wish I could make you believe that I am not quite such a heathenish savage as I appear."

"Only yourself would call you so," said Blanche, half laughing.

"No. But a great many would think me so.—And yet, I think, yes; I am sure," she continued, more seriously; "that I could be a friend—a true friend—a better friend to you than most people. Blanche, why do you feel yourself so lonely?"

Blanche regarded her with a smile of surprise; and Maude went on. "You are lonely, though you may not choose to own it; you have no one to sympathize with you, though so many love you; and you have fancies, and worries, and brooding thoughts.—I see it constantly."

"Are you sure you are not speaking of yourself?" asked Blanche.

"Never mind me; I am used to it. I am older, have seen more of the world, and have learnt to live in it by myself. But you have not. And you are not formed to battle with it alone, as I am."

"It may be the lesson I am to learn," said Blanche, gravely.

"No, no," exclaimed Maude; "that is one of your narrow views. We choose our own lessons, and shape our own lives. They do so, at least, who are worth anything. Determine that you will not be lonely,—that you will have companionship and sympathy, and you will find it."

"Have you done so?" asked Blanche.

"No; but it is because I do not need it—because I would rather stem the torrent of life's troubles by my own unassisted power; but you are formed to lean upon others and cling to them. Why must you condemn yourself to reserve and solitude?"

"I do not condemn myself," replied Blanche. "I enjoy sympathy when I can have it; but I do not need it as much as you imagine: or rather," and her colour slightly deepened as she spoke, "I have more than I can explain."

Maude turned away as if annoyed.

"Am I unkind?" said Blanche, following her.

"Incomprehensible, merely," was Maude's cold reply; "but I have no wish whatever to force your confidence. I might have known, from our conversation yesterday, how little our ideas accord." And yet, as she said this, Maude lingered in the room, evidently unwilling to break off the conversation.

"You are very kind to me, dear Maude," said Blanche, gently. "I wish I could make you believe that I really am obliged; perhaps, by-and-by, you will, when we understand each other; for, in some things, I think we agree more than we know. But, as regards confidence, I have none that I should feel it right to give to any one, except Mrs. Howard; or, perhaps, my aunt."

"Mamma!" exclaimed Maude. "Confidence to her!"

"I don't mean confidence, exactly," replied Blanche. "But there are some things which she could tell me, which would be a comfort to me; though I could not ask her about them just now."

"No;—certainly," answered Maude, with a satirical laugh. "Fond though she is of you, I would not advise you to put yourself in her way again, for some hours at least."

Blanche looked distressed, and said she was scarcely aware what she had done, though she supposed it was being so foolishly changeable, as to going to Senilhurst.

"I suppose it was that: but leave her to herself; she will come round again; and she will bear a great deal from you."

"I am glad she is fond of me," said Blanche; though she said it with an uncomfortable feeling or distrust and disappointment.

"Yes! mamma is always fond of persons she is proud of."

Blanche's face showed that she was puzzled; and Maude continued, laughingly, "Now, my dear Blanche, there is a certain limit to simplicity, beyond which it becomes silliness. You really are much too sensible not to know that you possess a great deal of which the world is proud—rank, wealth, beauty. Nay; don't shrink from the truth," she added, as Blanche suffered an expression of distaste to escape her lips. "I am not flattering you; I am not a man paying court to you; if I were, I should be wiser than to praise you to your face. But I long to see you make the most of yourself; and I am sure no one can ever do that who has not a thorough appreciation of his or her peculiar advantages. So you must understand that mamma is proud of you; and, as a consequence, fond of you; and if you choose to go and confide your griefs to her, don't let me prevent you. Only, I should have imagined—"

"What?"

Maude thought for a moment, and then answered, "I should have thought that your taste might have led you in a different direction."

"It is not a question of taste," replied Blanche. "If I did not love my aunt, she would still be the only person to help me now; unless, perhaps, Mrs. Wentworth could."

"Then go to Mrs. Wentworth," exclaimed Maude, hastily. "Cold, though she is, stiff, unbending,—go to her, Blanche. You wonder at me, and I shock you; but I am not thinking of my mother, as my mother—only as suiting you. Mrs. Wentworth will tell you more of what you wish to know than mamma will," she added, fixing her large piercing eyes upon Blanche, as if she knew her inmost heart.

"But I cannot go to Mrs. Wentworth; I cannot learn from one who is not a member of my family—"

"The secrets of that family," added Maude, quietly. "Suppose I could tell them, Blanche?"

"Do you know? Can you tell?" exclaimed Blanche, and the faint shade of colour in her cheeks went and came rapidly.

"If I cannot tell myself, I might learn," pursued Maude.

Blanche shook her head in disappointment. "No; you are very kind, very good; but it will not do."

"And there is to be no confidence between us, then?" said Maude.

Blanche did not answer. They had been standing together at the window, and as she was about to turn away from it, Maude laid a detaining hand upon her arm, and pointing to a bird which was winging its flight far into the blue sky, said, "I had a dream of two minds soaring together, leaving the delusions of this paltry world behind them, and seeking a higher life in the glorious light of truth."

Blanche sighed.

"Must it be a dream?" said Maude, almost tenderly.

Blanche raised her eyes timidly to her cousin's face, as she replied unhesitatingly, "There is a false light as well as a true one. Before we soar together, Maude, we must know which we are seeking."

"Truth," answered Maude. "In other words, spiritual, intellectual beauty, which is another name for truth."

Blanche passed her hand over her eyes, and said, with a faint smile, "I cannot talk as we did yesterday—my head aches too much; I cannot fix my thoughts."

There was a tone of indescribable depression and weariness in her voice. Maude looked at her compassionately and kissed her, and said she would not tease her; and the sympathy overcame the self-command which Blanche had been exercising, and large tears filled her eyes, and rolled down her cheeks.

Maude made her sit down. "Can't I help you?" she said. "Are you quite sure?"

"Quite sure; unless you know." She thought for a few moments, and then added, "Does my aunt ever talk to you about herself?"

"About past days?" said Maude. "Yes, sometimes; but not often."

"Not of interesting things; things which would interest me?" and Blanche looked up imploringly.

"I don't know," said Maude doubtfully; "that is, they would interest you in a way."

"But does she ever mention my mother?" The last words were uttered with painful unwillingness, and when they were spoken Blanche sat with her hands tightly clapsed together, as with an effort to conceal the working of some keen emotion.

The perplexed expression of Maude's face increased as she looked at her. "What is it that troubles you, Blanche?" she said. "Surely nothing connected with days so long gone by; sorrows that have so long ceased?"

"Then she was sorrowful; she was miserable," exclaimed Blanche, rising impetuously. "Oh, Maude, in pity tell me what you know."

"Sorrowful, miserable," repeated Maude slowly. "One must always fear it in such cases; but it may have been better than we think."

Blanche grasped her cousin's hand, and the brightness of her eye was terrible in its eagerness.

"There are sadder moments of sanity than of delusion," continued Maude, gently; and Blanche's fingers relaxed their grasp, and she fell back in her chair nearly fainting. Maude was not in the least hurried out of her usual steadiness of manner; she sprinkled some water on her cousin's forehead from a flower-glass near, and when Blanche a little revived, and uttered mournfully the word "delusion," answered, without any reference to her transient weakness, "I thought you knew it, dear."

"No, no; they kept it from me. But tell me now, quickly."

"Only delusion," answered Maude; "nothing more. Nothing to distress you, Blanche. Pray believe me," she added, as Blanche's eyes again filled with tears.

"But what delusion? of what kind?" asked Blanche, faintly.

"Quiet melancholy; only that, I assure you; nothing really hereditary to frighten you."

Blanche scarcely seemed to hear this comfort; she only said in reply, "Was she alone?"

"Yes, sometimes, when it could not be helped," replied Maude, with evident hesitation.

"Quite alone; sorrowful, miserable," murmured

Blanche, and she leant her head upon her hand, and cried bitterly.

"I will tell you all I know," said Maude. "She was not strong naturally, mamma says; and she was a great deal by herself; and she must have been like you, Blanche, fond of brooding over her own fancies, for they never could persuade her to see people and go out, except occasionally, when Lord Rutherford was here."

"And she went out then? she was happy then?" exclaimed Blanche, raising her head quickly.

"Yes, she went out a little to please him," continued Maude. "But you know he was absent a great deal, especially at last."

Blanche's head sunk despondingly. Maude's quick eye remarked the change, but she went on—"I do not think there was really anything to distress you so much; of course, she had every comfort, and her mind"—she stopped, considering how to approach the subject in the way least likely to give pain; but Blanche made a slight motion of the hand, and said, "I can bear it," and Maude continued, in a rather hurried voice, "It was not so very dreadful; not common insanity. She was very quiet, and gentle, and good. Mamma used to come and see her very often, and for a long time people said it was only melancholy, it came on so gradually. She used to write a great deal, I believe; but almost all her papers were destroyed when Lord Rutherford came back from abroad."

"But he was with her; quite at the last?" said Blanche, in a low voice.

"No; he was not here in time. It was very unfortunate; for the longing to see him was so great, it was worse than anything. But Blanche, my dear, I am doing you harm," she said, observing her cousin's look of intense suffering.

"No, no; go on;" was all that Blanche ventured to utter.

"There is not much besides to tell," answered Maude. "But indeed, Blanche, I am very anxious you should not think it at all worse than it really was. She was ill and depressed very long before it was thought necessary to have any one with her; a companion," she added, as Blanche slightly shuddered. "And, even to the very last, there were intervals when she knew everything and everybody quite well; and the only way in which they discovered when the attacks were coming on worse, was that she would then kneel for hours together in her room, repeating portions of the Burial Service."

Blanche put her hand before her eyes to hide the light of the glorious sun. Many moments elapsed before she spoke. Then she rose from her seat, and kissed Maude, and said, "Thank you; you have been very kind; you must not say that you have told me," and walked slowly out of the room.

CHAPTER XXIV.

MRS. WENTWORTH was sitting alone in her little room: the post was just come in, and she was busied in answering her letters. She looked particularly old that morning; perhaps her dress was unbecoming—perhaps her letters had been annoying; at any rate, her care-worn expression was sufficient to attract observation; and as Dr. Wentworth passed the window, and stopped to say a few cheerful words, it made him delay the business he was bent upon, and re-enter the house. "There is nothing amiss in them; is there, my love?" he inquired, taking up the letters on the table. "I did not read them through."

"Oh, no! nothing: they are mere chit-chat; not of any consequence. Why should you ask?"

"You seemed uncomfortable—that is all; but if there is nothing the matter, well and good. It must be the cap, I think, which makes you look different. I think I told you I was going to the Union this morning."

"Yes: you will be back to dinner, I suppose, at six o'clock."

"Say half-past; we shall be more punctual. Good-b'ye;" and Dr. Wentworth departed.

Mrs. Wentworth leant back in her chair, in a reverie, a strange and painful one. It carried her back many years, to that early romance of first love—that entire sympathy of thought and feeling, which she had imagined was to last undiminished for ever. Dr. Wentworth was a good man, an earnest man: his heart was given to his duties, first; his family afterwards. His wife did not wish it should be otherwise; but she did not resemble him. The romance of her early years had not, like his, been extinguished by the constant pressure of parochial cares. She was poetical, enthusiastic still, in secret. She had, as it were, two characters—the one of great imagination, the other of strong common sense. Her husband's affections had been won by the former; they were retained by the latter. Imagination, with him, had been the amusement of boyhood; with her, it was the present beauty of life: and if Mrs. Wentworth had been endued with a less portion of right feeling and self-command, the discovery of this essential difference in their characters might have been made at the risk of the happiness of both. As it was, it only served to throw her back into herself, to chill the outward show of enthusiasm, and to concentrate all the intensity of her hopes and interests upon her children. Perfect respect, and a true, though unimpassioned, love, were still her husband's; but she had learnt to live her inward life without him: and whilst sharing his pleasures, and sympathising in his sorrows, she concealed, as by a natural instinct, those keener, more sensitive feelings, which he would not have understood. There were times when this sense of uncongeniality was very oppressive. When Mrs. Wentworth thought of her children, she most felt the absence of that perfect sympathy, which would have supported and soothed her under the anxieties they occasioned. It was a fear for them which was now pressing heavily upon her spirits; that boding, shadowy fear which cannot be combated, because it assumes no tangible form. She indulged the reverie of the past for a few moments only. It was dangerous to her peace, and contrary to her strict conscientiousness; but, as it faded away, there rose up the long vista of futurity, and who can blame a mother's momentary longing to pierce into its secrets? It is so hard to persuade ourselves that the children whom we love so fondly, and guard so tenderly, must one day bear, as we do, the burden of this evil world. When we are sinking ourselves beneath pressing cares, we can least endure the thought that they must sink likewise. When we are struggling with the claims of conflicting duties, or worn with exertions for their happiness, we can least look forward to the same conflict for them. We watch them in their hours of mirth, and listen to their joyful expectations, and in pity suffer the delusion to last whilst yet it may; and at length we ourselves become sharers in it, and, closing our eyes to reality, whisper to our own hearts, "To-morrow shall be as this day, and much more abundant." Happy is it that a truer love and a wiser forethought is steadily, unshrinkingly, yet most mercifully, preparing for them the cup of trial which we would so weakly withhold.

A knock at the door disturbed the train of Mrs. Wentworth's thoughts. "Come in," was the order, spoken quickly and nervously; but Mrs. Wentworth did not look round.

"Did you want me, mamma?" asked Eleanor, standing as if unwilling to enter.

"Yes; if you are not engaged. Is Susan at her lessons?"

"She was just going to say them; but she can do something by herself, if you wish it, mamma," and Eleanor retired.

Several minutes passed before her return, more, it seemed, than were necessary, and Mrs. Wentworth had a hasty word on her lips in consequence; but it was not uttered, and served only to give a sadder tone to her voice, as she said, "I would not have interrupted you, my dear, if there had not been a necessity."

A little awkwardness was perceptible in Eleanor's manner as she approached her mother; and a certain consciousness that the necessity alluded to was not an agreeable one.

"You were very late returning from the castle last night, my love," continued Mrs. Wentworth. "I did not like to vex you by saying anything about it at the time; but I was sorry. I did not expect, indeed, that you would have stayed to dine."

"I did not mean to do it," replied Eleanor; "but we went out driving and riding, and came back late; and then Lady Charlton and Adelaide persuaded me, and I thought you would not be angry."

"Adelaide," repeated Mrs. Wentworth in a musing tone; but she made no other comment upon the familiarity. "I am not angry, my dear child," she added; "and, perhaps, I should not even be vexed if you were alone."

"You are afraid for Charles," replied Eleanor; "but, mamma, it is his only amusement."

"Yes, I know it; but it makes me very anxious."

Eleanor looked steadily in her mother's face, whilst a smile, which she vainly strove to repress, stole over her features, as she said, "You are afraid of his falling in love, mamma?"

"Falling in love, my dear! No!" and Mrs. Wentworth's lips curled in disgust. "I could never fear that Charles would fall in love with anything so vain and frivolous as Miss Charlton; but I am afraid of his being led on to say and do foolish things; to flatter and talk nonsense, and go further than he knows; to flirt, in fact: and I am afraid of your seeing it, and perhaps being induced to join in it in a certain way. I could not bear that sort of thing,

Eleanor; it would be so utterly against my taste, not to put it upon higher grounds."

"Charles likes Miss Charlton very well," said Eleanor; "but he does not really care for her."

"I do not see that it makes much difference whether he does or does not," replied Mrs. Wentworth; "for a young man just preparing for ordination to waste his time and lower his character by dancing attendance upon a silly girl, whom he does not care for, merely because he wants amusement, is, to say the least, unworthy."

"The Charltons will be going soon," said Eleanor. "Lady Charlton talks of spending the winter at Senilhurst, and taking Blanche with her."

"Indeed!" Mrs. Wentworth's face brightened instantly.

"Yes; it is nearly settled;" but Eleanor looked as much vexed as her mother was relieved.

Mrs. Wentworth observed the expression of her face: "My dear child, you must forgive me for being glad; I do feel for you."

Eleanor only drew up with an air of reserve, and said, "I am not disappointed; I have known that it must be so from the beginning."

"It will smooth every difficulty if they go," continued Mrs. Wentworth, evidently trying to be frank and unconstrained; "that was why I sent for you, Eleanor, to know if you could tell me anything of their movements. If they were to remain, I must urge your father to make some other arrangement for Charles. I have such a great dread of the intimacy. Can you not understand me?" she added, watching Eleanor's countenance narrowly. "I think you must see yourself how bad it is."

"Certainly," replied Eleanor, flattered by her mother's confidence, "Adelaide Charlton is not the person to improve him; but, there is more in her, mamma, than you would give her credit for."

"That may be; but Charles must have a superior wife, if he is ever to do anything in life. He must marry a woman whom he respects."

"And loves, too," said Eleanor.

"Yes, assuredly; but the love in which there is no respect is but a broken reed to rest upon. However, I need not take up your time any longer, my love. If Lady Charlton goes soon, all my trouble will be at an end; and, in the mean time, I must trust to you not to do more than you can help in bringing them together."

"I will not do anything you dislike, dear mamma," was Eleanor's reply; "if you will only look less anxious than you did when I came in."

"Anxious, did I? My face is not generally a tell-tale."

"I understand it always," answered Eleanor. "You have been uncomfortable very often lately."

Mrs. Wentworth did not contradict the assertion.

"I think you would be happier," added Eleanor, "if the castle was far off; and yet, mamma," and she hesitated, "you suffered me to be brought up with Blanche."

"Yes, I did; possibly it was a mistake." Mrs. Wentworth thought for a few moments, and then continued, "Yet I acted for the best at the time. When you first went to Mrs. Howard I was very ill; I could not take proper care of you myself. Mrs. Howard urged me to let you go for the sake of Lady Blanche, and for her mother's sake. At that time there seemed little probability that Lord Rutherford would ever settle permanently in England; or, if he did, that he would choose to reside at Rutherford. The circumstances under which he left it were such that I myself could not have contemplated his return. He has another place in the north; I imagined that he would have preferred it. Yet it might have been an error, a want of due forethought. Oh! Eleanor, you will not make me regret it!"

Eleanor's feelings were touched by the earnestness with which her mother spoke. "Mamma!" she exclaimed, "I have been foolish, I know, of late; but, indeed, you may trust me. I can only learn good from Blanche, and I cannot really be led away by a person like Adelaide Charlton."

"God forbid you ever should be, my love," replied Mrs. Wentworth. "You do not know all that such an influence brings; how it lowers, wastes, vitiates the whole tone of the character; how its effects are felt for years and years. Such a mind as yours, Eleanor, if it is not bent upon the highest objects destroys itself; it cannot rest in mean pursuits, and it turns inward and gnaws at the root of its own happiness. And you may be—shall I tell you what you may be?—what I have sometimes pleased myself by imagining you to be?"

"Something much better than I can ever imagine myself, I am sure," said Eleanor.

"Yet nothing beyond your power," continued her mother. "A woman with all a woman's tastes, and gentleness, and modesty; yet earnest, untiring, exalted in your aims, enlarged in your views, sufficient for your own happiness, from having fixed it where alone it may be safely centred, whilst living in the happiness of others, because your whole life is devoted to the promotion of their welfare; and having a power over their minds, because you have kept such a strict watch over your own. That is what you may be."

"And what shall I be, mamma?" The question was put in a tone of great thoughtfulness.

"Mrs. Wentworth paused," and her voice sank again into its quiet stillness, as she said, "One only knows."

"But tell me; help me, if you can," said Eleanor; "tell me what I must be if I am not what you describe. Mamma, it may do me more good than you can think."

"Would you wish to hear?" replied Mrs. Wentworth. "You will think me exaggerating, yet I have watched the downward progress of many characters like yours, and the general outline is alike in all. First, self-dissatisfaction and a longing for the respect which might be deserved, and then an endeavour to be satisfied with mere admiration instead; admiration becoming necessary, and sinking gradually into the craving of a miserable vanity; and this changing in old age into a sharp, cynical narrowness of mind, which is wretchedness to itself and others. I am not speaking in the least too strongly, Eleanor. I have seen it, and grieved over it; and the first symptom has always been that fickleness of action, though not of intention, in little things, which you are always regretting."

"And never amending," said Eleanor. "Mamma, I must do so, I will." The house-bell rang at that moment; Eleanor coloured deeply. "It is Adelaide Charlton," she said. "I did very wrong; I asked her to come."

"Mrs. Wentworth strove hard not to show her real annoyance."

"She shall stay but a few minutes," continued Eleanor. "She has only to look over some music, and she knows I shall be busy."

Miss Charlton was announced in the drawing-room.

Mrs. Wentworth rose and said she would receive her, and, collecting her letters, was preparing to go, when Dr. Wentworth's voice was heard. The meeting at the Union was deferred; he was returned unexpectedly, and he came to the window to say so.

"I want you, my dear, particularly. I must have you for a few minutes to go into the village with me."

"Is it really necessary? There are visitors in the drawing-room."

"What visitors? Only Miss Charlton. Charles and Eleanor will entertain her."

Mrs. Wentworth's conscience smote her for the pride which had made her shut up from her husband the anxieties which she imagined he could not sympathise with. Now, when she wanted his assistance, he was working unknowingly against her.

"Indeed, I must have you, my dear," he continued. "I am in a hurry."

Mrs. Wentworth could say no more; but she looked at Eleanor as she joined him, and Eleanor answered the look with, "Adelaide will only stay a few minutes. I shall not let her do so."

CHAPTER XXV.

"I HOPE I am not interrupting you," began Adelaide Charlton, as Eleanor welcomed her with a gravity of manner which she could not hide.

"Oh! pray don't name it. I shall find the music I mentioned almost immediately," and Eleanor began searching for it hurriedly; inquiring at the same time for every one at the castle.

Adelaide rattled on in her usual style. They must have had a bad night, she supposed, for they all seemed cross; but she made a point of never inquiring what was the matter. She had left Maude and Blanche in close conversation; but, of course, she did not know what it was about: they were becoming such desperate friends, it would not do to pry into their secrets.

Eleanor bent over the music-stand, and regretted that the lost piece of music was not forthcoming; but promised to look for it, and send it to the castle in the course of the day.

"Oh! it does not signify;" was Adelaide's indifferent reply. "One never really cares for any particular piece; I dare say you have a good many that I don't know. May I look?" She took up a piece of music, hummed a few notes, thought it seemed pretty, and seated herself at the piano to try it. "Awfully difficult all this style of music is, and not in good taste, people say; at least, Maude says so, and she is the oracle. After all, instrumental music is worth nothing compared with vocal. How badly your brother and I sang last night! We really must practise before we exhibit again. Don't you think it would be a good thing to have practising days?"

"If one had time, it might be," said Eleanor.

"Oh, but we must make time. I have no notion of persons not finding sufficient time for anything they wish. I protest, there is that enchanting trio we were talking of; you must try it."

"A trio for two persons!" said Eleanor, laughing; "that will not quite do."

"Never mind; just try your part."

She struck the first few chords; Eleanor grew hopeless of escape. Adelaide's visit was from her own invitation, and she could not summon courage to shorten it by confessing her engagements.

"You very good people are so methodical," continued Adelaide; "you quite put one to the blush. I declare, to see the way Blanche goes on is enough to convert one into an automaton. I must have some music this morning to put me in good humour."

"Can that ever be needed?" asked a voice from behind her; and, to Eleanor's extreme annoyance, her brother joined them.

Adelaide Charlton's manner showed instantaneously the working of her mind. There was a little blushing, a little bantering, a good many quick upward glances, interspersed with a few downcast modest ones; some pretty nonsense about music and flowers, and a pretence at shyness, when Mr. Wentworth asked her to sing, with an evident disinclination to leave off when she had begun. It was vanity, unmistakeable; and Eleanor stood by and compared Adelaide's flirting with her own dignity; and, in the pleasure of self-satisfaction, forgot her mother's caution and her own promises. And so the minutes went by, and Eleanor satisfied herself that the waste of time could not be avoided, and therefore it could not be wrong to enjoy it. And she did enjoy it in a measure.

There is generally something agreeable in that sort of light, quick conversation which accompanies music, and Adelaide Charlton was not deficient in talent of a certain kind. She had travelled and could relate amusing adventures herself, and assist Mr. Wentworth in remembering his; and she had seen more of the world than Eleanor, and laughed at many of her simple notions; she was older also, and had been presented at court, and was acquainted with people of rank and fashion. These were all ingredients of influence, especially when mingled with them was the thought "Notwithstanding all these advantages, I am the superior."

"And now, Charles, we really must be steady," was at length Eleanor's faint endeavour to stop the flow of the conversation. "I am doing very wrong in staying here, and you are doing very wrong too, Adelaide. I must be rude and send you away, or we shall both get into disgrace."

Adelaide started from her seat; "Go, must I? Well, I suppose I have been here an immense time. I did not mean to stay a quarter of an hour. Mr. Wentworth, I must trouble you to return my glove: you seem bent upon keeping possession of it; but I am afraid it will not be quite as useful to you as to me." She held out her hand, and to her surprise, the glove was given as a matter of course, and Mr. Wentworth, turning suddenly to his sister, said, in a tone of quiet politeness, "Eleanor, you do not see— Lady Blanche Evelyn."

Blanche was at the window, and Mr. Wentworth stepped forward to open it. His manner was quite different; thoughtful and respectful, as if some sudden spell had been cast over him. Yet Blanche was thoroughly at her ease, smiled and shook hands, and rallied him upon his musical mania. Perhaps he saw that the words were words of course, spoken to smoothe the little stiffness of the party, for there was no real gaiety in what she said. She looked ill and harassed, and when Adelaide declared her intention to return to the castle, Blanche made no remark, and allowed her to say "Good b'ye," without asking her to wait. So Adelaide, after a little more lingering and sighing, and laughing, departed, taking care when she had gone a few steps to attract attention, by an "Oh! Mr. Wentworth, I forgot;" which drew him after her, and induced him to accompany her more than half-way home.

Eleanor stood watching them until they were fairly out of sight, and then going up to Blanche, said, as she stooped to kiss her, "Blanche, I am thankful you are not your cousin Adelaide."

Blanche smiled, and replied, "Perhaps, I am glad too; and yet that is wrong," she added, correcting herself; though one may be glad one is not forced to lead the same life. But, Eleanor, I was not prepared for your having any one here; and I thought Susan's lesson would be over by this time. If Adelaide has been with you that of course is impossible."

Eleanor had seldom felt less inclined to attend to lessons, and, as an excuse to herself, said, that Susan could do very well without her for the present; she wished first to know what had brought Blanche to the rectory.

"Business that can wait very well," replied Blanche, "so please go, if you have anything to do, and I will sit here and write a letter till you are ready."

"But you look fagged and worried, Blanche; what has been going wrong?"

The eyes of Blanche filled with tears, but not one

was suffered to escape, and, avoiding a direct reply, she said, "I came here partly to tell you that we shall all probably go to Senilhurst immediately."

Eleanor's countenance betokened blank disappointment; she was not prepared for such a sudden move.

"Yes," continued Blanche quickly, as if anxious to avoid questions; "it is my aunt's wish, and I shall vex her if I refuse, and I don't think papa will dislike it. My aunt says it is the best thing for me; and, and I don't much care myself what ——" her voice failed her, and she burst into tears.

Eleanor was at her side in an instant, soothing and caressing her, and entreating to be told what was the cause of her grief. Blanche seemed distressed at her own weakness, but had no power of controlling it when she had once given way.

"Oh, Eleanor!" she exclaimed, "if they had only told me; if they had not brought me up in ignorance!"

"Ignorance, dearest Blanche! Of what?"

"Of everything; of what I ought to have known; what all the world knows except myself," replied Blanche, impetuously; a feeling of pride mingling unperceived with her sorrow.

"All the world! what? how?" inquired Eleanor, frightened at her unusual vehemence.

"You know," continued Blanche, and she grasped her friend's arm nervously, until Eleanor said, "I can know nothing which you will not tell me;" and then Blanche dropped her hand, and leaning her forehead upon the table, murmured, "I am unkind too! and I thought I had self-command!"

"You must not have self-command with me, dearest," said Eleanor. "If you cannot talk openly to me, whom can you go to?"

"No one; no one;" was the mournful answer. "But I think I could bear it better if I knew all. Oh, Eleanor! are you sure? did your mother never talk to you? did she never tell you of—of my own mother—my sweet mother?"—she paused, and her voice sank almost to a whisper; but it was a whisper clear and thrilling, and Eleanor's cheek turned pale, and a shudder passed through her frame as she heard, "Eleanor; she was insane."

There followed a long pause, until Eleanor said very gently, "Mamma, if it is true, would tell you all."

Blanche shook her head: "I could not ask her. I had a thought—a foolish one—that you might know."

"No, never. Could I have hidden it from you?"

"Perhaps so; they all did. They thought it right: it was a cruel kindness."

"Are you quite certain it is true?" asked Eleanor.

"Maude says so; and I feel it. I understand things now. Oh! if I could have comforted her but for one hour!" and Blanche groaned in agony for the past, whilst Eleanor trembled at the horrible train of thought which in those few moments had been conjured up for the future.

Blanche recovered herself by degrees. She related what had passed with Maude, and showed Eleanor how the fact was confirmed by her mother's papers, and the strange silence and mystery in which everything connected with her was involved. She seemed to shrink from any attempt to persuade her into disbelief. "It was better," she said, "to face the truth at once; that was what she was now longing to do entirely. A few days ago she could have gone to her aunt; but there had been an unhappy misunderstanding; she scarcely knew how it had arisen; from some foolish changeableness of her own, she believed. It had worried Lady Charlton extremely, and she had not recovered it. There is no one besides her, except your mother," continued Blanche, and Eleanor assented. She did not venture to ask why Lord Rutherford's name was not mentioned.

"And why should you not go to mamma?" she said, as Blanche again repeated her longing wish to hear the particulars of her mother's history.

The answer was given with some reluctance: "Because I am afraid of her."

"Afraid of her! so good, and gentle, and charitable, as she is. Oh, Blanche!"

"Yet still I am afraid. Do you know what it is to have an intuitive perception of being misunderstood—misjudged? Her interest in you absorbs her; and well it may. It is a mother's love." Blanche turned away her head to hide her unbidden tears. "I am very wrong to regret," she added, "only sometimes I think that, if my mother had lived, I might have been better; but then ——."

It was an awful thought which suggested itself to both, and Eleanor, willing to divert it, said, "Even a mother's love, Blanche, cannot always be our safeguard."

"It seems so, as if it must be," replied Blanche musingly. "Your home, and its quietness and peace; all your time marked out, and your duties fixed, and a friend to go to always;—it must be safer than mine."

Eleanor made no direct answer. "When do you go to Senilhurst?" she said abruptly.

"Directly, I think; but the day is not fixed."

This was said with an air of such melancholy indifference as to recall Eleanor from all thoughts of herself.

"You must be made happier before you go, Blanche," she exclaimed.

"That cannot be. I must try and bear it, and the pain may lessen."

"But not the ignorance and mystery; and if you chose, there would be nothing easier than to learn everything. Mamma would tell you every little detail, if she thought you were aware of the truth; and you would feel her value then."

Blanche recollected the request for her mother's picture, and was silent.

Just then Mrs. Wentworth came into the room, accompanied by Susan. Blanche looked nervous and agitated. Mrs. Wentworth spoke to her, but seemed to have an instant perception that all was not right; and addressing Eleanor, reminded her that the morning was fast passing away, and that Susan's lessons could not possibly be finished in time if she was left to herself. "I make no apology to Lady Blanche," she added; "she will not require it. I am glad you have been detained by her." A meaning stress was laid upon the pronoun, and Eleanor's sincere conscience would not suffer her to misunderstand it.

"Blanche has been here but a short time," she said. "Adelaide Charlton stayed longer than I thought she would, and Charles came in, and they sang."

"Oh!"

There was no further remark or comment. Eleanor kissed her mother, and the kiss was returned warmly; but the sigh which accompanied it spoke volumes of disappointment. Mrs. Wentworth sat down when she was gone; her manner was less self-possessed than usual. She asked a few unconnected questions, and when Blanche mentioned the plan of going to Senilhurst directly, she did not appear to take in the idea; her mind was wandering to another subject. At length, Blanche asked if she might stay and write a letter, and occupy herself till Eleanor was at leisure again; and this seemed to put Mrs. Wentworth at ease, and she placed the portfolio for her, and laughed at the bad pens which she had to offer, and afterwards, saying she would leave her at liberty, went away.

CHAPTER XXVI.

"YOUR master is much better this morning, Pearson," said Lady Charlton, addressing the civil man-servant, as he stood aside, condensing himself into the smallest possible compass, whilst she passed.

"Rather better, my lady. I am afraid he has been in a good deal of pain the last half-hour."

"But he is better, Pearson; a good deal. Mr. Stone said so yesterday. He will be able to go to Senilhurst soon."

"Certainly, my lady; certainly, if you wish it. Did you say soon?"

"Yes; very soon; next week. Your master will be quite ready for the journey by that time."

"Certainly, my lady;" and a faint smile played upon the lips of the well-instructed Pearson. "The change is to do him good, I imagine, my lady."

"Of course; and this weather will do very well for travelling; later in the season might be running a risk."

"Certainly, my lady; and it might be bad for your ladyship and the young ladies."

"Yes; in fact, we must be at Senilhurst next week. Lord Rutherford and Lady Blanche will accompany us." Pearson bowed low. "I shall see your master presently, Pearson." Another bow.

Lady Charlton went to the drawing-room, and Pearson repaired to the library, to see if the fire was getting low. The glance with which Sir Hugh repaid his attention was discouraging; so were his words. As usual, they were a reproach for the length of time he had been left, and, as usual, Pearson made no attempt at explanation, and only answered, "Very sorry, Sir Hugh; extremely sorry; might I be allowed?—I think I could put your pillow more comfortable."

"Not at all; I don't want to be comfortable. Left alone two full hours! it's unbearable."

"I was certainly forgetful," began Pearson.

"Forgetful! idiot, you forget everything! Where's my medicine?"

Pearson poured it out, and as he handed it to his master, ventured to observe that the day was so fine, he hoped it might do for a drive.

"Where is the good of driving?" muttered Sir Hugh, "the hills stop one at every half-mile."

"Exactly what I was saying to the bailiff just now, Sir Hugh. Mr. Denham, said I, this place is very different from Senilhurst. There we have a fine open country, where my master can drive about and get plenty of fresh air; beautiful soft in the valleys, bracing upon the downs. Trust me, if you could come to Senilhurst, you would never wish to go back to Rutherford."

"Then you talked nonsense, Pearson," exclaimed Sir Hugh more mildly than before.

Pearson did not seem to notice the interruption, but went on, "Mr. Denham is hard of belief; a very narrow mind; never has travelled at all, Sir Hugh. He wouldn't credit a word I told him of your crop of turnips the year before last." Sir Hugh leaned his head upon his hand in a soothed attitude. "Wonderful, those turnips were!" continued Pearson; "but, as I told Mr. Denham,—my master, said I, understands these things; he's an experiencing gentleman; he takes nothing upon trust."

"And Denham wouldn't believe you, eh?" said Sir Hugh.

"Wouldn't believe a word," said Pearson; "said there never was such a crop known, and he couldn't understand it. But, said I, Mr. Denham, it's not for you and me to try and understand these things. My master is a man of science, and what he does he does upon principle—strict principle; the turnips, d'ye see, grew upon principle."

"Hem, nonsense," muttered Sir Hugh, whilst the frown upon his forehead gradually subsided, and a pleased smile stole over his features. "Why don't you bring him to Senilhurst, Pearson, instead of trying to talk him over here?"

"Undoubtedly, Sir Hugh; it's the only thing to be done; but, as I said, if we are to stay the winter at Rutherford, there is no good in thinking of Senilhurst."

"And who said we were to spend the winter at Rutherford?" inquired Sir Hugh sharply.

"I understood from my lady," began Pearson; but Sir Hugh broke in, "I have told you fifty times before, Pearson, that you are to understand from me; your lady knows nothing about the matter."

"I imagined it was my lady's wish," began Pearson again.

"And what did you think then was my wish? Did you suppose that I meant to be cooped up here for the next six months, with nothing to do but to follow your lady's beck and call?"

"My lady seemed to think it was fixed," continued Pearson, "and of course it was not my place to say anything; though I could see, like every one else, Sir Hugh, that it would be better for you to be at home."

"And what is to hinder me from going home?" inquired Sir Hugh.

"Nothing, sir, nothing; if you desire it: only my lady——"

"Don't talk to me of your lady; my will is her will."

"Unquestionably, Sir Hugh; and no doubt my lady's health, and that of the young ladies, would be materially benefited. As I said to Mr. Denham, Senilhurst air is quite renovating."

"And what did Denham say to that?"

"He was amazed, Sir Hugh; never saw a man more so. Mr. Pearson, said he, Senilhurst must be a paradise. Mr. Denham, said I, it is."

"Hem!" muttered Sir Hugh; "Denham's got more sense than I gave him credit for. To see how he manages the estate here, one would think him an ignorant booby. Young Wentworth knows much more about farming than he does."

"Mr. Wentworth has had great advantages," observed Pearson, "going about with a gentleman of such experience as yourself, Sir Hugh."

"Wentworth's a sensible fellow," continued Sir Hugh; "he has his eyes about him, and he's not conceited. He has my geology pamphlet by heart; in fact, he's quite the life of the place."

"Mr. Wentworth would take a great interest in the farming at Senilhurst," said Pearson insinuatingly.

"Yes, he might; he would, I think. There would be a good deal for him to learn there;" and Sir Hugh fell into a short reverie, which was apparently caused by some difficulty in the contemplated return home, as he tapped his finger on the table and began reckoning—"Lady Charlton, one; Maude and Ady, three; young Wentworth, four; it's one too many."

"The earl and Lady Blanche will have a great loss in your absence, Sir Hugh," began Pearson, a little alarmed at not hearing their names mentioned.

"Well, yes; I suppose they will," said Sir Hugh,

stroking his chin; "the earl and I have pursuits in common, we are both literary men."

"There's a thought of his lordship and Lady Blanche remaining here through the winter, I suppose," said Pearson; "at least my lady seemed to say so the other day."

"What should your lady know about it?" exclaimed Sir Hugh; "the earl has no fixed plans, he told me so confidentially. If I were to ask him to Senilhurst he would go."

"And be delighted, no doubt," replied Pearson; "he has not been looking at all well lately."

"No wonder, living at this place. He and young Wentworth together."—Sir Hugh mused again, but whether upon the travelling plans, or the probable indignation of Lady Charlton if he presumed to give Mr. Wentworth an invitation to Senilhurst, it is impossible to say. The difficulty which perplexed him, whatever it was, seemed, however, to be insurmountable, for after the silence of a few minutes, he exclaimed, "It won't do; no, it wont do; and after all, spring is the best time for seeing a place. If we stay here a few weeks longer we shall help them on into the winter, and they can come to us early in the spring."

Pearson was in dismay; but he was a man of singular patience, and having reached the point from which he had started, he steadily set forth to traverse the same ground again; pulling Sir Hugh one way, in the conviction that he would be sure to go the other, until at length he had once more brought him to face the possibility of removing to Senilhurst immediately, taking Lord Rutherford and Lady Blanche with them, and giving an indirect invitation to Mr. Wentworth to follow at his earliest convenience. This last resolution, however, Sir Hugh did not fail to qualify by repeating, "I shan't invite him; I hate regular invitations. Only if he likes it of course he will be welcome. Mind, Pearson, I have no intention of inviting him."

Pearson assented both to the letter and the spirit of this declaration, and having arranged his master's pillows for about the twentieth time since the conversation began, ventured to suggest that Lady Charlton might be glad to know of Sir Hugh's definite plan. A gracious permission was given, and Sir Hugh raised himself in his arm-chair to look imposing, and spreading a blank sheet of paper before him, chose a new pen that he might make a legible list of imperative orders for the journey.

"Sir Hugh would be glad to speak with you, my lady," said Pearson, as he met Lady Charlton at the foot of the stairs. His face was impenetrable, but his self-satisfied tone showed that all difficulties had been smoothed away.

"I will be with him directly," was Lady Charlton's soft reply; and Pearson went off to the servant's hall, charmed at his own cleverness, in having ruled his master, pleased his mistress, and been instrumental in suggesting an idea, which he had good reason to think would gratify one at least of the young ladies; and all without committing himself.

CHAPTER XXVII.

It was not a long interview between Sir Hugh and Lady Charlton; no interviews of this kind ever were long; for Lady Charlton, when she had once gained a point, took care not to dwell sufficiently upon it to give time for a change of feeling. The determination of returning to Senilhurst was especially important to her at this moment, as the neighbourhood of the Rectory was, in her eyes, becoming every day more undesirable. Even if the earl and Blanche persisted in remaining at Rutherford, she had resolved to go; but independently of her own pleasure, their society would, she knew, be a great inducement to Sir Hugh to consent to her wishes. His vanity would be flattered by the idea of showing Blanche his own place and his own plans; and, as she had calculated upon this as the easy mode of obtaining her point, she was the more provoked at the indecision which Blanche had evinced. Still she did not doubt of gaining her object eventually. Pearson's skill was almost always successful in winning Sir Hugh's consent, even against his favourite wishes; and Blanche was too gentle not to be easily brought round. Yet Lady Charlton allowed no surprise or satisfaction to be visible when she entered the library. She was quietly indifferent, and even put a few obstacles in the way of a sudden removal; obstacles which, of course, only strengthened Sir Hugh's resolution, and gave him a sense of power in showing the clever way in which he could surmount them.

"Lord Rutherford and Blanche must be talked

over," he said; and Lady Charlton agreed; not even a smile betraying that the suggestion had been made to them previously.

The day of departure was next to be fixed. Sir Hugh named it—determined the hour of starting—wrote down the names of the few villages through which they were to pass before they reached a railway station, and the time which the distance might be expected to take; and then proceeded to copy out the after details of the journey from a railway guide, Lady Charlton assisting him by reading out 11·25, 12·50, &c., in due succession.

When, at length, the word Senilhurst was written, in legible characters, at the bottom of the paper, announcing the termination of the journey, Sir Hugh threw himself back in his chair and exclaimed, "There, my dear; now I think I have done my part. I have saved you all the trouble of arrangement, and you will have nothing in the world to do but just to obey orders—the easiest thing of all—just to obey orders—nothing more. We leave this place at half-past eight precisely; we reach Senilhurst at twenty minutes past six. Don't trouble yourself; don't distress yourself about anything: you see when a man is once accustomed to this sort of thing it becomes quite easy. You may tell Maude and Ady, if you like it; but it will be as well to leave Rutherford to me. Gentlemen always manage these things best with each other. I shall hint my wishes gently, and bring him round by degrees."

"Perhaps it might be the best way," said Lady Charlton, and she rose to leave the room.

"Stop, my dear Frances; Lady Charlton, you are in such a hurry. Sit down, will you. One thing we have forgotten—dinner. Let me see; we start at half-past eight; we reach Walton at 10; Ditchley, 12·35; Hoxley Road, 2·40; Sunbridge, 5·15;

reckoning a quarter of an hour for delay; Senilhurst, 6·20; that leaves us forty minutes—one hour and forty minutes till eight o'clock. Will one hour and forty minutes be sufficient? Consider now—to settle yourselves—dress—be, in fact, quite ready for dinner! Can you promise to be in the drawing-room by eight?"

Lady Charlton thought there would be no difficulty.

"Very well, then, that is another point decided. You may write to Mrs. Corrie, and tell her to have dinner ready at eight precisely. And, stay, don't I hear Lord Rutherford's voice?" The earl opened the door. "The very person I wanted to see. I must have a few words with you; I must consult you."

But Lord Rutherford interrupted him. "I beg your pardon; I will return to you, but, at this moment, I have pressing business. Lady Charlton, can you give me a few moments of your leisure?" The tone was unusually haughty, and before Lady Charlton had time to answer he was gone.

Lady Charlton followed him instantly, in spite of Sir Hugh's entreaties, that she would wait and consider what further arrangements were to be made.

Lord Rutherford went before her till he reached his private study, the door of which he opened, and motioned to her to enter it, and then closing and bolting it carefully, he sat down opposite to her. Lady Charlton turned pale. There was something in his countenance which would, in itself, have been sufficient to alarm her; a look of hardly repressed indignation, reproach, and over-excited feeling: a curling lip—a frowning brow—a fire in his flashing eye, only softened by the indescribable expression of mental anguish that pervaded his whole countenance. He did not speak for some moments, but sat resting his forehead upon his hand. Lady

Charlton tried to shake off her fear. She went up to him, laid her hand upon his shoulder, and said in a light, unconstrained tone, "You must not treat me in this way. I must know at once what is the matter."

He looked up and said sternly, "You can tell."

Lady Charlton's tone was unchanged as she replied, "You are mistaken. I know nothing that has happened to put you into this strange mood."

"Not that you have deceived me—betrayed me—broken your most solemn promise?"

A momentary indignation clouded Lady Charlton's face, but she subdued the rising feeling, and said gravely but calmly, "My dear Rutherford, this is not language which I ought to hear. I have not betrayed, or deceived you, or broken any solemn promise; and I have not the most remote idea what it is you refer to. I must insist upon your explaining yourself more clearly."

"You have told her," he said, "you have done the very thing which"—he stopped, and Lady Charlton said eagerly, "Blanche? do you mean that she knows?"

"All that I would have kept from her at any sacrifice. Frances, I thought I could have trusted you better."

Lady Charlton looked extremely pained, and the colour rushed to her cheeks as she said hesitatingly, "It was not I who told her."

"No," exclaimed the earl, "it was not you; it was Maude. But from whom did Maude learn such facts? and who put it into my darling's head to inquire?"

Lady Charlton recovered from her embarrassment when this question was asked reproachfully.

"You are still speaking mysteries," she said; "if you will say clearly what you refer to, I will give you the best explanation I can."

"They are simple facts," replied the earl, sarcastically; "Blanche was missing this morning when I wanted her; I went to her room, and found her in an agony of grief. When I would have forced her to tell me what distressed her, she said—you know what she said. She knew it. Her whole life is embittered—her happiness is blighted—her love for me—but I will not think of that—I dare not."

"And Maude told her?" inquired Lady Charlton.

"Yes, Maude told her."

"And what? how much does Blanche know?"

"Do you think I could bear to ask?" exclaimed the earl, bitterly, "Was it a story that I could endure to have the details repeated; that I could listen patiently whilst my child described her own misery?"

"It might have been as well," said Lady Charlton, coldly; "you might have spared me much pain, and yourself much after-reproach for injustice. Maude has heard from me little beyond what all the world is acquainted with. What she may have guessed or learnt from other sources I cannot answer for. She is of an inquisitive disposition; from a child she was strangely interested in the fate of my most unhappy sister. To satisfy her, I told her the bare fact of her melancholy depression of spirits; but of other sufferings,"—and Lady Charlton's voice became eager, and her eye kindled as she went on—"of neglect, loneliness, disappointed affection; trials which crushed her intellect, and brought her to an early grave, I said nothing."

Lord Rutherford sank upon a chair and groaned.

"It may seem cruel to upbraid you now with an error of judgment," continued Lady Charlton; "but, in my own justification, I must remind you that you were long since warned against the mistake of keeping from Blanche the secret of her mother's history."

"I did not wish to keep it from her," exclaimed the earl, starting from his seat; "but I would have prepared her for it gradually. I would, yes," he added, his voice sinking from its tone of proud excitement into an accent of the most mournful tenderness, "I would have won her to myself,—I would have made myself her all, and then I would have appealed to her love,—her reverence,—her devotion,—for pardon."

"You must have had sympathies in common first," said Lady Charlton, with a quiet sarcasm which escaped her almost involuntarily.

The earl writhed under the censure which he knew was intended, yet he answered firmly, "We have many,—art, and taste, and refinement."

"And religion!" added Lady Charlton.

Lord Rutherford bit his lip, and was silent.

"That is the key to her affections," continued Lady Charlton; "without it I fear you may find the barrier between you greater than you are aware of."

The earl regarded her steadily as if he would have said, Do not try me too far,—but Lady Charlton knew her own power—the power which almost necessarily accompanies the knowledge of a strong mind's weakness—and she went on, "If it were possible to humour her upon the point;—if you could, at whatever sacrifice, bring yourself even to appear"—but the earl broke in upon the observation.

"Appear!—to Blanche!—to my own child!—appear to be what I am not? Oh! Frances, how little you understand us both!"

"Blanche, at least, I understand," said Lady Charlton calmly—"she is like her mother."

The name acted like an electric shock upon Lord Rutherford. "Yes," he exclaimed shuddering, "like her in form—in feature—in mind—in fate." The last word sank into a whisper.

"There is little fear of it," replied Lady Charlton, "except in your own imagination, and in possible circumstances, which are entirely under your control. Loneliness and want of sympathy preyed upon poor Emily's mind. There was no positive hereditary disease. Her case might be the case of any one in the same situation. Loneliness, Blanche will never feel; want of sympathy she may not, if——"

"If," repeated the earl, bitterly. "I tell you, Frances, I have not the power, even if I had the will, to deceive my sweet child. Pure-minded, simple, transparent and true as she is; the very earnestness of her own feelings must make her alive to hypocrisy in others. Would not the tone of my voice—the turn of my sentences,—would not every action of my life betray me? No, better far that she should see me as I am—admire me for what I am—even hate me,—hate me, if it were possible, for what I am not—than be the dupe of professions which must, sooner or later, be discovered, and bring wretchedness upon us both."

"As you will," replied Lady Charlton. "It would be useless to try and persuade you, that I do not wish you either to deceive, or make a profession. All that I desire is, that you should not shock her—prejudices, as you call them—principles, as I call them." She paused, but the earl was silent. "You make the same sacrifice to the world continually," pursued Lady Charlton: "you mix with persons whom you dislike; you join in amusements which do not interest you."

"Yes," interrupted the earl vehemently; "I make a sacrifice to the world, which the world sanctions and understands. I speak its own language, and take advantage of its permitted customs. It is not deceived by civilities and professions. But religion—Frances, I was never a hypocrite. If I had been, I might have spared myself the bitterness of this hour."

"I think you are unnecessarily anxious," replied Lady Charlton.

The Earl did not notice the remark. He was engaged in his own reflections, and in an under tone he said, "Poor child! one could almost be inclined to envy her."

"Can you envy what you consider error?" replied Lady Charlton.

"Error!" repeated the earl, musingly.

"You think it so," said Lady Charlton.

He looked up quickly: "Have you never, Frances, watched a sunset, and seen mountains, and islands, and glittering lakes amongst the clouds, and looked till you believed—till you almost knew them to be real? So have I watched Blanche—daily, hourly, since my return. She has been to me a vision of beauty and purity beyond all that I have known, or could have dreamt; and I have gazed upon her until almost I could persuade myself that her enthusiasm was reality."

"It is real, doubtless, to a certain extent," replied Lady Charlton. "Blanche is young, and a little carried away by feeling; but her principles are unquestionably sound and high; and we ought to be most grateful to Mrs. Howard for having made her what she is."

A sudden check seemed to have been given to Lord Rutherford's earnestness. He drew himself up coldly, and said, "We have wandered very far from our first subject. I should be glad to be quite assured that you have not disobeyed my wishes."

"You are really provoking," replied Lady Charlton, petulantly. "I could never have taken upon myself such a responsibility. Blanche must have had her suspicions previously raised, and then exaggerated what Maude told her." Lady Charlton stopped and after considering for a moment added—"You told me you had given her her mother's papers."

"Yesterday: it was an impulse, after a conversation, a few words only which passed between us. I felt they might interest her, for I saw she longed for sympathy, and I thought they might be something of a bond of closer union between us. But I had long before determined upon doing so when I could summon resolution."

"They must have betrayed the secret," said Lady Charlton.

"Impossible! There were a few letters of my own, including some written years ago, and a journal; you must remember it. I thought it might please Blanche, but there was little in it beyond extracts."

"Are you sure that was all?" inquired Lady Charlton.

"Certain. I destroyed every paper which was in any way painful before I left England."

"Then it must have been Blanche's own fancy," said Lady Charlton, "or —"

The earl turned to her hastily; "Or whom?—what?"

"Or Mrs. Wentworth!"

"Yes," exclaimed Lord Rutherford, as if the idea had in an instant brought conviction to his mind; "yes, it must have been her. How could I have been so blind? But I thought she knew my wishes through you."

"I wrote to her," said Lady Charlton, "when you first thought of returning to Rutherford, impressing upon her the necessity of caution. Her reply was stiff and unsatisfactory, like everything she does or says; but I certainly oould not have imagined her capable of telling Blanche what you wanted to keep from her."

"She supposed it her duty, perhaps," said Lord Rutherford, with a sneer. "She is very much bent upon duty."

"Her own, and other persons too, in this case," observed Lady Charlton; "but you must not be hard upon her. Remember, we have as yet only suspicion."

"It shall be certainty, one way or the other, soon," exclaimed the earl; and without adding another word, he seized his hat, opened the window, and the next minute was walking at a rapid pace down the steep path which led to the rectory.

Lady Charlton looked after him for a few seconds, and then murmuring to herself, "Impetuous as ever! but I have diverted his thoughts for the present," she went to seek Maude, and give her a maternal and not very gentle reproof, for the extreme imprudence which had led her to divulge facts, only a portion of which had as yet been intended to reach the ears of Blanche.

Lord Rutherford and Mrs. Wentworth disliked each other, as persons must do who, without mutual sympathy or respect, have been compelled by circumstances to learn the secrets of each other's lives, without caring to know the secrets of the heart. Years before, when Lord Rutherford had brought his bride to her stately home, and offered her luxury and gaiety, she had turned from all to seek the companionship of Mrs. Wentworth. The earl was not jealous—he did not love sufficiently to care where his wife found happiness, as long as he was not called upon to give up his own wishes to contribute to it; but he chafed at the strictness of Mrs. Wentworth's principles, dreaded her influence, and was repulsed by the coldness of her manner—and the aversion was quickly reciprocal. If Mrs. Wentworth reverenced the Countess of Rutherford for her piety, and pitied her for her lonely position; she could scarcely feel cordial towards the selfish, worldly husband, who by civil unkindness blighted her hopes and mocked her affections. And, as years went on, and absence and neglect did their fatal work in wrecking not only the peace, but the mind of the unhappy countess, the first feeling of dislike almost necessarily deepened into intensity.

But that time was long gone by. The Countess of Rutherford was resting in her quiet grave, safe from the weariness of disappointment and the bitterness of unrequited love; and the earl was returned to his home, to begin, as it were, a new life, and repay the debt which he owed to the memory of his wife by the devoted affection which he lavished upon her child. The past was forgotten;—so it seemed to many but himself; forgotten by the countess's relations; forgotten, if it had ever been remembered, by the world. Yet, was it so?—does the tide of life indeed sweep by and bear away all traces of the joys and griefs, the good and evil, of our vanished years; or is there, even upon earth, a record of the deeds of former days, written upon the memories of our friends and companions, and bearing a witness which few can recollect and feel towards us as if such things had never been?

But Lord Rutherford did Mrs. Wentworth great injustice, when he considered her capable of biassing the mind of his daughter in any way against himself; or even of endeavouring to fix her affections upon her mother's memory at his expense. Even if Mrs. Wentworth had felt for Blanche as she had once felt for the countess, she would have shrunk from such an act as worse than cruelty. But, in truth, she was not sufficiently attracted by the gentle girl, who seemed to have no will but her father's, to attempt to gain an influence over her. She was interested in Blanche for her mother's sake and for Eleanor's; but being a person of strong impulse and prepossessions, and peculiarly alive to the impression which she made upon others, she could not help seeing, from the very beginning of their acquaintance, that Blanche was not likely to seek her confidence. This was an offence which Mrs. Wentworth was not inclined easily to overlook. It awoke a sense of injustice, as if something was denied her which she had a right to claim. Her natural stiffness and reserve also made her seek for the opposite qualities in others; and symptoms of shyness, especially in young people, were generally attributed to some instinctive difference of feeling, caused possibly by her own defect of manner, which it would be useless to endeavour to overcome. Thus it was that, when Mrs. Wentworth was met with more than her own cordiality, she could love, and love intensely; but when she did not love, she was indifferent, and not unfrequently prejudiced.

Lord Rutherford knew nothing of all this. He was not an observer of human nature in general; and seldom took the trouble to think what people were like, or why they pleased or displeased him. A spoilt child from infancy, he only knew what offended his taste, or shocked his self-esteem, and avoided it. It was always an effort to him to be with Mrs. Wentworth, and he would have shunned, instead of seeking, an interview, if he had not been carried forward by indignation and something like revenge. For it is pleasant to our unchecked natural instincts to have a clear cause of complaint against a person whom we dislike, and yet respect; and, by the time the earl had reached the parsonage, he had worked himself up into the persuasion, not only that the accusation against Mrs. Wentworth was true, but that no extenuation could be offered.

Blanche saw him pass the drawing-room window as she sat writing her letter and waiting for Eleanor, but she did not go to meet him. His look of anguish as he turned away from her, when in their short morning interview she told him the cause of her distress, was still present to her recollection, and she dreaded to encounter it again. In her simplicity, she could not read its entire meaning; but it had warned her that the subject must never again be alluded to, unless by him. The earl was shown into Mrs. Wentworth's morning-room; and through the thin partition Blanche could hear his voice, as the conversation began—first formal, and subdued, then gradually rising into energy and excitement; whilst Mrs. Wentworth's answers seemed only rather more decided than usual. The interview was soon over; Blanche heard, as she supposed, the parting words, and a pause followed. She thought her father was gone; but as she drew near the window to see, she again caught Mrs. Wentworth's voice. The words were distinctly audible—"Your lordship must forgive me, if I earnestly warn you to be cautious. No one knows better than myself the many reasons for being so; and, in pity to your child, you must remember, that the germ of the evil, at least, may be hereditary."

There was a faint, sharp cry of exceeding misery, and Blanche fell senseless to the ground.

END OF VOL. I.

Stevens and Co., Printers, Bell Yard, Temple Bar.

THE EARL'S DAUGHTER.

THE

EARL'S DAUGHTER.

BY

THE AUTHOR OF "AMY HERBERT," "GERTRUDE," "THE CHILD'S FIRST HISTORY OF ROME," ETC.

EDITED BY

THE REV. W. SEWELL, B.D.

FELLOW OF EXETER COLLEGE, OXFORD.

Life, ... is energy of Love,
Divine or human; exercised in pain,
In strife, and tribulation; and ordained,
If so approved and sanctified, to pass,
Through shades and silent rest, to endless joy.
The Excursion.

VOL. II.

LONDON:
LONGMAN, BROWN, GREEN, AND LONGMANS,
PATERNOSTER ROW.
1850.

LONDON:
STEVENS AND CO., PRINTERS, BELL YARD,
TEMPLE BAR.

THE EARL'S DAUGHTER.

CHAPTER I.

THAT evening, as twilight shades were gathering over the sky, and repose was settling upon the lovely valley of Rutherford—as happy children were returning from their play, and the husbandman was preparing to enjoy his evening meal, and the sleep which "to the labouring man is sweet, whether he eat little or much"—the young heiress of all that wealth, beauty, and prosperity can bestow, lay stretched upon her couch, striving to chasten her rebellious heart, and bring every gloomy thought, and fruitless wish, into submission to the will of her Maker.

Poor Blanche! she had not known, till that hour, that it was possible to feel more intensely for herself than for others. Unselfish, confiding, humble-minded, she had lived for her fellow-creatures, and in their joys and sorrows had found her own. But there are griefs which encompass us with a barrier that shuts out human sympathy, and forbids us to find relief in the thought that our affliction is less than that of many around us. "The heart knoweth its own bitterness;" and in those seasons of trial it is incapable of estimating comparative wretchedness.

Blanche lay quite still, her hands clasped tightly

together, and her eyes firmly shut; occasionally her lips moved, and the momentary contraction of the forehead, or a nervous action of the fingers, gave indication of some passing thought of misery, but the expression of the face was that of calm hopelessness. There was no one near her, no one watching her; the one wish she had expressed was for solitude; solitude with Him "to whom all hearts are open, and from whom no secrets are hid."

The door opened slowly, and Lord Rutherford stole gently to her side. Blanche just opened her eyes and closed them again instantly. He drew near and knelt down beside her, and took her clammy hand in his, and she turned her face towards him and tried to smile; but the parched lips quivered, and a mist gathered over her soft dark eyes, and then the bitter tears flowed silently and fast.

"Blanche," said the earl, "are you better?"

His voice was quite changed; low and husky. Blanche raised herself and put her arm round his neck, and kissed him; but she could not speak.

"My poor child," he said, "they told me you were asleep."

Blanche shook her head, and answered, faintly, "that she had been trying to sleep, but it was of no use."

"You must have an opiate," observed the earl; "I shall send for one," and he touched the bell-rope.

"No opiates for me, dear papa," said Blanche, stopping him; "they can do nothing—no one—nobody"—She paused, and put her hand to her head, as if to check the swift torturing current of thought which was about to rush over her.

"Blanche, can you forgive me?" and the proud earl hid his face upon her pillow, and sobbed like a child.

"Forgive you, my own papa; you who have been so kind, so good: what can I have to forgive?" And again she kissed him and fondly smoothed his hair, and whispered how dear he was to her; but the anguish of remorse was too keen for such consolation.

"Stay, Blanche! stay," he exclaimed; putting aside her hand, and rising with a sudden effort at self-control; "hear me patiently, calmly, if you can; let me tell you all."

"Yes, all, if you please, if you will," said Blanche, with a gentle but sad smile; "that is the greatest kindness; and, papa, I will try to bear it."

"And if it should be too much?" repeated the earl, thoughtfully. "They wished me not; your aunt says it is unwise. But, Blanche, neither you nor I can endure suspense."

"No, indeed; thank you so much for sparing me. Then, papa, it is—hereditary?" Her breath came quick and faint, and her glassy eyes rested upon her father's face with a look of intense eagerness, which made him turn shuddering from her gaze.

The earl paused for one instant. "We think not; we hope not; only—"

"Only you fear," said Blanche, quite calmly.

"No, no," he exclaimed, "I do not fear; others may, but I do not. Blanche, you shall hear my story and be comforted, even though it be at the sacrifice of your love for me." He sat down by her, and, without daring to look at her, went on: "Your mother was insane—I would not try to conceal or mitigate the fact—for many months before her death; and I—I am said to have been the cause. Yes, turn from me, and hate me," he exclaimed, as Blanche involuntarily caught away the hand which he had taken in his; "it is only what I deserve; but bear with what I have to say in my defence. There is no hereditary insanity in her family, but there is a peculiarity,—a tendency to morbid melancholy, on the female side—not on that of your aunt, they were but half sisters. It is this melancholy which I am accused of having aggravated; it may be, truly. But, Blanche, even for this—a grievous sin in the eye of man—it is possible that some extenuation may be found in the sight of God. Men call me cold and forbidding; I am so now, but I was not so always. Once, Blanche, I was loving, tender-hearted, enthusiastic, even as yourself. I was young then. I believed the world was made for happiness, and I thought that I had found it. Look!" and he drew forth a small locket, from which the hair that had been placed in it was gone. "This was a gift from one who was to have been my wife. It is the symbol of the heart she offered me—empty, valueless. She deceived me; and, in the madness of my disappointment, I married another. There was my first offence—the offence for which I cannot forgive myself, and for which the punishment of years has fallen upon me." Blanche stretched out her hand, and again he took it and pressed it to his lips, and continued: "Your mother had been known to me from infancy. We had played, and walked, and sang together, and outwardly shared many joys and sorrows; but we had never suited each other. So at least I thought till the hour of my great trial; then, for the first time, I discovered from the extent of her compassion that we had sympathies in common. Yet I did not really love her; I knew that I did not. I felt that our natures and our tastes were in their foundation totally dissimilar. But I was so lonely—so unutterably wretched; it was such a relief to be able to talk of my misery, that, forgetting how by the very act of marriage I must shut out all memory of the past, I offered myself, and was accepted. One great mistake! Oh, Blanche! how it mars all hope of goodness and greatness in life. From that hour I was an altered man; bound with an irrevocable chain; having lost the prospect of comfort in domestic life, and unable to rouse myself to interest in public matters. For your mother,—let me speak of her as she was," he said, gently, as Blanche heaved a sigh; "if I seem to blame her, remember that I am seeking to excuse myself to her child; your mother was not a person to be blind to the real state of my heart. She had a craving for affection, and a keen insight into the feelings of others. When she found herself disappointed she sank into a torpid, dreary melancholy, the more unendurable for us both, because the occasion of it was never alluded to by either. Whether by a different line of conduct she might at length have won my love I cannot say, but she seemed to have no hope of it herself; for she shut herself up from me. When I brought friends to the castle, she pleaded illness, and withdrew from them; and when I took her into society, she gave way to a depression of spirits which awoke constant remark." He paused, watching the effect of his words; but Blanche averted her face.

"That is all my complaint of her," he continued, hurriedly. "She was too good, too high, for me. If she had been more earthly we might have been happier. At least, I should not have to reproach myself with having been the murderer of an angel's peace."

"She was very good, then?" murmured Blanche.

"Good!" he replied; "I never knew her equal upon earth, until —" and he stooped and imprinted a kiss on Blanche's burning forehead. "Yes, she was a marvel, a miracle; but, Blanche, even for that very cause we were unhappy. It was a goodness which I could not comprehend; for it was exalted above infirmity itself, and yet saw evil in the most natural pursuits of others. A life of entire seclusion from the world was her ideal of real excellence, and she tried to carry it out, and did so. I do not say she was wrong," he added, as Blanche looked up with a disappointed expression: "it may have been, I believe it was, my own doing. This is not a moment for concealment: I drove her to it. My principles grieved her, and I did not try to soften them; and then she grew more strict, and the evil increased. We led this life for nearly four years," continued the earl; "and how wretched it was for us both I can never describe. I had friends about me; but they gave me no real comfort; and your poor mother took such an aversion to them, that she made it, at last, a point of duty to avoid them. Her only companion was Mrs. Wentworth. I doubted then whether the intimacy was wise; I am sure, now, that it was not. Mrs. Wentworth aggravated, instead of soothing, what was amiss. She made your mother think worse of me than I deserved, and fostered her strict notions till they became absurd. But you were born, Blanche; my own precious child: it seemed a new era in my existence; a bright hope, and interest for the future. People said that I was disappointed because you were not a boy; but they did not know me. If I was grave afterwards it was not for that reason. Your mother's spirits for a time rallied so much that I began to think she might soon become more to me than I had ever fancied possible. I tried to induce her to join more in society, and proposed that we should travel. I sketched out a plan, and chose a party to accompany us: she took some pleasure, or at least interest, in the idea at first; but when we came to enter into detail, all our former differences revived. Two persons more diametrically opposite in character and taste could never have been united; and unfortunately her prejudices were principles, and she would never yield them. Yet she loved me, Blanche; through all, she loved me. It is the bitterest thought of all, now that the past is irrevocable. Her very wish to travel with me alone, to keep me away from those whom she thought likely to encourage me in error, arose from love: but it irritated me beyond endurance; and—" the earl paused, and moved from his seat as if thus to escape the pain of further recital.

Blanche stopped him. She said, in a clear, firm tone, "Papa, you will tell me all now; we shall both be happier." And like a humble child he sat down again, and went on.

"Yes, I will tell all. Blanche, you are right; if we are ever to know peace on earth, it must be by openness. Yet you will shrink from me, even as I shrink from myself; for I was cruel to her—your mother! the mother of my only treasure. It was on a stormy, blustering day—how well I remember it!—I had been absent all the morning, riding with a party of friends,—some whom she particularly disliked. Perhaps their influence was not good, at least it did not work for good on that day. I returned home in better spirits than usual, and resolved to show myself independent, and insist upon your mother's giving up her prejudices and going with us abroad. I found her in her favourite room—the same which you were in yesterday. She scarcely ever left it, except to take her meals; she was sitting as usual, working, with the Bible open before her. I recollect she told me that she was glad I had come, and that the day had seemed long. We entered into conversation, and from her manner, at first, I fancied it a favourable moment for again insisting upon my wishes. She listened patiently whilst I urged the pleasure it would give me, and reminded her of a wife's duty; but I saw by the expression of her face, as soon as the subject was named, that her resolution was immoveable. If I would go alone she would accompany me; but on no other condition. The very fact of her silence exasperated me; I could have better borne a torrent of words, than that still, fixed look of determination. I upbraided her with inconsistency and neglect of the duty she owed me; and then, for the first time, she poured forth her long-hidden griefs. They were true and real. I had disappointed her affections, and treated her with coldness, and forced upon her society which she abhorred; but I was too proud to hear it: and, in my indignation, I told her that it was better we should part. The words were no sooner uttered than a sudden change passed over her; she stood before me, a silent, colourless statue; her limbs rigid, her eyes fixed on vacancy. I spoke to her, but she took no notice; and even reproach—for I ventured upon it to excite her—had no effect. I was more frightened than I chose to acknowledge, but I had no doubt that quietness would restore her; and, ringing for her maid, I left her. Mrs. Wentworth met me in the passage. I was bewildered and conscience-stricken, but I could not endure that she should see any symptoms of humiliation; and being determined to tell my own tale, I stopped her, and, related in few words what had passed, attributing your poor mother's change of manner to obstinate resolution. 'My will,' I said, 'was irrevocably fixed; as I could not make her happy, I was certain it was better for both of us to part.' Mrs. Wentworth received the announcement with her usual cold stoicism, and, merely asking me where she should find your mother, went to her room. I joined my friends, for the thought of solitude was dreadful to me. I had such horrible misgivings, which I could not subdue. After the lapse of about an hour, I sent to inquire for your mother; they brought me word that Mrs. Wentworth was with her, and that she wished to remain quiet. Can you believe, Blanche, that I was irritated by this? After all my indifference and cruelty, I hated the thought of Mrs. Wentworth's being her companion. I fancied how they would talk of me, and blame me; and I had pictured to myself despair and anger, rather than quietness. Hitherto I had triumphed in the knowledge of my power over your poor mother's affection; perhaps, but for that, I should never have tried her so far: but the seclusion and calmness reduced me to nothing. I was determined, however, not to betray what was going on; our party was as gay as usual, and we dined out; and in the course of the evening, as the plan for a continental tour was again brought under discussion, I was induced to say that I would not let anything interfere longer with the scheme, but that I would be ready to start in a few days. In my heart, I hoped that this determination of purpose would bring your mother to reason, and that a reconciliation would be the consequence. But it was otherwise ordered, Blanche," and the earl's voice became tremulous and hollow; "I never saw her again; never, until eight months afterwards, she lay dressed for her coffin, apparently the same colourless image from which I had parted.

"Yet it was not all my fault," continued the earl, more calmly; "Mrs. Wentworth may have acted for the best; I have tried to believe that she did: but she played a cruel part. She found your poor mother stunned at what had passed, and thought it right not to run the risk of allowing her to see me; but, instead of telling me of her real state, and so awakening my compassion, she sent me messages, which made me think your mother cold and obstinate: and soon so exasperated me, that the next day I set off for London, and sent her word that I was upon the point of leaving England. I think Mrs. Wentworth saw her error at last; at least she must have been convinced that she had miscalculated the amount of your poor mother's strength of mind, for it was gone then; the little that had remained from the time when I first spoke of separation fled, when she knew that I had actually left her. She became—oh! Blanche, you must not ask me to tell you what; I would not have you know it or think of it." He rose from his seat and paced the room, and Blanche closed her eyes and prayed. "It is not hereditary, you see—it cannot be hereditary," continued the earl, drawing near her again, and speaking rapidly; "you were then nearly a year old. Who gave you the notion that it might be?"

"Only Mrs. Wentworth in those few words," said Blanche, trying to keep under every symptom of agitation.

"My evil fate!" exclaimed the earl; "it is she who has been the destroyer of every hope. It must have been a letter to her that you told me you had read; yet I thought I had burnt all."

"The letter did not exactly frighten me," said Blanche; "it only made me unhappy; for it was very miserable."

"It must have been written towards the last," said the earl; "she was better then, but not happier. Would to God that I could think so! There again I did her grievous wrong; yet not entirely intentionally. The people about her sent me word at first that she was ill, but they said little of the circumstances. It was Mrs. Wentworth's great aim to keep all private; I do her the justice to believe from good intention—a regard to public opinion, and the feelings of the family, and a dread lest my return might do harm instead of good. She devoted herself to your mother, and scarcely any one else saw her: when at last the unhappy fact became more certainly irremediable and more generally suspected, Mrs. Wentworth wrote, still, however, vaguely, advising me to return for the sake of my own peace of mind; but that was all. I did not understand her allusion, and I desired a message from your mother, which she was in no state to give. Yet, I will not excuse myself; I would not know what I might have known. I did not learn because I would not inquire. But the shock came at last. I was at Venice, just returned from a wandering in the Tyrol, and planning a further tour in the East. Letters were brought me from England, and I opened them carelessly, for I expected nothing more than I had received for many weeks. She was dying;—her reason had returned, but she was dying. The one longing wish which haunted her, was to see me and forgive me. Blanche, she may have forgiven me in Heaven; but I was never permitted to learn it from her own lips on earth. Two hours before I reached Rutherford she died."

There was a silence of many moments. It was broken by Blanche. "Papa," she said, "you have made me happier; will you not be happier yourself?"

Lord Rutherford did not trust himself to look up; he had leant his head upon her pillow, and she felt the agitated beating of his pulse as his hand rested upon hers.

"Papa," she said again, "may I tell you what I really feel?"

He did not answer, and she went on.

"I was frightened this morning, for I was selfish; I had horrible thoughts about myself, and I was afraid—it was very wrong, but I thought there was something more dreadful about—about you. I feel so sorry now, and I am not unhappy: I can trust, and I will try not to think of what may be."

"May be—may be," exclaimed the earl, passionately; "I will never have those words repeated again."

"Yes; may be, dear papa," said Blanche, firmly; "for it may be the will of God, and then we would neither of us murmur."

Lord Rutherford rose impatiently; but Blanche

detained him with a look of the most earnest entreaty for his assent, and added, "We could not think it hard if it was ordered; could we?"

"Not hard!" and the earl smiled scornfully; "not cruel, that my innocent child should suffer!"

Blanche sighed heavily; yet it was only a momentary feeling of despair, and again gently and seriously she said, "I can trust, and hope, and try to be happy; and, if I wish it, will not you do so likewise? You are so very kind always."

The earl's eyes glistened; "I would do all in my power, my child," he said, "for your sake, and for my own. Oh, Blanche, you little know the weary life that has been my punishment since those fearful days. If sackcloth and ashes could atone, as men fondly deem, for their offences, there should have been no greater penitent on earth than him whom men have called the proud Earl of Rutherford. But I have atoned, and I will atone, in the only way left. When kneeling by your mother's coffin, I vowed to redeem the past by the sacrifice of every wish of my heart to the happiness of her child; and that vow, in the sight of God, I now repeat to you. Ask what you will, Blanche—do what you will—it shall be granted and allowed; only let me feel that the curse which I have brought upon myself is revoked—that the visitation which has once been sent upon my house will not return to it in judgment again."

Blanche caught her father's hand; but he turned away, and in a firmer and altered voice entreated her to rest for the present, and, if possible, to exert herself so as to appear at the dinner table. "We may understand each other, but there is no need for others to understand us," he said, as he left the room; and Blanche, though longing for further conversation, dared not ask him to remain.

CHAPTER II.

A GAY party was assembled on the lawn at Senilhurst. Lady Charlton, and a few elderly ladies and middle-aged gentlemen, chaperoning an assemblage of younger ones. Luncheon was just ended; some guests were departing; some, who were staying in the house, were settling rides and drives for the afternoon. Lady Charlton was making herself agreeable, as she always did in her own house. There could not be a more easy, unaffected, kind-hearted manager for every one,—quite unequalled, apparently; for she was good-humoured, sympathizing and considerate, with just enough strictness and particularity to suit sober-minded people; and just sufficient vivacity to enjoy and keep up the mirth of the more thoughtless. And Senilhurst was precisely the place in which Lady Charlton could show herself to advantage. There were no deep windows, suggesting retirement and reflection; no antiquated pieces of furniture, with traditional stories attached to them; no haunted chambers or dark melancholy passages. It was a bright, smiling, sunshiny house, large and handsome, built on the side of a hill facing the south. There was a genial southern aspect over everything about it. Greenhouse-plants flourished in the open air; vines were trained over trellised work, and formed green arches and shady walks; the sloping lawn was smooth and soft as velvet; the clear stream of water reflected every leaf and branch of the large beech and ash trees which grew on its banks. At a season when almost every one else was sighing at the thought that summer was over, Lady Charlton was exhibiting her garden in full beauty. It was a triumph she peculiarly enjoyed, for it involved no offensive vanity, and Lady Charlton shrank from all personal display. It was so pleasant to hear the different remarks made upon the charming situation —the splendid colours—the beautiful outlines, couched with the suggestion that nature had done much, but art had done still more; and Lady Charlton felt herself so unpretending and indifferent, in the midst of such delicate homage to her taste, and was so courteous and modest; in fact, she became quite young in her garden.

"You must be entirely spoilt for other places," suggested Colonel Lorton, a new acquaintance, and a man of large fortune, who was endeavouring to ingratiate himself with Lady Charlton for the sake of a rather idle and wilful son.

"Every spot has its peculiar beauty," was the careless reply. "Senilhurst is certainly pretty; but, Colonel Lorton, you are not going to leave us this afternoon. The riding party reckoned upon your assisting them in exploring the Warham Woods."

Colonel Lorton bowed, but regretted that he was under a special engagement. If he might be allowed—if it would not be an intrusion to leave his son as his representative—he thought, indeed he was quite sure, that he would be a most safe guide.

Lady Charlton felt it necessary to be slightly distant and hesitating in her manner of conferring a favour which she had determined upon beforehand. "Of course," she said, "every one would be glad of such an escort. It was just possible that her daughters might be obliged to give up their horses to some friends, but that would make no difference to Mr. Lorton—and she would immediately inquire what was settled." And Lady Charlton glided away to insist upon Adelaide's joining the Warham expedition, at all events.

The party set off;—a pleasant, merry one. Lady Charlton watched them as they rode through the park, and congratulated herself on her good management. Mr. Lorton might be a little silly, a little dissipated; but he had family and fortune in his favour. The intimacy might or might not have results—that was not the question; but it would amuse for the moment, and drive away all thought of Mr. Wentworth; and though Lady Charlton could not but own to herself that it was a balance of evil, what was to be done? Adelaide was so giddy and headstrong there was no possibility of keeping her out of mischief, except by skilful management. Principles she did not and could not understand, and if it was not a very high-minded, delicate species of domestic diplomacy, it was only the way of the world; and people who live in the world must follow the maxims and customs of the world.

Lady Charlton congratulated herself upon her cleverness, and went, with a lighter heart, to inquire into the movements of the remainder of her visitors. Two riding-horses were still standing at a side-entrance; and she heard Lord Rutherford ask if any one had seen Lady Blanche.

Lady Charlton went up to him: "You are not waiting for Blanche, are you? She is gone, I believe. I am nearly sure she was one of the Warham party."

"She has changed her mind then very suddenly," replied the earl; "an hour since we settled to ride together."

"Oh! but, of course, that was all nonsense. When the Warham Woods were talked of, you could not expect her to keep to a first engagement. And it would not be right—you must not really be so exacting."

"I wish her only to do as she likes," replied the

earl, gravely; "she told me she preferred riding alone with me."

"But, my dear Rutherford, you don't surely take literally all that the poor child says. She is so devoured by duty, that she has not space left for any thought of pleasure; and therefore we must think for her. Just fancy what a very agreeable ride she would have missed. Mr. Lorton, Sir Charles Trevanion, Mrs. Cuthbert Grey and her very nice daughters, and that first-rate Lord Erlsmere; it would have been cruel to make her leave them."

"Dear papa, have I kept you waiting? I am so sorry," said the gentle voice which was sweeter than the most delicious music to Lord Rutherford's ear. Blanche was standing on the steps, dressed in her riding-habit; her colour was brighter than usual, her eyes were lighted up with pleasure, or perhaps something better than pleasure—peace—the peace of a mind at rest in itself, and having nothing externally to disturb it. It was a lovely picture which she made, leaning against a column of the portico; the peculiar and very exquisite beauty so lavishly bestowed upon her by nature, enhanced by the brilliant sunshine and the colouring of the flowers which filled the entrance hall; and Lady Charlton whispered to the earl, that it was a perfect study for an artist. She thought to please him, but he did not answer her; his eye rested upon Blanche for a moment, and a sigh, audible only to Lady Charlton, followed, and without saying another word he assisted Blanche to mount, and they rode off.

And Blanche was then happy! with the certainty of her mother's trials and fatal malady, the want of congeniality in her father, and the disappointment in her aunt, whose character she was now beginning to understand, and whilst living amongst worldly people, and hearing worldly maxims, tempted by all that earth holds most precious, she could still smile, with the holy, innocent smile of her happy childhood, and rejoice in "the peace that passeth understanding." It may be hard to imagine, so few there are who enter upon the scene of life's great delusion with a sufficient safeguard against its snares. But if Blanche had great temptations to battle with, she had also great support, not only in that inward strength which is never denied to those who seek it, but also in the outward circumstances which were Providentially provided for her. Senilhurst was, indeed, her first experience of the pomps and vanities of the world; she found there luxury, flattery, refined dissipation, disguised selfishness; but her mind was pre-occupied, and in consequence much that was evil passed by unnoticed.

Blanche had grown very old since that one conversation with her father which had revealed her mother's history. The first knowledge obtained in early youth of the great mistakes by which the happiness of life may be destroyed, makes us strangely thoughtful: it opens a new world, by drawing aside the veil which, in childhood, hides from us the hearts of our fellow-creatures, and induces us to believe all persons happy who have not lessons to learn and teachers to obey. Blanche saw that her mother had erred; and, painful as the conviction was in some respects, it was not without its accompanying comfort; for if the countess had been reserved and exclusive her husband might at least be excused for his want of sympathy. There had been faults on both sides; yet not such as to destroy a child's respect. Blanche felt that, if her mother had been spared, it might have been possible to bring about not only reconciliation but harmony between her parents. Since that blessing was denied her, it remained only to devote herself to her father, and make it the object of her life to render religion as winning to him now as formerly it had been distasteful. The resolution was made calmly and solemnly, after long thought and earnest prayer; for Blanche knew that it was not without its dangers. In her desire to make duty agreeable she was likely to be betrayed into a sacrifice of principle. It is the evil which we constantly see in persons who try to gain the favour of the world, and yet to have a conscience clear of offence before God. But Blanche's singleness of purpose saved her; she did not desire to please her father for the sake of his affection, precious though it was; she had one aim, one motive, infinitely higher, by which to solve every question of casuistry, and it was fortunate for her object that it was so.

Inconsistency is never winning. The most inveterate opponent of religion has no respect for the halter "between two opinions." Talent, grace, beauty, sweetness of temper, unselfishness, all are in the end powerless, as means of influence, where there is a want of fixedness in principle: for the world is quick and keen in its perceptions, it is particularly gifted with what is called common sense; and however it may openly flatter and fawn upon its double-minded friends it most surely visits them with scorn in secret. Yet there was nothing in Blanche's mode of life at Senilhurst likely to attract remark. Lady Charlton saw that she was more cheerful, and attributed the improvement to change of scene, and Adelaide found that her cousin could enjoy many things which at Rutherford she had fancied would have no interest for her. All went on naturally. If Blanche contrived to occupy herself with Lady Charlton's school, it was in such a way that it brought no thought of peculiar goodness or self-denial. She said that she liked it, and made no mystery of anything she did there, and her visits were taken as a matter of course; and when she joined in the afternoon's amusements and made herself often the life of the party, it did not occur to any one to complain because she had absented herself in the early part of the day. So again, when she gave up some scheme of enjoyment to ride or walk with her father, it was impossible to think she had made a sacrifice. There was not a shadow of disappointment upon her bright face; it was supposed that she followed her own inclinations, and no sympathy was thrown away upon her.

And yet Blanche was learning to fashion her life, in this new world of temptation, upon a strict and most self-denying rule. Her hours of devotion were fixed; her duties marked out day by day; and the one motive of her father's happiness influenced her in the most trifling circumstances.

Lady Charlton was a strict observer of all the customary forms of a religious household, and Blanche was never absent from family prayers. Adelaide laughed, and said, "She was dreadfully good;" but it was not such an extraordinary effort as to create much wonder; and no one knew or thought of inquiring how much time Blanche had redeemed from unnecessary sleep to prepare herself, in private, for the day's trials. When so many were going and coming—talking, drawing, singing—it was not seen that Blanche followed any order in her occupations; yet the day was carefully divided, and seasons for self-examination and retirement were as watchfully, if not as methodically, kept as if she had been a member of an order set apart from the world: whilst, amidst all, as a duty of religion as well as of affection, Blanche was ever striving to make her father read with her, talk to her, and interest himself in her engagements. The first hour after breakfast was always spent with him, looking over his letters and trying to gain some insight into the business connected with his property. Blanche had begun the practice playfully, and seemingly only from curiosity; but, in a very short time, she made herself really useful; and, even when questions were too complicated for her opinion to be of consequence, Lord Rutherford found a satisfaction in talking them over with her. So, in other ways, whatever engaged his attention occupied hers; and, though at first it was difficult to believe that this interest could ever be reciprocal, Blanche endeavoured to make it so, and in a great measure succeeded.

She always took it for granted that her father cared to know what she liked or what she did. She gave her opinions upon people and things freely to him in private, and brought out, in return, many of the lesser feelings and sympathies which form the cement of family life, but which reserved people are apt to bury in their own bosoms, and scarcely perhaps to remark even in themselves.

It was scarcely possible for such an intercourse to continue day after day without working some effects, visible even to Blanche, and giving her hope that their principles might eventually accord.

Lord Rutherford had begun by thinking her a child to be loved and fondled, and treating her accordingly; but, as time went on, his sentiments towards her insensibly changed. Respect blended with his affection; respect for her judgment, discrimination of character, and delicacy of feeling; and something approaching to awe at the high, unworldly views which she did not hesitate to put forth, though so unobtrusively as never to offend his taste, or to jar upon his sense of a parent's position of superiority. And Lord Rutherford was now at ease with Blanche. There was nothing more to reveal. The worst, both for himself and for her, had been told; yet she could love him still: and, what was equally essential to his happiness, she could still smile without any apparent foreboding of evil to come.

Lord Rutherford little knew the constant check upon the thoughts by which this calmness was attained. He only saw the result, and was satisfied, and he had reason to be so.

After the first shock of discovering her mother's insanity was past, Blanche's fears had naturally reverted to herself; not so much with a definable dread, as with a vague horror of the future, which was perhaps worse to bear. She was too young and inexperienced to understand fully the government of her own mind, and fancies and fears oppressed her, which might have brought lasting consequences of evil, but for a warning from the only friend to whom she ventured to reveal the extent of her fears.

Mrs. Howard could feel for Blanche, the more deeply as she had herself, up to that period, been kept in ignorance of the nature of the countess's illness; but her advice was given with a calm decision, which in itself served to strengthen Blanche's failing spirit. "It was not," she said, "a case for resignation simply; for that, under such circumstances, would imply submission to a certain evil; and the first thing for Blanche to do, was to realize to herself, as clearly as possible, that the evil was not certain. And this must be done not by taking the opinion of others, but by using her own reason."

"Put the question aside as belonging to yourself, if possible, my dear child," wrote Mrs. Howard; "and try to look at it as if it concerned another. Our trials are often exaggerated to at least double their real magnitude, because we have not courage to view them in their full extent. Whatever the evil may be which presents itself, face it; see it as well as may be in its true light, without any distortions of hope or fear; then determine how it may be avoided or endured. If you do this, you will see that when the circumstances are fairly considered, there is little to justify uneasiness in those who love you best. If there were, do you think I could write as I am now doing? But you will say, and very naturally, that the dread still remains! I believe it must. I do not think it is in human nature to escape it; and it is in this that I feel for you most deeply. Yet it may be converted into a blessing. If, when the idea of a dreadful possibility presents itself, you can turn away from it as a matter of duty, you will acquire a power of self-control, which will be—I cannot say how useful to you in other instances. I do most earnestly trust that you will try and do this. Pray never read books upon the subject; and when you find yourself fancying what may be, and beginning to torture yourself with picturing scenes of misery, remember that for you that sort of reverie is as mischievous as real evil might be to others. It will be most difficult at first, I know, to keep this constant watch over yourself; but it is not at all impossible, and your happiness unquestionably depends upon it. I should be much comforted if I thought that you were likely to lead a very active, useful life. Constant employment—devotion, in fact, to any object out of yourself—would be a great help to you. And especially, my dear child, I must warn you not to try and hide from yourself that there is something which you dread. It would be a very vain attempt. Only, when the fear comes, as it must and will no doubt, overwhelmingly, at times, until you have learnt thoroughly to command yourself, carry it where alone it can be soothed. Do not reason or talk, or even endeavour to distract your thoughts;—but pray. If you have not words at command, yet the very attitude of kneeling will give you comfort. A child in its grief hides its face in its mother's lap, and so may we hide our faces from the worst of this world's sorrows under the shadow of God's love."

The quiet tone of this letter had a great influence upon Blanche. She was a little disappointed in it at first, and thought it cold; but, on reading it a second and third time, she saw that it only appeared so because Mrs. Howard was not really uneasy. Her naturally buoyant spirit revived as the impression deepened, and although miserable thoughts would often rush upon her mind, and a continued check was required for her wandering thoughts, yet she did by degrees succeed in keeping down, though not entirely crushing, all sad forebodings.

In effecting this her life at Senilhurst was certainly as great an assistance as even Lady Charlton could have desired; for it was a very new, interesting, amusing life; with frequent arrivals and departures and never-ending schemes of pleasure, and merry dancing and musical evenings; the pervading gaiety being varied by clever discussions upon books, sparkling wit, and occasional arguments upon grave and important topics. There was nothing in all this openly to shock Blanche's principles, for Lady Charlton was fastidious in her choice of visitors, and liked to have it considered a privilege to be admitted at Senilhurst. She contrived also very cleverly to mix up her parties, so as to bring together persons who were likely to suit; and with Lord Rutherford and Blanche as the guests, for whom she was most interested, she had taken particular care to exclude all persons who had not something of intellect, or refinement, or accomplishment, or, what she valued more than all, goodness, to recommend them.

Yes, Lady Charlton liked goodness extremely—so only that it had a name. She could bear with a considerable amount of oddity, or shyness, or even rough sincerity, if it was coupled with a little respectable authorship, or well-known zeal, or, what perhaps was as useful as either, a certain amount of persecution. Blanche met with several very excellent and thoroughly simple-minded, unworldly persons at Senilhurst; persons whom she could admire heartily, and long to imitate: and they were a great safeguard to her, though in a way which her aunt never intended when she brought them together.

Lady Charlton was a managing, scheming person; really very unconsciously: management with her was an instinct. She had managed her own marriage to escape from an unhappy home, and the marriages of her sisters and of almost all her intimate friends. She intended to manage her daughters' also; and, as a matter of simple duty and kindness, that of her niece.

True, Blanche was extremely young to think of such a thing; quite a child in many of her tastes; very ignorant of the ways of the world, and not yet regularly introduced into society; but there was no harm in being on the watch. If it would not do as yet to fix upon any person to encourage, it might be well to take care that she should not be put in the way of any whom it might be right to discourage; and, following out her own notions of what might not be wholly undesirable, Lady Charlton collected at Senilhurst as many persons as she could, of sufficient rank and fortune, and respectability of character, to make the society pleasant without being dangerous.

Of one danger, indeed, she never thought—the danger of the flattering homage which grace and beauty, when joined to high birth and great wealth, can scarcely fail to receive.

That was no danger in Lady Charlton's eyes; rather it was the tempting prize, for which every effort must be risked. Blanche was exposed to it without a thought of caution; with no shield except the simplicity of her own heart and the devotion of her time and thoughts to other objects.

But with these she was safe. The pursuits which chiefly interested her were such as brought her in contact with persons whose superior intellect and high tone of mind raised her standard of what men might be; whilst their age and position in life prevented all idea of romance or admiration. Blanche felt keenly the difference between such men and the ordinary worldly, though refined and accomplished, persons who visited at Senilhurst. She saw they could understand and sympathize with her, although as she deemed far above her in mind and excellence. And such intercourse saved her from the delusion, which sometimes fatally misleads young persons, of believing, that because the generality of persons are careless in their conduct and lax in their principles, therefore no real purity and goodness exist, except in cases of special retirement and abstraction from ordinary pursuits.

Blanche was beginning to learn, from her own experience, that men can mingle in the common intercourse of society and retain their simplicity and devotedness. She saw before her true, single-minded, earnest goodness, and no discovery of its counterfeit could henceforth shake her faith in it.

It might be that such a conviction rendered her fastidious and indifferent. Some persons said she was so, and blamed her. They could not comprehend the quiet, unexcited way in which she received the attentions paid her by men whose admiration was generally considered of great value. One or two ladies, more harsh judging than the rest, declared that she was proud; others, suspicious of evil, became conscious of it, and yielding to it, stated their conviction that Blanche was, in her heart, as vain and "flirty" as any other young lady of her age; but the greater number—men as well as women—yielded to the spell of her pure and gentle dignity, and treated her with the cautious respect shewn to the innocence of a child, which we shrink from sullying even by a thoughtless word.

CHAPTER III.

"BLANCHE," said the earl, as they passed through the park gates, and caught sight of the riding-party ascending a hill at some little distance, "I am afraid you have disappointed yourself to keep your promise with me. You wanted to go to Warham, I know: I wish you would have told me."

Blanche laughed. "And made you uncomfortable and myself too, dear papa. I did want to go to Warham, certainly; but one day is as good as another, as far as seeing the country is concerned; and I had two reasons for not desiring to be with them to-day. One, that I liked the thought of a ride with you; and the other, that I did not much fancy the party."

"What, not Mrs. Cuthbert Grey! and, as your aunt calls him, that first-rate Lord Erlsmere?"

"I like Mrs. Cuthbert Grey very well; not very much," said Blanche, hesitating. "I wish one could go through the world without judging people; but I have never liked her very much since—such a very little thing, I really am ashamed to mention it."

"Well! since what? I can keep a secret," replied the earl, smiling.

"Since I heard her talk so strictly against operas to Archdeacon Fanshawe, and found out afterwards that she always engages a box for the winter. It gave me a notion of her not being true. I don't think I could ever like a person very much who was not true. But I was not thinking of Mrs.

Cuthbert Grey when I said I did not fancy the party."

"Of Lord Erlsmere, then, perhaps?" said the earl.

"No, nor of Lord Erlsmere. I don't care about him, except that he is rather tiresome to talk to, and always asks me if I don't look forward to my first London season. But, papa, I do very much—I hope it is not wrong—I really dislike very much, indeed, to go without you or my aunt, when Adelaide and such a person as that Mr. Lorton are together. I cannot tell why it is, but they make me feel so stiff and so cold; I am quite worried with myself. And it vexes me the more, because Adelaide is particularly kind to me, and makes a point of arranging that I shall be with her when she is going anywhere. Can you understand?"

"Your taste is offended," replied the earl; "that flirting manner of Adelaide's is unlady-like. I cannot imagine how your aunt can endure it. I should lock her up if she was my child."

"I wish she would," exclaimed Blanche, and then, laughing at her own eagerness, she added, "I wish she would do anything, I mean, to keep Adelaide quiet. And I wish," she continued more gravely, "that my aunt could win Adelaide's confidence, and persuade her to talk to her as she does to me."

"Is there confidence between you, then?" exclaimed the earl, in a tone of surprise, and slight displeasure. "I never supposed your cousinly intimacy could go quite so far as that."

"I don't know whether you would call it confidence," replied Blanche; "I suppose not, for it is not at all reciprocal; but Adelaide seems to like to say odd things to me, and now and then she does say very odd ones; startling, quite, if I could believe them. But she rattles on so fast, one never knows whether she is in earnest."

"She is a silly, vain girl, who never says a word worth listening to," exclaimed the earl, impatiently. "I hope, Blanche, you don't trouble yourself about her."

"I cannot help myself," replied Blanche.

"Oh! yes, my love, indeed you can. If you were not so unnecessarily good-natured, you would by this time have found out how to rid yourself of silly people."

Blanche put her horse into a canter, and they rode on. The thread of the conversation was for the moment broken, but the earl resumed it. "I hope you will remember that, my dear child, when you go more into the world; remember, I mean, to keep clear of boring, absurd people. It is the only thing I am really afraid of for you. Such a person as Adelaide may hang about you like a dead weight, if you don't make an effort to shake her off."

"Poor Adelaide!" exclaimed Blanche, "there are very few persons to care for her; I wish there were more, heartily. But, papa, do you know there does not seem such a great difference to me between her and a good many other persons I have seen here, and whom my aunt calls superior. She only does openly what they do quietly."

"So you have discovered that, my love, have you?" said the earl, smiling; "but you will learn by-and-by, that it is a great virtue in the world to conceal one's object dexterously."

"I should be sorry to have any object to conceal," said Blanche.

"Heaven forbid you ever should have, my darling; but it would be impossible: for you could never be on a par with the managing, manœuvring people one meets with everywhere; it is not in your nature. You will go on dreaming, Blanche, I suspect, and leave it to your aunt and me to fall in love for you."

Blanche laughed. "I suppose it is a sort of thing one might be very glad to do by proxy," she said, "as most people say they are so wretched all the time. But, papa," she added, slightly blushing, "I don't see that it is quite necessary to fall in love, as a great many of the young ladies I meet here seem to fancy."

"Not necessary," said the earl, unable to repress a smile; "only most natural and probable, as you will understand in due time."

"Then I would rather leave it to due time before I think about it," said Blanche. "I should not like to believe that I could not be quite happy without it; without being married, I mean," she added quickly: for the recollection of the one fatal instance of a marriage without affection rose as a phantom of evil before her.

"Yes, leave it, leave it!" exclaimed Lord Rutherford, quickly. "It will come too soon for my happiness, whenever it does come: but I would not be selfish."

"It will be sent," said Blanche gravely, "I like to think that, because then one feels so satisfied either way."

"What do you mean by sent?" asked the earl, shortly.

"Ordered; arranged for one, by Providence," answered Blanche. "I remember, when I was quite a child, asking Mrs. Howard, why every one was not married, and whether she thought that I should ever be; and she said to me, 'God knows, and He will tell us by-and-by;' and so I thought it a duty to wait till I was told, and I think so now; and, besides," she added, her voice sinking into an under tone, "so many other things may happen; one may die."

They had just then reached an open common, upon which stood a few scattered cottages and a school built by Sir Hugh. It was a very inviting place for a quick canter over the soft turf, and Blanche was gathering up the reins as a preparation, when two women came slowly out of the school-house, carrying between them a little boy, about five or six years of age; he was lying apparently senseless in their arms, his head drooping and his face deadly pale. Blanche thought she recognised him as the son of the lodge-keeper at Senilhurst, a sickly child who had often attracted her notice and pity for his ill health, and in whom she was particularly interested as being the nephew of the blind girl at Rutherford. The women stopped to rest, leaning against the gate of the school-ground, and water was brought to recover the child; and as Blanche and her father rode close up to them, he revived a little; Lord Rutherford asked a few questions, and heard that "he was faint—that it was a common thing with him, for he was very weakly—he would be better soon, no doubt, and then he would go home, they did not know how, it was some distance; but he would manage it, of course, for he always did."

The earl looked at the boy, and said "Poor little fellow," and would have gone on, but Blanche begged that they might delay, just for a few minutes, till the boy was really better.

She should like to dismount, she said, if she might; and as the school could not well be left, she would stay and watch him herself, and then they might arrange to have him taken home, for it must be bad for him to walk.

Almost as soon as the words were spoken, and before her father could assist her, she had alighted. Lord Rutherford acquiesced in the idea; though, if the suggestion had been made by any one but Blanche, he might have laughed at it as ultra-benevolence—perhaps he thought it so then in his heart—yet there was something that touched his better feelings, in this ready sympathy with suffering; this weakness, it might be, which could not "pass on the other side," and leave a sick child to the chance of ordinary care. And it was like Blanche—it was consistent; and however far removed he might be from sharing his daughter's principles, Lord Rutherford could still value them for this one reason. That which never failed as a guide, which directed the least as well as the most important actions of life, and gave stability to a disposition so gentle and otherwise yielding, was becoming, even in the eye of the man of the world, an ingredient of value in the formation of character.

The schoolmistress and her companion went away, and soon afterwards the boy was able to answer Blanche's questions himself; but his countenance belied his words, when he said that he was really well; and as he tried to move he staggered, and put his hand to his head and complained of pain. It was evident that the attack was not a common one.

"They ought to send him home at once," said the earl, with some impatience of manner: "it is folly to talk of his being able to walk. There must be a cart, or something, which will take him; but these people are wonderfully indifferent about such matters. I shall tell them they must do something with him directly."

He went into the school-house, and returned almost immediately, followed by the mistress, who was speaking eagerly. "Yes, certainly, his lordship might depend upon her doing her best. Carts were not so easy to be had; but she would try. No doubt something would be managed. It was a great pity his lordship and Lady Blanche should have been delayed; but Lady Blanche was so very kind always. Johnnie Foster would be quite sorry when he came to himself, to think of how much trouble he had been giving."

Johnnie Foster seemed perfectly conscious of this fact already, for he tried to raise his head, which was laid against Blanche's shoulder, and a smile came over his little pale face, as he thanked her for being kind.

The earl regarded him with more interest than before. The expression of the countenance was singularly sweet and intelligent, as he fixed his blue eyes upon Blanche, with a mixture of shyness, wonder, and pleasure, at the notice she was bestowing upon him. "We will look after him at Senilhurst," he said, addressing Blanche; "but we must not wait now, or you will lose your ride completely."

Blanche had a request upon her lips; for she thought the ride a very secondary object to the child's comfort. Yet she hesitated in making it, since it was against her desire of consulting her father's wishes.

"You would rather stay," he said, reading her inclinations quickly.

"No, not stay; for I do not think I can be of much use, as he is better; but if there is any difficulty about sending him home, I should like to let his mother know, and she might come, perhaps, in Sir Hugh's spring-cart to fetch him. And then we might, if you did not care, go on the other way to Cobham, and let the doctor know he is to come and see him. I should like to be sure that he was taken care of," she added, "and to feel one had done all one could."

The schoolmistress began to remonstrate against this very unnecessary trouble, as she called it, repeating again and again that Johnnie would do very well, and they should "manage somehow;" but Blanche was urgent, when she saw that her father did not object to the idea, and, after seeing the child carried into the house again and laid upon a little sofa in the mistress's parlour, she again mounted her horse to return.

Cobham was the post town of Senilhurst, a small place, a few miles from the railway station. The road was dull, and the town dirty and uninteresting; in general, Lord Rutherford made it a point of duty to avoid it; but this afternoon, although it was growing late and chilly before he and Blanche reached it, his usual complaints were silenced. Yet he was not amused by conversation; little had been said, by either, for nearly half an hour, the time which had elapsed from their leaving the lodge-gate at Senilhurst. Blanche had seen the mother of the sick child there, and advised that he should be sent for immediately, and had undertaken to give notice to the doctor at Cobham, and then she seemed satisfied, and would have talked as usual to her father upon other topics, but she found a difficulty in fixing his attention, and presently gave up the endeavour. The medical man was not at home. Lord Rutherford wished to give a verbal message, but Blanche asked to write it.

"It was more certain," she said, "and she was afraid the child was worse than his mother fancied;" so a card was left, with "Lady Blanche Evelyn's compliments," and once more Blanche turned her horse's head towards Senilhurst.

"And your mind is at rest now, Blanche, is it?" said her father, as they rode off. "Do you mean to go through the world taking as much pains about everything? You will have hard work if you do."

"I should not care for that," replied Blanche; "if I could do it as it ought to be done. I should like to think that this sort of thing was work."

"It is troublesome and disagreeable enough, at all events," replied the earl. "Not that it has been disagreeable to me, my child; don't think that; but

I see in you so often, Blanche, an over-tasking of your mind, an exhausting energy which will wear you out if you don't take care; and it makes me anxious about you."

Blanche checked her horse, in her surprise, as she exclaimed: "Anxious lest I should overwork myself! my dear papa! why I have nothing to do all day but to consider my own pleasure."

"And your pleasure is to labour for others. I see it, my love, when you don't imagine it. From morning till night you give yourself no rest. There is always a thought of duty before you."

Blanche waited for a few seconds, and then said; "I wish I could believe it was so; but even supposing it, one must live for some purpose, with some aim, to be happy; and I should certainly like to know that I was doing my utmost, if that were ever so little. I can't imagine resting in anything short of the utmost."

"It is a strange notion for such a child," said the earl, regarding her with a look in which an intense affection was mingled with wonder and respect; "but it will scarcely make you happy, Blanche, as you suppose; because your notions of the utmost are unattainable."

"But I would try; I would strive," exclaimed Blanche, her face flushing with eagerness; "and my rest would be in striving. There is so much to be done and to be accountable for; and life may be short," she added quietly.

"Yes, it may be," replied the earl, "but it may also be long; and there can be no reason to shorten it by over exertion."

"I would not do that," said Blanche; "and if I could see any danger of over exertion, I would check myself as a matter of duty. But when I look at other people and see how they are circumstanced, how they are obliged to work, I feel that it would be absurd in me to think over exertion possible. I am forced to live such a comfortable life, that the only satisfaction I can find in it is, when anything in the shape of a duty comes in my way, doing it thoroughly."

Lord Rutherford repeated the word "thoroughly," in a tone of much thoughtfulness; it seemed to have aroused a new train of ideas.

"I think sometimes," continued Blanche, "that people must be better and happier who are born to work, or at least to be useful in some definite way. It seems as if a great responsibility, and a great difficulty must be taken from them."

"But why work, my dear child?—why fret yourself about such subjects?—why not take the world as it is given you, and amuse yourself as your age points out?"

"Because—" Blanche began her sentence twice, and paused with the effort to repress some rising feeling—"because one should be so sorry if the time came that one were not able; that is, one might die, or—or—it might not—the power might not be allowed one; and if it were so, and then at the last, perhaps just before one's death, one had to look back upon this time wasted, it would be so dreadful." Her voice grew quite composed as the sentence concluded; but the earl read the secret dread which prompted the thought, and his face was in an instant convulsed with an expression almost of agony. Putting spurs to his horse, he galloped on, without venturing upon another word till they reached Senilhurst.

CHAPTER IV.

"BLANCHE, where are you going? here are letters for you," said Lady Charlton, the following morning, as Blanche came into the library, dressed for walking.

Blanche received her letters, and was going to take them away, when her aunt again made the inquiry as to where she was going. "It is too damp, my love, for you to be out. The weather is quite changed—really wintry. I must have you careful of yourself."

Blanche was only going to the lodge to inquire for the little boy, and had no intention, she said, of remaining out long.

"Oh! but, my dear, we can send quite easily. Pray don't give yourself the trouble of inquiring, and don't tire yourself, especially to-day. We shall have such a charming importation of visitors at dinner; people you will be sure to like, so don't wear yourself out beforehand."

"Any one I know?" asked Blanche.

"Oh! yes—know by name quite well;" and Lady Charlton ran over a short list, consisting of a poet and a poet's wife; an historian, his sister, and a brother-in-law, all delightful people; and to crown the whole, Mr. Johnstone, of Oakfield; "it is the greatest favour in the world for him to come," she said, her eyes lighted up with excitement. "He is so immensely busy, and so entirely devoted to his parish, and the bishop makes so much of him, and gives him such a quantity of work to do, I quite despaired of him, though I longed for you to see him, Blanche. But I tempted him with the petition that he would give an opinion about the restoration of the chancel which you heard Sir Hugh talk of. Those good men are so very hard to get at, it is quite a triumph when one can seize upon them for a day."

"And will Mrs. Johnstone come too?" inquired Blanche. "Eleanor Wentworth knows her, I think; I remember hearing her say one day that she was a particularly nice person."

"I believe she is very nice,—extremely quiet and domestic; good she must be to be his wife; but I don't know much of her; she seldom leaves home."

"Then Mr. Johnstone will come alone," said Blanche.

"Mrs. Johnstone is to come, if it is not too wet, and to bring a friend; but I must confess she is a very secondary consideration. He is charming, however. I shall persuade him to stay to-morrow, if I possibly can; but I am afraid he will be obstinate. But that must be left; all I wanted to say to you, my love, was to give you a warning not to over-fatigue yourself, as I should give Ady warning before a ball. So much for difference of taste! By the by, have you seen Ady this morning?"

"No," replied Blanche; "she was not down-stairs when I left the breakfast-room."

"Shockingly bad habits!" exclaimed Lady Charlton, shaking her head. "I wish you could give her a little of your energy and steadiness, Blanche; or, more properly, a great deal." Then assuming an air of confidence, she added,—"I need not say to you, that Ady gives me a great deal of anxiety."

Blanche assented by a look of sympathy, for she did not know what to answer.

"She is very giddy," continued Lady Charlton,

"and wilful too. I was in hopes that taking her from Rutherford might have done some good, but I am half afraid. Pray, have you heard from Miss Wentworth lately?"

Blanche held a letter from Eleanor in her hand, and Lady Charlton began to excuse herself for having kept her so long from reading it; looking, at the same time, as if she very much wished that it should be opened in her presence.

"London!" exclaimed Blanche, in surprise, as she broke the seal, and examined the date; "that must be quite a sudden plan."

Lady Charlton's countenance showed some uneasiness. Blanche was too much occupied with her letter to notice it; yet she read out passages occasionally, from the consciousness that Lady Charlton was standing by, listening and expecting. Eleanor, it seemed, was in London, staying with a cousin who was about to sail for India, and had insisted upon her paying a short farewell visit.

"She does not write in good spirits," said Blanche, commenting upon the letter as she went on; "Rutherford is so dull, she says, without me. I was afraid she would miss me; she wants so much to know what I am doing." Here followed an extract from the letter, and rather an unfortunate one, for it brought Blanche into the middle of a confidential sentence, before she exactly knew where she was, and when it was equally impossible either to go forwards or backwards, without explanation: she stopped and coloured; and then, laughing at her own awkwardness, exclaimed, "I don't know why I should be so shy with you, Aunt Charlton? I am sure you will understand. Eleanor and I were talking one day at Rutherford, about being separated all the winter; and we said it would be so nice if she could come here for a little time: but we both agreed it could not be, because we knew you were uncomfortable about Mr. Wentworth and Adelaide. Now, Eleanor says she cannot help thinking about it, and longing for it, because London is so near, and the Johnstones have asked her to go to them, which would bring her into the neighbourhood. Her brother is not with her, so that there would be no real objection, if I could manage it. But you must not think about it, please," continued Blanche, affectionately. "I would not worry you on any account, and I know the house is full, and it may be very inconvenient; and as to her visit to Mrs. Johnstone, she does not say she is going, only that she has been asked. I merely mentioned it that you might see there was no mystery. I need not let Eleanor know that the idea was ever suggested to you."

It was a great effort to Lady Charlton to conceal that the visit of any person of the name of Wentworth would be disagreeable to her; but she was really extremely fond of Blanche, and anxious to make her happy, and if Mr. Wentworth was out of the way, there could be no actual objection to Eleanor herself. Still she hesitated; it was opening the door, and no one could foresee the consequences.

"If I were quite sure about Mr. Wentworth," she began.

Blanche interposed with an urgent entreaty that she would not allow the subject to trouble her for an instant. She could quite understand; so would Eleanor. And, after all, even if the invitation was given, Mrs. Wentworth might not like Eleanor to accept it; and Lady Charlton acquiesced, but not as if she was satisfied with the decision; it seemed unkind, and all Blanche's assurances to the contrary failed to restore her to equanimity.

Poor Blanche heartily repented her imprudence in

reading the letter aloud too hastily. It was a lesson for the future, but the experience was bought dearly. Lady Charlton was, to use the common expression, "put out;" and there is nothing which effects this more surely with people who seek popularity, and pique themselves upon good-nature, than being obliged to appear ill-natured. She endeavoured to change the subject, and spoke again of the guests who were expected in the evening; but she showed plainly what was burdening her mind, by saying, as she left the room, "You know, my dear, I could not bear to be ungracious; but it would be a mere compliment to ask Miss Wentworth here merely for two or three days, and next week we shall really not have a bed to spare."

Blanche had nothing more to say, and nothing to do, but to try and forget her disappointment as best she might. She left the house, intending to go to the Lodge, but the sky was clouding over, and before she had gone any distance, large drops of rain fell, and she was obliged to return.

Misfortunes, every one agrees, never come alone, and this disturbance of her plans was a great increase to Blanche's annoyance. She was lingering under the portico, trying to persuade herself that black clouds and faint glimmerings of light, swiftly appearing and vanishing, meant fine weather, when Adelaide Charlton came to the hall door, and seeing that Blanche had been walking, asked what the weather was likely to be. Blanche was a little startled by the question, for she had not thought that any one was near, and turned rather quickly to answer it. At the same moment Adelaide dropped a letter, which she was reading. Blanche stooped to pick it up, but Adelaide stepped forward in a great hurry to prevent her.

"Thank you; don't trouble yourself," she said,

hurriedly,—crumpling the letter in her hand, and evidently much discomposed; "have you had letters this morning?—any from Mrs. Howard—from Rutherford?—but I forgot, there is no one to write to you there; that is I suppose,—I imagine—is Miss Wentworth at home?"

"No," replied Blanche, a little surprised at Adelaide's confused manner; "she has been on a visit to a cousin, in—"

Blanche did not say where, for a little dog, a pet of Mrs. Cuthbert Grey's, just then came running up to her, and jumping upon her dress, diverted, for the moment, the current of her ideas.

"And Miss Wentworth is going to remain—how long did you say, in London?" inquired Adelaide, still lingering, with the pretence of watching the weather.

"I don't know, exactly," replied Blanche, not observing, in her simplicity, the knowledge which Adelaide showed of Eleanor's movements.

"She will not have time to come here, I suppose," said Adelaide, carelessly.

Blanche did perceive something unusual in this remark—in the tone rather than the words. She looked at Adelaide more attentively. There was anxiety in her face; an anxiety which she was trying to hide by a forced coolness. She bent down to caress the dog, and again the letter fell from her hand. Blanche did not offer a second time to pick it up; but, as it lay for an instant on the ground, she thought the handwriting was Eleanor's.

"It won't do for excursions to-day," said Adelaide, advancing to the top of the steps; "we must make up our minds to amuse ourselves as well as we can within doors. It is a happy thing we have not very stupid people to entertain: the Cuthbert Greys are invaluable on a wet day."

"And there are so many coming to dine and sleep," observed Blanche: "with such a set of geniuses, we ought to be very agreeable."

"Geniuses!" exclaimed Adelaide; "of all things in a country party, I hate geniuses; people who force one to count the letters in every word one utters, lest one should shock them by one's ignorance: and who, after all, are generally the dullest persons one ever meets."

"Then you must have goodness instead," said Blanche, laughing. "Mr. Johnstone is more famous, I believe, for his goodness even than for his talents."

Adelaide made no reply, but ran down the steps, regardless of the rain, and declared that it was certainly going to be fine.

"You will be very wet; do come in, pray Adelaide do," remonstrated Blanche. But Adelaide's fancy, at that time, was to be considered strong. On other occasions she sometimes chose to be thought delicate. She stayed just long enough to prove that she would have her own way, and then ran back into the house, leaving Blanche provoked by her absurdity, and rather mystified by her manner.

CHAPTER V.

A WET day in a country house is undoubtedly a trial; often of the spirits, and always of the mental resources of the party assembled. Senilhurst was as pleasant a house, under such circumstances, as could well be imagined, for there were books for those who chose to employ their minds; music and drawings for any who enjoyed and appreciated them; and billiards for idle gentlemen who had no other way of killing time. Mrs. Cuthbert Grey sat near a window, ostensibly for the benefit of the light upon her embroidery frame,—really, that she might be able to see all that was going on. The Miss Greys wrote letters and worked, and tried to make Lord Erlsmere talk, and to persuade Maude to sing. Adelaide was unusually quiet; it was supposed because she was interested in a new novel; and not even the entrance of an occasional refugee from the library—tired of prosing with Sir Hugh, and hoping to find relief in the society of ladies—induced her to exert herself to be entertaining. Lady Charlton came into the room frequently; gossiped a little with Mrs. Cuthbert Grey, and admired the Miss Greys' work, and wished earnestly that she could find time to be as industrious; and then turned to Lord Erlsmere, with some question about the post-office, or the railroads, which brought out his accurate information upon all matters of public interest. "But there was no resting-place for her there," as she said herself with a tragicomic shake of the head, which implied that she was overpowered with business.

"The poor little new schoolmistress had come to make a complaint to Sir Hugh about her chimney; and Mrs. Foster, at the Lodge, wanted advice about her boy; and many other little matters, too numerous to be mentioned, were all requiring her presence elsewhere. She wished earnestly that she could have a day's quiet—but home and quietness were not synonymous terms"—and, with a resigned sigh, Lady Charlton flitted from the room, leaving her guests in a very agreeable state of feeling—compounded of pleasure at the delicate flattery administered to themselves—and admiration of the energetic, self-denying, and useful life of their hostess.

"Lady Blanche does not give us much of her society in the morning," said Miss Caroline Grey to Maude, after they had been silent for some minutes, and were, as she thought, in danger of becoming victims to dulness in consequence.

"She spends a great deal of her time with her father, I imagine," observed Mrs. Cuthbert Grey, in a soft voice. "One cannot be surprised at it. Such a sweet young creature as she is!—he must take great delight in forming her character."

"Her character is formed, I should think," said Lord Erlsmere, who, if not a first-rate person in point of interest, was certainly so in his love of truth and simplicity.

Mrs. Cuthbert Grey sank from rapture into pity.

"Yes, Lady Blanche's character, she supposed, might be said to be formed; formed in a peculiar way for so young,—so very young a person; but that would scarcely prevent Lord Rutherford from being anxious about her. Poor man! he had great cause for anxiety;" and Mrs. Cuthbert Grey sighed, and again repeated, "Poor man;" and concluded with observing, "that it must be a comfort to him, under the circumstances, to see his daughter so cheerful, and with such even spirits." An observation which made Lord Erlsmere look up with a perception of some secret meaning.

Mrs. Cuthbert Grey worked very diligently after this, only pausing every now and then to inquire how her eldest daughter was progressing in her studies; for Miss Grey had, within the last few minutes, laid down her pen, and commenced the perusal of a political pamphlet which Lord Erlsmere had been heard to recommend strongly. This brought on a discussion, deferential on the part of Miss Grey, and animated on that of Lord Erlsmere; in the midst of which something very like a groan was heard to escape from Maude—and throwing down her book, with an ejaculation at its stupidity, she left the room apparently in a fit of impatience.

There was a gleam of hope in the prospect of the weather; a little blue sky in the west, and symptoms of dispersion amongst the clouds overhead. Maude stood in the portico, as Adelaide had done before—her own countenance very like a thunder-cloud—and her voice, as she hummed the first few notes of a German song, not very unlike its distant rumbling. Yet it was not the thunder-cloud of anger only—sadness and weariness were mingled with it; and when, a few minutes afterwards, she went to put on a bonnet and shawl, intending to take a solitary walk in the colonnade, it was with a listlessness which proved that the walk, in itself, was no object to her. Many times she paced up and down—slowly and decidedly—stopping every now and then as the sound of wheels caught her ear; but even in this, there was the same indifference and languor. A carriage at last entered the park, and was driving up to the house; Maude turned a corner to avoid being seen, and then looked—she did not know why; visitors were not of any importance to her, and this was a hired carriage—a fly;—probably some people come to stay;—the Johnstones possibly—they were expected before luncheon. Yes, so it was;—Mr. Johnstone, with a pleasant, clever, rather eager face; and Mrs. Johnstone, with a face which none would remark. And there was a friend too—a tall, elegant-looking girl, her features were not seen at first, she lingered behind Mrs. Johnstone; but Maude caught a full view of them, as some remark was made which induced her to look towards the colonnade, and saw—she could not be mistaken—undoubtedly it must be—Eleanor Wentworth. Maude's impulse was a strange one;—it was less surprise than irritation;—it made her rush down the steps from the colonnade, and hurry away into the thick shrubbery, and from thence into the park; and away—she scarcely cared where—so that she might be certain of solitude.

The clouds were now gathering together again, and a driving mist was settling into rain; but Maude was at no time as mindful of weather as her health required, and though she was tired with her walk, went on, until a pelting shower convinced her how unwise she had been, and induced her to think seriously of shelter. The lodge was near, and she hurried towards it, and opened the door unceremoniously. The next moment she repented of her haste, for she was an intruder. She saw it directly, as Blanche rose from a seat by the side of the sick boy's bed, and closing a book from which she had been reading to him, said, "I will come and finish it to-morrow if I can; and you will try and think about it, Johnnie, and be patient, wont you?"

Her hand was laid upon the little fellow's burning cheek, and she bent over him and whispered, "God bless you!" and as Maude came forward to speak to the child herself, she perceived Lord Rutherford also. He was standing behind a projecting wall, and gazing so earnestly upon Blanche, that he had not noticed Maude. He came into the light as she spoke, and laughed at their meeting, and said a few words in his usual tone, but there was deeper thought beneath the outward indifference, and the glance of his eye was softened as it rested upon Blanche into the expression of a woman's tenderness.

"We can go now, I think, dear papa," said Blanche, drawing near to him.

He was generally cold, even to her, in the presence of others; but now he put his arm around her and kissed her. They stood together by the side of the child's bed. Maude watched them with an indefinable feeling of repose.

"We will come again to-morrow," said Blanche, appealing to her father.

"Yes, to-morrow, if we can. He will be better then we hope; and we must remember what he wants. I will speak about it myself."

"Thank you—thank you," said Blanche;—"so very much:" and the child tried to sit up, and thanked him also; and Lord Rutherford turned hastily away, for he would not for worlds it should be seen that a tear glistened in his eye.

"This is not weather for you to be out in, Maude," said Blanche, as, the shower being over, they left the cottage together, the earl lingering behind. "I was half afraid of it myself, and I am much stronger than you are."

"It is better at least than the weather within," replied Maude, shortly. "You seldom sit in the drawing-room in the morning; so you don't know what it is. But I wonder you ventured so far from home when you were expecting Eleanor Wentworth."

She said this bitterly; and, when Blanche turned round in extreme surprise, she saw that Maude's lip was curling with pride and anger.

"I don't want to blame you, Blanche," began Maude again; but Blanche interrupted her with questions as to her meaning. Could she be sure that it was Eleanor? did she know whether Lady Charlton was annoyed? and similar inquiries which were a very evident proof that Eleanor's visit was entirely unexpected. Maude's irritated face was gradually soothed as the conviction strengthened, yet her only reply was, "One can't doubt you, Blanche; but don't hurry on in that way. Must you see Miss Wentworth immediately?"

"Yes; no; there is no absolute necessity. Why must I not go?" inquired Blanche.

"Simply because I must speak to you first," answered Maude. "Can I not have a few moments of your precious time?" she added, as Blanche seemed inclined to wait for Lord Rutherford.

"Yes, of course, presently; but I must not leave him to walk home alone;" and Blanche turned back and put her arm within her father's. They walked on silently. Blanche was too much perplexed and annoyed at Eleanor's unforeseen arrival even to mention her name.

"I may come to you before dinner, papa; may I not?" she said, as they reached the house, and Lord Rutherford stood, apparently expecting her to enter.

Maude touched her arm impatiently, "If you stay here, Blanche, you will be seen. I must have you; this way"—and she would have drawn her into the colonnade.

Blanche resisted. "I may come and seal your letters, papa, at five o'clock; may I not?" she inquired again. Lord Rutherford smiled. Maude, eager as she was, could not help noticing the fondness of his manner.

"Good-b'ye," said Blanche, lightly. "I am going with Maude now."

She followed her cousin through the colonnade, and Lord Rutherford stood at the door, and watched them till they had turned the angle of the building; and, even when they were out of sight, he still lingered, as if unwilling even for those few minutes to lose sight of her.

"And now, Blanche, answer me," exclaimed Maude, when they were alone, "only once, tell me plainly, did you not expect Eleanor to-day?"

"I have told you in all but the exact words—why do you ask me again?"

"Because—the world is a strange world—more strange every day—more irritating, aggravating, enraging." Maude walked on so rapidly, that Blanche found it difficult to keep up with her.

"Adelaide, and the Cuthbert Greys, and that bore Lord Erlsmere, and Eleanor Wentworth—they are all alike; not one better than the other," continued Maude. "If they were twenty times your friends, Blanche, I must say it."

"But, my dear Maude, pray—if you would only be clear—only tell me what you are thinking of. You really make me impatient!"

"Then I make you what I am myself," answered Maude. "I need not do that either," she added in a lower and graver tone; "but you are too good for them, Blanche; and I cannot bear to see you deluded. Why do you put faith in Eleanor Wentworth?"

"Eleanor! she is my friend; we were brought up together: whom can I put faith in besides?" inquired Blanche, in rather a frightened tone.

"In me," exclaimed Maude, sarcastically. "I should not treat you as Eleanor Wentworth does."

Then, seeing that Blanche was silent from astonishment, she added, "You did not know that she was expected to-day; but Adelaide did." Blanche remembered the handwriting she had seen, and could not doubt the assertion. "I am not jealous," continued Maude. "I don't want to win your affection, or any of that romantic nonsense; so you need not think I have any double meaning."

"Double! oh, no! impossible!" interrupted Blanche.

"Not so impossible as you may think. People don't tell tales of one another, generally, without some meaning. Mine is to put you on your guard, and make you see that Eleanor Wentworth is too much a friend of Adelaide's to be a friend of yours too."

"But indeed, Maude, you wrong me very much," exclaimed Blanche. "I know that Eleanor is what some people would call a friend of Adelaide's; that is, they are glad to see each other, and laugh and talk together; but that sort of thing is totally different from her feeling for me. I cannot imagine how it should stand in her way."

"Has it not stood in the way?" inquired Maude, coolly. "Why did not Miss Wentworth tell you she was coming here to-day?"

"Because—for a thousand reasons. I will go and ask her;" and she would have hurried away, if Maude had not detained her.

"Blanche, how long will you be a child, trusting and deceived? I tell you I know Eleanor Wentworth better than you do. She is Adelaide's friend; and like her—vain, frivolous,—worldly; that is the word you will understand."

"No; that she never was, and never will be," exclaimed Blanche with energy. "I will not listen to you, Maude; it is unfair to Eleanor. She was my first friend, and I will not hear her spoken ill of without giving her the opportunity of defending herself. I will ask her for an explanation."

"Ask, ask, if you will," answered Maude; "and make her tell you why she keeps up a constant correspondence with Adelaide; and why Adelaide's letters are never to be seen. Ask her whether she is not encouraging her in that utter folly which went on at Rutherford; the very thought of it would make me ill, if I did not know that Adelaide can carry on as many flirtations as there are days in the year, so that there is no real danger; but Miss Wentworth should never have demeaned herself to bear any part in it; she should ——"

Blanche broke in upon the sentence. "Maude," she said earnestly, "you are making me very unhappy; any facts would be better than these vague hints."

Maude's tone of angry sarcasm changed into one of quiet seriousness, when she saw that Blanche was really distressed. "I have spoken in this way," she said, "because I have no actual facts to bring forward; only convictions of my own, from observation. You know as well as I do how Adelaide behaved at Rutherford, and how annoyed mamma was. I did not tell you, Blanche, half how disgusting the whole affair was to me. I don't know whether I am more fastidious than the rest of the world, but when I see that sort of thing going on it makes me hate myself for being one of the same race. Mamma thought it would be all over when Adelaide came here, which was more than I did; at least, I was sure that if she did not flirt with Mr. Wentworth, she would with some one else; and so she has done, as you may have seen. Adelaide is one of those persons who can't look or speak without flirting; but I did not know, till a few days ago, that she has not given up the old folly. I suspected it from seeing letters come frequently in Miss Wentworth's handwriting, and I taxed Adelaide with it, and she tried to turn off the subject, but she could not deceive me. And now suddenly, without any invitation from my mother, they have contrived that Miss Wentworth shall come here. What for, I can't pretend to say; but I should have supposed that pride alone might have prevented her from intruding herself where she must be aware she is not welcome." Maude paused; but Blanche, without venturing to reply, walked slowly and thoughtfully towards the entrance of the house. "You will not believe me, now?" said Maude, following her.

Blanche turned round quickly, "What would you say, if I believed accusations against you, before I had given you the opportunity of explanation?"

"You would believe them instantly," exclaimed Maude; "but your affection deceives you in this case."

"And have I no affection for you, Maude?"

There was a quivering movement about Maude's harsh decided mouth. She threw herself upon a bench, and when Blanche stooped to kiss her, her cheek was wet with tears.

"Dear Maude," said Blanche kindly, and she sat down by her. A proud struggle was visible on Maude's face.

"Not pity!" she exclaimed. "Save me from pity. After all, what does it signify to me, if the world is made up of hypocrites. I don't mean you, Blanche," she added, laughing in spite of herself, at poor Blanche's expression of wonder and horror; "You don't belong to the world; but it is so wearing to live day after day with people one despises; to see no beauty, no goodness anywhere, except—I see it in you; but it is weak goodness—superstition."

"Yet I am happy," said Blanche quickly, "and you are not."

A crimson flush dyed Maude's sallow cheek, and then it faded away to a deadly paleness, and she answered, "If I am not happy, it is because I was not born to be deceived."

"Suspicion is deceit," said Blanche; "because it makes us believe evil to exist where it does not."

"But it does exist; one sees it everywhere," exclaimed Maude; "only it puts on a mask. Look at that woman, Mrs. Cuthbert Grey, my mother's idol. Such a good churchwoman! a perfect example! reads sermons by the hundreds, and buys good little books by cartloads. I have heard her talk, until, if I had not known her, I could have supposed she was St. Cuthbert, instead of Mrs. Cuthbert; but I sat in the drawing-room this morning, and watched her toadying Lord Erlsmere, in hopes of making him fall in love with her eldest girl, until I could bear it no longer. If I had had a scourge I verily believe I should have used it."

"One might be tempted to do so, sometimes," said Blanche, smiling, "if one might begin upon oneself."

"Oneself!" and Maude's face became very sad; "but I must leave that, and I did not intend to talk of Mrs. Cuthbert Grey, only the woman drives me wild. You may as well go, Blanche; you won't be undeceived, so you must follow your own course."

Blanche did not like to go, Maude's face was so worn and harassed that it grieved her to look at it. "I should like to make you happier, Maude," she said, still lingering.

"Then close my eyes and stop my thoughts," replied Maude, bitterly. "Thought!" and she put her hand to her forehead, as if it ached terribly. "Oh! if one could only cease from it but for one day."

"Yet it is the great object of education, so people say, to make one think," observed Blanche.

"Is it? I don't know; I never was educated. No, never," she repeated, answering her cousin's look of surprise. "I was left to bad governesses, and never went out of the school-room. I learnt just what I chose—what I could teach myself;—history and geography sometimes—thought always. I began thinking when I was a child—when people supposed I was playing with my doll: I thought about the doll,—why it did not speak—why it had no mind—how it differed from me, and I have gone on thinking ever since: yes, on, and on, and on, until—Blanche, have you ever thought till you felt that the next step would be insanity?—That is what I have done," she continued, without waiting for an answer; "and I have found others who have done the same—clever men, men I thought I could reverence. I met with them abroad; but they were all alike—all disappointing in practice and differing in theory. There was no rest; what one believed the others disbelieved."

"Can there ever be rest in the systems and theories of our own forming?" said Blanche, gently.

Maude shook her head. "Ah! Blanche, there is our difference. I cannot walk blindfold. I cannot bow my intellect to forms and superstitions."

"I hope I could not either," replied Blanche; "but I am afraid we can scarcely understand each other; we have been brought up so differently. I was told what was true, as a child; I was not left to find it out for myself. I was taught to obey, too, before I knew the reason why. Now that I am beginning to think for myself, I see that what I learnt agrees with the Bible; and if I try to follow it, it makes me happy; I have no room, therefore, for doubts."

This was said so simply and confidently, that Maude looked up in astonishment. "We do differ, indeed," she said, proudly. "Like you, I am a Christian; but I must put my own interpretation upon the Bible. To yield my opinion to the judgment of others, I must be a child again."

"Must you?" and Blanche waited for a few moments in thought, and then added,—"A grown-up person might pray to be taught rightly, and might go to Church regularly, and read the Bible, and try to be good as far as he knew, in spite of the difficulties, and then, perhaps, they would go away."

"And that is what you would have me do," said Maude, quickly.

"Yes, it would be better, I think—safer than argument—because—"

"Go on—go on," said Maude, impetuously.

"Safer," continued Blanche, more firmly, "because we cannot doubt for ever."

"No, there will be certainty before long for us all," said Maude, gravely.

"And if it should be the certainty of all being true which we doubted and thought difficult to understand," pursued Blanche, "it would be very horrible." Maude's brow contracted as with pain.

"Very horrible! would it not?" repeated Blanche. "If, I mean, we had gone on following our own will, because we had not all the certainty we wished for."

Her voice was very tremulous as she said this; and Maude saw that she turned pale. "You are ill," she observed. "I have kept you standing too long."

"No, not ill; only cold," replied Blanche; and she wrapped her shawl round her.

"And I have kept you from Miss Wentworth," said Maude, a little sarcastically. "That was wrong in me, too."

Blanche tried to smile, but it was not a subject for amusement.

"You really don't look at all well," continued Maude. "You ought not to have gone out this damp day, and I have kept you standing and walking till you are tired to death. Do go in and rest before you see Miss Wentworth."

Blanche repeated that it was only the cold; a fire would make her quite well; but Maude was not satisfied, and, forgetting her own grievances, hurried her into the house, and insisted, with the most persevering and even affectionate attention, on seeing that she was resting comfortably in her own room, before Eleanor Wentworth went to her.

CHAPTER VI.

No one who had seen the Senilhurst party that evening would have discovered any signs of unusual annoyance or uncongeniality, unless upon close inspection, and after intimate knowledge of the characters of the persons collected together.

Blanche, indeed, sat in an easy chair, looking pale and talking little; and Lord Rutherford hovered about her to ward off all that might disturb her. But Blanche smiled and seemed contented, and her father had evidently no wish except to be near her, and was quite satisfied when he found her pleased in listening to Maude's exquisite singing, and in the intervals when there was no music taking a part in a conversation he was carrying on with Lady Charlton and Mr. Johnstone, respecting a living in his gift which was likely soon to be vacant.

So far all was well; and what if Adelaide's manner was absent and Maude's cross, if Eleanor Wentworth was shy and Lady Charlton distant; these differences were not visible to the common eye. There was the same polish of refinement and courtesy over all, and the drawing-room at Senilhurst might well have been supposed to contain as large an amount of comfort and freedom from restraint and care as could be found amongst any similar portion of English society.

Blanche could not suspect evil; it was not in her nature. She was, besides, far from well, and did not feel equal to thought. She had not seen Eleanor for nearly half an hour after her conversation with Maude; but, when they did meet, the explanation of her sudden arrival was simple enough to put to flight all the suspicions which Maude would have raised. The visit to Mr. Johnstone had been, Eleanor said, quite unexpected. She had arrived only two days before; Mr. Johnstone had insisted upon bringing her to Senilhurst, as Lady Charlton had given him a "carte blanche" to introduce any of his friends; and her name had not been mentioned merely to cause an amusing surprise to Blanche. Certainly, she allowed that the secret had been entrusted to Adelaide, but this was because—she did not know why, exactly; she had been executing commissions for Adelaide in London, and was writing to her about them, and that put it into her head to name it. She quite supposed that Adelaide would have mentioned her being in London; but it was just like her to forget.

Nothing could be more satisfactory, and Eleanor was so pleased, and bright, and affectionate, so enchanted to see Blanche again, so full of all the parish news of Rutherford, that it would have been impossible to quarrel with her. Blanche thought, as she watched her that evening, how superior she was to every one else in the room; graceful, intellectual, brilliant, amiable; even Lady Charlton was obliged to acquiesce in the praises that were lavished upon her, although the next moment she relapsed into coldness, as unpleasant recollections forced themselves upon her.

"Frances, my dear," said Sir Hugh, who sat opposite to Blanche, in a gouty chair, trying to believe, and to make other persons believe, that he was quite well; "Frances, my dear—my dear Lady Charlton—Frances;" Lady Charlton was bending her head low, to catch a passing observation of Mr. Johnstone's; music was going on at the time: did she not, or would she not hear?—"Frances—pshaw!—Maude, tell your mother I want to speak to her."

Lady Charlton did hear then; she smiled sweetly

upon Mr. Johnstone, and promised to return in an instant.

"You wanted to say something to me, Sir Hugh. Shall I ring for Pearson?"

"Pearson—folly! what are you talking of?"

"Every one will excuse you," continued Lady Charlton, quite amiably; "I was saying to Mr. Johnstone, just now, that you were much later to-night than usual."

Sir Hugh very nearly knocked away the pillows in his gouty chair; "I tell you, Frances, I am not going. All I wanted to say was,"—his voice sank confidentially,—"that now Miss Wentworth is here, we may as well persuade her to stay. It is not worth while for her to go back with Mr. Johnstone."

"Very well—yes, we will see; to-morrow will do. Lady Charlton was hurrying away as fast as possible.

"But listen, Frances, listen," and Sir Hugh laid a detaining hand on her dress; "I shall ask her presently; I think it is right. Dr. Wentworth is an old family friend; Mrs. Wentworth too; very good people, highly respectable."

Sir Hugh was gradually working himself into a fit of excitement, and Lady Charlton was in an agony lest the brilliant variations upon the piano should suddenly cease. "Very well—yes, we will see," she repeated again.

"I like her," continued Sir Hugh; "she is very handsome, dresses well." Lady Charlton's fidget increased every moment; in another minute, Thalberg's variations would infallibly come to an end; "We will settle it at once and then I shall go to bed."

"But, my dear Sir Hugh, hush—pray be quiet; trust it to me."

"It is the right thing to do," pursued Sir Hugh; "it will please Blanche—please Lord Rutherford; it is the sort of thing one is bound to do."

"Yes, yes, of course; we will talk about it—only just—of course you will have your own way. I will go and say a few words to Mr. Johnstone first."

Sir Hugh allowed her to depart; but she heard him mutter to himself—"It's right, quite right; for ten days or a fortnight we shall manage very well. Her brother can come and fetch her."

Just then Eleanor left the piano, where she had been standing to turn over the leaves of Miss Caroline Grey's music-book.

Lady Charlton kept Mr. Johnstone's few words for a better opportunity; and seizing upon Eleanor, carried her off to the ante-room.

She must apologise, she said, for being a little unceremonious; but she really was anxious to obtain Miss Wentworth's co-operation in a plan for detaining Mr. and Mrs. Johnstone a day or two longer at Senilhurst. She was afraid it might be inconvenient. Blanche had told her that Miss Wentworth's stay in that part of the country was to be very short; and she could not, under the circumstances, say anything, however glad she should have been to have had the pleasure of a long visit at Senilhurst. No doubt Mrs. Wentworth must be very anxious for her daughter's return, and they must look forward to a future occasion—a more fortunate one—when engagements on both sides would not be so pressing. But there were a few days free now, before the house would be full. Could not Miss Wentworth persuade Mr. and Mrs. Johnstone to remain with her at Senilhurst, if it were only till Saturday—from Wednesday till Saturday? Surely a clergyman might spare two days; and she would let them return quite early on Saturday morning, if it were necessary. Miss Wentworth would join in the request, there could be no doubt of its being granted; and Blanche, and every one, would be pleased. "Poor Blanche! she is not at all well, I am afraid," concluded Lady Charlton. "It was very imprudent in her to go out to-day. I think, for her sake, you must consent."

Eleanor Wentworth was, in general, peculiarly self-possessed; but there was a mixture of pride and awkwardness in the cold politeness of her manner, as she thanked Lady Charlton for the invitation to herself, but feared it would be difficult to persuade Mr. Johnstone to agree to the proposal, since she knew that his time was just then particularly occupied. Lady Charlton instantly grew eager to carry her point. It would be vexatious, provoking, in every way disagreeable, to be refused. She must have it settled at once: she could not rest till it was. Might she only say that Miss Wentworth did not object? And in answer to the acquiescence which followed the question, Lady Charlton was so grateful and cordial, that Eleanor found herself compelled to reciprocate civilities, and be extremely obliged for an attention which was the very least she had a right to expect.

A short conversation of entreaty with Mr. Johnstone followed, and Lady Charlton presently returned to Sir Hugh, pleased and placid. She had gained the point he wished, Miss Wentworth was going to stay; how long she did not say, and Sir Hugh happily did not ask; but soothed by the apparent obedience to his will, consented to retire for the night.

Blanche had observed part of the progress of this arrangement, and understood it. She had little to do on that evening except to observe, and there was considerable food for thought in all she saw, even though much lay concealed from her usual unsuspiciousness. Maude's face was one which particularly engaged her attention. It was more than commonly sarcastic. She spoke but little to Blanche; and, when she was not called upon to sing, devoted herself principally to Lord Erlsmere, whom she engaged in a disquisition upon universal suffrage, which kept him engrossed for more than half the evening, much to the annoyance of Mrs. Cuthbert Grey. Blanche could scarcely help smiling at the cleverness with which Maude managed to defeat all the mother's manœuvres in her daughter's favour. Yet it left a very disagreeable impression upon her mind, unfavourable to all parties except Lord Erlsmere. Blanche, did not feel obliged to Maude for having withdrawn the veil, and given her an insight into what was going on behind the scenes. It was low, unlady-like, to say nothing more, and as she looked on, and found herself attributing motives, and suspecting double meanings, she felt ashamed of herself as if she also was, in a measure, a party to the conduct which she disapproved.

"I think you had better go to bed, my love," said the earl, coming behind her chair, when the time-piece struck ten o'clock. "You can slip away without being noticed."

Blanche prepared to go, for she was very tired.

Maude, who was standing near the door, stopped her when she was leaving the room. "Are you going, Blanche?—good night."

"Good night," said Blanche, cheerfully; "will you tell Eleanor to come to me presently?"

"If you wish it—if I must."

"Why, is there any objection?" asked Blanche; "I shall not keep her long."

"Forewarned, forearmed," said Maude, coldly.

Blanche looked seriously annoyed, and answered, "You cannot make me suspicious, Maude. After all you said this afternoon there was nothing that could not be explained."

"Time will prove," said Maude, in the same provoking tone.

Blanche turned away angrily; but she could not

bear to part in such a spirit, and the next instant she smiled, and offered her hand to her cousin.

The hand was retained, and Maude, looking at her anxiously and kindly, said, "You must be better to-morrow."

"Yes, I hope so; I am nearly sure I shall be."

"And you will promise to sleep well?"

"Yes, if I can; the extent of this world's promises."

"Well, then, good night, once more," and Maude walked away to the piano, and Blanche left the drawing-room.

CHAPTER VII.

BLANCHE was not at all sorry that the evening was over. When she sat down alone in her room, she looked and felt wearied in mind and body, and was quite startled at the haggard expression of her own face, as she caught sight of her features in a glass. Illness might be one reason for her being depressed; there was nothing else particularly to cause it, but she felt very solitary, all the more so, perhaps, because there were so many about her. Yet she ought not to be solitary when Eleanor was in the house; a year before she would have said that she needed no other companionship. And why should she now? What change had come over her? Her mind travelled back to the days that were past: long past they seemed, but that was a delusion; it was but a short time; yet the grey, weather-stained walls of the old manor house, the green walks, the trim holly hedge, the antique dial and all the associations connected with them, were as the clear, yet faded visions of a distant land; and the voice of the friend who had loved her from infancy, though sweet to her recollection, was very faint, as the dying notes of music which we shall never hear again. It is hard to realize the death of our own life; we never do so whilst our childish associations are unbroken. The thought of it came to Blanche's mind with awe and sadness, as she tried to recall the forms of those by-gone days from which the spirit had departed to bear an undying record before God. Happy they had been, very happy and blest—more blest than the present—more innocent and guileless; and they could never in any way return;

years could never restore ignorance, they could never make to her unknown what once was known; they could never bring back confidence where it had been disappointed. Years—they stretched far, far out, interminably it seemed; and they must be met, endured, with all their possible trials, with the risk, the possibility of — Blanche shuddered, her heart grew faint; it was a real, physical faintness, for the next instant a sharp pain shot through her frame, and she leant back in her chair, and gasped for breath.

Eleanor Wentworth knocked at the door. Blanche said, "Come in," as loudly as she could. The pain had been only momentary, and she did not like to think of it.

"Not undressed, Blanche," said Eleanor, as she came up to her; "that is very naughty."

"I sat by the fire, thinking," replied Blanche, "and expecting you. Why did you not come before?"

"I did not miss you at first when you went; and your cousin Maude only told me to come to you a few minutes ago," replied Eleanor.

"Maude is very strange," said Blanche, thoughtfully. "But tell me, Eleanor; I understood a great deal that went on down-stairs, though I only heard half. How long are you to stay?"

"Two days," answered Eleanor, shortly.

"Two days only?"

"Lady Charlton has not given me the opportunity of staying longer."

"It is vexatious," said Blanche, "very."

"Yes, and to find you not well, besides; and to have seen so little of you all the evening. However, one must bear it, and be thankful, I suppose."

Blanche was chilled, for Eleanor's tone was petulant. "We shall be able to talk to-morrow," she said, soothingly; "and, Eleanor, you must not be hard upon my aunt; she has reasons, you know, for not being quite as cordial as one could wish."

Eleanor's cheek flushed with deep crimson, and she exclaimed, "Of course, I know. She does not consider the son of a country clergyman a fit connection for her family. Yet I could tell her that the Wentworths are an older race than any other in the county."

"It is not the question of family; indeed, you must not think that," said Blanche, earnestly. "If your brother —." She stopped, for the observation might have been an awkward one.

"I understand what you would say," replied Eleanor, with an air of great candour. "If my brother was a dashing man of fashion, with his four or five thousand a year; or even if he had the promise of a good living, with a deanery or bishopric in perspective, Lady Charlton would not let the question of family interfere; but being as he is, about to take orders, and live a quiet, serious life, as a curate in a country village, she does not deem it a suitable prospect. I do not blame her; I do not know that any one could; only, Adelaide may go farther and fare worse."

Blanche was more perplexed than before what to say. The tone Eleanor was adopting was quite new to her. She seemed to think the affair serious.

"You do Charles injustice yourself," continued Eleanor. "When you saw him flirting—for he did flirt, I grant, at Rutherford—you put him down as a silly, vain young man: he is very far from that: or, at least, if he is vain, he has great counterbalancing qualities. All that frippery and folly will go when he is ordained."

Blanche was silent.

"What are you thinking of?" asked Eleanor. Her voice was nervously eager, and she repeated again,—"What are you thinking of? I must know."

"Should it not go before he is ordained?" asked Blanche, quietly.

Eleanor drew back for an instant; then she answered, hurriedly,—" Yes, yes, certainly; before—at the time when he is ordained. He will be quite a different person by-and-by, you will see."

" But will by-and-by do?" pursued Blanche. "Can it ever be right to take such a responsibility without being very devoted—very good, beforehand—a long time beforehand?" she added, becoming bolder.

Eleanor's face showed much more vexation than the occasion seemed to warrant; but she only replied,—" Well! well! we won't talk of it now, Blanche. You are prejudiced, I am afraid; so is Lady Charlton. We won't spoil our few hours together by discussion."

Blanche looked sorry, and observed, it was very foolish of her to say such things; it must seem unkind, when Eleanor was so fond of her brother; but it was hard to keep back her opinions, where she had been accustomed to tell them so openly.

Eleanor was standing near the fire. She bent down and kissed Blanche, and fixed her eyes upon her intently, but without speaking.

"I may tell you all, I think; may I not?" said Blanche, answering the look.

There was another pause. Eleanor's eyes glistened; she seemed lost in thought.

" May I not?" repeated Blanche.

" Yes, all; undoubtedly. You are very tired: shall I ring for your maid?"

" In a minute; only I am so afraid I have pained you."

Eleanor answered by another kiss—warm, affectionate as in the years of their happy intercourse at St. Ebbe's.

The bell was rung, Eleanor departed, and Blanche was left to think over what had been said, and to ponder upon the cause of that sharp, warning, momentary agony;—what did it mean?

CHAPTER VIII.

ELEANOR'S step, as she moved along the gallery from Blanche's room, was stealthy and quick; but she paused at the top of the staircase to listen to what was going on below. All the guests not staying in the house had taken their leave; and now there were parting good-nights and cheerful last words said as the rest of the party broke up. She heard Mr. Johnstone and Lady Charlton speaking of the plans for the next day. That was a satisfaction, as it showed that he had not changed his mind about remaining at Senilhurst. Eleanor had a half inclination to go down again and inquire of Mrs. Johnstone, to be quite sure of the fact; but the sight of Maude coming up the stairs had a sudden effect upon her intentions, and with the same quick and quiet step as before, she went on, reached the further end of the gallery, and, opening a door which led to the apartments in the east wing, found her way amidst passages and turnings, to a small sitting-room, out of which two doors opened. A hasty double knock at one of these was answered by Adelaide Charlton, who exclaimed, "Come at last, Eleanor!"

"Hush! hush!" and Eleanor put her finger to her lips. "Maude will be here in one instant; let me in."

Adelaide threw open the door, which Eleanor took care to bolt again, and then Adelaide, motioning to Eleanor to sit down by the fire, said, "Well! what success? what does Blanche think?"

"My dear Adelaide! how wild you are. Blanche, of course, thinks nothing, and knows nothing."

"What, have you not asked her?"

"No, not this evening. I only sounded her a little."

"Sound!" repeated Adelaide, in a tone of vexation. "But, what is there to hinder you from speaking out at once? Why can't you say, Your father will have a living in his gift soon, and I wish he would promise it to my brother?"

"Oh! Adelaide! can't you understand?—to ask a favour!—to put oneself under an obligation!—there is nothing more difficult."

"But not between friends—persons like you and Blanche, who were brought up together."

Adelaide threw herself back in an easy chair, and angrily pushing aside a footstool, continued, "I see how it is; we are resting upon a broken reed. I told Charles it would be so long ago."

"You may say what you will, Adelaide," replied Eleanor, with some dignity of manner. "If you will not trust me, you must take your own way; but one thing I am quite sure of, that mine is the only right and wise one."

"I don't see why he is to be tied down to that odious profession," observed Adelaide, petulantly.

"Merely because his whole education has been a preparation for it," said Eleanor; "and that it would break my mother's heart if he were to give it up."

"But he does not like it; he is not fit for it," said Adelaide.

"Yes, begging your pardon, he does like it, and he is fit for it, when you do not influence him against it."

"A thousand pities he ever knew me then," said Adelaide, sharply.

Eleanor did not contradict her. She only answered,

"It is too late to think of that now, when you are engaged."

"Who brought on the engagement?" asked Adelaide, satirically.

"Do you repent it?" said Eleanor.

"Repent! oh dear, no! not in the least! What a strange notion! do you?"

Eleanor was silent.

"Do you?" again repeated Adelaide; and Eleanor was compelled to answer.

"I should not, if you would be what you have promised."

"What I have promised to be when I am married," repeated Adelaide. "It will be time enough to think of that by-and-by."

"It would be better to begin at once."

"We wont sermonise," exclaimed Adelaide, impatiently. "You know I have an insurmountable objection to sermons. If any harm comes of our engagement, Eleanor, you will have no one to thank for it but yourself. When Charles and I were at Rutherford, we had no more idea of anything serious, than we have now of travelling to the moon. It was entirely through correspondence, and messages, and that sort of thing, that the affair came to a point. I declare I should have forgotten him by this time, if you had not so constantly reminded me of him."

"I was obliged to repeat what he said," replied Eleanor; conscience reproaching her for untruth as she uttered the words.

"Well! obliged or not obliged, you managed to make me think of him, and this is the consequence; and, having led us into the scrape, all you can possibly do now is to help us out of it. The idea of going to mamma with the news that I am engaged to a man, without any prospect but a country curacy, is an absurdity; I wont do it."

"But if you must?"

"There is no must; I don't acknowledge any."

"And the alternative will be—what?"

Adelaide laughed heartily. "I am not going to let you into all our secrets, Eleanor; you know too much already. Trust us, if you will not manage matters for us, we shall manage them somehow for ourselves; and soon, too. I have no notion of hanging on, from week to week, in this way. It destroys all the pleasure of one's present life, without giving one a prospect of anything better."

"Charles is obliged to you," said Eleanor, gravely. "I should have thought that, being certain of his affection, you might have been well-contented to wait till he can come forward openly."

"His affection! yes, of course, I am certain of that, and satisfied. But it is a little,—however, I won't frighten your propriety; only, perhaps you can understand that now and then it is just a wee bit uncomfortable to go about the world with one's hands and feet tied; and not to be able to mention it. One moves awkwardly."

"There may be something in that," said Eleanor, thoughtfully. "But, what is still more important, I am sure it is not quite right. Your mother and my mother ought to know it. I, for one, should be miserable at the concealment, if there were not such good reasons for it at present, and if—"

"Well—what? What salve have you found for that very fidgety conscience of yours?"

"Very sufficient salve," replied Eleanor. "You and Charles settled your affairs yourselves. I was no party to the actual engagement."

"That is," exclaimed Adelaide, her eyes sparkling with irritation, "you showed us the road, and led us to the point, and gave us a little push, and then hurried away, that you might be able to say you did not see. Oh! Eleanor."

Eleanor blushed; yet she could not rest without a further effort at self-vindication.

"You are exaggerating," she said. "I did not know what was going to happen. I scarcely ever suspected it. When Charles told me you were engaged, I was utterly amazed.

"Then, what did you think we were about?" inquired Adelaide. "What pretty game were we playing?"

Eleanor was too much ashamed to reply. How could she own that she had calculated upon Mr. Wentworth's unsteadiness of disposition, and Adelaide's habit of flirting, and suffered herself to encourage them in folly, whilst deluding herself by thinking it would come to nothing? And all this partly from a weak wish to please her brother; partly from finding a silly pleasure in watching an affair of the kind for the first time, and feeling herself a person of importance; and partly from the secret desire to keep up an acquaintance which promised a good deal of amusement, and possibly an introduction, by-and-by, to gayer society than she could meet with at Rutherford.

It was very unlike the conduct to be expected from Mrs. Howard's pupil; but, perhaps, the person whom it would least have surprised, was Mrs. Howard herself. Eleanor was not so very different now from what she had been in former days. Circumstances had brought out the weak points of her character, and rendered their consequences more important; but the original faults were the same;—vanity, and love of excitement—known and acknowledged, but never thoroughly struggled against.

"I don't like this new mood of yours," said Adelaide, after a pause, finding that Eleanor sat abstractedly gazing on the fire. "I had looked forward to your coming as the end of all my difficulties. I thought you would go at once to Blanche,—entreat her compassion; and then, when we had engaged Lord Rutherford's interest, that the thing would have been known and settled."

Eleanor could not help smiling in spite of herself. "Adelaide! when will you learn common sense? How can you imagine it possible to settle a business like this in a minute? Even supposing I could bring Blanche over to your side, and supposing Lord Rutherford were to promise Charles twenty thousand a-year, instead of a living worth twelve hundred,—how can you suppose that Lady Charlton would be brought round in such a moment?"

"Oh! there are two strings to that bow," replied Adelaide. "If mamma will not consent, papa will; that I am quite sure of. Pearson told my maid, the other day, that he was wonderfully fond of Charles, and meant to have him asked here. I don't want that, though, just yet."

"No, indeed;" and Eleanor inwardly trembled at the storms which might arise from so imprudent a step.

"I don't see why you should say, No, indeed! in that tone," exclaimed Adelaide. "I don't want it to be just yet; but I don't know why you should be so afraid. We are not quite such babies as not to understand keeping our own counsel."

"There are eyes about you," said Eleanor.

"Mamma! yes, she is a regular Argus."

"And your sister."

"That is to be considered, certainly; I am awfully afraid of Maude."

"So am I," replied Eleanor.

"She is a person to be afraid of; tough, leathery," said Adelaide. "She never did a foolish thing from the time she was born. And she can look through one when she chooses it. I declare, if it was not for her German metaphysics, I could not live in the house with her. Happily, they make her so puzzle-headed that she only sees one-half of what is going on."

There was a loud angry knock at the door. Adelaide started, and exclaimed, "That is her knock."

Eleanor turned pale. "Are you sure she does not see more than one-half already?" she asked, in a whisper.

Adelaide made no answer. Eleanor took up her candle to go. "Adelaide and I have been gossiping," she said, as an explanation to Maude, when the door was opened. "It is very foolish, I own."

Maude took no notice. "You have some books of mine, which I want, Adelaide," she said.

Eleanor felt herself growing nervous; and, to hide her confusion, would have pretended to search for the volumes wanted; but Maude prevented her. There was no occasion for Miss Wentworth to trouble herself, she said. Adelaide knew quite well where the books were; and, as she spoke, she placed herself near the doorway, in such a position that Eleanor was compelled to confront her. Her glance was proud and searching; and Eleanor shrank from it.

"Good night! Adelaide," she said, in as light a tone as she could assume. She would have given her hand to Maude, but it was not taken.

"Good night, Miss Wentworth," was repeated, haughtily; and Eleanor went to her room, humbled and unhappy.

CHAPTER IX.

It was about a week from that time,—the weather was cold and bleak, even for the autumn, and as the rough blasts howled round the old parsonage at Rutherford, and the rain pelted against the latticed windows, Dr. Wentworth drew his chair near to the fire, and congratulated himself that his work for the day was over—that there was no case of illness in the parish requiring his attention, and that it was not a night for the evening school, or for any other duty which would expose himself or his parishioners to such inclement weather.

"I wish Charles was equally safe from it," said Mrs. Wentworth, who sat at work opposite to her husband. She was cutting out baby clothes, and from the full attention which she bestowed upon the occupation, it might have been supposed that she esteemed it the most important duty of her life.

Dr. Wentworth looked up in answer to the remark, and said, in an apologetic tone, that he had not forgotten Charles, but that young men thought nothing of weather when there was a dinner party in question.

"And I should hope not when many other things are in question," replied Mrs. Wentworth; "but that does not prevent one, I am afraid, from thinking of it for them. However, Charles must accustom himself to brave a great many worse trials than weather; so it may be as well for him to begin at once."

She relapsed again into silence, and Dr. Wentworth read to himself. Nearly half-an-hour went by in this way; Mrs. Wentworth worked unremittingly. There was something almost painful in the energy with which she cut, and folded, and squared; placing piece after piece in a basket that stood on the table by her side. To look at her face, with its expression of intellect and resolution, one might have said that it was a waste of power to throw so much vigour into a mere mechanical employment.

"A quarter to ten," observed Dr. Wentworth, looking at his watch;—"time for the servants to be called in, my dear."

"Yes, if you please; will you ring the bell?" and with the same quiet determination of manner, Mrs. Wentworth moved away her work to another part of the room—placed a Bible on the table—arranged the chairs for the servants, and prepared to join in the nightly family service. It was very simple and short; a few verses from the New Testament, with a few words of comment, and prayer. Yet there was something very touching and impressive in the earnest exhortation which besought all who were present to cast their care upon One who cared for them—whether it were care for others or themselves—for the needs of the body, or the claims of the imperishable soul. Mrs. Wentworth sat with her hands placed one upon the other, and her eyes bent upon the floor; not a muscle of her features moved, and her voice, as she joined in the supplications which followed, was clear and firm, until the petition for the absent and the loved. Then, for a moment it sank; but no one noticed the change, for none saw the secrets of the mother's heart, save He who had formed it.

"Do you mean to sit up for Charles, my dear?" said Dr. Wentworth, when the service was concluded.

"I had thought of doing so; he promised to be home early."

"But you will do him no good, and will only tire yourself; you had much better not."

"I have some work to finish," replied Mrs. Wentworth, preparing to resume her former employment.

Dr. Wentworth saw it was useless to remonstrate. He said, half playfully and half in a tone of vexation, "Well! you must have your own way;—wilful women always do. Only don't ask me to sit up with you."

Mrs. Wentworth smiled, and disowned all intention of inflicting such a penance upon him, and Dr. Wentworth went away.

The room looked dreary then. It is strange how much there is in association;—how different a solitary hour is before a household has been broken up for the night and afterwards. Though the fire may blaze just as cheerfully, and the lamp give the same bright light, a sense of loneliness, almost of awe, insensibly creeps over one. Mrs. Wentworth might have experienced something of the kind, for she soon gave up her work and tried to read, and after a time, putting aside the book, walked about the room, and listened for the trampling of a horse,—though she knew her son was not likely to return for the next hour.

That hour and another passed, and he did not come. Mrs. Wentworth was not at all anxious; she was not a nervous person, and she did not think that any accident had happened; but she did think that Charles had been induced to stay longer than he had purposed. It was a slight fault, if it could be called one; but she was not in a mood to be lenient to slight faults. She grew more and more restless—more and more visibly annoyed; and when, at length, the bell rang, and her son appeared, she greeted him with,

"You are an hour and a half beyond the time you mentioned, Charles. Has anything happened?"

"Nothing—nothing at all,"—was the answer. "Am I so late?—I did not know it." He took out his watch—"Not much more than an hour—I really could not help it."

Mrs. Wentworth did not directly reply, but as she lighted her candle to go to bed, she said:—"It is a great pity, Charles, that you cannot learn to be exact. If you had told me you should not be home till twelve, I should have known what to expect."

Mr. Wentworth looked provoked. "My dear mother, I really beg your pardon, but—you must excuse me,—I did not ask you to sit up." He had no sooner said the words than he was vexed with himself for it. He saw that she was offended.

"Good night, Charles. I will take care not to give myself unnecessary trouble again."

"My dear mother!" and he went up to her and kissed her. "I cannot bear this. It was very silly; very wrong only—"

"Only!"—and Mrs. Wentworth gave way for an instant to her hitherto repressed feelings—"Only, Charles, you were tempted, and you yielded."

"It is not such a very great offence," replied Charles, relapsing again into his former tone of indifference. "It was impossible to get away sooner; as it was, I was one of the first to go; and really it was no case of temptation. The party was immensely stupid; not a single person there whom I cared to meet, except young Johnstone."

"Was he there?" exclaimed Mrs. Wentworth eagerly. "Did he say anything about Eleanor?"

"Yes; he told me what I knew—that she had been staying with his father and mother; and that she was with ——; she was at Senilhurst now."

There was a hesitation in Mr. Wentworth's manner, which however did not occasion any remark.

"I was in hopes Eleanor might have left Senilhurst by this time," said Mrs. Wentworth. "It is vexatious her being there at all; but I suppose she could not help it; and now the staying for this party is not what I like."

"Eleanor is to go back again to the Johnstones," said Mr. Wentworth; "and it struck me—I must go to London before long—I might just as well bring her home."

"London! my dear Charles! you must go to London before your ordination! What are you thinking of?"

Whatever Mr. Wentworth's thoughts were, that was not a moment for confiding them to his mother; yet it might have been a relief to him, and he evidently felt so, for his countenance assumed for an instant an expression of openness and confidence; but Mrs. Wentworth's tone, as she repeated to herself, "London! what a strange notion!" threw him back upon himself, and he replied shortly, "I have business there."

His mother did not press the inquiry beyond the observation, that it was a very sudden and incomprehensible idea, and took no notice of the suggestion respecting Eleanor, till it was made a second time. "She could not tell; she could not decide;" was all she would say upon the subject. "Eleanor would probably return almost immediately."

"But I am thinking of going immediately," persisted Charles; "our plans will just suit."

"We must first know what Eleanor's are," continued his mother. "She says that she has been induced to remain at Senilhurst to keep Lady Blanche's birthday. She hopes I shall not be angry. Poor child! she need not be afraid of that; vexed I might be, but not angry. In this case there seems to have been a train of events almost forcing her to do as she has done. Her visit to Senilhurst at the very first was unforeseen."

"I should be thankful, my dear mother, if you would make the same excuses for your son that you do for your daughter," said Charles, in a tone of pique.

Mrs. Wentworth softened instantly in manner, though she sighed as she replied, "If I could see the same reasons for excuse, my dear Charles, you would not be more thankful for it than I should be."

"And are there not the same reasons?" exclaimed Mr. Wentworth impetuously. "Is Eleanor to go where she likes, even to the very place which you profess to dread for her, and must I not even remain for an hour at a dinner party beyond the time fixed?"

The case was too glaring not to strike Mrs. Wentworth's sense of justice, and she said instantly, in a tone of apology, "I was vexed then without cause—at least without sufficient cause. I am sorry for it; but if you knew, oh, Charles!" and tears started to her eyes; "those little things—they indicate so much to my mind. If you cannot keep to engagements and rules in your daily life, how will you ever submit to them in serious matters? How can you be fitted for the self-denial required of a clergyman?"

"Perhaps I am not fitted for it," began Mr. Wentworth, but his mother's distressed look stopped him, and in a milder tone he added, "When I am talking to you, I always fear that I am not."

"Fear would be your safety," said Mrs. Wentworth.

"Then I am safe beyond the possibility of danger," exclaimed Charles eagerly. The same expression of openness passed over his features as once before, but again his mother spoke, and the momentary courage vanished. This time, however, she was not chilling.

"You are safe, I hope and trust," she replied very earnestly, "because you know your faults, and have striven against them; but for that your father and I could never consent to your ordination. And if I am hard upon you, Charles, it is only from my love; my longing to see you what a clergyman ought to be, what your father is."

"Yes; I know it, my dear mother. I am quite aware of it. I wish you would not apologize."

"I always own when I am wrong," said Mrs. Wentworth. He drew near to wish her a good night, and she looked at him with a mother's proud fondness. "A few weeks more and you will be a clergyman. Then the greatest wish of my heart will be granted."

"Always supposing the fitness," said Charles, almost moodily. He sighed very heavily; his mother thought for an instant that something was weighing upon his mind, that he had a secret which he wished to tell; yet he only recurred to the often-repeated question, "How would she feel if he were to give up the idea?" Mrs. Wentworth's heart was too full to answer, but her silence was sufficient. She was a person of few interests, few wishes; but those she had were intense. It would break her heart if he were to disappoint her.

CHAPTER X.

THERE are some fortunate individuals—fortunate in the eyes of the world—whose success in all they undertake is proverbial. Lady Charlton was one of these. Whether it was from tact and cleverness, or real unselfishness and kindness, she almost universally carried her point. Such persons insensibly become despotic. Their irritation when thwarted is naturally in accordance with their certainty of victory. But, happily for Eleanor Wentworth's comfort, there were two considerations which neutralized in a degree, in Lady Charlton's mind, the feelings excited by Sir Hugh's announcement that he had insisted upon Miss Wentworth's remaining to keep Lady Blanche's birthday. One was the increase of gaiety in the society at Senilhurst which her presence caused; and the other was the hope of inducing Mr. Johnstone in consequence to come to Senilhurst again, and be the lion of a grave dinner party which was shortly in contemplation. It was a peculiar faculty in Lady Charlton, that of seizing upon the advantageous points of every incident, however apparently untoward. The loss of half her fortune, or the illness of her dearest friend, might have affected her to despair for the moment; but she would infallibly have extracted satisfaction from them the next minute. Either she would be an object of universal sympathy; or her friend, if she died, would leave her a valuable legacy; or—no matter what—there was always something to be gained. Not that this "something" mollified the first burst of resentment or annoyance. Lady Charlton was thoroughly cross with Eleanor for half a day, and with Sir Hugh for several days; but the considerations before-mentioned had the effect of supporting her in the endeavour to hide what was displeasing to her from her guests, and in making her to all appearance the same kind-hearted, bright, charming person, which she was generally allowed to be.

As for what took place behind the scenes, in more private domestic intercourse, or in that still greater privacy—the sanctuary of the heart,—it was not the business of any of the visitors at Senilhurst to inquire.

And so the world went on—cheerfully in the morning, busily in the afternoon, and merrily at night; and Mrs. Cuthbert Grey worked worsted-work, and moved gracefully, and spoke softly; and Miss Grey finished the "getting up" of the political pamphlet, and was rewarded by hearing that Lord Erlsmere thought her a very sensible person; and Miss Caroline Grey laughed at nothing, and exercised her fingers violently on the piano; and Maude, and Adelaide, and Eleanor, did just what every one else was doing, and Blanche—

"Why is not Blanche at breakfast?" asked Lady Charlton of Maude, when they met one morning about ten days after Eleanor's first arrival. Eleanor was sitting next to Maude: she had an impulse to answer, but she would not, because Lady Charlton had not chosen to address herself to her.

"Blanche's throat is uncomfortable this morning, I think," replied Maude. "Her maid told me that was the reason she was not getting up; she had a bad night."

"Her throat!" repeated Lady Charlton. "I never heard of it. What is the matter?"

"Somers will see her to-day," said Lord Rutherford. "I have sent to him."

Lady Charlton looked from one to the other in displeased surprise.

"Lady Blanche has not seemed quite well for the last week," observed Mrs. Cuthbert Grey.

"A cold; only a cold," said Lord Rutherford, quickly. "You know she has often a sore throat," he added, turning to Lady Charlton.

Lady Charlton did not know it; she was not aware that anything was amiss; it made her extremely uncomfortable; in fact, if she might be excused, it would make her happier to go at once and see how Blanche really was—and she left the room.

"Colds are awkward things," said Mrs. Cuthbert Grey to Lord Erlsmere, who was sitting next her; "and Lady Blanche looks so delicate."

She did not intend Lord Rutherford to hear, but he did hear, and remarked, in answer, in a tone of—what for him was—great irritation, that people who looked delicate were very often not at all so. He was happy to say that Blanche had never known a day's serious illness since her birth.

Mrs. Cuthbert Grey smiled with polite incredulity, and hoped it might be very long before the spell of such good health was broken.

Lord Rutherford did not thank her; he only rang the bell hastily, to inquire whether the man was gone to Cobham with the note for Mr. Somers.

Maude had been sitting silent for some time, seemingly without paying any attention to what was passing; but, upon hearing that Mr. Somers' note was not gone—only going, when some John, or Joseph, or Stephen was ready, she turned round quickly, and said, "Let them take my pony and set off directly;—directly," she repeated, as the servant hesitated, in surprise, apparently, at an unusual order. "I shall not ride to-day."

"Thank you," said Lord Rutherford, from the opposite side of the table. He pushed aside his plate, leaving his breakfast half untouched, and went to the window; and, after a few minutes' consideration, said, laying his hand upon the bell a second time, "I shall go myself—these people are so stupid. If Mr. Somers is not at home, the note will be lost."

The words were spoken to Maude; she did not try to dissuade him; only she observed that it might be as well to wait and hear what her mother thought about Blanche.

Lord Rutherford sat down again, and conversation continued around him, but there was no life in it. Eleanor asked Maude a few questions about Blanche; but Maude would not say a word more than was necessary, and even then answered in a short, disagreeable way, which was no incentive to pursue the subject.

Lady Charlton returned, after rather a long absence. Lord Rutherford did not inquire how Blanche was, but she said of her own accord, that there was not much the matter—a cold, caught from imprudence: all young people's colds originated in the same way. There was no inducing them to guard against the weather. Blanche had got wet about ten days or a fortnight before, and had not taken proper care of herself.

"It was the day we met at the lodge," said Maude: "she was not well, if you remember, that evening."

"And she has not been looking well since," again repeated Mrs. Cuthbert Grey, in a pleasant, cheerful voice, as if she was making the most agreeable remark possible.

Lord Rutherford said he did not see why people should trouble themselves about the origin of colds. Blanche had one—that was sufficient; she must get rid of it. Were there any commands for Cobham? he was going there immediately.

"For Mr. Somers?" inquired Lady Charlton.

"Yes, partly; that is, I shall call just to see if he is at home. It is satisfactory to put things into a medical man's hands at once, if only one's finger aches. It saves one from responsibility."

"And if anything does go seriously amiss afterwards," remarked Mrs. Cuthbert Grey, "one is freed from self-reproach."

Lord Rutherford rose, and saying, he should see Blanche before he set off, left the breakfast-table.

"So strange it is!" observed Mrs. Cuthbert Grey to Lord Erlsmere, lingering for a tête-à-tête, when every one else was gone; "so curious! almost amusing! to watch people trying to deceive themselves! Lord Rutherford thinks he is not anxious; poor man!"

Lord Erlsmere said, "Poor man!" also; but with a very different feeling from Mrs. Cuthbert Grey.

Blanche appeared at the luncheon-table, looking so like her usual self, so bright and simple and happy, that even Mrs. Cuthbert Grey did not see any cause for pity. Lord Rutherford took real pains to announce Mr. Somers' opinion. Lady Blanche was not well, certainly, she was delicate, and required care; she had been rather imprudent, and must make up her mind not to be out late, and not to sit up at night; she must take strengthening things; "in short, she is to be treated as an invalid for the present, to keep her quiet," he added with a smile, and with this dictum all were satisfied, and all went their own way.

Blanche went hers; it was to her own room: she did not feel as others thought she felt; yet it was not easy to complain, when there was little definite to complain of, beyond a sore throat, which any person might have, and a sense of languor and weakness which might be more indolence than anything else. She was almost vexed at becoming more comfortable, as she sat writing to Mrs. Howard, and began to think herself fanciful. The quietness and solitude were very pleasant, and she wrote and read and worked, till it grew dark, and then, tired with exertion, sat by the cheerful fire thinking till she fell asleep. How long she slept she did not know, but she was awakened suddenly by pain—that sharp indescribable pang which had once before so startled her; the involuntary cry which she uttered was answered by a kiss from her father. He was bending over her with a face of the fondest anxiety.

"My dearest child, you frightened me," he said; "but you are sitting uneasily; that is the matter, I suppose."

"Yes, I hope so; I suppose it may be," said Blanche; but she was very pale, for the pain continued, though not so intensely. Lord Rutherford laid her on the sofa, and placed the pillows for her to rest; she smiled cheerfully then, and told him she was better. It was only pain for the moment, which she had felt before, and, no doubt, it would soon be gone. He was not satisfied, but scarcely choosing to acknowledge his uneasiness to himself, he said, with an endeavour to divert his thoughts, "I was coming to tell you about my afternoon's business. I have been to the lodge, and inquired after your little friend; and there I met Lord Erlsmere, returning from a short ride with one of the Miss Greys; so I persuaded them to join me and go as far as Cobham, where I made Miss Grey choose some books and toys, which are to be sent home for you to see; and to-morrow we will go and give them."

Blanche held out her hand to him, and said, "Thank you," very earnestly; but her voice was faint.

"Your hand is so hot, my child—quite feverish,"

said the earl. "I wish Somers had sent the medicine he talked of."

He was going to ring and inquire, but Blanche would not allow him. It was pleasant, she said, to have him for half an hour to herself, and she could inquire about the medicine afterwards; for, if he thought it would not look fanciful, she would rather not go down stairs that evening.

Lord Rutherford acquiesced; he sat down by the sofa again, and went on talking to her about the little boy. He seemed to know everything about him—how he had slept, and what he had eaten—and as Blanche, from time to time, smiled, and was pleased and interested, he became quite eager, almost impatient in his wish to show her what he had bought. "I shall come to you again, after dinner," he said, when the dressing-bell rung; "that is, if you are not gone to-bed; but you must not sit up late. If you do not nurse your cold now, you will not be fit for your gay birthday."

Blanche had no doubt that she should be quite well the next day—her colds were never of much consequence; and Lord Rutherford agreed with her, and went away happy, as he tried to believe; but the world was not quite so sunshiny as it had lately been. Perhaps, it was that he missed Blanche in the drawing-room and at the dinner-table.

CHAPTER XI.

"So we are not to have the pleasure of seeing Blanche this evening," said Sir Hugh to Lord Rutherford, when, after a good deal of exertion and endurance on the part of Pearson, he had been moved from the drawing-room and settled at the dinner-table. "A great loss, that! We shall all feel it. But we must hope; if she will take care of herself now, we may anticipate the gratification of welcoming her in full beauty on her birthday."

"That will be, when?" asked Lord Erlsmere. A laugh went round the table. Lord Erlsmere must certainly have been living in the clouds; or, as Maude whispered to her next neighbour, in that which is the nearest approach to them—the House of Commons—not to have learnt that the next Tuesday was to be a gala day.

"Oh!" Lord Erslmere was guilty of a slight blush—for he undoubtedly had not been paying that full attention to the affairs of this lower earth, or, at least, to the affairs of Senilhurst, which might have been expected from a person supposed, of course, to be either destined for Lady Blanche or desperately in love with Miss Grey. "Wednesday is the day—the day, par excellence," said Sir Hugh, graciously. "Lord Rutherford has done us great honour in allowing us to keep it here; and the fact reminds me—"

"Sir Hugh," said Lady Charlton, in a tone which was quite melodious from its gentleness; "you are overlooking your neighbour. Miss Caroline Grey has eaten nothing." Sir Hugh was all attention in an instant.

"Wednesday, is it?" said Mrs. Cuthbert Grey to Lady Charlton, with an air of surprise and disappointment. "I have made a great mistake, I thought you said Tuesday."

"No; Wednesday, the 29th. I am right, am I not, Maude? Wednesday, the 29th, the grand day," exclaimed Sir Hugh, returning to the subject with renewed vigour; "and I was about to observe—I was about to remind Lord Rutherford—" The earl was seized with a sudden interest in an observation made by Eleanor Wentworth, who was sitting by him. Sir Hugh looked from one to the other, but the tide of conversation had received an impulse which it was not easy to avert.

Mrs. Cuthbert Grey's next remark was made in an under tone to Lady Charlton. She was really vexed, she said, to find that Wednesday was the day, for she was very much afraid that some plans which she had formed would be incompatible with what would otherwise have been a great wish. She had set her heart upon Adelaide's returning with her, and as she must go on the Wednesday, she was afraid this notion of the birthday would interfere.

"But Wednesday is the very day: you are not going then; we could not let you go," exclaimed Lady Charlton. "I could not entertain the idea for an instant."

Mrs. Cuthbert Grey professed herself as vexed and disappointed as Lady Charlton could possibly have desired; but again repeated that her plans were so fixed they could not under any circumstances be altered. It was business, indeed, which required her presence at home on the Thursday, and business which could not be set aside. "But you will perhaps spare Adelaide to us after the party," she added.

"The distance is not very great; and possibly, if Mr. Johnstone is coming here again, he might bring her back part of the way; for you know they are near neighbours of ours—only at two miles' distance."

Lady Charlton was not inclined to make any such arrangement. She was too much provoked at losing the guest whom she especially prized on the precise day of her intended party. Her only comfort arose from perceiving that Mrs. Cuthbert Grey was as much annoyed as herself. There was perfect sincerity in the regret she expressed at the unfortunate mistake.

"Mamma may break her heart; but it is more than I shall do," said Maude, in a low voice to Eleanor. But Eleanor did not answer; she was looking across the table at Adelaide, who was bending forward and listening with a strange eagerness of manner to her mother's decision.

"I hope I shall have inclination to plead for me, as far as you are concerned, Adelaide," said Mrs. Cuthbert Grey smiling at the interest so unconsciously shown. Adelaide started, and coloured crimson, and answered, laughingly, that she had set her heart upon it: but there was no sign of anxiety given after this, for, during the remainder of the dinner, she kept up a flighty conversation with Miss Caroline Grey, which had the effect of chilling into gravity nearly every other person at the table.

The dinner was ended, and Eleanor and Maude went to Blanche's room together. Each wished the other absent. They had but one feeling in common—that which centred in Blanche. Maude took up a book, as was her wont, and Eleanor rallied her for being unsociable; but still she read, or pretended to do so; whilst Eleanor sat by, amusing Blanche with little incidents of the day. She was very quick and clever in description; and Maude was attracted by her against her will, and whilst holding a volume of travels in her hand, could not avoid adding an occasional remark or an explanation.

"Come, Maude, resign yourself, and be agreeable," said Blanche, playfully, as Maude turned towards the light, seemingly determined upon being studious; "you really cannot help yourself."

"No one is agreeable who is told to be so," replied Maude, shortly. "Besides you don't want anything when Miss Wentworth is with you."

"Yes, I do; I want you for my own pleasure, and to scold Eleanor for saying a good many things she ought not."

"What things?" asked Eleanor; and Maude put down her book, and gazed steadily on the fire.

"Lectures are for a tête-à-tête," answered Blanche; "and, moreover, they are not in my way."

"Thank you, for supposing them in mine," observed Maude; "but I am used to it: it has been my character from a child to be fond of giving them—and I think I am. Miss Wentworth thinks so—she cannot deny it."

Eleanor did not attempt to do so; she only said that she had never had the honour of receiving one.

"That may be because she considers you incorrigible," observed Blanche. "I always deem it rather a favour to be lectured by people I care for; it shows that they have not quite given one up."

"Miss Wentworth is not likely to profit by any lectures of mine," said Maude.

Eleanor tried to laugh at what might be supposed the double meaning of this speech; but it was an awkward attempt, for she felt much the coldness, the rudeness indeed, of Maude's manner.

Blanche looked at her cousin reproachfully. She could make allowance for Maude's defect of temper, and the faults of a neglected education; but this want of courtesy towards her friend, and Lady Charlton's guest, was almost more than even her gentleness could bear.

"You have no cause to be angry with me, Blanche," said Maude, replying to the look.

"I only say what I mean; I am not the person to lecture Miss Wentworth, *if* she deserves a lecture:" the marked emphasis upon the *if*, was evidently intended to show that, in Maude's opinion, the lecture was deserved.

Blanche was quite afraid to reply. Eleanor sat very still, and very stiff, and Maude returned to her book, having thoroughly succeeded in stopping the conversation, if that was her object.

A knock at the door, at this instant, was a seasonable relief. "It must be papa," said Blanche, "he promised he would come to sit with me after dinner." But the knock was repeated, and Adelaide put her head in at the door and called Eleanor away. There was nervousness and conscious secrecy in Eleanor's manner as she answered, "Coming, in one moment; go to your room, and I will follow you." Adelaide still stood at the door without entering; and, after hoping that Blanche was better, said aloud, to Maude. "The Cuthbert Greys' plans are settled, Maude; they go back to Oakfield on Wednesday night, after the party; hard work it will be, but it is quite settled."

"Is it?" said Maude, without raising her eyes; and, before Blanche could ask the meaning of the information, Adelaide beckoned again to Eleanor, and both left the room.

Then Maude threw aside her book, and standing before Blanche, whilst her eyes flashed with indignation, exclaimed, "Why did you stop me from saying what I would have said? Is it good for Miss Wentworth, that no one should have the courage to tell her the trnth, and make her ashamed of the part she is playing ?" Blanche was lying on the sofa, very tired and worried; she had not strength or inclination to enter upon the subject, and Maude's vehemence chilled her, it seemed so misplaced. "I thought you had more in you, Blanche," continued Maude; "more courage and energy."

Tears were in Blanche's eyes as much from fatigue as vexation. "I don't know what you are talking about, Maude," she answered; "it is all such a mystery. Perhaps you will leave it till another time, for I don't feel very well to-night."

Maude became more gentle, but she did not seem willing to defer what she had to say, and continued, "It may be very cruel, Blanche, to put you up to the ways of the world. You are walking through it blindfold, happily for you; happily for all who can do so. But remember you have been warned; and if you will still allow yourself to be infatuated by Miss Wentworth, the fault is not mine. Yet I should have thought," she added, "that anything like manœuvring would have been foreign to your nature."

Blanche was completely roused for the moment. "Manœuvring!" she exclaimed. "Maude, this is only a repetition of the charge you made against Eleanor before. I thought I had told you that I would not bear to hear it brought forward without proof."

"And you have not seen any proof, then, during the fortnight you have been together," said Maude sarcastically. "Well; I suppose it is possible—wilful blindness is greater than any other. But, if you have not, I can assure you that I have. Every look and word of Miss Wentworth's convinces me that she has a double-meaning in her visit; that she is manœuvring for her brother and Adelaide; and, what is more, that she wishes to draw you into her schemes. I could not tell you all the facts from which I draw my conclusions. Some things I see, some I hear.

It may be all folly now, but it may be serious by-and-by; and you, Blanche, true and simple though you are—so true and so simple, that I would give all I am worth to resemble you—may be led to join with them; they will reckon upon your good nature."

"If they do," began Blanche indignantly—but she stopped, and added, "no, I will not, I cannot believe it."

"Do believe, do think," said Maude, persuasively. "Believe whatever may save you from being like them, from being anything but what you are."

"You make me very unhappy," replied Blanche; "I wish I knew your object. Why, if you suspect anything amiss, do you not go to your mother, instead of speaking mysteriously to me?"

"And have you, then, really lived so long with us without understanding us?" exclaimed Maude. "Can you be childish enough to suppose that I should go and make vague complaints, and aggravate my mother's temper, in the hope of inducing Adelaide to behave as a woman of sense, instead of an idiot? My dear Blanche, there is not in the house, at this moment, a single individual—I say it calmly and advisedly;—no, there is not one, yourself excepted, whom I would trust to act with common prudence as far as Adelaide is concerned. They are all —"

"I do not wish to hear what they are," said Blanche firmly; "and I would rather that you should not make me the exception. It is quite impossible that any one of my age, and with my ignorance of the world—which you know, Maude, you are always reminding me of—should know how to act or advise in such a case."

"No," said Maude, more quietly; "it is not impossible. You have influence over Miss Wentworth; and you have also the one qualification—the basis of all good judgment—you are true and consistent."

"I would try to be so," was Blanche's reply.

Maude stood in silence for a few instants, her large cold grey eyes riveted upon the lovely features of her young cousin, which now bore the expression of pain, both of body and mind.

"To-morrow," said Blanche, "we will talk more of this." Maude did not notice the words; a cloud of thought seemed passing over her. "To-morrow," repeated Blanche; and Maude started, like one awakened from a dream.

"To-morrow did you say? Yes, if you will; but, oh Blanche! in pity do not let me be deceived in *you.*" The tone in which she spoke was strangely different from the chilling bitterness of her former voice.

Blanche raised her eyes to her, and asked, "Why are you afraid for me?"

Maude did not answer the question. She knelt down beside her, and said, "I have talked too long. Can I help you in any way before you go to bed?"

"Thank you, no; I shall not go to bed yet. I could not sleep."

"You will lie here and think; that will be very bad for you," said Maude.

"How can I help it? to be suspicious and distrustful! to doubt Eleanor! Maude, you should not put such thoughts into my head."

"It was necessary," replied Maude. "But drive them from you, at least to-night. Let me read, and make you think of other things." She took from the table the same volume of travels which she had been looking at before the conversation began.

Blanche smiled, and thanked her; but added, "I had better read to myself."

"Because you are afraid of troubling me; but I should like it. Shall it be this?" and she held out the book. Blanche hesitated. "You would prefer something else, only tell me what."

"I am too tired and too vexed for common reading," replied Blanche. "You had better say, good night, and ask papa to come to me."

Maude turned round almost sharply, and said, "If I were any one else you would like me to read the Bible."

"I should like you to read it, very much, I cannot say how much, if I thought you would like it," said Blanche.

Maude only replied by putting a Bible into her cousin's hands. Blanche opened it, and pointed to one of the concluding chapters of St. John's Gospel. It was read without hesitation, and ended without comment, and Maude went away.

CHAPTER XII.

BLANCHE could not sleep, as she had feared would be the case. Even the words of unspeakable comfort, of unutterable love, that had soothed her when read by Maude, failed to chase the wearying thoughts, which partly from feverishness, and partly from the evening's conversation, harassed her mind. If she fell asleep, it was only to mingle in confused scenes of distress with Adelaide and Eleanor and her aunt; or to imagine herself guilty of some unknown offence, or involved with others in some great punishment. She awoke continually, and still the distant sound of voices in the drawing-room below, or the notes of the piano or the harp, reminded her that she was the only person who had as yet retired to rest. There came at last a pause, as the party was breaking up, and Blanche in that interval fell asleep again, and when she again unclosed her eyes, it seemed as if she had slept a long time. She sat up to look at her watch. It was just eleven. She had not then slept so very long, and on listening she could still hear a few movements in the house, and murmuring voices near; yes, very near, in the gallery by her dressing-room, the door into which was partly open. They were very low, and Blanche could not at first distinguish them; but after the lapse of a few minutes, a push, it seemed an angry one, was given to the dressing-room door, and Adelaide and Eleanor, both speaking together, entered. Blanche was startled for an instant, and then, supposing they were wishing to see if she was asleep, laid her head again on her pillow, expecting them to come into the bed-room; but there was a delay.

"Remember, Adelaide," she heard Eleanor say eagerly, "you may carry your amusement a little too far. Mrs. Cuthbert Grey will never countenance any folly."

Adelaide laughed lightly, and replied, "We shall not do her the honour of asking for her countenance; besides, if you are afraid, you know the alternative." Silence followed for some seconds, when it was again broken by Adelaide, "You need not trouble yourself to-night," she said. "Talk to her to-morrow quietly, and bring her round; and I have given my word of honour, so has Charles. Your difficulty will be at an end."

"Will it?" asked Eleanor, thoughtfully.

"Yes; do you doubt us?"

"Charles is so rash; so fearfully rash," said Eleanor. "He will not hear of delay."

By this time Blanche had become aware that what was said was not intended for her ears. She coughed to give the idea that she was awake, and repeated Eleanor's name; but, in the eagerness of conversation, she was not heard, and she could not help catching Adelaide's reply, "We are both sick of delay; and if you will not do anything for us, you must expect us to do something for ourselves."

There was a movement as if Adelaide was going. It seemed that Eleanor detained her, for in a voice of anxious entreaty she said, "Adelaide, have you no pity for my mother? If you encourage him to any rash step, it will kill her; it will be sad enough as it is," she added, in a lower tone.

Adelaide only burst from her, closed the dressing-room door hastily, and Eleanor was left alone.

All was very still then: Blanche could hear the beating of her own heart as she waited for Eleanor's coming. She could have thought that nearly a quarter of an hour had gone by before there was the very gentle tap and the stealthy footstep, as of one who was afraid of intruding ;—so many thoughts and such painful misgivings were crowded into a few moments. What could be the meaning of all she had heard? Why did Eleanor come to her at all? Was it only kindness, or had she some secret, something to ask or to tell? and could it really be wrong, could there really be a foundation for Maude's warnings? could Eleanor,—but she had no more time for such questionings, Eleanor stood by her bedside, shading the candle which she held in her hand, so that the light scarcely fell upon her features, whilst she asked, hurriedly, whether Blanche had been asleep, and if she was feeling at all better. The inquiries were made as a matter of course, and Blanche answered them in the same indifferent manner. She could think of nothing but of what might be still to come.

"Then I can do nothing for you, dear," said Eleanor, stooping down to kiss Blanche. The light fell upon her face as she raised herself: Blanche had never seen her look so wretched. She kept her hand, longing to speak, but not knowing how to begin.

"Good night," said Eleanor, trying to withdraw herself.

"Good night," repeated Blanche. A pang of conscience followed the words, as if she was deceiving Eleanor, and she added, "Must you go?"

"I think I must. Do you know how late it is?"

"After eleven; but can't you stay a few minutes?" Eleanor sat down.

"It seems selfish, too," continued Blanche, affectionately. "You look very fagged. Had you a pleasant evening?"

"Yes, very;" but Eleanor could not bring herself to give any particulars of it.

"Is Adelaide going to Mrs. Cuthbert Grey's?" begun Blanche, hoping to bring round the conversation by degrees; but contrivance was so opposite to her character, that in the pause which preceded the reply, she exclaimed, "Eleanor, I must tell you one thing; I could not sleep or be happy if I did not. I heard what you and Adelaide said; I could not help it." She expected a burst of indignation; but the stillness of the hour was broken only by a stifled sob, as Eleanor leant her head upon Blanche's pillow, and cried bitterly.

"I did not understand it; and I do not wish to know any thing, dearest," said Blanche, fondly. "Only forgive me. I know it could not be wrong—just say that it is nothing wrong," she added, in her simplicity betraying the doubt which pained her. Eleanor put aside the arm which was thrown round her, and apparently ashamed of her weakness and wishing to hide it, said as she sat upright, "What did you hear, Blanche?—and how did you hear it?"

Blanche repeated, as well as she could recollect, the substance of what had passed, saying again, as she concluded, "Don't explain; I would rather you should not."

Eleanor's lips became white with agitation. She looked steadily at Blanche for an instant, and then answered, "Blanche, you will trust me, I am sure. I have trusted you from childhood. Grant me what I ask."

"If I can,—tell me only what I am to do," said Blanche, frightened by her manner.

"But, before I tell—now—promise me."

Blanche drew back. "Before! it is impossible."

"Not to me, in whom you have so much confidence!" exclaimed Eleanor, reproachfully.

Blanche could scarcely bear to realize her own doubt, and she continued, " It is wrong to promise anything in ignorance; therefore I cannot."

" But ignorance may be your good," said Eleanor; " it may save you from pain."

Blanche looked at her with sadness and surprise; then she answered almost coldly, " A year ago, you would not have asked this. You know I cannot consent." It was a tone and manner which it was impossible to mistake, for it spoke a fixed decision; and Eleanor had long since learnt that Blanche, gentle and yielding though she appeared, possessed much of the resolute spirit of her family.

" Then, if you will not," she exclaimed, " we will leave the subject for to-night. You can hear more another time, if you wish it."

" No," said Blanche, eagerly, yet very seriously, " we will not wait; you have led me so far, that you are bound to be candid."

" It is a small request," answered Eleanor, in a musing tone. " It will not injure you or inconvenience you; and you will do more good by it than you know or think."

" Only let me know it," repeated Blanche. " If there is nothing wrong, there can be no cause for hesitation."

" You are suspicious," exclaimed Eleanor. "Blanche, I would not suspect you."

Blanche was silent.

" Maude Charlton has made you so," continued Eleanor; " she hates me. If it had not been for you, Blanche, I would not have borne her behaviour; and now, to find that even you have turned against me!"

Blanche would not attempt to vindicate herself—she only said, in a faint voice, " I should like to know what I am to do."

"I would not ask a favour for myself," began Eleanor, proudly; "but it is for Charles and for my mother. Oh! Blanche!" and her angry tone changed into one of the most earnest entreaty, "forgive me for being so hasty; I am very wretched."

Blanche drew her affectionately towards her, and said, "What am I to grant?—all I have is yours."

"It is but to ask for—to persuade Lord Rutherford; he has in his gift—" she paused, hoping that Blanche would conclude the sentence; but no help was given her, and at length, slowly and with shame, came the words—"the living of Whitfield is vacant; if it might be for Charles—promised him, kept for him, I mean"— she added. "Such things are done." Blanche did not speak. "It is a very little thing," repeated Eleanor: "I wonder I was so shy of asking," and she laughed that cold empty laugh which betrays an aching heart.

Blanche was strangely silent and still.

Eleanor was frightened. "It is but a trifle after all," she repeated again: "so you will say, Yes, dearest; and I will go."

But Blanche caught her dress as she was about to take up her candle, and said, in a very quiet, low voice, "Don't ask it again."

Eleanor did not catch the full meaning of the words, and replied, "Yes, you are right; we can't talk of it now; it is so late. I would not have told you, if you had not insisted upon it."

"But, Eleanor, Eleanor, listen;" and Blanche kept her hand, and grasped it tightly, "I cannot;—that was what I meant;—I cannot."

Eleanor put down the candle and sat down on a chair, with a face of blank dismay.

"I can scarcely ask you to understand," said Blanche, her courage returning with the effort she had made; "but it is such great, great pain to refuse."

Eleanor covered her face with her hands, and seemed buried in thought. When she looked up she was very pale and agitated, but not as Blanche had feared; there was no anger.

"I think, perhaps, you will know why I cannot," said Blanche, gently, "when you consider more. I do not know your brother well; he has not been tried; he may not be fitted for it; and the responsibility would be so great, if I were to do as you desire. Is there nothing else I can do?"

"Nothing; but to forget the request was ever made."

The tone in which this was said was despairing, and a sudden perception of the truth crossed Blanche's mind. "Eleanor," she exclaimed, "you are asking this for Adelaide Charlton."

"I am asking it for myself," replied Eleanor, in the same cold tone of wretchedness, "and for my mother, and my father—for all our happiness; and you refuse it. Good night."

"Oh! Eleanor! how cruel!" exclaimed Blanche; "but you do not mean it."

"I mean that my happiness and my mother's are in your hands," said Eleanor. "Good night."

Blanche could bear this no longer. "In pity, Eleanor!" she said, "do not keep me in mystery. Why are you so miserable? How is it that so much is involved in this one request?"

"Will you know?" asked Eleanor, her eyes lighted up with a gleam of hope.

"Know? yes, anything; if I can only comfort and help you."

Eleanor paused.

Blanche waited, tremblingly, for her reply. She did not see—for it was not a time of reasoning—that her refusal was founded upon grounds which nothing ought to shake.

"We may trust you," continued Eleanor, speaking more to herself than to Blanche; "you could not betray us. Yes, I am sure we may trust you." She paused again, and then added, "Should you be very much surprised—would it seem very strange if—if you were to hear that Adelaide and Charles were engaged?"

"Engaged!—actually engaged?" was all that Blanche could say; and there was more surprise, and even displeasure, in her tone than Eleanor was prepared for.

"You shall hear about it," said Eleanor. "I was afraid you would be vexed; yet I could not tell you before."

"I am not thinking of myself," replied Blanche, quickly; "but, quite engaged! who allows it?"

"They allow it themselves," answered Eleanor, with a faint effort at a smile. "But, Blanche, dearest, I will tell you as shortly as I can, and then,—" she did not dare to utter her hopes, but Blanche understood them—"it was soon after you left Rutherford they wrote to each other," began Eleanor; "that is—not themselves at first"—she waited for a moment, and then continued, passionately, "I must say it all out plainly: it is my doing—my folly. Oh! how bitterly I have repented it. I let them send messages in my letters; I don't know why; it was mere idle nonsense. I never thought for an instant that anything serious would follow; and Charles did not give me the least notion of what he was going to do; but he proposed quite suddenly: a sort of impulse, he told me afterwards, seized him. He proposed, and she accepted him, and they were engaged."

Blanche looked at her quietly and simply, and asked, "And what did your mother say?"

"My dear, dear Blanche! what are you thinking of? Of all persons on the face of the earth, Charles dreads my mother. He would have borne torture rather than acknowledge the fact to her."

"But she must know it," said Blanche.

"Yes, in time; when she is prepared. But you can scarcely understand what her character is like—so strong, so stern, and devoted; so rigidly bent upon duty, and yet so excitable, and her one object in life her children—Charles especially; that is her object of anxiety; she has less fear for me," and Eleanor sighed deeply.

"She would not like the marriage, I can believe," said Blanche.

"No; she is very much prejudiced: she has a dislike to Adelaide; and, independently of that, she has a horror of anything which would interfere with Charles's duties; which would make him less earnest just as he is going to be ordained; and she would feel—it would half kill her, I believe, if he were to do anything rash, now."

"Yes," said Blanche, thoughtfully; "a marriage with a person like Adelaide at such a moment would be very sad."

"Quite dreadful, in mamma's eyes," exclaimed Eleanor; "and that is what I am bent upon preventing."

Blanche looked at her for a further explanation.

"You will scarcely see what I am aiming at, at first," pursued Eleanor; "but there is one hope, and only one. Both Adelaide and Charles are wild, I believe: they think they can live upon nothing. Charles might, by the interest of an uncle, get into the army; but neither he nor Adelaide will now let me fully into their plans. Adelaide dreads the thing being known, and says her mother will never hear of her marrying a country curate, and she encourages Charles in the notion of the army."

"It is very strange to me," said Blanche, "that a

person like Adelaide should ever have engaged herself to a country curate."

"She is so thoughtless," replied Eleanor; "I really suspect she scarcely knows what a country curate means; only that it is something Lady Charlton would not like; and then, to do her justice, she is not mercenary, and, I believe, cares for Charles as much—as much as she can care for any one. You will understand, Blanche, what a very awkward state of affairs this is."

"Very," replied Blanche; in her heart thinking it so awkward that she heartily repented having been made acquainted with it.

"Now," continued Eleanor, "I know Charles well enough to be quite sure he will not go on in this way long. He might persuade Adelaide to a private marriage, even: I would not trust him."

"No, no," exclaimed Blanche; "you must be unjust to him. It would be such a bitter grief to his mother."

"It would be worse than that," said Eleanor, very gravely; "it would nearly kill her just now, on the very eve of his ordination: she, who has such strict notions on all these subject, to be so disappointed in him. Blanche, it would be very, very dreadful for her to bear." There was a silence for several moments, and at last Eleanor raised her eyes timidly to Blanche's face, and said, "You can prevent it." There was no need for Blanche to seek for an explanation; Eleanor had reached the point she had been aiming at, and in a hurried voice added, "If Charles had any prospects in the Church; if he had the promise of such a living as Whitfield, for instance; his circumstances would be so altered that he would not be ashamed to come forward openly, and Adelaide would not be afraid, not so much afraid at least, to acknowledge their engagement. Sir Hugh would take her part, if Lady Charlton did not."

"And your mother and Dr. Wentworth?" asked Blanche.

"They would be very grieved; they would think it infatuation; but, if there was nothing clandestine or underhand, they would be more inclined to excuse it."

"But at such a time, just before his ordination," persisted Blanche.

"They would not know it was thought of now," replied Eleanor. "If Charles had any certainty before him, he would wait. Christmas is near; he would delay mentioning the subject until he was ordained, and then he would prepare them for it by degrees. It is only this lingering uncertainty which frets him and drives him to desperation. And one thing, Blanche—if things go on as they are, I am convinced that he will never take orders. Adelaide's influence will lead him in a contrary direction; and, if the engagement were to be known, both my father and mother would dissuade him from it, at least for the present—they would say his mind was not in a fit state, and he might go into the army; into a merchant's office—into—I don't know what he would do; but mamma would be miserable for life."

"But Eleanor, Eleanor," exclaimed Blanche, and she sat up and looked at her friend as if distrusting the evidence of her reason as to the meaning of what she had heard; "surely, if your father and mother would not consider him fit, he is not so; he cannot be so in the eye of God; and to induce him to take such awful vows!—to encourage him in any way to such self-deception!—indeed, you do not see what you are doing."

"I was prepared for this," said Eleanor, calmly; "remember you are judging Charles without knowing him. You say he cannot be fit for holy orders now, because his heart is set upon this unhappy engagement. But I know him a great deal better than you do. Let him once feel himself bound, and I venture to say there is not a clergyman in England who will do his duty more conscientiously. And consider, after all, there is no great sin in what he is about. He is in love; you and I think it very strange he should be; but then, you know, we cannot understand half the marriages that take place—we wonder at them constantly. I do not think we, either of us, are able to make excuses for him, such as persons would do who were more used to such nonsense."

"But Eleanor," said Blanche, earnestly, "I don't think being in love, as it is called, is nonsense. It involves all the happiness of a person's life; and if people do not act rightly when they are in love, I cannot see how they are to expect a blessing when they are married."

"There is no harm in being in love, that is all I am contending for," said Eleanor. "It does not follow that Charles is not to make a very good clergyman, because, unfortunately, he has lost his heart to Adelaide Charlton."

"Oh! Eleanor," exclaimed Blanche, reproachfully, "you are trying to argue with me as you used to do at St. Ebbe's. You are keeping to the letter of my words, and missing the spirit." She turned away her head, as if to put an end to the subject; but Eleanor would not be thus silenced.

"Listen to me once more, dearest Blanche," she said in an altered voice, "I will not argue in the way you dislike. I will grant all you say, if you wish it; but my mother was your mother's best friend—the only friend who helped her in her hour of need. For the sake of my mother, and in remembrance of your mother, grant what I have asked." Blanche looked round with an expression of such intense suffering in her countenance, that Eleanor could almost have wished the allusion withheld.

Yet she pursued her advantage selfishly, mercilessly; she thought that she was seeking the happiness of others. "It is no exaggeration," she said; "mamma is no common person; she has for years dwelt upon the hope of seeing Charles a clergyman, and she has had no other great interests to distract her from it. Her anxiety for him, during the last two years, has weakened her health, and I would not answer for the consequences of a disappointment. If you persist in your refusal, I have no expectation whatever that Charles will ever take orders; he will be driven to some desperate step which will bring misery upon us all; on the other hand, give him a certain hope, and he will be patient and good, and bend his thoughts to his duties; and after he is ordained, and quietly settled down as a clergyman, he will break the matter to papa and mamma; and though there might be a good deal of fuss and difficulty at first, all will be well in the end. Oh, Blanche! surely you cannot refuse now." Blanche was silent. "You shall think of it," persisted Eleanor. "I have kept you awake a great deal too long to-night; but to-morrow morning you shall tell me that you will agree. It is the first great favour, the first real favour, I ever asked of you." Blanche returned the kiss, which accompanied these words, warmly; but her face was burning with fever and agitation, and her cheeks were wet with tears. For the moment Eleanor reproached herself; yet even then her eagerness got the better of her real affection, and as she wished Blanche good night, she added, "Remember, my mother's happiness rests upon your decision."

CHAPTER XIII.

"AND now, my dear Lady Charlton, you really will let me persuade you," said Mrs. Cuthbert Grey, the next morning, as she sat at the writing-table, sealing letters for the post, and professing that her necessary correspondence was the very torment of her life; "you really will let me carry off Adelaide. I quite see all your objections; the awkward time, just after your party, and the long night drive, and the discomforts; but you know I will take uncommon care of her, just the same as I would of my own child."

"There was no doubt of that," Lady Charlton said, though not very cordially.

"Then what are the obstacles? if I could only know them and obviate them, I should be so glad."

"I am not sure that I could say why I object," replied Lady Charlton, assuming an air of frankness; "it is a question of feeling more than of principle. Adelaide is so unfortunately thoughtless."

"Yes—young, girlish—you could not be afraid of her with me."

"Of course not; you must not think so: but I am always more happy when Adelaide is under my own eye. A mother's anxiéty you know!" and Lady Charlton sighed.

"Certainly; no one can enter into that more than I do," replied Mrs. Cuthbert Grey; "left with two dear girls—not a person to look to—no Sir Hugh to manage for one; at times the burden is indescribable.

Agnes, love," and she turned to her eldest daughter, who was working at the other end of the room, "I think you had better be dressed for your ride before luncheon. The days close in so fast now, you will have no time if you don't set off directly afterwards."

Miss Grey expressed a doubt whether some change had not taken place in the general plans since breakfast. Lord Rutherford, she thought, was to have gone with them, but Maude had told her he had changed his mind, so perhaps there would be no riding that day.

"Oh, yes, my love, put on your habit; I won't hear of you staying at home, if there is a possibility of going out. So delicate as she is," continued Mrs. Cuthbert Grey, addressing Lady Charlton, "it would be quite wrong to miss such a day as this; and some one will be certain to take pity on her. But why was the party broken up, my dear; do you know?"

Miss Grey did not know, but she believed it was Lord Rutherford's doing. He had come into the room about an hour before, looking very uncomfortable; and, after that, she had heard from Maude that he was not going.

"He is anxious," said Mrs. Cuthbert Grey, carelessly.

"Lady Blanche ought to be better this morning," observed Miss Grey; "she is down stairs, and has been sitting with Lord Rutherford."

"Yes, for nearly an hour," observed Lady Charlton, n a particularly grave voice.

Mrs. Cuthbert Grey instantly changed her tone, and inquired whether Lady Charlton thought there was any cause for anxiety.

"Not exactly," was the reply. Mr. Somers had assured them there was not anything seriously amiss, only care was required. And naturally enough with an only child, even a slight indisposition was a subject of uneasiness.

"Lady Blanche is going out, I rather think," said Miss Grey, "and Lord Rutherford is to drive her."

"Going out!—impossible!" exclaimed Lady Charlton. "My dear Miss Grey, why did you not tell me before? I must instantly prevent it." She hurried from the room as Miss Grey said, in an under tone, "Prevent it, if possible; but that is not quite the order of the day."

"Then what is it?—What is the matter, Agnes, my love? Is Lady Blanche seriously worse?" inquired Mrs. Cuthbert Grey, with some curiosity.

"Not that I know of," replied Miss Grey; "at least Maude told me she was not; but I caught a glimpse of her for a moment, and she looks ten degrees at least worse than yesterday."

"And they are uneasy, then," continued her mother. "Well, that is not to be wondered at; though really, if I were Lord Rutherford, I could be happier to see her dying of consumption, than to know that she was to live to be what her mother was."

"Lady Rutherford! there was nothing the matter with her, mamma, more than ordinary illness, was there?" inquired Miss Grey, quickly.

"Only that she was out of her mind," replied Mrs. Cuthbert Grey; "and that there is every probability that this poor child, if she lives, will be the same."

Miss Grey looked very much shocked. She had never heard the fact before.

"It is not generally known," continued Mrs. Cuthbert Grey; "the family tried to keep it as quiet as possible: but things will get abroad through servants, and there is no doubt poor Lady Rutherford was quite insane; a kind of melancholy madness, which took a religious turn."

"Lady Blanche is very religious," observed Miss Grey.

"Yes; and it is that which would make me so uneasy. Lord Rutherford is not satisfied himself, I am sure; he watches her unceasingly; I have observed him particularly the last few days."

"Lady Blanche looked melancholy enough this morning," observed Miss Grey: "she was coming down the stairs, wrapt up in a shawl; and I thought her the picture of misery; and just at that moment Miss Wentworth met her, and she seemed so hurried and fluttered, I really pitied her."

"I should not like it," said Mrs. Cuthbert Grey, shaking her head. "Those peculiar notions of hers are just the things to turn her brain. I don't mean that there is any likelihood of such a calamity, at the present time, poor child! It would be dreadful if there were; but if she were to fall into ill health, and these morbid fancies were to increase, I should not be in the least surprised: it was precisely the case with her mother. People said Lord Rutherford did not treat her well; but he had a great deal to bear, I suspect. I hope it won't be the same thing over again now."

"Every one is out of sorts this morning," observed Miss Grey; "Maude Charlton is shorter and sharper than ever. Really, if it were not for her splendid voice, no one would bear with her: and Adelaide is in such a strange mood, I can't in the least make her out. One minute she laughs and talks as if she was in the highest spirits, and then she seems quite abstracted."

"Whimsical, my dear, whimsical," said Mrs. Cuthbert Grey, oracularly. "Adelaide likes being odd; but we will carry her away with us, and we shall soon bring back her spirits."

"If she will go," observed Miss Grey. "She seemed doubtful at first, when I spoke about it this morning; but there will be an attraction for her in the neighbourhood. Miss Wentworth and her brother will be at Mr. Johnstone's."

"Her brother!" repeated Mrs. Cuthbert Grey: "I never heard of him."

"Oh, mamma!" and Miss Grey laughed. "I thought every one knew about Adelaide's flirtation with Mr. Wentworth."

"I think I have heard something," was the reply; "but you know, my dear Agnes, if one is to be always *au fait* upon the subject of Adelaide's follies, one must make it the labour of life. A great pity it is such a nice girl as she is, in many ways, should have been so carelessly brought up. I must not keep you, however, my love. Put on your riding habit, and you will be sure to find some one to accompany you. And remember, dear, if it should chance to be Lord Erlsmere, and you should be talking of Lady Blanche, you must not speak quite as plainly as I did just now about the unfortunate malady. It does not do to give more than a hint upon such topics; especially where it is possible the subject may be a tender one; though, for his own sake, one could wish that he knew the facts well. Now go and dress quickly as you can."

CHAPTER XIV.

Miss Grey's observation, that every one was out of sorts that morning, was quite correct. A much stronger expression indeed might have been used to describe what seemed the prevailing spirit of indefinable gloom and uneasiness. With one, the most innocent and guileless of all, it was a melancholy which could not be concealed or cast off; and there were those about her, who, from different causes, were so influenced by her as to feel their own spirits rise or fall with hers. Lord Rutherford did not believe, with Mrs. Cuthbert Grey, that his child's religious notions were in themselves likely to injure her mind. He had already seen too much of their soothing and strengthening effect to indulge such fears. Perhaps, if he had been asked, he might even have allowed that they were the ballast to a disposition naturally too excitable; but the one dread which —though he shrank from owning it to himself—was never entirely absent from his thoughts, made him look with suspicious anxiety upon every indication of depression or inequality of spirits, as being the possible precursor of that morbid sadness which had caused so much of the misery of her mother's life. Of physical illness he thought far less. Blanche was delicate; but not, he imagined, more so than many who seemed likely to live to old age. He had never permitted himself to deem it possible that she could be taken from him; it was an idea so dreadful, that if, for a moment, it crossed his mind, he discarded it as weak, self-tormenting. Blanche was his one treasure—that for which alone life could be endured—and it could not be—so he had at times said to himself—it could not be, that she should be removed, and he be left desolate. Why it could not be he never inquired—why he was to be saved from a trial to which thousands before him had been subjected, or what he had done to deserve such an exemption. Suffering had for years been present to him only in remembrance; and he could not yet believe, that, except under one form, it might again be inflicted in the mercy or the wrath of God.

Yet something did come before him that morning, as he sat alone with Blanche in the study within the library, where his mornings were usually spent—a shadow, though faint and distant, of coming evil.

Blanche had dressed earlier than he expected; and he thought, when he saw her in her room, she must be better—at least she did not complain; and when he begged her to come down stairs, and stay with him quietly instead of remaining by herself, she had consented readily. There seemed less to cause uneasiness than even on the preceding day, as regarded her health; but there was a change in her manner which he could not help noticing. She was so very quiet, so wrapt up in her own thoughts; and any attention to what he said was evidently such an effort. He hinted several times his fear that she was fretted, anxious, uncomfortable; but there was always the same sweet smile and bright glance of gratitude and love in answer, and for the moment he was satisfied that it was mere fancy; yet a little more observation brought back suspicion. Something was weighing upon her mind causing melancholy and reserve; and the supposition which would have crossed the mind of another, as a natural annoyance, gave a pang sharp as a dagger's thrust to the sensitive spirit of Lord Rutherford.

And it was no fancy : Blanche was unhappy—more unhappy than she had ever been before from any but external causes. Eleanor's last words—"My mother's happiness rests upon your decision"—were the first which occurred to her remembrance when she awoke after a restless and unrefreshing sleep. The thoughts that accompanied them—harassing and confusing—made her long to lay her head again upon her pillow, and forget. Pain and disappointment came, with the recollection of Eleanor's conduct—shame, at the consciousness of having been made privy to a secret in which there was so much to disapprove; and, above all, a distracting doubt when the question arose as to her own determination. For there was much to be said—she could not help acknowledging it when she tried to think upon the subject dispassionately — there was much to be alleged, at least, in excuse for Eleanor's wishes. To prevent a great evil—to save her brother from a rash step, which he might regret for life—and to spare Mrs. Wentworth a trial, the effects of which no one could foresee—were reasons quite sufficient to account for the earnestness with which Eleanor pursued a request that, under other circumstances, she would herself have been one of the first to condemn. No one had in general higher views than Eleanor, of the awfulness and importance of a clergyman's duty; or of the lasting evil which arises from any carelessness in the bestowal of Church Patronage. Blanche had heard her speak almost uncharitably of an instance of indifference upon this point which had come under their own notice. She had herself taken in a degree the part of the accused, and suggested extenuations which Eleanor could not be induced to accept.

It might, therefore, naturally be supposed that, in the present instance, Eleanor saw reasons sufficient to satisfy her that she was not doing wrong in supporting her brother's wishes. Blanche, indeed, did not comprehend them. Mr. Wentworth to her appeared very unfitted to take orders. He gave her the idea of a vain, unsteady, though clever and agreeable, person. But Eleanor said he was much better than he appeared; and who could be so good a judge as a sister? Then, again, she was not called upon to decide the question of fitness. Dr. Wentworth—a very excellent, sensible person—did not object to his son's being a clergyman. Mrs. Wentworth, of whose goodness there could be no possible doubt, encouraged the notion. Why was Blanche to put her judgment against theirs, and refuse to do a kindness, because the individual who asked it had, unfortunately, fallen in love,—and engaged himself to a person not likely to make a good clergyman's wife. It seemed—really it seemed upon consideration—that she might, at least, please Eleanor by asking the favour of her father; and that the responsibility of the decision might be left in his hands. If the petition were granted, the gift would be Lord Rutherford's, not hers; —if it were denied, no blame of unkindness could attach to her; and, whatever consequences might arise from the impatience and imprudence of Mr. Wentworth and Adelaide, she would have done all that lay in her power to prevent them. So Blanche reasoned with herself at one moment; so she almost persuaded herself to remove the weight upon her mind, by speaking to her father on the first opportunity. But she was standing by her dressing-table, putting round her neck the chain and locket which Mrs. Howard had given her. Her eye fell upon the date inscribed upon the locket—the date of her confirmation. How many—many thoughts were suggested by it!—thoughts of holiness and purity, and that single eye to the glory of God which can alone assist us to a right determination. Again, Blanche knelt in thought at the Cathedral altar, and renewed the vow of her baptism; again, she seemed to listen to the warning against even the "appearance of evil;" and to recall the intensity of purpose with which she had sealed the public profession of her devotion, by the secret vow which, in that glorious temple and that awful Presence, appeared doubly sacred and binding. She had been told, then, that no action could be safe that appeared doubtful when she thought of the Judgment: her present difficulty could be tried by that test. When the account of all things done in the flesh should be rendered before God, how would she feel if she yielded to the present temptation? Before that dread Tribunal would meet the rich and the poor—the learned and the ignorant—the giver and the receiver; there, the true consequences of every action would be fully seen; and there, the curse of the hundreds who might be ruined by the evil example of an indifferent or negligent clergyman would fall, also, upon her head. No kindness or affection for individuals would, in that day, plead her excuse. If she wilfully and knowingly aided in confiding such a solemn trust to a person whom she had reason to believe unfitted for it, she could not be held guiltless of the result.

Thoughts like these were easily encouraged and treasured up in solitude, and, when Blanche left her room, her determination was so fixed that she was comparatively at peace. She wished that Eleanor had come to her earlier, so as to be assured that any further hopes were vain; but Eleanor delayed, and Blanche dreaded seeing her, and when they met accidentally, as Miss Grey had noticed, Eleanor's countenance and manner gave her a pang which she could scarcely bear; and, in an instant, all the former suggestions and doubts returned.

To a person in perfect health this state of indecision would have been very trying; but, to Blanche, never very strong, and at that time suffering from serious indisposition, it was crushing. She sat in her father's room, with a book resting upon her knees, scarcely able to appear to read, and finding it difficult even to reply to common questions; whilst pondering over and over the arguments for and against her decision; and even, whilst feeling herself right, not able to rest satisfied without reviewing her reasons, repeating all that could be said on the opposite side of the question, and tormenting herself with imagining all the possible consequences of her refusal, and the responsibility it seemed she was incurring.

Lord Rutherford tried in many ways to engage her attention. He showed her his letters, consulted her upon some improvements which were to be made at Rutherford, and, at length, finding every attempt fail, sank back in his chair with a heavy sigh and a face which showed uneasiness of no ordinary nature.

"You are going out this afternoon, are you not, papa?" said Blanche, aroused, at length, to a consciousness that his change of manner was caused by her.

"Yes, I thought I should; but I don't know now. I can't go with all that party."

"You will not stay in for me," said Blanche, affectionately. "I should be quite vexed if you were to do so."

"There is no pleasure in going out without you;" and Lord Rutherford left his seat, and walked slowly up and down the room. Blanche cast her eyes again upon her book; for she felt perplexed, as if she did not know what to say even to him, and in a moment the current of her thoughts had returned to its former channel. When she looked up again, after several minutes, her father was standing by the fire, resting one arm upon the mantelpiece and watching her narrowly. She could not bear this, and tried again to enter into conversation.

"You will go out to please me," she said, with an effort to speak lightly.

He did not smile or make any answer in return for a few moments, but then he exclaimed suddenly, "Your aunt was wrong in urging me to bring you here. Rutherford was your best home."

"It was my happiest home," said Blanche, quietly. "I was more useful there."

The earl started, as if a new idea had been suggested to him. "Yes, occupation; of course, occupation," he murmured to himself; then again, recurring to the former subject, he repeated, "Rutherford was your best home; we will go back there."

"May we? shall we?" replied Blanche. Her eyes brightened with pleasure, for in leaving Senilhurst she thought she should leave temptation and trial.

"Do you wish it?" said the earl, eagerly, almost hastily. "You should have told me before."

"It is not a fixed wish; only at times," said Blanche; "but I should like to feel that I could be doing something. There is nothing but amusement here, except, just now, the little boy at the lodge; that is the only thing I seem to have particularly to attend to. I should like to see the toys that were bought for him."

"How could I have forgotten!" exclaimed the earl, ringing the bell violently. That one slight allusion to a wish was a command. He threw all his energy, in an instant, into the subject, ordered the parcel to be brought, and drawing Blanche's chair to the table, knelt on one knee beside her, with his arm round her waist, and spread the little toys before her, and discussed which it would be best to give, with an earnestness most touching, yet most sad, for it was the earnestness of idolatry.

Blanche's thoughts were a little diverted for the moment. She was particularly fond of children, and the little fellow in whom she now interested herself was singularly engaging. She had seen him several times since the first day of his serious illness; as often, indeed, as the weather and her own health would permit:—for the lodge was within a short walking distance, and she could often go there when she was not able to attempt anything beyond. She thought him very ill, herself; though the parents would not allow it, and even the medical man spoke sanguinely of his ultimate recovery: and, with this idea, she exerted herself for him more than perhaps was always prudent.

In a place where there was so little opportunity for personal exertion, this one case seemed to have a peculiar claim upon her.

But Lord Rutherford was not inclined, on that day, to think of prudence. As soon as he saw that Blanche could smile and take pleasure in consulting for the child's amusement, his whole heart was bent upon gratifying her fancy to the utmost; and, notwithstanding Lady Charlton's entreaties, he persisted in the idea of driving her to the lodge, after luncheon, instead of riding, as he had intended.

This gleam of sunshine, however, was but transitory. When the question of the toys was settled, Blanche returned to her book and her restless thoughts, and Lord Rutherford to his watchfulness and foreboding. The luncheon-bell rang, and Blanche proposed to join the rest of the party. "It was making less fuss," she said; "and she need not stay long."

The earl was relieved at the suggestion: anything was better, for her, than sitting alone; anything was preferable, for himself, than to witness even the faintest possible shadow of that melancholy love of solitude which had been her mother's characteristic.

The dining-room was filled when they went in. Miss Grey, dressed in her riding-habit, was acting extreme surprise and disappointment at the breaking-up of the afternoon's engagement, and looking wistfully at Lord Erlsmere for sympathy, which he did not appear inclined to give, his attention being engaged by a chance visitor, who was believed to have considerable parliamentary influence.

Blanche, however, had neither care nor thought for any one except Eleanor. She did not see her at first, for they were on the same side of the table and far apart; and, after a little time, she began to feel faint and nervous, and repented having come into a crowded room. The talking and laughing that were going on around her made her head dizzy; and it was an effort to her to try and catch Eleanor's voice, and judge if she was really as wretched as she had looked in the morning.

However, something was said, at length, which effectually aroused her from the dreamy state into which she was sinking. It was a speech addressed to Lord Rutherford by Sir Hugh.

"My dear Rutherford, you will excuse me: I hope it is not intruding—not trespassing too much upon the rights of private patronage; but, pray, what have you settled as to that great living of yours, Whitfield?"

The knife which Blanche held in her hand dropped from it, as she sat, motionless, to hear the answer.

"Nothing."

Sir Hugh was a little daunted by its shortness; especially as Lady Charlton, at the same instant, sent a lightning-glance of caution across the table; and, nearly as quick, a message, by a servant, to beg that Sir Hugh would tell Pearson where to find a curious collection of parliamentary tracts, for Lord Erlsmere and his friends to look at after luncheon. But Sir Hugh returned to the charge. "It was a famous piece of patronage—that living; one of the best in England. Some people considered it the high-road to a bishopric, since two bishops had, within a few years, held it. Not that he was of that opinion; he had made many observations upon the subject; more, he suspected, than most people. He had kept lists of all the bishops made within his recollection, and traced out the causes of their election. It was not every one who could do so; but, with his extensive acquaintance—his connection with the late premier—his—" Sir Hugh had quite lost himself; but he nodded his head, oracularly, and ended with—"depend upon it, there is a good deal of mystery in the appointment of bishops."

Lord Erlsmere caught the last words, and turning to Sir Hugh, asked if he had heard that Dr. —— was certainly to have the next vacant seat on the Bench.

Sir Hugh supposed and inferred, and thought it most probable, from his own private means of information; and he had a great many, a very great many, as Lord Erlsmere must be aware; but, he was not then thinking about bishops, he was merely giving his opinion about the living of Whitfield, one of the largest livings in England.

"Oh yes, by-the-bye;" and Lord Erlsmere innocently appealed to Lord Rutherford for information, not being aware that the decision was still uncertain, and that the earl disliked all curiosity upon what he deemed his private affairs.

The answer was as unsatisfactory as before; but it had not the effect of setting aside the subject, which was now fairly established. The value of the living, its claims, and its responsibilities, were all discussed; not earnestly by any one but Lord Erlsmere; yet the facts brought forward, of spiritual destitution, ignorance, and crime, were very startling and dreadful to Blanche. She had never heard of such details before; and, as she listened to them, it seemed that even Eleanor, with all her fondness for her brother, could scarcely put his interest in competition with the welfare of thousands. Unconsciously a sigh escaped her; it reached the quick ear of her father, and in an under-tone he asked if she was tired; but she scarcely heard him, so intent was she upon a story, a horrible story, of suffering and misery, which Lord Erlsmere was telling Lady Charlton. It was suffering from a clergyman's neglect. In her eagerness Blanche leant forward, her eye caught Eleanor's, and the next moment Eleanor pushed back her chair, and excusing herself to Lady Charlton, by saying that she did not feel well, left the room by herself.

"You shall not go with her," said Maude Charlton, going behind Blanche's chair; as, with a face of anxiety, she was about to rise and follow. She laid her hand firmly upon Blanche's shoulder and continued in a low voice, "Trust me, she is not really ill."

Blanche tried to free herself, but Maude still kept behind her, and addressing Lord Rutherford, begged him to carry Blanche away to his study. "I shall take care of Miss Wentworth myself," she added.

Blanche looked up with a feeling of irritation, and answered, almost haughtily, that it was her wish to go to Eleanor; she did not mean to exert herself, but she must go. And Maude drew back coldly, and suffered her to pass from the room without another word.

CHAPTER XV.

ELEANOR was kneeling by her bed, her face bent down upon the coverlid; an open letter lay on the ground; and Blanche saw that it was from Mrs. Wentworth.

"Eleanor, dearest," said Blanche, and she stooped down and kissed her; and Eleanor rose, and pointing to the letter, answered with a bitter calmness, "Judge what you are doing."

Blanche took up the letter; her limbs trembled, and she sat down to read it, whilst Eleanor stood by, watching the changes that passed over her face.

The bold legible handwriting was the transcript of Mrs. Wentworth's mind: yet lines of weakness and suffering might be traced in it; for it was the outpouring of a mother's uneasiness. The letter had been written upon the day on which Charles had left the rectory for the avowed purpose of transacting business in London. What business no one knew, or could understand; no one at least at Rutherford. But it was possible that Eleanor was better informed, and her mother wrote to request, even to entreat, that if she could throw any light upon her brother's movements, she would, in pity both to Dr. Wentworth and herself, do so without fail.

"It is not a mere wish to seek out all that Charles does and thinks," wrote Mrs. Wentworth, "which makes me ask. At his age there may be subjects upon which he may not wish to be open; though, strictly speaking, there ought to be none which a son should fear to confide to his mother; but I would not strain the point. Only, at such a time, to have mysteries and concealments! — it makes my heart sink. I fear lest we are mistaking him; lest, after all his outward professions and his real improvement, there should not be that stability of character which is essential to the right performance of a clergyman's duties. Feeling, I am quite sure he has—the very strongest; but feeling will not carry him safely through the dangers of the world; neither is it a sufficient guarantee for the performance of his ordination vows. I am very unhappy, perhaps causelessly. Your father does not view things in the same light. He says, we ought to be satisfied with Charles' conduct of late; for that he has done all that could possibly be required to prepare himself for a clergyman's life; and that he is certain of his conscientiousness. I would give worlds to feel the same; but I recollect all that went on in the summer —that folly with Adelaide Charlton; and I fancy that perhaps something of the same kind is in his thoughts now. God grant my fears may be groundless. I scarcely know why I have them so strongly; perhaps it is from the very fact of the misery the reality would cause me. It would be the destruction of the one day-dream which has cheered me amidst all the trials of my life. I have lived upon the hope of seeing Charles a clergyman, in heart as well as in profession. If this is not to be—if he is to be lukewarm or worldly—let him go; let him choose the army, the law, a merchant's office—anything, I shall never live to see the error of his ways, for my heart will break."

Blanche was about to refold the letter, but Eleanor turned to the other side, and pointed to the postscript, written by Dr. Wentworth.

"Your mother is not well; which, I think, is one cause of her worrying herself so much about Charles. She had a slight attack, yesterday, of one of those fits which she was subject to years ago, at the time of poor Lady Rutherford's death. I have had a long conversation with Mr. Dawson about her to-day, and he assures me there is nothing to alarm us, but that she must be kept quiet. I only mention this in order that you may write cheerfully about Charles. As to his London business, no young man likes to be asked the reason of everything he does. I did not like it myself when I was his age, and I begged your mother to let it pass; but she would question him, and then made herself wretched because he was annoyed and did not like to answer. We shall expect you both home together, the earliest day you can manage to come; only give us notice beforehand. You will hear from Charles immediately, I imagine."

When Blanche had finished, and given the letter back again into Eleanor's hands, there was a silence of some moments. Each dreaded to say what was uppermost in her thoughts.

"You see," said Eleanor, at length, with a forced quietness of manner; "I did not exaggerate."

"There seems no cause for immediate alarm," replied Blanche, feeling, as she spoke, that her words were cold.

Eleanor remarked the tone directly, and exclaimed —"Oh, Blanche, can you be so changed? is my mother's health—her life—of no value to you? Do you not know that it was sorrow for your mother, and anxiety and fatigue in nursing her, which first undermined her strength?"

Tears gathered in the eyes of Blanche, but she tried to check them, as she answered, "I know you do not mean to be unkind, Eleanor. You would not willingly make me wretched. Try me in any other way; tell me anything else that I can do."

"Anything except the one thing; the one only

favour which will save my mother's life," exclaimed Eleanor. "Yes," she continued, as Blanche shuddered and drew back, startled at the expression; "what I said last night, is nothing to what I must say to-day. It is all hastening forward so rapidly: in another week it will be too late to interpose. I have heard from Charles myself; he is in London; he does not venture to let me know his plans; but he writes in desperation. He will not see that mamma is unequal to bear any shock; he believes that it is my fancy. His present life, he says, is wretchedness, and he knows but one way of extricating himself; that means," and Eleanor's voice shook, "that he will marry Adelaide privately, and break my mother's heart."

Blanche's cheek became very pale, and she looked faint and exhausted; but she said, firmly, "Any sacrifice but that of conscience. Eleanor, you cannot ask that."

"I know it; I feel how hard it is," exclaimed Eleanor, changing her tone. "When we were listening to what was said at luncheon, I felt certain of the effect upon your mind. But, Blanche, when Charles has done an act of which he will repent for his whole life; and when my father's happiness is ruined, and my mother is—I dare not say what she may be—it is paralysis with which she is threatened: when all this has come, will it never cross your mind with regret, that one word of yours might have prevented it? I speak my deliberate opinion," she added. "The last words of Charles' letter are: 'Give me but the hope of being able to come forward honourably and openly, before another three months have passed over my head, and I will be contented to wait; if not, delay is useless.'"

Blanche leant her head upon her hand to hide her tears.

"My answer must go by to-day's post," said Eleanor. "I have left my letter open, waiting for your final determination."

"It will not help you," replied Blanche, in an accent of great suffering.

"Yes, indeed, indeed, it will," exclaimed Eleanor. "Pray do not think that; it will, at the least, be delay, and a thousand things may happen in three months; the engagement may be broken off. If it is not, still Charles will have taken orders, and my mother will be spared the shock I dread for her. Oh! Blanche, what fearful evil you have it in your power to prevent!"

A message from Lord Rutherford interrupted them. He had ordered the pony-chaise, and hoped that Lady Blanche would be ready to go with him in ten minutes' time. Eleanor received the message, closed the door again, and bolted it; and going up to Blanche, said, as she grasped her hand in the agony of entreaty, "Think, only once more. If I do not write to-day, he will come down; not here, but to the neighbourhood. He will see Adelaide, and it will be all over, for them and for me. Not for my mother, but for myself I ask it. Blanche, it has been my own doing, and the consequences ——," her voice sank into a deep whisper, and Blanche caught only the words, "Save me; save me from them."

For a moment Blanche wavered. Eleanor pursued her advantage; but it was one step too far. "Indeed you may trust me," she said; "all that I have told you is truth. Only grant my request, and everything will be right. If nothing should break off the engagement, Charles will be quite open, and Sir Hugh will support him. We know it; we are quite certain of it," she added eagerly. "Pearson has told Adelaide's maid, who is obliged to be a little in the secret, that Sir Hugh is devoted to Charles."

Blanche started from her seat. It seemed as if a veil had been suddenly withdrawn from her eyes. "I will leave the affair in their hands," she said, with a cold quiet dignity. "Thank you for letting me know who are your counsellors." She walked to the door; but her gentle nature was not proof against Eleanor's look of despair, and once more returning to her, she said, "Eleanor, you have tempted me very far; almost to act against my conscience. I trust there is no one else who would have led me in the same way; but let me tell you my true opinion of this business. You say that Adelaide's maid is obliged to be in your secret. Pearson, of course, must suspect it. A gossiping girl and a fawning man-servant! And you are forced to entrust to their discretion facts which would make your mother miserable, and my aunt indignant. A few months ago the very thought of such a thing would have disgusted you. I am sure it must disgust you now. I do not wish to hear how much or how little they know; but, for myself, I would rather give up rank, and wealth, and friends, and beg my bread in the streets, than suffer my name to be mixed up with a clandestine engagement, and my character for sincerity and delicacy, and all that one holds most dear, to be at the mercy of my servants."

"And if it is too late to retract?" said Eleanor.

Blanche paused. "It cannot be too late to amend," she said, after a moment's consideration. "I do not see how, now, and I have not time to think; but something must be possible."

Eleanor shook her head. "One way there is: grant my request, and you may impose your own conditions."

She was not answered. Blanche turned away as from a temptation which she dared not encounter again.

CHAPTER XVI.

If Lord Rutherford had seen cause for anxiety in the morning, when Blanche sat alone with him in his study, he could scarcely be more satisfied when she came to him prepared for her drive. The change even in that short time was painful; she looked quite haggard; her eyes bore the traces of tears, and her whole manner was that of a person bowed down by a weight of care. The earl could not delude himself any longer by thinking that she was merely languid and uncomfortable from not being well; a much deeper cause there must be, he was certain, for such strange depression. Or was there no cause?—nothing but indefinable wretchedness—the precursor of more lasting misery?—and swiftly, in a moment, his thoughts travelled back through the long lapse of years, whilst striving to remember the first indication which had struck him of his wife's morbid temperament. His thoughts made him silent during the short drive; and Blanche was only too willing not to be obliged to exert herself. She was sorry when they stopped at the lodge, for the fresh air was reviving; but the afternoons closed in quickly, and she had but a short time allowed her. Lord Rutherford followed her into the cottage. It was strangely natural to him now to be there; he who had once never entered the house, even of one of his own labourers, except when business made it necessary, was now a recognised and welcome guest in the sanded kitchen, where, stretched upon a low pallet, lay the sick child, his pale face flushed with pleasure, and his little thin hand stretched out to welcome the lady whom he had not seen for many days. The earl seated himself by the fire; when Blanche was present he had no wish except to watch her, and listen to her, and yield himself to an influence so different from all which for years had governed him, that it seemed to present to him a new phase of existence. Yet it was not very much that Blanche said. She was shy before her father, and the disquietude of her mind gave her a tone of unusual reserve. But the child was not aware of any difference of manner; he only knew that some one was near him who was kind to him, and had brought him toys to play with, and pictures; and, with the simplicity and openness of his age, he made his remarks, and called for her attention, until insensibly Blanche's interest was absorbed, and she forgot that there was any other care or duty to be thought of. Then she talked freely and cheerfully, and the boy grew more and more happy to have her with him; and discovering, by a natural instinct, where his wondering and childish, yet reverent, thoughts would meet with sympathy, asked questions which if, at times, they were hard to answer, yet betokened a mind strangely beyond his years. The pictures, he told her, he liked so much—the Scripture ones—those which were about people being made well; and, raising his eyes to Blanche, with an expression of great awe, he said, as he laid his finger upon a figure representing our Lord, "It must have been so pleasant to be with Him; He looks so kind." Blanche tried to give him a personal feeling of gratitude by speaking of the blessings which had been granted to himself.

"Yes," he said, "there were a great many. His mother was good to him, and his sister; and they made his bed comfortable when he was tired: but he knew it was our Saviour who taught them to do it.

"And he makes you come and see me," he added. "Do you like to come?"

Blanche could scarcely repress a smile at the eagerness with which the question was put; as if a sudden doubt had crossed his mind.

"I like it, and the gentleman likes it too," she said, looking towards her father. "It was he who went to Cobham to buy the toys for you."

The child fixed his eyes upon Lord Rutherford, with a half-timid gratitude which he dared not speak; and the look drew the earl from his seat by the fire, and he went to the bed-side.

"Thank you!" said the child, fancying that he had come to be thanked. "Sissy and I shall play with them by-and-by; and I must say, 'Thank you,' to our Saviour too; mustn't I?" he added, appealing to Blanche, "because He told him to do it; like your coming to see me." Then taking up one of the prints, he held it before the earl, asking whether he would not like to see it—it was so pretty. "That is a little boy saying his prayers," he continued. "I say my prayers too, when I can; when I am very tired, Sissy says them for me. Do you think you could say them for me?"

"I dare say the gentleman could, if he knew what to say," interrupted Blanche quickly: "or I might, if you liked it. But, I suppose, Sissy says your prayers for you at night before you go to bed?"

"But I should like to have them said now. I should like to have you to say them;" and the wish having once suggested itself, the child grew quite excited, his cheek flushed, and his breathing became quick. "You would say them better than Sissy; and sometimes she looks about; I don't like her to look about."

"People should be quite still and keep their eyes shut, or else look down upon their books, when they say their prayers," said Blanche. "I dare say Sissy will when she grows older. Does she ever read to you?"

"Yes, sometimes; but mother reads at night, about the beautiful city. That's where the clergyman says I'm going. Should you like to hear about it, if the lady reads it?" he added, turning to Lord Rutherford.

"The lady is tired," answered the earl; "don't you see how white she is?"

The little boy gazed at Blanche steadily, and after a few moments of thought said, with a very earnest voice, "She looks like me when mother puts the glass before me. Is she going to the beautiful city, too?"

Lord Rutherford's countenance changed. He caught up Blanche's cloak from a chair, and wrapping it round her observed that they must go.

"Then you can't say my prayers for me to-day?" asked the child, with a disappointed air.

Blanche looked at her father entreatingly. "If he wishes it so much," she said, "might I not stay five minutes? His little prayer can scarcely take so long. What is it you say, Johnnie?"

"'Our Father!' and 'I pray God to bless mother and Sissy;' and the clergyman taught me another," answered the child.

"And if I were to say 'Our Father!' for you, should you like it?"

The little pale face brightened with pleasure, and Blanche, after one glance at the earl, who was standing passively waiting her will, knelt down. There was a moment's pause; and the child, touching Blanche's arm, asked, "Doesn't the gentleman say his prayers too?"

Blanche made no answer, she repeated the prayer. The little boy joining in it with his hands clasped and his eyes closed. When it was ended, and she rose up, Lord Rutherford was kneeling by her side, his head still bowed in the attitude of devotion.

"And now, good b'ye," said Blanche, gathering her cloak around her and preparing to go.

The child kept her hand, "Thank you for saying the prayer, and next time you will read about the beautiful city, where I'm going; wont you?"

Blanche kissed his forehead, and as a smile passed over his features, he whispered, "I hope you will come soon, for I know you will be happier." They were his parting words. Lord Rutherford hurried Blanche into the pony-carriage, and seizing the reins drove rapidly homewards.

Maude met them at the hall-door, fretted apparently, and full of business. Scarcely noticing Blanche, she said to the earl, "Mr. Johnstone has been here, waiting for the last quarter of an hour: he says he must see you before the post goes out, if possible."

The earl looked anxiously at Blanche. "Take care of her," he said to Maude. "I have been very foolish—mad, I believe,—keeping her out so late, till she is half-dead. Mr. Johnstone wants me, did you say? Oh! yes, I remember, about the Whitfield living."

He was going, but Blanche's voice stopped him. "Papa, may I ask? what did you say?" and in an instant the colour had mounted to her cheeks, though only again to leave them of a more deadly hue.

"The living of Whitfield, my child; that is all: nothing to disturb you. Mr. Johnstone has made application for a friend."

"A friend! what friend? — a good one?" said Blanche, hurriedly.

"A good one, of course. Mr. Johnstone, every one says, is to be depended on. But, my dear love, you are quite excited: do you want the living for yourself?"

Blanche laughed faintly: her knees trembled very much, and she sat down on one of the hall-chairs. Maude scarcely assisted her. A sudden gravity had gathered upon her face, and she folded her hands, awaiting what was next to be done.

"We must have your maid, my love," said the earl. "She must take care of you, and you must lie down and rest. I will ring for her; and then I must go to Mr. Johnstone."

Blanche still detained him. Would he let her know — if it was not wrong — if she might be told — would it all be settled to-day about the living?

A strong warning grasp was laid upon her arm, as Maude, stooping down under pretence of picking up her glove, said, in an under voice, "So miserably weak!—oh! Blanche!"

Blanche started; her eye caught her father's, full of strange sadness. She felt quite bewildered. What did he mean? and what did Maude mean? Was she doing anything wrong? Were they vexed with her? Did they know her secret? She was so tired, so ill, so worn, that all her natural strength of mind gave way, and she burst into tears.

Maude's manner softened a little; but the earl spoke sternly; so it might have been called, but for an involuntary quivering of his lip. He wished her to go to his study, he said; it was quite close, and it would be the best place for her, and Maude might beg Mr. Johnstone to wait. There was time; if there was not, he could not come to him: he must wait.

Maude lingered for a moment, apparently seeking for one more word with Blanche; but Lord Rutherford gave her no opportunity for it, and, opening the study door, led Blanche into the room, and said, with the quietness of great self-control, "Blanche, my child, we are alone; now, you will be open with me. There is something amiss. If it is a wish ungratified, you have only to speak."

Blanche could not answer him.

Eleanor's despairing tones of entreaty were again sounding in her ears; and weak though it was to waver, it was agony to resist.

The earl waited in silence for a few seconds, his countenance showing more and more plainly the distress of his mind. "You cannot fear I shall refuse," he said at length, almost reproachfully. "Is it in my power now? Will it be so hereafter? Can money purchase it, or time, or influence, or exertion? Only, in pity, tell me."

Blanche shook her head: she tried to find words for an answer—anything to satisfy him; but it seemed impossible.

The earl withdrew himself from her, and stood moodily by the fire.

"I do not doubt, indeed, papa, that you would give me everything," said Blanche, forcing herself at last to speak.

"Then why may I not be told?" he exclaimed, quickly. "If it is a request—"

"But it is not; I have nothing to ask; only, if I knew what was right; if I could be quite—quite sure."

Lord Rutherford's impetuous manner was subdued; but there was far greater sadness in his tone than before, as seating himself on the sofa beside her, and drawing her towards him, he said, "My poor, poor child; is there no peace on earth, then, even for you?"

"If I could be quite sure—quite certain," repeated Blanche.

"And is that all? Is it nothing definite?" asked the earl. He waited breathlessly for the answer, and at that moment to have been told that Blanche was suffering under the burden of some overpowering calamity would have been a relief from the foreboding which made his heart sicken with dread. But again there was no rest for his fears; for a few moments of recollection had brought to Blanche the remembrance that she had no right to awaken suspicions which might eventually betray the secrets of others, and she was silent.

Lady Charlton's knock was just then heard at the door. "Mr. Johnstone," she said, "was becoming uneasy," and she begged Lord Rutherford not to delay seeing him.

As she spoke she glanced at Blanche in surprise and some curiosity; but the earl scarcely heeded her. His whole thought was centred in Blanche; and, as soon as the door was again closed, he said, "Then there is something—a wish—a want unfulfilled; or is it disappointment? You spoke of it once; you said that the world was dreary. Oh! Blanche, is it through me that it is so?—through my fault? God knows it may be my penalty."

"Papa! papa!" exclaimed Blanche; "pray do not speak so or think so; it is not through you; I could not be so ungrateful."

"But you may be afraid; your wish may seem a difficult one to grant," continued the earl, "yet solemnly and sincerely, I would repeat what before you may have thought to be mere words. As the one only atonement which I can make for the misery of your unhappy mother, ask what you will, and if it is in the power of human effort to obtain it, it shall be yours."

Blanche threw her arm around his neck, and answered, "I want nothing."

Again they were interrupted. The door was hastily opened by Eleanor Wentworth. Agitation and excitement were visible in her countenance, but she apologized calmly. She had understood Blanche was by herself, and she was wishing to speak with her.

Lord Rutherford was leaving the room, but he returned to give a parting kiss to Blanche, and whisper, "Remember, you have only to ask."

He was gone, and Eleanor and Blanche were alone. Eleanor's errand was quickly told. This was her last effort—her last moment of hope. Blanche listened again to her former arguments, her reiterated miserable entreaties. They were more plausible, more urgent than ever. "Ten minutes more—only ten," she said, pointing to the timepiece, "and it will be useless to ask. Mr. Johnstone is certain to carry his point; he is to write by this day's post. Lady Charlton supports him. Lord Rutherford is already inclined to listen to him. In remembrance of all our happiness, and our love which was to last for ever, Blanche, have pity on me."

Blanche was lying on the sofa, without the power of argument, but she had strength to say, "Leave me, and return in five minutes;" and Eleanor, seeing a ray of hope in this apparent yielding, left her.

They were five minutes of intense wretchedness; Blanche was not able to compose her mind sufficiently for thought, the consequences of her decision crowded upon her. Misery for Eleanor—despair for Mrs. Wentworth—recklessness and folly for Adelaide and Charles. Even the ticking of the clock was distracting, and in the greatness of her distress, she threw herself upon her knees and prayed for certainty. God answers our prayers, but not as we expect.

Eleanor re-opened the door, and Blanche started up; but, before a question could be asked, Lord

Rutherford returned, accompanied by Mr. Johnstone. A number of letters were in his hand, which he threw upon the table, with an exclamation of fear, lest they should not be sealed in time for the post.

Eleanor stopped as she was hurrying away, and asked if she could be of any assistance? Certainly, if she would be kind enough, it would be a great help; and Lord Rutherford lighted the taper, put his seal into her hand, and then, relieved from a tiresome task, turned to Blanche and said, "I could scarcely prevail upon Mr. Johnstone to come and see you, he was afraid of tiring you; but I insisted upon it. You know his business; he is a very able advocate, and I think I cannot do better than follow his opinion: still I have a fancy,—it has haunted me whilst we have been talking,—that you have some wish of your own in this affair. I have told him that if it is so, the decision must rest with you."

"Is this letter to be sealed?" asked Eleanor; the direction was in Mr. Johnstone's handwriting.

Mr. Johnstone smiled. "It is for Lady Blanche to determine," he said; "the letter is to my friend; it contains the promise of the living. I could not have asked it for him if I had not known him to be fitted for it. Earnest, energetic, humble-minded, accustomed to the necessities of a large manufacturing population. But there may be others as fitted, and I cannot believe that Lady Blanche would wish to incur the responsibility of entrusting such a charge to one who was not."

A pause followed; Eleanor stooped down, and pushed a footstool towards Blanche, and whispered, "My mother."

"Speak, my child," said Lord Rutherford. "Tell us if you have any wish, or feeling even upon this matter. Is there any one whom you have ever desired to benefit?"

Blanche's heart beat so quickly that her breath was almost gone. Lord Rutherford looked alarmed, he rang the bell for some water. The servant was already at the door, he was come for the letters for the post; Lord Rutherford put them into his hand, all but the one unsealed. Again he referred to Blanche, "Shall I seal it? Are you quite sure?"

Blanche waited for one moment only to gather strength for the effort, and then, with a firm voice, said, "Yes, quite sure; thank you for asking, but I have no wish to have a voice in the matter."

The letter was sealed and sent. Blanche talked quietly with Mr. Johnstone for a few minutes upon indifferent subjects, and then went to her room; but no one, not even her father, saw her again that evening.

CHAPTER XVII.

It was a brilliant spectacle, when the long suite of rooms and the great hall at Senilhurst were lighted up in celebration of the seventeenth birthday of the Lady Blanche Evelyn. Many who saw it kept the remembrance of it as a scene to be described to their children, and their children's children after them; and some few, who knew the circumstances of that evening, and the events which followed, recurred to it with melancholy interest, to marvel at the mockery of human happiness and the strange contrariety that so often exists between the outward and the inward phases of this mortal life.

Yes, it was a brilliant spectacle—with the dazzling lights shining amidst evergreen leaves, and the choicest flowers that art could force from nature, wreathing the glasses which reflected on all sides forms of elegance and beauty; and exquisitely sweet were the strains of music that echoed through the lofty apartments, furnished by wealth and taste, with all that could minister to the enjoyment of the senses.

The seventeenth birthday of Blanche Evelyn! they who looked upon her said that it could scarcely be. So childlike and simple she seemed, so unconscious of her own position, so easy and unreserved in manner, and not even shrinking from notice because she was unaware of attracting it. And they said also that she was happy; that her laugh was the laugh of a light heart, that the flush upon her cheek was caused by gay excitement, and that her occasional restlessness and eagerness were the natural impulses of a child upon her first introduction into society. And so she was watched and criticised, and mothers coveted her grace, and daughters envied her beauty, and a few turned to mark an eye which was following her with proud delight, and shook their heads and sighed, that a father's hopes should be centred in one whose very loveliness and purity were marked with the tokens of an early grave.

Shall we look upon the truth? There is a lesson to be learnt in the most delusive scenes of the world's joyousness, as striking, it may be, as in the closet or the church.

The evening's entertainment was just beginning. A few early guests had arrived, and, together with one or two of the visitors in the house, were assembled with Lady Charlton in the drawing-room. Conversation was rather dull; it usually is so at the first opening. Lady Charlton found it difficult to avoid pauses, and heartily wished for further arrivals; and the appearance of Mrs. Cuthbert Grey and her two daughters was hailed as a great acquisition.

Mrs. Cuthbert Grey looked particularly young in her evening dress; it was not easy to believe that she could be the mother of two tall girls, and the consciousness of this gave her a certain vivacity of manner which was just then particularly needed.

"It is quite pleasant to see you here;" began Lady Charlton, addressing her; "I thought this afternoon that we should lose you after all."

"Not willingly," was the reply; "you know where my inclinations have led me from the first. Nothing but absolute necessity would have taken me home; besides it would have been unkind to Adelaide. You are aware we have really determined to carry her off with us to-night." Lady Charlton did not dissent, in words at least; and Mrs. Cuthbert Grey went on : "It is a perfect charity to spare her, for Agnes and I are engaged to dine and sleep at Weston on Thursday; and Caroline would be left quite alone."

Lady Charlton seemed a little startled at this announcement ; but, before she had time to speak, Miss Caroline Grey interposed : "You know, mamma, it is not absolutely certain I shall be alone ; those cousins of ours, from Wales, are coming almost immediately. They may come to-morrow, there is only a possibility of my being alone."

"Still it is a possibility one should be glad to escape, my dear ; and Lady Charlton is very kind in sparing Adelaide. Indeed, I cannot say how obliged I am."

Miss Caroline Grey paid but little attention to her mother's remark. She was seized with a sudden interest in Lady Blanche, and a desire to learn who had seen her lately, and if it was quite certain that she would be well enough to appear that evening. The mention of Blanche's name caused a general interest, and Lady Charlton was only too pleased to be called upon to answer the many inquiries as to what had been the matter; whether she was strong, whether the air of Senilhurst agreed with her, and if she was likely to remain during the winter.

Her niece had been ill, she said. She had indeed made them all a little anxious; but she had improved very much since the preceding day, and had insisted upon joining the party that evening. "She is not to dance much, or exert herself," added Lady Charlton, turning to Mrs. Cuthbert Grey. "Her doctor gave special orders upon that point; in fact I suspect if he had had his will, she would have kept to her room, but she had set her heart upon being present. Poor child ! very natural at her age ; her first ball and in her own honour ! and she would not hear of its being postponed."

Lord Erlsmere here joined the party, and remarked that he had just met Lady Blanche going to her father's study. He was quite struck with her, he said, she had such an unusual colour, and looked so much better than when he last saw her.

Lady Charlton was engaged with some more guests, and Mrs. Cuthbert Grey whispered to Lord Erlsmere, "Ah yes! poor thing! excitement—all excitement; the earl sees it quite plainly. He has been wretched about her the last two days. You know how she has shut herself up, and now she comes out quite well, as it seems; just like her mother. She had all those fancies. You never could depend upon her spirits from one hour to another."

Lord Erlsmere looked very grave; it was so sad a prospect, he said, for such a lovely young creature; and when he was with her he could never believe it possible. Her mind seemed so peculiarly well-disciplined, her temper so equable.

"Oh! but they are not symptoms to be depended on," continued Mrs. Cuthbert Grey. "I could tell you things—Agnes, my love, what was it you were saying to me about poor Lady Blanche, just now?"

"Oh! nothing, mamma, nothing; really I did not mean to mention it to any one, except yourself;—but it was strange."

Lord Erlsmere could not avoid a little curiosity.

"It was what her maid said," began Mrs. Cuthbert Grey.

"Oh! yes, yes, mamma," interrupted Miss Grey, hastily. "But it is not fair to repeat such things to Lord Erlsmere; only her maid is a great gossip, and told our maid that Lady Blanche had cried incessantly for the last two days, and that she thought there was some fuss between her and Miss Wentworth; for that Miss Wentworth had not been near her! Poor thing! I dare say she is a little wayward."

"And to-night you see she has shaken it all off, and comes forward as if nothing was amiss," said Mrs. Cuthbert Grey. "Well! one can only feel for her; but I am glad I am not Lord Rutherford."

Miss Grey touched her mother's arm.

Lord Rutherford had just come into the room, and was asking if any one had seen Blanche. His entrance attracted notice, but he was not aware of it. To one or two persons he bowed distantly and mechanically, but his eye wandered anxiously around; and a moment afterwards he was gone—to his study—there Blanche was waiting for him.

A father's love is blind; yet Lord Rutherford might well have been pardoned if, as he looked upon Blanche dressed for that evening's entertainment, he deemed her faultless. In her simple white dress, almost without ornament, she might have moved amongst the loveliest and the most splendidly attired of her rank and age; and in her exquisite grace, her perfect unconsciousness of beauty, have outshone them all. The earl could not praise; he could not even say that he was satisfied. Admiration was not the idea which presented itself in looking upon Blanche. But he imprinted a kiss upon her forehead, and blessed her; and the blessing brought a thrill of untold delight to Blanche's heart.

"It is so good of you, my child," he said, "to wait for me. I thought I should have tired you, and that you would go to the drawing-room without me; but I was kept. Sir Hugh took a fancy, an hour ago, about some of the arrangements, and would interfere; and your aunt was quite fretted with him. So, in pity to her, I carried him off to the library to discuss an old quotation. So immensely absurd he is! But you are not doing too much

I trust; you look better to-night—a great deal better, I think."

Blanche said she did feel more equal to the effort than she had done all day; and her father did not remark that she avoided saying she was better.

"There are a good many arrivals," continued the earl. "I looked into the drawing-room a few minutes ago—your aunt seemed quite in her element. I don't know any person who manages a thing of this kind better than she does. But they are all expecting you, Blanche."

"Must we go just this minute?" she asked. "It is very quiet and comfortable here."

He regarded her with a slight uneasiness. "You are tired, my love, already. It is too much for you, I believe, after all."

"No, no," and Blanche roused herself from the languor which was stealing over her. "I shall do quite well, indeed; but I thought there was no hurry, and I wanted to stay just for a few moments; I was hoping to hear—"

"What?—anything I can ask for you?—anything I can inquire?—let me go."

"Oh! no," said Blanche, with a half smile; "but I sent just now a message to the lodge. Little Johnnie is taken worse, and I had a great wish to know"—tears started to her eyes, but she added cheerfully, "one can't help being interested about him."

Lord Rutherford made no reply; but he drew an arm-chair towards her, and Blanche sat down by the fire, and fixed her eyes upon the bright flames, and the strange caverns, and hollows, and precipices of the glowing coals. There was silence for several minutes. Once or twice Blanche looked round, thinking the door was opened; but no one came.

"I hear music," said the earl, at length; "they

are impatient to dance. Are you sure your message was taken to the lodge?"

"Barnes promised me she would send some one directly," replied Blanche; "but it does not signify; I can go;" and she was about to rise.

"We can wait," said the earl; "only"—he took out his watch—"I think we really must go; it will look so strange."

Some one came to the door and tapped gently.

Lord Rutherford uttered an impatient "Come in;" but it was not a servant that answered him—it was Maude; very grave—very stiff and cold; and dressed in a manner but little in accordance with the gaiety of the evening.

"They are wondering what is become of you, Blanche," she said. "Mamma sent me to find you. She had a fancy that you were not well. But you are well—very well, I declare, after all. Quite a colour there is in your cheeks; or is it only that you have been burning yourself over the fire?"

There was a colour in Blanche's cheek, for it was crimsoned with the conflicting feelings excited by Maude's accent of sarcasm.

"We were just saying that it would not do to stay here any longer," said Lord Rutherford; "but Blanche had a fancy to wait till she could hear about a message which she sent to the lodge to inquire after the little boy."

"They can bring it to her in the drawing-room," said Maude; "there is no use in waiting here, and the dancing cannot begin without Blanche."

"No, no; thank you," exclaimed Blanche, and she rose immediately. "I would much rather not have it brought; it does not signify; at least I would rather not hear. Indeed, I would rather not," she repeated, as Lord Rutherford was going to ring the bell.

Maude stood by coldly, merely saying, that every one was expecting Blanche; it was her own evening.

"Yes; I ought to have been in the room. It was wrong of me to wait," said Blanche. "Papa, I am quite ready."

She trembled as she stood up; and he observed it, and laying his hand upon hers, said fondly, "You are nervous, my child; but you will not care after the first moment."

Blanche smiled, and opened the door. A full burst of music sounded from the great hall; a murmur of many voices—laughter and conversation.

"Stop! here is your messenger, after all," said the earl.

A servant was coming hastily along the passage.

"May we go back to hear it?" asked Blanche. She seemed really agitated now; it was not mere nervousness.

"You have been to the lodge. Tell us quickly," said the earl. "Lady Blanche is anxious. How is the child?"

A little girl of about twelve years of age stepped forward from behind the servant, and came close up to Blanche. "I was to tell, myself," she said. "Johnnie said I was. He sent his love to my lady, and he's gone,—he's gone to the beautiful city, and he begs her to come soon." And bursting into tears, she sobbed as if her heart would break.

"Come," said Maude, drawing Blanche forwards. "Poor child! we cannot help her." Blanche stood still for an instant: the light of a lamp fell full upon her features; they were of a deadly paleness. "Come," again repeated Maude, authoritatively.

Blanche started, and turned to look for her father. He was leaning against the wall, at a little distance, with his arms folded. Blanche went up to him, and said gently, "Papa, I am ready now;" but he did not answer, only he caught her hand, and holding it for an instant, looked wildly in her face; and then dropping it suddenly, walked back to the study, and closed the door. Blanche made no remark; she stooped to caress the poor little girl, who had thrown herself upon the floor in an agony of grief, and in a tone of quiet sympathy, spoke a few words of comfort, and gave an order that the servant should take her back to the lodge, and said she hoped to see her mother the following day. Then addressing Maude, she added with perfect composure, "We had better not wait for papa," and putting her arm within her cousin's, went with her to the drawing-room.

Again there was a crimson flush upon Blanche's cheek; again her eyes shone brightly, and the silvery tones of her voice fell with cheerfulness upon the ear. The evening was wearing on. She had talked and danced, even laughed and sang. It was beautiful to watch her; beautiful and inspiriting, except when occasionally a passing word seemed to jar upon some inward chord, and then for a moment a look of anguish flitted across her lovely face, and a mist seemed to gather over her eyes, and whether it were in the dance, or in conversation, a sudden vagueness and abstraction would come upon her, and she would pause, as if unknowing where she was, or what she was saying, till recalled by a gay reproof, or a glance at her father's countenance. For Lord Rutherford was "himself again;" whatever might have been the rush of foreboding excited by that untimely message from the bed of death, it was gone now; charmed away by the spell of his child's apparent enjoyment, and the proud happiness of beholding the admiration she inspired.

"Lord Rutherford must be satisfied now," said Lord Erlsmere to Mrs. Cuthbert Grey. He had been watching Blanche for some time; longer than Mrs. Cuthbert Grey approved.

"Yes; satisfied for to-night at least. But it is not real; all that cheerfulness, I mean, which poor Lady Blanche puts on. She will suffer for it to-morrow."

"So do many people suffer for a night's excitement. There will be nothing to wonder at in that."

"Yes; but even now it is forced—evidently forced. I have lived longer than you; and I have seen more—of young ladies, at least. Look, now; see what a change there is."

There was a change, certainly; a remarkable one. Blanche had been standing at the lower end of the room, talking to her partner. Now he had left her, and there were several people near her, but no one especially addressing her. Her face was turned away, but Mrs. Cuthbert Grey and Lord Erlsmere caught a side view. She had laid her hand upon some one, who was standing in front of her, and was speaking with an eager haggard look of entreaty, which seemed to have changed even the outline of her features.

"She is talking to Miss Wentworth," said Lord Erlsmere. "I fancied they had quarrelled."

"Yes; quarrelled I suspect they have; she is conscious of it probably, and trying to make it up. Those apparently very sweet tempers are not much to be depended on."

"If Lady Blanche Evelyn's temper is not sweet, I must distrust the evidence of my senses for the rest of my life," said Lord Erlsmere, earnestly.

Mrs. Cuthbert Grey smiled expressively.

"The quarrel is made up at any rate," said Lord Erlsmere, as he saw Blanche rise and walk with Eleanor across the room.

"Or reserved for a more private explanation," observed Mrs. Cuthbert Grey. "Miss Wentworth is not, I suspect, to be won over so easily."

Lord Erlsmere did not pay much attention to this remark—his interest was attracted by Eleanor and Blanche, and to Mrs. Cuthbert Grey's discomfiture, he made some excuse for going away, and followed them through the door by which they had departed. It led into the hall. A few people were walking up and down, taking refreshments. Adelaide Charlton and Miss Caroline Grey amongst them. Eleanor and Blanche were passing them just as Lord Erlsmere came into the hall. Adelaide tried to stop Blanche, and said something ludicrous, and Blanche's face for a moment wore an expression of great annoyance; but she went on, and Adelaide and her companion laughed only the more heartily. Lord Erlsmere could not see more. A dance had just ended, and persons were crowding into the hall—some to refresh themselves, some to find partners, and Mrs. Cuthbert Grey to collect her party and prepare for an early departure. She laid siege to Lord Erlsmere again.

It was growing very late, she said; and they had a long drive before them, and arrangements to make—packages, and boxes, and numberless things to collect; it was such an unnatural undertaking to leave a place where you had been staying, in the middle of the night. Would Lord Erlsmere try and find her daughter, Agnes?

Lord Erlsmere could not but be most happy; yet he delayed for a moment, with a lingering curiosity, to watch what had become of Eleanor and Blanche.

"You lost sight of the two friends in this crowd, I imagine," said Mrs. Cuthbert Grey, cleverly reading his thoughts. "People come and go like meteors. Stay—there are Adelaide and Caroline; do bring them to me."

Lord Erlsmere crossed the hall, and delivered his summons. Adelaide was talking lightly with one of her partners as he came up.

"I have orders from Mrs. Cuthbert Grey," began Lord Erlsmere.

"Orders? oh! yes, to go, I suppose—Caroline," and she looked round for her friend.

"Can I be of any service? can I give any message, or find anything for you?" asked Lord Erlsmere.

"No, thank you, nothing; nothing at all. We must go; the sooner the better," she added, with an accent of peculiar melancholy—almost regret—which Lord Erlsmere, unobservant though he usually was, could not help remarking.

"You are to be absent for some time," he said. "I shall scarcely have the pleasure of seeing you again, I am afraid."

"Thank you, no; I think—I believe I am going for some time. Caroline,—where is she?"

Lord Erlsmere offered her his arm to lead her to Mrs. Cuthbert Grey.

"But, mamma and papa; I must see them; I must say good b'ye to them," said Adelaide.

"There will be sufficient time," replied Lord Erlsmere, trying to check Adelaide's haste by his own steady pace. "The carriage is not ordered yet; you will scarcely get away for the next three-quarters of an hour."

Adelaide sighed, and the next moment burst into a fit of laughter, declaring that she was so fearfully tired, she had nearly lost her senses.

"You are not the only tired person, I imagine," said Lord Erlsmere. "Your cousin, Lady Blanche, for instance."

Adelaide coloured crimson. "Blanche!" she exclaimed; "oh! yes, Blanche is very tired, I believe."

"She looked so just now, when I saw her," continued Lord Erlsmere. "But I will tell her, if you wish to see her before you go?"

"Oh! no, no, thank you;" and Adelaide's manner became even more impetuous. "I would not trouble her for the world. Besides, she is with Miss Wentworth. It is better she should be with her; she will only be flurried."

"And you do not wish to see her; to say good b'ye?" said Lord Erlsmere, with a little curiosity to know why Blanche was so little of a favourite.

"Thank you, I don't care; it does not signify. They are talking together there, I believe," and she pointed to a little room which had been occupied by some of the attendants during the evening; "but I would not disturb her. Please let me go to mamma," and, hurrying from the hall, she threaded her way amidst the maze of guests, and through various rooms and passages, till they reached the drawing-room.

CHAPTER XVIII.

THE little waiting-room, to which Eleanor and Blanche had made their way, was quite deserted. It had been used merely as a temporary convenience, whilst the refreshments were handed about, and there was no fear of interruption in it. But, even if there had been, Blanche was not in a state of mind to have much thought except for the moment. When the door was seen to be open, and the room empty, she entered it as a place of refuge and relief; and, regardless of Eleanor's warning that the room was cold, and that it was not fitting for her to remain, exclaimed, "Now, Eleanor, let me hear."

"It is too late," said Eleanor, moodily. "Yours is but a mockery of sympathy."

"Pity—have pity," said Blanche, and she looked pleadingly in Eleanor's face.

"I have nothing to tell," continued Eleanor; "at least, nothing but what you may well guess. All things are as they were; only, hastening to their end."

"And is there no hope?" asked Blanche. "Has nothing happened these two long, long days that you have kept away from me?"

"You are unjust in your reproaches," said Eleanor. "What comfort could my visit have been? You have cast off sympathy, and have destroyed the happiness of those as dear to me as my own life."

"Yes, it may be—it may be," said Blanche, in an

accent of utter wretchedness. "I know you have a right to be angry; but I thought you would not go on being so."

"It will make but little difference to you, I imagine, whether I do or not," said Eleanor: "no one watching you this evening——"

"And are you too deceived?" interrupted Blanche. "Then, indeed, I can act well."

"There is no cause for acting," said Eleanor, bitterly. "Lady Blanche Evelyn, beautiful, prosperous, wealthy, without a single care,—nay do not stop me; I am only repeating what I have heard said by fifty persons this night."

"But you shall hear me for myself," exclaimed Blanche. "Before you think me so cold, so heartless, you shall judge me from my own lips."

"My own eyes will be the better judges," replied Eleanor. "Laughter and talking and dancing are sufficient indications of the state of a person's mind."

"And it must be laughter and talking and dancing to the end," said Blanche; "the end," she repeated again, thoughtfully, "which may soon be here." Eleanor looked at her wonderingly, and a feeling of returning love and tenderness stole over her as she saw the sunken eye, and the pale cheek, now no longer bright, and flushed with excitement; but, marked by the undeniable signs of great mental suffering. "Do you think I could be here to-night?" said Blanche, "if I followed but my own will. With so great a weight upon my mind, could it be my wish to join in such a scene, even though it is in my own honour? But you have thought for your mother, Eleanor; and I have thought for my father. He is very unhappy—very anxious; God knows whether there is cause," she added; her voice becoming almost sepulchral; "but I have felt to-night that there might be."

"He is anxious for your health, I know," said Eleanor.

"Not for my health of body," replied Blanche; "but there is another fear. He thinks I am like—my mother." She paused for a moment, and continued hurriedly: "He tries to hide it; but I have seen it. I saw it the other day,—that day," and she gasped for breath, "when we were together. His very eagerness to please me—I understand it, I know what it means; and he shall please me; I will be happy. If I am not"—her voice grew faint—"he shall never have the misery of knowing it."

"Blanche," said Eleanor, in a tone of alarm, "you must not let yourself be excited in this way; it will do you a great deal of harm. After all you may be fanciful."

"No, no," exclaimed Blanche, shuddering; and coming up close to Eleanor, she added, in a tone of quiet despondency which made Eleanor forget for the moment that they had ever had a word of difference, "he told me so himself, yesterday. He came to my room, and I was crying, and we talked together, and I made him own it. Oh, Eleanor! he was so wretched, and so kind—so very, very kind."

Eleanor kissed her and whispered: "Dearest," and Blanche, with the tone and manner of a weary child, laid her head upon her shoulder and said: "Let me be miserable with you; with him I must always seem happy. Several persons at that moment passed the door, and some one was heard to inquire for Mrs. Cuthbert Grey's carriage. Blanche started up. "We must not stay here," she said. "Only tell me that you forgive, that you understand me."

"Yes, I will forgive; that is, I will try to think you meant rightly," said Eleanor, her own trial returning again to her recollection. "But you cannot go on in this way, Blanche. No mind could bear the constant effort."

Blanche smiled sweetly; but very sadly. She stood for a moment thinking silently, and then her thoughts were uttered aloud, and she said abruptly, "Johnnie Foster is dead; did they tell you of it?" Eleanor looked at her in astonishment. "Yes, he is dead," repeated Blanche, in the same dreamy tone. "He sent me a message; we will go and see his mother to-morrow."

"Any one here?" inquired a servant, opening the door. He drew back and apologized. He was looking for Mrs. Cuthbert Grey's maid. She was wanted particularly. Mrs. Cuthbert Grey is going then," said Eleanor.

"Yes, immediately," was the reply: the carriage had been ordered a long time; and the servant went away. Eleanor sank into a chair and covered her face with her hands. Blanche walked up and down the room in great agitation.

"Fool that I was!" exclaimed Eleanor. "I might have seen the result from the beginning."

"There is no result yet," said Blanche, in a voice quite different from her usual tone.

Eleanor looked up sarcastically. "When a vessel is driven against a rock, there can be but one end."

"How can you be sure?" asked Blanche.

"How can I doubt, rather?" exclaimed Eleanor, with something of indignation in her manner. "When Adelaide Charlton takes Caroline Grey into her secrets, and hides them from me; and when Charles has come into the neighbourhood, desperate and full of wild schemes; it is mockery to ask if I am sure. My poor, poor mother!"

"It must all be stopped, it must be prevented," exclaimed Blanche.

And Eleanor answered, bitterly: "It could have been."

"Lady Charlton ought to know, at least she ought to be put on her guard," said Blanche.

"There is nothing to tell," replied Eleanor, coolly; "except the engagement. There we are both bound in honour to be silent."

A pause ensued. Eleanor rose to go. "Stop," said Blanche, detaining her. "I cannot see why you should be so miserable to-night."

"Because I am sure there is mischief plotting, and I cannot discover it. But it must come; it is not my doing; no, whatever happens, it is not mine. They never told me. Charles never asked my advice. They have taken their own way, and they must answer for it. Oh! if they had never, never met!—if I had never sent a message, never encouraged them! But I did not think. I did not suppose what it could come to. My poor mother!"

Blanche dared not speak. Every word which Eleanor uttered added to her own distress. "You will come and wish them good b'ye, of course," continued Eleanor. The softness of manner which had stolen over her whilst attempting to comfort Blanche's grief was now quite gone.

"I will wish papa good night and go to bed," said Blanche; "no one will miss me."

She looked extremely ill, and Eleanor offered to go with her. "No, you will be wanted; you had better find out Adelaide—or Maude; can't Maude help you? she knows something."

"She knows they are idiots, and she thinks us hypocrites," said Eleanor; "that is all. For your comfort she believes you the worst of all."

"Me!—a hypocrite!" and Blanche was for the instant roused from unhappiness to indignation.

She has heard some servant's gossip, and thinks

you are in league with me to support Charles, and make him propose to Adelaide," said Eleanor; "but you may bear that share of blame, Blanche. It is little enough, and your conscience will tell you, you have not helped us."

This last sarcasm was the overflowing drop in poor Blanche's cup of trial. She sat quite motionless, in a kind of stupor. The sound of carriage wheels had been heard frequently during the conversation. Music was still going on, but many of the guests were departing. Lord Rutherford came along the passage, and Eleanor heard him ask whether Lady Blanche's maid was with her. He thinks you are gone to your room," said Eleanor; "it is the best place for you."

Blanche did not answer.

"Perhaps you had better stay here for a few minutes," pursued Eleanor, "and I will send your maid to you."

Still Blanche remained with her eyes fixed on vacancy, leaning back in her chair, and her hands resting helplessly in her lap.

Eleanor was a little frightened. She thought of what it would be best to do, and supposing Blanche was over-fatigued, said, "I will go and find Barnes, and wish Adelaide good b'ye, and then I will come back."

Blanche half smiled in acquiescence, and Eleanor was satisfied and left her.

Several minutes went by, and Blanche continued in the same confused state of wretchedness and exhaustion. She heard people hurrying to and fro, and voices sounding now at a distance, and now quite near, and she was conscious of being alone, where no one would think of finding her; where it would be considered strange that she should be; yet she had no inclination to move. At length the medley of sounds rather died away, the music in the dancing-rooms ceased, and from the frequent repetition of Mrs. Cuthbert Grey's name, it was evident that at length she was really going. Blanche had an impulse to say good b'ye to her and to Adelaide; it seemed as if it would be kind and civil; and she had a thought—it could not be called a hope, it was so vague—that she might do or say something, or discover something which might help to comfort Eleanor. But it was all dreamy and misty, and when she stood up, her head swam, and her eyes were dim, and it was an effort to her to make up her mind what she was to do. She remained at the door debating with herself whether it would not be better after all to go to bed. She had never felt so ill and strange before, but there were persons talking in the passage, and she had a dread of meeting any one, so she stood still till they should be gone. They did not, however, seem inclined to go; they were talking rather eagerly, but in an undertone. They might be Adelaide and Miss Caroline Grey, for Blanche caught a few words about a cloak, and mamma, and looking in the little room, and then something else was said about forgetfulness, and one of them—the voice was very like Adelaide's—observed, "It wont do to be forgetful now; if one is careless for the rest of one's life." "No," and there was a laugh. "We must both have our presence of mind about us certainly, to-day and to-morrow, and then."—"Yes, then,"—a sigh followed.

"Nay, you must not begin to sigh yet," was the rejoinder. "There will be time enough for that when the mischief is done; but, really, I don't think there is the least cause for sighing."

Blanche went back into the waiting-room, for she felt that she had better not hear more. Immediately afterwards Adelaide and Caroline looked into the room, glanced round, without seeing Blanche, who was behind the door, and seeing no trace of the missing cloak were going away.

"Miss Adelaide Charlton's cloak to-night," said Caroline Grey, in a half whisper. "Mrs. Charles Wentworth's on Thursday. Fancy how absurd, and for mamma and Agnes to be so very amiable,—to leave us just at the very moment we wish to be left."

Blanche started, almost exclaimed, and stepped forward to show herself; but the rustling of her dress alarmed the two friends, and they rushed away laughing nervously. Blanche stood motionless; disgust and fear struggling in her breast. The next impulse was to follow Adelaide, and implore her to give up her schemes. Excitement caused a momentary energy both of body and mind, and she hurried through the passage and entered the hall, which was empty. There she paused to consider what was next to be done, for she heard Adelaide's voice in an adjoining room, where several people were talking. She sat down on a bench.

Eleanor came into the hall, and Blanche beckoned to her to come near, and said, "I think I know it all now. They have a plan for to-morrow, or the day after, when Mrs. Cuthbert Grey and Agnes will be out. Can that be possible?"

Eleanor turned quite white. "How did you know it? So soon! Yes, it may be. Oh! Blanche! Blanche!"

"I will stop it," said Blanche, in a hollow voice.

"How?"

"I will see Adelaide."

"But she is gone."

"No, not gone; only going.—Hark!"

"Yes, she is there; but there is not time; and she is wilful beyond imagination."

"Then my aunt —"

"No, no, we cannot; indeed, we cannot betray them."

"Good b'ye," said Mrs. Cuthbert Grey, approaching the hall. "The carriage is at the side entrance below, I think you said."

"Yes," replied Lady Charlton, who was following behind her: "it was more convenient for the luggage. You will not mind our passages, I hope; they are all well warmed."

They moved on, accompanied by Agnes and Caroline Grey, and Adelaide. Two or three gentlemen were with them, but not Lord Erlsmere.

"I must go with them," said Eleanor. "Will you come too?"

Blanche made a faint effort to move.

"No; you had better remain," continued Eleanor, watching her.

But Blanche stood up, and said "I will speak to Adelaide."

"Now? Impossible."

"But I must—I must," repeated Blanche, vehemently. "If she knows that I know, it must frighten her."

"Probably it might, if there had been time; but it is too late," and without waiting for Blanche's reply, Eleanor hastened to follow Mrs. Cuthbert Grey.

Blanche delayed for an instant to consider; but the instant seemed a year. The voices and footsteps grew fainter along the passages, and as they died away she became desperate, and, resolved to warn Adelaide at all hazards, rushed from the hall, as fast as her failing strength would allow, towards the side entrance.

She was met by Lord Erlsmere at the top of the staircase which led to the lower part of the house. "Lady Blanche!—here alone! I thought you were ill. I thought you had retired long since," he exclaimed.

Blanche only shook her head, and, without an answer, would have hurried on. The light of a lamp fell upon her features: their expression was wild and ghastly, and Lord Erlsmere, putting himself before her, said, "Excuse me; something very much is the matter: you are ill."

"Ill? yes, very," and Blanche tried to pass him, saying, eagerly, "They will be gone; I must see them: will no one tell them to stop?"

"Mrs. Cuthbert Grey's party, you mean," said Lord Erlsmere, looking at her steadily.

"Yes, Adelaide; I must see her; I must go to her."

"But not by yourself, in the cold. Pray, wrap a shawl round you, or let me take a message."

"No; I must go myself—no one but myself," exclaimed Blanche, more agitated than before. "There is not a moment to lose."

She was growing very faint, and Lord Erlsmere saw that her steps tottered. "You must take my arm," he said; and Blanche did as she was told, for she could scarcely stand alone.

"Come, come," she said, and she tried to draw him forward; and, as she spoke, Mrs. Cuthbert Grey's warning flashed upon his mind with horror. They reached the foot of the stairs; a cold draught rushed along the passage from the side entrance.

"This is death to you," exclaimed Lord Erlsmere; but Blanche laughed faintly, and said in a strange voice,

"Did you hear them? they are there; they are not gone."

Lord Erlsmere stopped at an open door. "This way," he said; "this is the best way," and Blanche mechanically followed him, and entered a small room.

"You must wait here," said Lord Erlsmere, assuming a tone of authority. "I will not take you into the night air."

Blanche sank upon a chair, and clasping her hands, exclaimed—"Fetch her; fetch Adelaide. Beg her to come. God grant she may listen."

Lord Erlsmere paused, irresolutely. "If you would be calm," he began gravely; "and could tell me your message."

"Bring her to me,—only let me speak to her; only bring her. Have you no mercy?"

Lord Erlsmere moved slowly to the door; opened it and listened. There was a confused sound of voices; then a momentary lull, and then the quick rattle of carriage wheels.

"They are gone," said Lord Erlsmere quietly, and in a tone of relief.

A fearful change passed over Blanche's face, and as blood gushed from her mouth, she sank down apparently lifeless.

CHAPTER XIX.

Two days after the ball! It was growing dusk; the bell had been rung for candles in the drawing-room. Lady Charlton rang, not for herself, but for Sir Hugh. She was with him alone. All the visitors were gone. Maude was sitting in Blanche's room, whilst Lord Rutherford was trying to sleep. One might have heard every footstep in the house, as the servants moved cautiously through the long passages; their slow tread in the distance, the one only sound disturbing the general stillness. It was very oppressive —very deathlike; and when the footman brought a small lamp, only just sufficient for Sir Hugh at his table, no fault was found. The dim light at the extremity of the large drawing-room seemed all that could be needed that evening.

"Dr. Lawson gone?" inquired Sir Hugh, looking up.

"Yes; a quarter of an hour ago. She has been asleep since."

"Asleep, has she? she will do very well then. She will get over it. I always thought so. These sudden attacks are just like what I used to have when I was a boy. Much more dangerous indeed mine were. I used to lie for hours"—

"Yes, yes; I remember," began Lady Charlton.

"No, my dear, begging your pardon, you can't remember, for you did not know me. I was going to tell you about them."

"You had better not move to your own room before dinner, Sir Hugh," interrupted Lady Charlton. "Let

Pearson settle you here; though, certainly, this room is dreadfully cold. I shall go up-stairs, and see how things are going on there. You wanted to read this, didn't you?" she added, opening a book with uncut leaves.

Sir Hugh seized it eagerly,—"The very thing! Where did it come from?"

"Mr. Johnstone sent it yesterday by the fly which took Miss Wentworth away."

"Oh! yes, to be sure. Johnstone and I were to have had a discussion upon it; and Rutherford too. Poor fellow! Well! I suppose we must wait; but she will get over it; there is no question about it. She is not half as ill as I was; and I don't see myself why every one should have left us in such a hurry, Miss Wentworth especially. A very fine girl she is; she looked beautiful the other night."

"Miss Wentworth went of her own accord," said Lady Charlton; muttering in an undertone, as she walked away, "the only symptom of good taste I have seen in her."

Sir Hugh finding himself without a listener, betook himself to his book, and soon afterwards, being persuaded by the discreet Pearson that the library was the best place for him on such a cold evening, retired, and left the drawing-room fire for his wife whenever she chose to return to it.

Lady Charlton walked up-stairs quietly, moved quickly along the gallery, opened the door of Blanche's room noiselessly, but still with energy; and looking around her as she entered, saw at one glance all that had been done, or was wanting to be done. It was little enough, but it was sufficient to occupy her for several minutes in giving whispered orders to the maid, and mute suggestions to Maude; and then she went and stood by the bedside, and looked upon Blanche's pallid face, now calmed by the half-repose of exhaustion. She was not a person in general to show much feeling; sometimes, it was said, that she had none; but this was an injustice. Perhaps the most unselfish of all her affections, was that which centred in her niece, and no one could have seen Blanche then, and thought of the intensity of happiness or misery that depended upon her life without deep emotion.

Whilst Lady Charlton was still in the room, Lord Rutherford came in, and stood by her. Tears had stolen down her cheek, almost unconsciously, before; but now she took her handkerchief and turned her face to the light, and whispered with a look of sympathy, "Poor child! we must be thankful she can sleep. Maude tells me she has been very quiet for the last hour."

"Yes," said Lord Rutherford, shortly; and he moved away without even going to look at Blanche, and sat down in an arm-chair by the fire.

Maude left her seat, and pointed to her mother to occupy it; but Lady Charlton could not sit and watch, except at night, when she was exerting herself to do what no one else was equal to. Her tears were gone now, and she was, as before, full of business, obliged to go and see about a hundred things; and after another compassionate glance at Blanche, she whispered to Maude to let the maid take her place when she came down to dinner, and departed.

Lord Rutherford and Maude were fit company for each other. They had no wish for sympathy. It might be that each felt there were depths of suffering, which no comfort, no comfort at least which they knew, could reach. Into the causes of a father's grief there is no need to search. They who have loved as Lord Rutherford loved—who have staked their last hope of happiness upon an earthly idol, and feel that they may be about to lose it, can alone tell the anguish of that awful suspense between life and death which language may not venture to describe.

But Maude had no life-long interests at stake. Whether Blanche lived or died, she had yet home, youth, talents, friends, and many of the allurements of the world, to brighten her prospect of the future. Yet there were feelings, selfish, perhaps, in some respects, but bitter and uncontrollable, which made the weary hours of that evening so desolate, that Maude would almost have been contented to exchange them for the earl's keen sorrow.

There is excitement in some griefs; we struggle with them manfully; the world's sympathy is with us, and we either conquer or die. There is hopeless monotony in others, and we bear them day after day, beneath a calm exterior; and years of endurance go by, and they are buried with us in our graves, and none guess the secret of their existence.

Maude had never experienced a bitter grief; her natural temperament was not open to it. She had never loved deeply, for she was slow to excite, and cautious, and criticising even when excited. There was within her a capacity of strong affection, but it had never been called forth. She did not think now that Blanche was going to die, but if she had thought so, it would scarcely have made her more desolate, for hers was the desolation of the mind as well as of the heart; the feverish, parched, dryness and barrenness of a spirit, which is for ever longing to rest upon some oasis of beauty and truth in the desert of life, and when it thinks that it has found the object of its desires, discovers that it has trusted to delusion. Maude had often been disappointed before she knew Blanche. She had often imagined perfection, and found imperfection; imagined truth, and discovered falsehood; and she had said to herself that she would never trust again, yet she had trusted—unconsciously; she had watched the light of Blanche's example, until something of clearness had spread itself over the darkness of her own mind; and the path of duty, and the way of truth, had opened themselves, though indistinctly, before her. But it was all dim now, all gloomy and doubtful as before. The light had been extinguished, for the thought of Blanche was mixed up with schemes and deceptions, irresolution and inconsistency; and Maude could better have borne a great offence, than a weakness which diminished her reverence.

What Eleanor, and Adelaide, and Mr. Wentworth might be doing or planning, she scarcely considered except as she believed them to be associated with Blanche. It was for her that she had been anxious and suspicious, and it was for her that she now grieved, as over one who had consented to take part in conduct unworthy of her education and her principles. The occurrences of the last few days, Blanche's wretchedness and disquietude, her uneasiness respecting the disposal of the living, and the reserve she had strictly maintained as to the cause of her distress afterwards; had convinced Maude that, in some way—how she did not know, and could not inquire—Blanche had, notwithstanding the warning given her, fallen into the snare prepared for her, and was pledged to exert her influence in Mr. Wentworth's favour. More than this she did not guess, but it was sufficient to make her feel that her trust in Blanche's stability of character was at an end; and to throw her back upon her own desponding doubts, whether any real firmness and goodness were to be found on earth: and now she sat by the fire, in the dusky twilight, thinking of Blanche, and knowing that she was very ill, and that even if she recovered this present attack, its consequences might eventually be fatal, yet not able to rouse herself to any feeling but that of gloomy depression at her own dreariness of heart.

It was a time when a person of a different character might have been roused to exertion, in the hope of putting a stop to anything amiss as regarded Adelaide; but Maude was a theorist. From the height of her philosophy she looked down upon Adelaide and Eleanor with contempt; and, if occasion required, she could have discoursed eloquently upon the indulged faults which led to the conduct she condemned; but it was not in her way to interfere with what she called other people's affairs, unless, as in the case of Blanche, urged by some peculiar personal interest. Silly persons would be silly, she knew, in spite of all she could say or do, and it was one of her favourite, comforting sayings, that the world must go its own way, and she must go hers; and in this spirit of indifferentism, she abstained from inquiring minutely into what was passing about her; contented with knowing that it was folly, and therefore beneath her notice. But we cannot thus cut ourselves off from our fellow-creatures, the members of one family, especially, cannot do so. By the inevitable decree of Providence, the sin of one will be felt in its punishment by the others; and woe be to us, if, whilst evil is working around us, we passively fold our hands and close our eyes, and say, it does not concern us.

There was one fact, however, which gave Maude great relief—Eleanor Wentworth was gone. She had left Senilhurst to return to Mr. Johnstone's, the previous day, upon the pretext of fearing to be in the way when every one was so anxious about Blanche. Maude smiled to herself at the apparent coldness of heart which could allow her to go at such a moment; but she was only too well pleased to be saved from the annoyance of her presence; and poor Eleanor departed with a weight upon her heart, which Maude, proud and unsympathizing though she was, could scarcely have forborne to pity, if she had known it.

Lord Rutherford and Maude sat together for nearly half an hour without speaking or moving. Then Blanche roused herself and seemed a little refreshed; but it was an effort to her to say anything. Maude took out her watch and pointed to the hour-hand, and observed to Lord Rutherford that it was dinner-time.

"Is it?" was the answer.

"Yes; I will send Barnes to take our place." She waited for him to assent, but he did not seem to hear her, and she could not speak to him again. There was something in his face, which repelled her. Maude looked round to see that everything was comfortable; she was a good nurse; continued ill health had taught her what illness requires; but perhaps she was a little fidgety; at least Lord Rutherford seemed to think so, for his eye followed her impatiently, as she went about the room.

"Then Barnes will come," she ventured to say, as she was going away.

"I will send for her when I want her," was his reply; he followed her to the door, closed it behind her, and returned to stand by Blanche's bed. Their eyes met, but his were turned away in an instant; she was lying uncomfortably, and he raised her, and placed her pillows right, and smoothed the coverlid, and moved the lamp; and afterwards poured out her medicine slowly, lingering over the action, and doing everything with a curious precision. When it was all finished, he brought his chair near to sit down, but that was a great effort, and he could not bear it; and leaning his head against the side of the bed, he cried.

Barnes looked into the room to know if he was coming down to dinner.

"No," he answered, at first; but Blanche made a little movement with her hand, as if begging him to go. He stooped down and kissed her, and said he would rather not, he was better with her.

But she whispered, "Please," and her soft eyes were fixed on him entreatingly; and submissively, without another word, he went down-stairs.

They were but a small gloomy party in the large dining-room; Sir Hugh prosed, and Lady Charlton found fault; and Maude wrapped a shawl round her, and complained bitterly of the cold; and the solemn men-servants moved round and round the table, offering dishes which scarcely any one, but Sir Hugh, tasted. Lord Rutherford ate nothing, though he took care to place enough on his plate to avoid the notice of Sir Hugh, who not only made a point of eating a good dinner himself, but considered it incumbent on his guests, as a matter of civility, to do the same.

"I am glad to hear your patient is improving," he said to Lord Rutherford, as the interval between the first and second courses allowed him to turn his attention to something besides fish and soup. "I have no doubt myself that it will all come right, and I have had a good deal of experience in such matters. The fact is, young people will be imprudent. We ought to have shut her up the night of the party."

"I urged it," said Lady Charlton, with some bitterness, "but no one would listen to me. Some people are destined to be Cassandras."

"Blanche came down stairs because she was told she might," said Lord Rutherford. The tone made even Sir Hugh feel that the subject had better be dropped. He turned to another part of the same topic—to introduce a new one was not easy.

He had been trying, he said, to reckon the numbers of the party exactly; but he was puzzled. Lady Charlton had forgotten to give him the answers to the invitations. Would Lord Rutherford help him to recollect?

The earl groaned audibly; and Maude came to his relief and said, "They might make a list after dinner."

"We were one gentleman short," said Sir Hugh; "it was very provoking. I meant to have had a secret—a surprise; nothing so pleasant, on these occasions, as a surprise."

Lady Charlton drew herself up, and her eyes sparkled; but she managed to say very gently, that she was not fond of secrets in general, and she supposed this could not be a very important one.

"Why not?—my dear?—why not?—why am I not to have important secrets; or rather, who has ever had so many as myself? When the late premier —he was my great friend—you remember," added Sir Hugh, appealing to Lord Rutherford; "when the late premier came"—a dish was placed before Sir Hugh —and the late premier was deferred for the moment.

"We shall hear from Adelaide to-morrow, I suppose," said Lady Charlton, hoping to get the conversation, if such it could be called, into her own hands. "I shall be glad to hear what she is doing at Oakfield. A first visit is always rather a trial."

"They must make up a very pleasant society at Oakfield," observed Sir Hugh. "I don't know any where a more agreeable, sensible woman, than Mrs. Cuthbert Grey; and very fine girls her daughters are. They, and their neighbours the Johnstones, and Mr. Wentworth"—he paused and looked round him significantly.

"Miss Wentworth, you mean," said Maude.

"No, my dear, excuse me; I know my own words —Mr. Wentworth. Mrs. Cuthbert Grey, Mr. and Mrs. Johnstone, and Miss and Mr. Wentworth will form a very agreeable society."

Maude involuntarily glanced at her mother. Lady Charlton's lips turned very white. She poured out a glass of water, and drank it quickly. No one spoke for some moments.

Then Lady Charlton said slowly, " You did not think it necessary to tell me that Mr. Wentworth was to be in the neighbourhood."

" No, my dear; no certainly, Frances, my love," began Sir Hugh, in a frightened tone, and his eyes glanced up and down quickly from his plate to his wife's face. " A little secret—nothing but a little secret—every one likes a little secret. Johnstone told me the other day, that young Wentworth was coming, before very long, to fetch his sister home; and I gave him—that is, I said if he happened—if he should just chance to arrive before the 29th, he was to send him over. A young man is always an acquisition—always welcome on such occasions. In fact," and growing bolder as he went on, his tone became rather that of defiance, " in fact, it was my wish—I thought it a compliment due; old friends you know, and his sister here, and in fact—in fact; but he did not come, my dear. So there is no harm done."

"It is not a matter of much consequence, I suppose," said Lord Rutherford, drily, and not raising his eyes to see the expression of the different faces. In that he was very unlike Lady Charlton. She could see in all directions, one might almost say, at once. Now, she saw opposite to her the twinkling intelligent eyes of one of the servants; the effect was that she replied, with an air of nonchalance, " Of course not. The coming or going of a young man like Mr. Wentworth can be of no consequence to any one."

It was provoking and humiliating to see the footman bite his lips to suppress a smile. Lady Charlton could have found it in her heart to order him out of the room.

"Hark! there is a ring at the bell," said Lord Rutherford. "It must be Dr. Lawson come again." He pushed aside his plate, and, without the thought of an apology, hurried away.

"It is not Dr. Lawson," observed Maude. "He said he should not be here till to-morrow."

"Some parcel or message from Cobham, I suppose," remarked Lady Charlton. "I wonder people can't find their way to the side entrance."

"I intend to make a fuss about it, my dear," said Sir Hugh. "It is a great deal too bad—an infringement upon private rights. I shall take some steps the very first opportunity. You may depend upon it, my dear, it shall be prevented. Let the Cobham people know," he added, speaking to the servant, "that if they continue to come to the hall door, I will—I will—I vow I will see what can be done to prevent them."

"It was not from Cobham, Sir Hugh," said the footman, respectfully, yet with a very meaning curl of the lip. "I heard the horse come up the other road."

Lord Rutherford returned, hurried and disappointed. There was no Dr. Lawson, but some message; he did not know what. He sat down again at the table. A silence of expectation followed.

"They are a long time bringing the message," said Lady Charlton. "Foster, go and see what is the reason."

Foster went to the door, and as he opened it received a note, just come, brought from Oakfield.

"From Oakfield?" said Lady Charlton, a little anxiously. "So late! nothing amiss, I hope."

The note was taken to Maude. It was strange—

generally self-possessed as she was—her hand quite trembled when she took it up.

"To ask how Blanche is, I suppose," said Lady Charlton. "I dare say they were anxious, and did not like to wait till to-morrow."

The seal was broken. Lady Charlton looked at the envelope. The feelings of a mother, usually so dormant within her, were awakened by a vague foreboding. "That idle child; how badly she writes! What does she say of herself, Maude?"

Maude looked up wildly.

"What does she say of herself, Maude? What is it?"

Still no answer.

Lady Charlton caught the note from her daughter's hand.

Maude started. "Mamma, pray wait one moment."

It was too late. Lady Charlton's eye had fallen upon the signature—Adelaide Wentworth, and she sank back almost unconscious.

Maude tossed the note to Sir Hugh, motioned the servants from the room, and turning to Lord Rutherford, said, as she went to her mother's assistance, "She is married! She is Adelaide Wentworth! God forgive her!"

Sir Hugh held the note in his hand, vainly trying to read it. "Adelaide what, my dear? Adelaide who? What is the matter? What has happened?"

"Let me go to him," said Maude to Lord Rutherford, giving a glass of water into his hand. "Mamma will be better in a minute. It is a note from Adelaide, sir," she said, speaking to Sir Hugh; "she has been doing extremely wrong. She ought to be ashamed of herself."

"But what has she been doing? What does she mean? Why does she call herself Adelaide Wentworth? Read the note: let me hear it."

"It is very short, and I can't make it all out," replied Maude, muttering to herself. "She thinks I shall help her. Intense, unutterable folly! The note is not worth reading," she said aloud; "but she is married, sir—that is what it is; married to Mr. Wentworth. She is Mrs. Wentworth."

Sir Hugh caught up the note again, raised himself with difficulty from his chair, drew the lamp towards him, and began stumbling through it:—

"My dear Maude,—I write in immense haste. You will be shocked, of course; but there was nothing else to be done, and no good in delay. You will break it to mamma. Papa, I hope and believe, will feel with me. You must try and understand this, for we trust to you to help us. We were married this morning, and are just starting for London. Make mamma forgive me, or I shall be miserable.

"Yours affectionately,

"ADELAIDE WENTWORTH."

Sir Hugh threw the note from him, with a fearful exclamation of anger. "Feel with them! I feel with them! Runaways! outcasts! Young Wentworth! Scoundrel! They shall never darken these doors—never! They shall never have a farthing from me. Write to them, Maude, and tell them. I feel with them, indeed! I vow your mother was right. Impudent scamp! my son-in-law! marry my daughter! marry into our family! and that woman! that Mrs. Cuthbert Grey!"

Maude had returned to her mother, who was slowly recovering; but as she heard the last words, she picked up the note from the floor, and showing the postscript, said, "Mrs. Cuthbert Grey is not to blame; that is her writing. 'I cannot attempt to comfort or excuse now; only believe that it was entirely without my knowledge.—A. G.' I believe that," continued Maude, speaking to Lord Rutherford. "For example's sake she would have been ashamed; but some one must have known it."

"The pleasant details will come to-morrow," replied the earl. "It is a perfect mystery to me; I can't believe it!"

"Poor mamma can't believe it either," said Maude, as Lady Charlton opened her eyes, and looked round her inquiringly.

Sir Hugh managed to hobble to the other side of the table. "Take her to bed," he said, almost tenderly. "There is no place like bed; let her go to sleep. Poor thing! poor thing! It is a horrid blow—most unexpected. Ring for some one, Maude, to help her up-stairs;" adding, as he bent down and actually kissed her, "we will talk of it to-morrow, my dear; but you had better go to bed. I shall write to them, and tell them they need not expect anything from me."

"Yes; my own room. Let me go, Maude," said Lady Charlton, faintly; and, whilst the bitterness of returning recollection rushed upon her as a flood, yet striving to keep up a proud composure. "Only let me never hear her name again; she has disgraced it."

CHAPTER XX.

A SAD and trying week went by at Senilhurst. Every one knows that the first moment of a great shock is not the worst; and the blow inflicted by Adelaide Charlton's marriage was no exception to the rule. It was not indeed one of those events which could be justly called a misfortune, by persons who regarded it in a worldly point of view. Mr. Wentworth was a gentleman by birth and education, and if he had no money himself, Sir Hugh was quite rich enough to assist him. He was also a person of unstained reputation, and, except in this one act of his marriage, of supposed high principle. Adelaide might undoubtedly have done worse. After all her levity and flirting, she might consider herself fortunate in not having been led into a much more undesirable engagement. This was what the world said; and in consequence, it gave Lady Charlton but a small portion of commiseration. But Lady Charlton herself did not view the subject in the same light. Her pride was wounded; and not in one point only. Family and fortune were inestimable advantages in the eyes of the world, and for them she would have sacrificed her daughter's happiness, and thought she was but consulting her best interests. But character, propriety—that indescribable delicacy and dignity which act as a shield from public remark—were scarcely less precious, because they were valued by those whose good opinion she was always seeking—the wise and good. It was their censure which Lady Charlton had dreaded when Adelaide flirted, and it was their censure which she feared now. A daughter's fault must in a measure recoil upon the mother who has had the charge of her education; and bitterly now did she repent the carelessness and blindness which had induced her to bring Adelaide very early into society, and give her almost unchecked freedom of thought and action. But it was for herself that Lady Charlton repented, not for her daughter. It was for the loss of her own position—her character as an excellent adviser, and a sensible guardian and friend. No one would henceforth appeal to her as a person whose cleverness, and judgment, and experience, gave value to her opinion upon education. One who had evidently made some great mistake in the training of her own child could not be competent to counsel others. Lady Charlton felt lowered. That is a feeling hard to bear—insupportable, except when we can carry it in humility to our Maker, and own it as our just meed and punishment. Lady Charlton could not do this. She struggled against it, and resolved to conquer it. No one should say that deception and imprudence, and the absence of womanly dignity, were sanctioned by Lady Charlton. As Adelaide's conduct was the subject of general remark, so also should be her mother's displeasure. Mr. and Mrs. Charles Wentworth might go their own way, and follow their own course; but they should not be admitted at Senilhurst. And Lady Charlton, as she made the determination, smiled scornfully, in the conscious stateliness of virtuous indignation.

The worst was over then; since, for once, almost the first time since their marriage, Sir Hugh and herself were agreed.

Both Adelaide and Charles had made a great mistake in supposing that Sir Hugh would support their cause against all opposition, if once they were married. Sir Hugh was a vain man; vain persons will do anything to assist those who choose to consult and flatter them, but they will almost infallibly turn against those who choose to act without them. Sir Hugh's vanity was as much piqued by Mr. Wentworth's neglect, as Lady Charlton's pride was by Adelaide's imprudence, and the mortification found its solace in the same revenge.

A short note was sent to Adelaide, telling her that since she had chosen a companion for life, for herself, she must, for the future, look to him, and to him alone; as her parents did not feel it consistent with their sense of right to sanction her conduct by receiving her at Senilhurst; and then, Sir Hugh and Lady Charlton felt themselves at liberty to announce their sentiments publicly, and hold themselves up to admiration, as martyrs to the cause of filial obedience and propriety.

All this appeared very inconsistent to Maude; and was of very little consequence to Lord Rutherford. In the eyes of Maude, Adelaide's foolish marriage was but the natural end of her previous foolish conduct. After the first moment, she almost wondered at herself for being startled at it. It was extremely wrong; disobedient and selfish; but, to her own knowledge, Adelaide had never been taught to be anything else. Her principles were the principles of the world; and Maude, keen-sighted and cool-judging, had long since discovered that it was in these they had both been nurtured from infancy. Lady Charlton might talk, and seemingly act religiously; she might praise daily services, give money to build churches, teach in parish schools, cultivate the acquaintance of men distinguished for learning and piety; but the stamp of the world was upon all.

Lady Charlton liked popularity; Adelaide liked admiration. Lady Charlton talked gravely, and believed she should be thought serious-minded; and

Adelaide laughed and chattered, and supposed she should be considered clever. Lady Charlton put a cross upon her prayer-book, because it was the fashion; Adelaide put an ornament upon her dress from the same motive. Lady Charlton went to church; Adelaide went to balls. Lady Charlton liked the occupation, and the attendant excitements, and the food for conversation, and the consciousness of being noticed; Adelaide liked the same.

Where was the difference between them? Maude could not see it. She thought her mother harsh, and she said so; and, in return, received a lecture upon female decorum, which, to a person whose offences were entirely on the side of stiffness, coldness, and fastidious reserve, became almost an absurdity.

A gulf, wider than ever, was opened between Maude and her parents; and, unhappily, the subject of difference could not be avoided. It was brought forward daily, by letters, visits, and suggestions, and all that marvellous want of taste which neighbours and acquaintances so often show in their strained efforts to be sympathetic.

"The pleasant details of the marriage," as Lord Rutherford had termed them, came in due time; certainly exculpating Mrs. Cuthbert Grey from any share in the plan, but throwing great blame upon one of her daughters. It was Miss Caroline Grey, who had entered into the scheme, and furthered it; and had actually been present at the marriage. Of course her mother was duly shocked and distressed; but no regret could undo the past. The intimacy between the two families must inevitably be stopped for the future; and Mrs. Cuthbert Grey's excuses and apologies were received and dismissed coldly, and with an openly avowed satisfaction on the part of Lady Charlton, as she spoke to Maude of the obstacle which would, in consequence, be interposed to the designs upon Lord Erlsmere, with whom Mrs. Cuthbert Grey had no acquaintance except through their meetings at Senilhurst.

Maude could not enter into such feelings; they were, to her, petty and unbecoming. She did not look at them deeply, as a person of high religious principle would have done; but she was disgusted. She longed to bury the subject for ever in oblivion. She heard that it was proposed for Mr. Wentworth, if possible, to enter the army, and she hoped he might be ordered abroad. That was what, in her heart, she most desired. Anything to remove them from her mother's thoughts; to prevent the constant, exasperating recurrence to the same unhappy topic. As regarded Adelaide, they had never been sisters in more than name; and Maude could not feign a regret at her loss, which she had no reason to feel.

Yet Senilhurst was very changed. Something was gone from it; not money, not rank, not any external advantage: but the life, the spring and motive of excitement, were absent. Adelaide had been an excuse for visits, parties, amusements; and though Maude professed not to like these things, she had been so long accustomed to them that she did not know how to do without them. She looked hopelessly round for some object, something to do or to care for, or at least to think of. Accomplishments and study were left her, and Maude had once boasted that with these she could never find existence wearisome. But they were not sufficient now. There was nothing soothing and satisfying in them. She might read, but to what purpose?—she might study, but where was the benefit, if reading and thought did but send her forth on a journey of intricate speculations, and distracting difficulties? Maude leaned upon her own mind, and it failed her.

That was the state of the outward world at Senilhurst, sharp, irritated, and gloomy. There was another, an interior world, which none saw, save those who watched in the sick room, where day by day, and hour by hour, the changes and flickerings of disease brought hope or despair to the heart of the Earl of Rutherford. There is, perhaps, no self-deception so universal as that which is discovered in our anxiety for those we love. If Lord Rutherford's case had been another's he would have been the first to discover all that he had to fear. But he was a father, watching over his only child, and who shall blame him, if as he saw Blanche partially regaining her strength, able to eat, able to be moved, able occasionally to converse, he flattered himself with the belief, that the illness was like many other illnesses, dangerous for a time, and requiring care; but giving no definite reason to doubt that she would, when the winter was over, regain her former health.

"Your cough is better, my love, to-day," he said, as he came to see Blanche when she was dressed, and sitting up for a few hours in her own room. "Barnes tells me that it has not been half as frequent as it was."

"I have scarcely coughed at all this morning," replied Blanche; "and I was only really disturbed by it once in the night; and then I think it was because the wind changed."

"But you have not eaten anything," said the earl, observing her untasted dinner placed on a tray near her.

"I have no fancy for anything just now. This being kept to one room takes away one's appetite; but I shall be better when I go out."

"Yes, of course. We must get you out the very first day we can, and then you will improve rapidly."

"Were there any letters to-day?" inquired Blanche, wishing to change the subject.

"One or two from Rutherford upon business."

"But any for me?"

Lord Rutherford hesitated a little. "Yes—no—there may have been. But, my love, if there should be, you know we agreed that you were not to trouble yourself about them."

"But I should like it, if I might. It would be an amusement to me," she was going to say, but she stopped;—the dread of something unpleasant which the post might bring came over her. She had been so ill,—utterly weak and helpless, that she had scarcely remembered anything till within the last few days; and even now, when she could try to recollect, it was difficult to bring her anxieties into a definite form. The last hour of excitement on the ball-night had left only indistinct memories of lights, and music, and crowds of people, and of an under-current of great physical and mental suffering to herself, and there was no one whom she could ask to make it clearer for her. Eleanor, she knew was gone, and there had been no letter from her; only inquiries for herself through the Johnstones. And there was also a rumour that Eleanor had returned to Rutherford; but how, or when, or why, no one would say. She was always entreated not to talk, and warned that her ultimate recovery depended upon her being kept perfectly quiet, but they who said this little thought how much worry of mind they were causing. "I am really much better to-day, dear papa," she continued, looking up at him with a smile, which it was almost impossible to resist; "and I should very much like to have my letters, if there are any. Did you say there were?"

"I think and I believe there may be. But, my love, I should be pleased if you would wait. I am sure it would be better, unless you were anxious—there is nothing you care particularly to hear of, is there?"

"I have been wishing very much to hear from Eleanor. If there was a letter from her I should be glad to have it." Her cheek flushed a little as she spoke; and the earl looked at her uneasily, and remarked that even the thought of the letters had done her harm, and he was sure she was much better without them. Blanche tried very hard to acquiesce willingly. She said if he wished it, she would not ask; she would wait till the next day: but a tear glistened in her eye, though she was ashamed of being so childishly weak. Lord Rutherford offered to read. He had not read the Psalms for the day to her; and he did so regularly now. It came quite as part of his duty as her nurse; and he was beginning to look forward to it as something quieting and refreshing. Blanche thanked him, and said she should like it very much, and he went to another table to fetch the Prayer-book, which had been moved away when the dinner was brought. Blanche wiped away her tears hastily, that he might not see it; but he turned round at the instant, and that peculiar look of sorrowful eagerness came over his face, which was always to be seen when Blanche was disappointed. He put down the Prayer-book, and came up to her instantly, and said, had she really any wish or fancy about the letters? he would fetch them for her directly if she had.

"Only for Eleanor's!" repeated Blanche. "I was very anxious to hear from her."

Lord Rutherford thought for a moment, and then he replied, "There is a letter from her, but I am afraid it might be worse for you than any others, because it would be so likely to excite you."

"I am more likely to be excited without it," said Blanche, "because I lie here and think so."

Again Lord Rutherford pondered for a moment, and Blanche watched his face, and read it; and laying her hand upon his arm, said, "Papa, you have something to tell me."

"Not about Miss Wentworth exactly—only about her brother and"—

"Adelaide," said Blanche hurriedly, and at the moment a veil seemed to be taken from the past, and it stood out clearly to view.

"You guess then," continued the earl, and a smile involuntarily began to play upon his lips; but it changed as he saw the expression of Blanche's face: it was that of extreme distress; and closing her eyes as if to shut out some painful vision, she sank back upon her pillow, and exclaimed, "Then it is over! Shall I ever be forgiven!"

A sudden thought, startling, unendurable, crossed the earl's mind; he repelled it, and sitting down by Blanche, said, "Will they be forgiven, you mean. I hope it may all turn out better than we expect; but it is a sad business." Blanche still kept her eyes closed; she was repeating something to herself; the anguish of her countenance was inexplicable: could it be that she was involved in such a secret? With her delicacy, simplicity, and refinement, was it possible that she could have been a party to the intended marriage? The earl shrank from the suggestion as if a serpent had stung him; but in a moment a flood of corroborative circumstances rushed upon him. At another time he would have been the first to consider prudence; but this suspicion, this possible taint upon the object of his idolizing affection, goaded him beyond endurance, and he exclaimed, "You did not know it? Blanche, my child, you could not have had anything to do with it?" For the first time since they had been together his tone was severe.

It fell with a painful shock upon poor Blanche, uprooting her unconscious trust in her own power over him. "I did not mean to do wrong. I acted for the best," she said, meekly. "Please do not be angry with me;" and at the mention of anger Lord

Rutherford started, as if he had been accused of some grievous crime, and the love which even when it lay dormant in his breast was the moving spring of his daily life, came back with a torrent of bitterness to reproach him. He told her that she was his hope, his treasure; the one only joy of his life; that it would be a sin to doubt her; and Blanche listened in fear, and prayed that the love which was fixed upon her, might in mercy find a surer resting-place, and then humbly asked if she might tell him all that she had done.

It was a tale soon repeated, soon understood, and Blanche was happy when she heard her father's whispered blessings; but she did not discover how much cause he had for thankfulness himself. She did not remember the load which must be taken from his heart by the knowledge of the cause of her depression; and she did not perceive the reverence which her firmness and consistency of character inspired. Lord Rutherford thought little of religion himself, but he could now appreciate it as a principle in others; and with Blanche he would have shrunk from the careless bestowal of his patronage, as from an injustice against a charge entrusted to him.

Silence followed: the peaceful silence of hearts which are one in affection and confidence. "Blanche," said the earl at length, "it was excitement which made you so ill. Your aunt says you ought not to have come down-stairs, the night of the ball."

Blanche looked up at him and smiled. "Ought I not? but you like to see me cheerful."

She meant nothing particular; but he repeated the last word quickly. "Cheerful! who told you I thought about it?"

"Your voice, your manner." She hesitated; they were treading upon dangerous ground.

"When? the day that I gave away the living?"

"Every day, and always," and involuntarily there was an accent of sadness in Blanche's tone. Another pause came, not happy and peaceful as the former.

"Blanche," said the earl, again, gravely, "you must not try to read my thoughts."

Blanche tried to smile as she kissed him, and answered, half reproachfully, "How can I help it, when you have given me the key to interpret them?"

Alas! for the transitory nature of earthly peace. Those few sentences had re-awakened the bitterness of the earl's remorse and anxiety. It was he then who had caused her illness; he, who by the very intensity of his solicitude for her happiness, had compelled her to an exertion which might be fatal.

The curse he had so long dreaded had fallen upon him, though in another form, at last.

CHAPTER XXI.

It was the bright spring time at Rutherford Parsonage. The smooth, neatly trimmed lawn, the flower-bed gay with anemones, auriculas, and polyanthuses—the first fresh green buds upon the trees, were all telling of the genial inspiriting influence of a morning in May. In a light hand-carriage, which had been drawn into one of the most sunny walks, reclined a lady, whose grey hair, sunken, worn cheeks, dim eyes, and wrinkled brow, would at a distance have given the idea of much greater age than could be traced on a nearer approach. Her features were good—once they might have been handsome, for their outline was very striking; but there was a strange, stony, impassive look in the eyes, which gave in general a cold, even vacant look to the countenance. Only, at times, a flash, as of some returning brightness, some gleam from past memories, flitted over it; and then, for an instant, it was beautiful with intellect; but the gleam gone, and the set features returned to their former listless gravity, and the helpless hands, and the querulous voice, seemed but the fit accompaniments of an age of disease and dreariness.

"It is pleasant to-day, dear mamma," said Eleanor Wentworth, bending over her mother's chair: "don't you see how forward the flowers are?"

Mrs. Wentworth looked round for a moment, and said, "Go on, into the shade."

"But this is the warmest spot, mamma," continued Eleanor; "and you know we are expecting

Blanche, and she must not go into the shade. You will like her to come and see you; wont you?"

Mrs. Wentworth looked up quickly and said, "Yes, we must make her happy, for he doesn't treat her at all well. It is very sad. Tell your father I want to see him."

"Papa will come presently," said Eleanor, her lip quivering; "but we will go on, dear mamma, if you like it, into the shade."

"Yes, that will be best; go on;" and they went on.

Dr. Wentworth was standing at his study window. He perceived them and came to them. "It is pleasant to see you out to-day, my love," he said, addressing his wife. "You are all the better for it, I am sure." Unconsciously his tone was that of a father speaking to a child; and there was something of a child's simple trusting love in Mrs. Wentworth's way of putting her hand into his, and telling him to keep close to her, and not to let them go too fast.

Eleanor left her mother's side, and came round to her father. "Are the letters come?" she asked, in a very low voice; but, low though it was, it reached Mrs. Wentworth's ear.

"Letters?" she repeated; "give them to me; we must answer them. We have a great deal to do. We had better go in and answer them. Tell Jones to stop."

"Yes, presently, dear mamma; presently, my love," said Eleanor and Dr. Wentworth, in one breath. "We will go in presently."

"But," continued Dr. Wentworth; slipping a packet of letters into Eleanor's hand, "I should like you just to be drawn round the orchard once; and Eleanor can go and fetch my hat." Mrs. Wentworth sank back again in her chair, and Eleanor, carefully concealing the letters, went into the house. Nearly ten minutes elapsed before she returned, and then her eyes were red with crying; but she kept her face steadily averted from her father, until her mother's attention was occupied by what she thought was a new shrub. Then, as they stopped to examine it, Eleanor walked on a few paces with Dr. Wentworth, and said: "He must not see her; I am afraid. It would do her great harm!"

Dr. Wentworth tore off a twig from a tree, and casting it from him, replied, "Let him go. I had only one wish in his seeing her."

"It would break his heart," said Eleanor.

"It might sober him for life," replied her father.

"He will not come without Adelaide," said Eleanor, taking advantage of a narrow part of the walk still to walk a little before the carriage, and side by side with her father.

"Then he will not come at all," was the bitter reply. "Your poor mother shall never, with my consent, be harassed by the sight of her."

"Eleanor," called out Mrs. Wentworth, in a shrill, plaintive voice, "I wish you would inquire about the letters. There wont be any time to answer them, and you know I must go up to the castle this afternoon. She is not so well, you said. I promised I would go."

"Lady Blanche is coming here, dear mamma," said Eleanor, with a particular stress upon the name. "You know she has had a bad cough, and is very ill; and she is coming to wish you good b'ye before Lord Rutherford takes her to the sea-side for change of air."

"Ah! yes, I forgot," and Mrs. Wentworth looked at her husband wonderingly. "I don't know how it is I forget so. I know they told me she had been ill. She has been so a long time, has not she?"

"All the winter," answered Dr. Wentworth. "She broke a blood-vessel when she was at —" a rapid, cautionary glance from Eleanor stopped him, and he finished the sentence, "when she was away."

"And they did not think she would live then," continued Eleanor, not allowing a moment's time for a question; "but she was better after a time, and they brought her to the castle; now she is going away for change again."

"A long change," said Dr. Wentworth, gravely. "It is a cruel thing in those doctors. Poor child! why not let her die at home?"

Eleanor was silent, but she drew back from her mother's chair, and walked for some paces alone.

"One more turn, my dear, round the orchard," said Dr. Wentworth, arranging his wife's cushions, and giving a sign to the gardener to go on. Then he rejoined Eleanor. "I shall write to Charles by to-day's post: you may write too, if you will. I don't want him to feel himself cut off; but he must not come here."

"It seems very hard," said Eleanor.

"Hard!" and Dr. Wentworth paused, impatiently, in his walk. "Look at *her;*—look at your poor mother; and then say who has been treated hardly?"

"Yes," said Eleanor, speaking in a low, crushed voice; "but she would be the first to forgive, if she could."

"And I forgive, too," said Dr. Wentworth, solemnly. "God forbid that I should not; even as I hope to be forgiven myself. It is not from anger that I say he must not come. If he were alone I might risk it; but if he insists upon bringing that —"

"Papa, dear papa," said Eleanor, entreatingly.

"You are right; you are right, replied Dr. Wentworth; "we must be charitable. If she were sorrowful—if she could feel what she has done—I could be so easily. But she is a flirt; a cold, heartless flirt;" he repeated. "She was so before she married; she is so still."

"Yes, that is the worst of all," said Eleanor, with a heavy sigh; "and one cannot help pitying Charles all the more."

"A soldier in a foreign land," continued Dr. Wentworth, "with a wife whom he must despise; feeling himself scorned by her family, and having utterly shipwrecked the happiness of his own; he may well be wretched."

"He is very wretched — very miserable," said Eleanor.

"But what could he expect better?" pursued Dr. Wentworth. "What has any man a right to expect when he trusts his happiness to a woman who could behave like Adelaide Charlton?"

"People may do worse things than Adelaide has done," said Eleanor, sorrowfully, "and not be blamed half as much."

Dr. Wentworth looked at Eleanor kindly, for he understood her. "My poor child!" he said, and as he put up his hand to wipe away a tear, he added, "I can take infinite blame to myself. I was too secure, too certain that all was right. I allowed him to have his own way, and I shut my eyes to his faults. Your poor mother was the only person who saw him truly. But one thing I can be thankful for—that he was saved from entering holy orders. To have induced him to be a clergyman, and then to have discovered his unfitness, would have been a misery to me for life."

Mrs. Wentworth's voice was just then heard, in a querulous accent. She was wondering where they were gone; why they did not come and walk by her side; and, as they hastened to her, she burst into tears, and said it was a miserable day; every one neglected her.

Eleanor pinned her shawl comfortably, and settled her cushion again, and as the sound of carriage-wheels, and of a bell, were heard at the entrance, exclaimed, "Hark! there is Blanche. Dear mamma, you will like to see her for one minute."

"I don't know—I don't want to see any one. Why do they bring her down here? Isn't she very ill?" said Mrs. Wentworth, her eyes moving rapidly from side to side; and then, in a startled voice, she added, "Does he come with her?"

"Blanche will come alone, if you like it," said Eleanor; and going round to her father, who was walking a little behind, she whispered, "You must keep Lord Rutherford. Blanche will only stay a very few minutes, dear mamma;" she added, returning to her mother, and trying to occupy her attention whilst Dr. Wentworth went to receive the earl. "You know she is scarcely allowed to stand still at all out of doors; and she is so very soon tired."

"Yes,—yes, I know," replied Mrs. Wentworth, and murmuring to herself, she added, "she is going; it is all best; there is no care there."

The garden gate opened, and closed again. Eleanor looked round.

"Are they coming?" said Mrs. Wentworth, growing excited. "Make me look neat, Eleanor; you didn't dress me properly. The earl always makes remarks."

Eleanor bent down her head, and busied herself with her mother. It might have been that she could not bear to watch the feeble footsteps with which Blanche, supported by her father, moved slowly along the walk. Dr. Wentworth and Maude Charlton were behind her; but as they drew near to Mrs. Wentworth, the earl stopped and gave up his place to Maude.

"Blanche, Blanche!" repeated Mrs. Wentworth, with an effort at thought. "Is she like her mother?"

Eleanor made no answer; for Blanche was standing by her. One silent kiss she imprinted on her forehead, and then leading her round to the front of Mrs. Wentworth's chair, she said, "Mamma, it is Lady Blanche Evelyn, come to wish you good b'ye."

Mrs. Wentworth looked up with an unmeaning start of surprise, and as her eye caught the pale brow, and dark, glittering, sunken eye, and the hollow cheek—which were all that could be seen of Blanche's sweet face—a smile of pleasure lit up her own features, and she said hurriedly, "I was coming to you to-day. Will he be out, and shall we have an hour to ourselves?" Dimness gathered over Blanche's eyes, and her voice was choked.

"It will not do," said Eleanor; "but I thought when she saw you it might be different."

"Will you not know me?—will you not wish me a safe journey? Dear Mrs. Wentworth, I am Blanche Evelyn;" and Blanche bent down that her face might be more clearly recognised. Mrs. Wentworth caught her hand, and looked at her sternly and fixedly.

"Yes," she said; "yes, I know you. You are going."

"Going where we shall meet again, I trust," said Blanche, calmly.

A gleam of intelligence brightened the vacant face. Mrs. Wentworth smiled, and raising the hand of which she still retained the use, to Blanche's head, she gently stroked her forehead, as a mother might that of a petted child; and said, "God bless and keep you, my dear, and bring you back better. And Eleanor," she added, firmly, " give her her mother's picture—she will like it."

It was the utmost effort of remaining intellect. Mrs. Wentworth's hand dropped, and her head sank back; and when Blanche gave one parting kiss, a wondering stare was all that met her gaze.

CHAPTER XXII.

GLORIOUSLY beautiful was the splendour of the setting sun, as it slowly sank to rest that evening behind the steep hills which closed the ravine at the foot of Rutherford Castle. Far over hill and valley streamed the flood of its golden rays; and the rugged mountains in the distance were wrapped in a veil of glittering mist, whilst their peaks caught and transmitted from point to point, the light which they gathered from the glowing skies. And nearer, where the radiant colouring of the higher hills had melted into the purple shadow of rock and wood, there still gleamed a faint path of light upon the deep-flowing stream, winding its way ever and onwards, without pause or rest, like the course of that awful river of Time which, lit by the reflection of Heaven, is carrying us all to Eternity.

The Earl of Rutherford walked alone on the terrace of the castle. Alone! that word suffices to tell the tale of his misery. What matter to him, that the gorgeous sun-set illuminated a princely domain which owned him for its lord? What matter that, as far as the eye could reach in hamlets, and villages, and towns, and the remote recesses of the distant hills, wherever his name was heard, men bent before it with respect, and envied him his greatness and his power?—he was alone; and Blanche was dying.

It is long before we allow the meaning of that word to force itself upon our minds. It had been long before Lord Rutherford would own to himself the realization of the fear which haunted him from the first moment of his child's illness. But it was all clear now—all true and vivid. There was death written in the hectic colour of her hollow cheek—in the glassy brightness of her dark eye—in the burning touch of her long fingers; and the quick, short cough which came but for a moment to leave behind it the echo of a funeral knell.

Blanche was dying. She might linger—she had lingered—from day to day, from week to week—no great change marking the progress of disease; sometimes apparently better, able to work and read—sometimes exhausted and feverish; no one day exactly like, or widely differing from, the other. But the end was certain. It was in vain that physicians gave flattering hopes, and friends related wonderful recoveries. There was one fact to which no one who watched Blanche constantly could be blind—she did not improve. Every week something was taken from her strength; every week something was given up which she had before been able to enjoy. The incipient disease, which might have been warded off at first by care, had received a fatal impulse on the night of the Senilhurst ball; and the changes, though imperceptible at the moment, were nevertheless very rapid.

For a time Lord Rutherford had flattered himself that the weather was in fault. When snow lay upon the ground, in the month of January, he looked forward to the spring for her recovery; and when the spring came, and the east winds blew keenly, he said that they could expect no real amendment till the summer. A warm summer in England and a winter abroad would quite set her up. But summer approached, and the weather was unusually favourable; and still, though Blanche might rally for a few days, there was no real progress: and then the earl looked more careworn, and said less; only he thought she would be better at Rutherford, and to Rutherford they prepared to go.

That at least was a satisfaction to Blanche. She pined for home, with an indefinable, eager longing. She did not say to herself that she should be well there; perhaps she did not in her heart think so: but in her sad moments—the hour of weakness, both of body and mind—which are the greatest trial of such diseases, she fancied that it might at least bring her a respite.

The air of Rutherford, the lovely views, the peculiar comforts of her own rooms, the interests which were to be found in the village, and, above all, the hope of seeing Eleanor, and returning to the friendship, which, though interrupted, had never been lost—all gave a charm to the prospect of return. If she could be at Rutherford again, she felt that she might live; and the thought sent a bounding thrill through her veins. For life is very pleasant to the young, and Blanche had just tasted of its enjoyments.

Then came the departure from Senilhurst—the hurry of preparation—the unavoidable excitement—the last thoughts, and last farewells. Blanche could not escape them. She was sorrowful and depressed, without apparently sufficient cause; and they told her it was weakness—that she would be a different person at Rutherford, and would return again to Senilhurst quite well: and she smiled and said, she would not call it a real good b'ye,—she did hope to come again very soon; and she had left a box and some books to be kept for her. She begged her aunt would write to her, and say how she managed without Maude. It was so very, very kind to spare Maude. It would be such a comfort till she was better; but she would not keep her a day longer than was necessary.

And Lady Charlton struggled against her rising tears, and kissed her tenderly; and Sir Hugh waved his hand, as she was assisted down the steps—and she was gone.

It was two days' journey from Senilhurst to Rutherford; when they had travelled before it was but one. Then Blanche was able to enjoy the novelty of the road, and to look forward with expectation, and hopes of pleasure: now she was laid on cushions, too tired to speak or think. When they had left Rutherford, she had bounded down the staircase, eager to be useful and kind to every one: now she was lifted in her father's arms, and carried to her own apartments, fainting.

That night, the night of their arrival at home, the earl first felt that she would die. And that night, also, as Blanche laid her head upon her pillow, she prayed that she might be taught to die. Nearly a month had passed since, and another change had been proposed. The air of Rutherford was thought too keen; and a removal to the sea-coast was considered desirable. It was the advice of a first-rate London physician: the earl and Blanche acquiesced without a word of objection; but when the physician was gone, they looked at each other and said, "He may be right: it is of little consequence, so that we are together." That was their one thought—that they might be together—that the earl might sit by her, and raise her when she wished for change of posture, and bathe her forehead when she was exhausted, and read to her when she was able to listen, and mark the hours for her daily drives—her food—her medicine; and that Blanche might thank him in whispers, and smoothe his hair, and press his hand, and lift her eyes to his, with a smile on her pale lips, and a prayer of unutterable thankfulness in her inmost heart, for the mercy which in leading her to death, was leading her father to heaven.

Lord Rutherford was said to be determined in his opinions, rigid in his self-formed principles, proud of his influence, and exacting in his demands upon the submission even of his equals. He might have been, he was all this and much more: haughty, indifferent, unsympathising, selfish; as that man must be who has reached the middle of life without contradiction or self-examination: but he was honest-minded. Whatever were the errors of his practice or his belief, he was no self-deceiver: and from the fatal moment when he stood by the inanimate body of his wife, and felt the conviction that he had been the murderer of her peace, if not of her life, he had carried with him a goading thought of self-reproach to shield him, as by a secret spell, from the intoxication of earthly splendour. He had lived with Blanche now for months only; to him they seemed years,—since he could not realize what life had been without her; and in that time, secretly, and without word, or argument, or entreaty, new principles and motives of conduct had been gradually stealing into his heart. He scarcely knew it himself; he did not understand the power which influenced him; and, when he thought of it at all, he supposed that it was a father's natural affection for a child like Blanche; and so at first it was. When Lord Rutherford began to read to Blanche and talk about things which interested her, and take trouble for the poor, he did it merely because it was her fancy, and it gave him pleasure to listen to her remarks, and hear her thanks; he did not care for the subjects in themselves; and satisfaction like this was very unreal, and to a person less true might have been very deceptive. But Lord Rutherford was too clear-sighted to believe that he resembled

Blanche, or was actuated by her motives, because he was beginning to approve what she approved. He would even have been annoyed if such a thought had been suggested: for he was proud and self-confident, and Blanche was to him only "as a very lovely song of one that hath a pleasant voice," exquisite to the senses, but not reaching the heart.

But they were to part. The decree had gone forth, to all human knowledge absolute and irreversible. She was to be taken from him; it might be in a few weeks, it might be in a few months, it could scarcely be—in a year. And whither was she going? Lord Rutherford had no doubt in his reply. When the thought first came, as he looked at his angel-child, when she had fallen asleep whilst he was reading to her, her fingers clasped in the earnestness of the prayer with which she had followed his words, and the brightness of heaven's peace resting upon her fair young face, he knew that she was safe. The voice of a messenger from above could scarcely have increased his confidence. And he said to himself then, and many times afterwards, that she was too good for this world. He said it to Dr. Wentworth when he came to see her; he wrote it to Lady Charlton, and he fancied that it gave him comfort. But did it do so?

In the anguish of the long nights, as he lay awake listening for every sound, conjuring up visions of dread, and knowing that the very worst which might be sent to startle him could only be the anticipation of an inevitable certainty—his past life rose up before him. The carelessness of his boyhood—the open irreligion of his manhood—the cold hardness and insensibility of his advancing age; all marked by certain positive offences, and mingled into one huge mass of sin, by the misty memories of his half-forgotten offences. If the God whom he professed to worship was a God of mercy; if in calling Blanche from an evil world, He was but calling her to early happiness; was He not also a God of judgment? and could the innocent and the guilty, the holy and the unholy, hope to meet again in the same heaven?

It was a question which, when once suggested, could not be put aside. It followed him by day as well as night; it intruded into his transient intervals of peace, when Blanche seemed more at ease, and he was able to interest and amuse her; it pursued him, as a spectre, in his solitary moments, and he could not speak of it, or find relief in human sympathy; for he had lived to himself, until the very thought of unreserve was abhorrent to him. Yet misery did not make him cold and harsh; that could not be when he was watching over Blanche. The very tone of her voice was soothing and softening to him, and sometimes a strange, momentary hopefulness crossed his mind, when she in any way alluded to the future, as if even for him there might also be pardon and rest. But it could not stay, for was he not under punishment at that very hour? Had not the curse of his early sins followed him through long years of dreariness; and had it not fallen now, chiefly by his means, upon the only being whom he had left on earth to love?

And with these thoughts Lord Rutherford walked alone upon the terrace of his castle.

CHAPTER XXIII.

Blanche watched the sunset also from her sofa, which had been drawn near the window that she might enjoy it. Maude was with her; she was her constant nurse in Lord Rutherford's absence, and Blanche had no longer reason to dread her cousin's moodiness and sharpness. Soon after the announcement of Adelaide's marriage, Maude's manner had quite changed. Blanche thought it must be from pity: but Maude's sympathies were not easily called forth, even by illness; and many times before, when Blanche had needed it, she had withheld it. Neither was pity the proper term for Maude's devoted attention. It was too silent and thoughtful, as if offered to a superior; and Blanche, in her humility, would not have supposed it possible that Maude could look upon her in such a light. The firmness of character she had shown, and which was made known to Maude by conversation with Lord Rutherford, had produced an effect which Blanche would never have imagined; for Maude could not be brought to confess that she had suspected unjustly; and if, from that time, she pondered more deeply upon the principles by which Blanche was actuated, and oftener asked herself whether they might not, after all, contain the truths for which she was herself seeking, no one was allowed to guess the thoughts that were working in her breast, except by her actions.

They were reconciled without explanation; but Blanche many times wished herself strong enough to bear a recurrence to those painful scenes; and

Maude's conscience, when it reproached her for false shame, urged her at least to make reparation in deed, by insisting upon accompanying Blanche to Rutherford, and nursing her during her illness. This was no act of self-denial; for self-denial, except when it involved some tangible good to others, was not part of Maude's creed of duty. But she knew that she might be of use, and thought it probable that she might be a comfort; and, for herself, the fascination which had drawn her towards Blanche in health, acted with tenfold intensity in illness.

To be with her was to find rest, at least for the hour—rest from the despairing search after truth by the light of her own intellect, in the calm, abiding faith, of one who had received and followed it from infancy.

Yet they were mournful days for Maude; this one especially had been trying. The farewell visit to Mrs. Wentworth had been a greater effort than Blanche was equal to, and she had suffered much in consequence. In itself it must, at all events, have been very painful, and the pain was increased by the recollections which it excited, and which Blanche could not entirely overcome; although she had been assured again and again, by Dr. Wentworth himself, that gratitude rather than reproach was due to her. Blanche tried to believe that she had acted rightly; she did believe it in her heart; yet the sight of Mrs. Wentworth's vacant countenance, the wreck of all that had once been so noble, was a fearful shock. The question would arise, in spite of herself—Had she not in some way been instrumental in causing it? And it was not till after a visit from Dr. Wentworth, who came to her in the course of the afternoon, that she could in any degree recover her former composure.

Still she did not regret the exertion she had made. It had been her own wish to pay the last respect that might be in her power to her mother's early friend; and Eleanor had entered into the idea, with the faint hope that the excitement might produce a favourable effect upon Mrs. Wentworth.

Maude had urged delay. She said that Blanche was leaving Rutherford for a time only, and might return better able to bear the interview. But Blanche would not allow herself to trust to this hope. Hope, indeed, it could scarcely be called. She knew her own symptoms too well, and could read the countenances of those about her too truly to admit of hope. Her daily prayer, her daily lesson, now, was not to desire it.

We may believe that there is always one last trial to be endured, one last grace to be acquired by those whom God visits with lingering illness. They to whom life is fraught with care, and the thought of the grave full of the rest for which they sigh, can little know the awfulness of that moment which first brings the young and the hopeful in sight of death. Blanche's short life had been burdened with many disappointments, many anxieties; and, in the time of health, she had often thought of the blessedness of an early removal from temptation, and believed that she could welcome it. The blessing was sent, and she trembled at it. It was not strange. She did not know till then how dear life was to her; she did not know how she valued the familiar faces of those even whom she supposed did not suit her; she did not understand how much she clung to sights, and sounds, and associations, and memories, which came and went almost without notice, but which constituted the amusement of existence. She did not know how precious her father's love was, how she rested upon it and trusted to it for protection. The prospect of death at a distance, and the actual waiting for its approach, were very different.

She gazed upon the sunset now, with Maude sitting beside her, and supporting her that she might be better able to watch it; but they were both silent. Blanche's memory had travelled back to the evening when she first saw that glorious view; when her father welcomed her to her home: and Maude's thoughts had wandered onwards into the dark future of earth and the dim awfulness of eternity.

Maude was the first to break the silence. "One should like to follow it," she said; "to know where it goes. One cannot imagine it still lighting up this world."

"I should be sorry to realize that it did," answered Blanche. "Sunset has always been my most vivid idea of heaven."

"It is too sad for heaven," said Maude. "Even as a child, one felt its sadness."

The eyes of Blanche filled with tears. "It ought not to be sad," she replied; "so beautiful it is in itself, and with hope to make it more so. If one did not regret this world, it would be joyful."

"Yet there is little enough here to tempt one to regret," said Maude.

"Do you think so?" asked Blanche, earnestly, and with a touching, child-like simplicity, as if really wishing to hear Maude's answer.

It was not given directly. Maude's eyes dwelt upon the crimson light, which, although the sun had sunk behind the hills, still flooded the western horizon, spreading itself far and wide, till it melted imperceptibly into a faint ethereal blue. "It is glorious, most glorious," she exclaimed; "but it is too much; one cannot grasp it."

"And one can grasp earth," said Blanche, with a sigh.

"Grasp it, and find it ashes," replied Maude, bitterly; "some do, at least; not you, Blanche."

"I have had a very happy life," said Blanche; "every one has been very kind to me. I should like to thank them."

Maude turned round quickly; "Now do you mean? Because you are going away?"

"Not to-night; I am so tired: but I should like every one to know that I have thought about them. If you come back again, Maude, will you tell them so?"

"You must tell them yourself, then, dear child," said Maude, kissing her.

Blanche looked earnestly in her face, and answered, "I should like to say things out plainly to you; but I cannot; if you do not understand."

"I do—I do understand," replied Maude, her voice sounding hollow with the effort to appear calm.

"I shall not come back," said Blanche. "Even papa does not really think so; and I should like to tell you now what to do with some of my things—my books, and pictures, and ornaments. I think about them a good deal, and I don't wish to do so; and if I might say to you what I should like to have done with them, it would be off my mind."

"But not to-night, dearest," said Maude.

"No; perhaps not to-night: but to-morrow; the first thing, I should wish it. You see, Maude, I may not have very much time before me, though papa and Dr. Granville say the sea-air will do me good; and if I could settle about it all, and say good b'ye to every one, and thank them, I should not have such wandering thoughts; at least I hope not."

Maude bent her head upon the sofa; her tears were uncontrollable. Blanche put her arm round her, as she had sometimes been wont to do in her days of health, and speaking quite calmly said,

"You must not fret about me, Maude, and fancy I am worse because I speak so; I only do it because of something Dr. Wentworth said yesterday. When he has come to see me lately he has been very kind, and I have been able to talk to him; and he understands—he knows what I feel."

"About being ill?" asked Maude.

"About death!" said Blanche. She waited for a moment, and closed her eyes as if praying mentally; then she said, "If I were very good, I should not be afraid; but I cannot quite help it."

"No one can help it, I should think," replied Maude.

"Yes, indeed, some persons can: but Dr. Wentworth says they are generally persons who are older and have suffered more; and you know, Maude, I have always had some one to depend upon, and take care of me; and—but that is wicked—because I have no faith," she added.

"If I were like you," began Maude, quickly; "and had lived the life you have—"

Blanche interrupted her; "Maude, dear, you will not say things which vex me, now we have so little time to be together. But I don't think the fear I have is so much about all I have done wrong; there is such great, great hope of forgiveness. But, even then, it is so awful, so lonely; if some one could go with me—papa, or Mrs. Howard, or you. I have never been alone all my life. I wonder what it will be like. Oh, Maude, can you think?" she covered her face with her hands, as if shrinking from the thought; when she looked up again all was peaceful. "It is over now," she said, heaving a sigh of relief; "it comes and goes—the dark hour, as Dr. Wentworth calls it. But he says I shall feel it less if I pray: and, Maude, you will do to-morrow what I asked? because I am to put away my cares for this world, even the very little ones, and then there will be nothing to come between me and my Saviour."

"There can be very little now," said Maude, tenderly.

Blanche shook her head. "Ah! Maude, you don't know. I did not know till lately; but you will hear all I have to say, and promise to do it all; will you not? and now, please, if papa will come and read to me, I should like to go to bed."

Maude went to call the earl; and, whilst the last gleam of sunlight was fading away, they knelt together and joined in the few short prayers, which were all that Blanche could bear after that day of excitement. Then Maude kissed her, and said, "Good night," and the earl lifted her in his arms and carried her to her room.

CHAPTER XXIV.

MAUDE remained by herself, thinking. At other times she could philosophize upon general principles, abstract theories, the ultimate destinies of mankind; but there was only one question now for her consideration—the question which must sooner or later be brought before us all—what was to be the ultimate destiny of each individual soul—of Blanche, of herself?

How she longed then for Blanche's simple faith! the vividness with which she must realize all that belonged to the unseen world, to be able to say so quietly and confidently, "There will be nothing then to come between me and my Saviour."

It was true, actual, as if she had spoken of an earthly friend. And even her fears were natural, neither exaggerated nor excited, only the awe which one so young, and tender, and helpless, could scarcely fail to experience in the first near prospect of entering upon a new existence.

It was very strange to Maude, a problem she could not solve, for it was not merely the result of education, the having been taught to believe. She had been taught also; but what to her was an idea, solemn and important, yet still only an idea, was to Blanche an all-absorbing reality. Some real difference there must be between them; and that not a difference which might safely be borne with, like any other diversity of taste or sentiment—death was a fact which admitted of no "halting between two opinions." If, in order to support the prospect of it, calmly, a life like that of Blanche was necessary, then Maude's dreamy, philosophical speculations and indolent practice, must be dangerous. Maude's inherent energy of mind was aroused by the thought. Hitherto, it had been spent in the study of abstruse questions; now, it was directed to practice. And she had full leisure for consideration—for the twilight sank into darkness, and the darkness was exchanged for the brilliancy of moonlight, and still she was alone with her own thoughts and the awfulness of the silent night. Lord Rutherford came to her once, but it was only to say that she must not mind being left by herself, for Blanche wanted him; and Maude knew well what that meant. It was the case every evening. He professed to be with her when Blanche was gone to bed, but he never remained for more than a few minutes. If Blanche was wakeful, he sat in her room fancying she would want him; and if she was asleep, he lingered in the outer apartment listening for any sound or movement. Since they came to Rutherford he had chosen to sleep in a room close to hers; but this did not satisfy him, and again and again, in the course of the night, he would steal into her chamber to look at her, as if fearful that during those short hours of absence, death would remove from him without warning the treasure in which his heart delighted.

The next day was to be the last but one of their stay at Rutherford. Afterwards they were to move by easy stages to the sea-side, as Blanche could bear the journey; and, if she found herself sufficiently strengthened to endure a further change, it was proposed to take her for about a fortnight to St. Ebbe's, that she might pay a parting visit to Mrs. Howard before leaving England. So they planned—the earl, Dr. Granville, and Maude—when she was called in to the consultation, neither choosing to allow what was in all their thoughts, and satisfying themselves by the expectation that sea-air would bring a respite of the evil day, though it could never work a restoration to health. Blanche gave no voice on the question; she had but one wish—to do what was considered best. Submission was her last trial of duty, and the little energy which remained to her was exercised in disciplining herself into quiet acquiescence with whatever might be deemed beneficial. And there was one part of the projected plan which, as the earl had anticipated when it was formed, reconciled her to it in the whole. Even her love for Rutherford was scarcely equal to the depth of interest and gratitude with which she thought of St. Ebbe's. When life is failing, and the future in this world becoming blank, memory returns with affection, tenfold increased, to the scenes and the events of the past: and where could Blanche find any recollections so calm, and holy, and bright, as those which were associated with St. Ebbe's? Once more to see it; once more to see her earliest and truest friend; once more to thank her for her loving care, her prayers, her counsel; to tell her, if time should be granted, the short history of those few months—few in number but infinite in importance—which had constituted the actual trial of her young life, and then to die;—where, when, how—as God in His wisdom should appoint; that was her last eager wish, the last earthly craving of her heart.

They were together again, Maude and Blanche, the following morning. Business which the earl could not postpone had called him for an hour away, and Blanche, feeling stronger after her night's rest, was sitting nearly upright on the sofa, with her jewel-case on a little stand by her; whilst Maude, with a pencil and paper in her hand, was writing down her wishes respecting her ornaments. They were both very quiet and composed; no one coming into the room would have supposed that they were engaged in anything more painful than usual, except at occasional moments, when a torrent of recollections rushed upon Blanche as she looked at some present from her father, and putting it aside would say perhaps that she could not give that away; she would rather he should keep it as part of herself.

"You shall let him have the paper, dear Maude," she said, when the task was nearly completed. "He will like to see that it is all done himself, by-and-by; though I cannot talk to him about it now. And if there is anything left that I have forgotten, and he does not know quite what to do with it, will you and Eleanor help him? for you will be friends with poor Eleanor for my sake, wont you?"

Maude's reply was inarticulate, though she tried to speak.

"And one thing more may I say to you, dear Maude?" continued Blanche, earnestly. "I long to have it all off my mind this morning, that I may tell Dr. Wentworth I have done what he wished when he comes this afternoon."

"If you talk much you will not be able to see him," said Maude, kindly. "You are quite overworked as it is."

"It will take but a few minutes," replied Blanche, "and to-morrow I should like to have quite free, because —"

"Yes," interrupted Maude, quickly; "I know. Go on, if you wish it."

Blanche waited for an instant. A thought of bitterness was to be struggled with and conquered; that her father, changed though he was in many ways, shrunk from the idea of being with her when she received the Holy Communion. Presently, she said to Maude, "That was a sad time at Senilhurst. I don't like thinking about it; but I am afraid sometimes that I must have seemed wrong in what I did, and I know I was cross with you. Wont you give me a kiss, now, and tell me you forgive me?"

It was all Maude could do to answer; but she did say, "It was I who was wrong and cross, and want to be forgiven;" and then she gave the kiss that was asked, and both were happier.

"There is a bracelet for Adelaide in my dressing-case," said Blanche, after a short pause. "It is too gay for your taste, Maude; she will value it, at least I hope she will, by-and-by, because my aunt gave it me."

"A long by-and-by that will be," observed Maude, speaking her thoughts aloud.

"Not so long, I hope, as you fancy," replied Blanche, cheerfully; adding, in a graver tone, whilst she looked steadily at Maude to see whether she understood her, "I could almost blame myself sometimes, when I think of the break-up of all your family happiness."

"There never was happiness with us," replied Maude, with emphasis; "never, as far back as I can remember. When I was a child of seven years old, I felt the hollowness and unreality of all about me. Nothing that you could have done or said, Blanche, would have made things better then they are."

"I hope not," replied Blanche; "yet even if I could——"

Maude finished her sentence; "you would not have been right in yielding; no, indeed, I feel that: you must be quite assured I do;" and Maude smiled brightly, and almost sweetly, for even this slight acknowledgment was a weight removed from her mind.

"If I had given way, I should have been very sorry afterwards," said Blanche. "That is one thing for which I have so much cause to thank Mrs. Howard, that she taught me in difficulties to look at actions as I should look upon them when—when I was as I am now—dying."

Maude's face showed, though unconsciously to herself, the pain which any allusion to Blanche's state gave her.

"I did not mean to grieve you, dear Maude," said Blanche, taking her hand affectionately: "but it is always in my own thoughts, and so I forget that it may not always be in others. And it makes all things so different; so very, very different. I can't exactly tell you what it is like; but, in a way, it is as if one had been amusing oneself with what seemed to be a a doll, a plaything, and suddenly, whilst one held it in one's hand, it had started into life, and become a living being. All the past is so awfully real. I feel," she added, her cheek becoming flushed with excitement; "I feel that it cannot die with me—that it must live on here—working for good or for evil. That one action, especially, would have been very dreadful, Maude, to think of now; would it not? To have been the means of bringing harm upon hundreds; and to know that, when I was resting in my grave, it would still be spreading. Oh! Maude, sometimes I think that even Heaven itself could not be Heaven with such a thought."

Maude was saved the pain of reply, for Lord Rutherford came into the room. Blanche hastily closed her jewel-case, and welcoming him with a smile, told him she had been better all the morning, and was better then; only she had tired herself with giving some directions.

"You were unwise to trouble yourself, my darling," was the earl's reply; "trust to Maude and Barnes; I am sure they will do everything you wish."

Blanche was silent. Lord Rutherford's eye accidentally fell upon the paper which Maude had been writing;—it was merely a list of different articles, with names attached to them: but love has a piercing sight; he understood it in an instant.

"I will take it," he said, holding out his hand as Maude folded the paper, and was going to put it hurriedly aside. Maude gave it him and left the room.

Blanche raised her eyes to meet her father's; he was very pale, but his voice scarcely trembled as he said, "It shall all be done;" and placing the paper carefully in his pocket-book, he walked to the window.

CHAPTER XXV.

AND now it was all arranged, all settled, and ordered; and Blanche had gone through the trying service for which she had been preparing, and said her last words of gratitude to Dr. Wentworth and told him he had comforted her and helped her, and begged him to write to her when she was away; and Maude had received every minute direction as to her cousin's wishes, in case she should never return to Rutherford; and the earl had pleased himself—for the moment it was really a pleasure, though a melancholy one—in contriving everything for the journey, so as to save Blanche, as far as lay in the power of human ingenuity, from the otherwise unavoidable fatigues of a journey. His spirits rather rallied under the pressure of occupation; and a flickering hope began again to burn feebly in his breast. The physician had spoken so confidently of the benefit of sea-air; he thought it might work an improvement, or it might at least delay the progress of disease; and Blanche had, undoubtedly, appeared stronger the last few days; she had borne the preparation for removal much better than any one anticipated. It was a natural delusion, and neither Blanche nor Maude were unwilling to foster it. Both felt that even a deceitful hope was better, at that moment, than the despairing certainty which would have rendered exertion almost impossible.

True, they might under such circumstances have remained at Rutherford; but Blanche herself was beginning not to wish for this. She thought it likely that the sea-air might invigorate her, and enable her to visit St. Ebbe's with something of enjoyment; and she looked forward to the possibility with that last lingering of earthly satisfaction, which even the near prospect of Eternity cannot quench in the bosom of the young. And there was another reason for her wish, very different and wholly unselfish. If she left Rutherford now, there was, she was well aware, no probability of her return. When and where her last moments would be spent, God only knew; but at least her father would be spared the pain of associating them with his home. He would not watch over her, day by day, and accustom himself to see her in the same room, the same position, and then suddenly miss her from her place. Dreary as Rutherford would, under any circumstances, be without her, the shock of the separation would be broken by their present removal; and her father would not so probably be tempted, as she had sometimes feared he might be, to rush from it in despair; and again, leaving the sphere of his duties, find refuge in solitary misery abroad. Yet the last evening in that her only real home was a grievous trial, for it was the first step towards the final breaking-up of earthly ties which she knew was before her. As she lay upon the sofa by herself, whilst Maude was engaged with her maid in the bed-room, and Lord Rutherford was talking to the steward in his study, she had leisure for thought, if she had been sufficiently strong. But she was not; she could only suffer fancies to pass before her; she could not control them: they were almost all of one kind—of her father, and her mother—her unhappy, but dearly cherished mother—the thought of whom seemed to give a resting-place to her human affections, when she fancied to herself the entrance upon another world. Leaving Rutherford seemed almost like deserting the countess's memory. It was the only place in which Blanche had learnt to know her. She wished she could go again into her room, to say farewell, as it were, to that which mostly had belonged to her. It was a strange mixture of feeling; the vision of her mother, at rest as she believed her to be, and waiting to receive her, was less vivid than the earthly image conjured up by her books and pictures, in the dreary desolate chamber, which told so truly the history of her life. Sight triumphed over faith, and tears of pity rose to Blanche's eyes; and all other feelings were forgotten in the intensity of longing, that she had been permitted to know her, to live with her and comfort her. That would have changed the whole current of her life; it might have made her a different person. Yet it must have been, in a measure, a barrier between her and her father, and Blanche turned away from such a thought; for how dearly she loved him she was just beginning to feel. Oh! if they could but have been as one! If now, when about to leave her father alone, she could at least restore to him the peace of mind of which the remembrance of her mother had robbed him! Then, it seemed, she could die happy, for she would leave him at rest; and something whispered to her that, if the bitterness of remorse was soothed, his mind would be more open to the principles and hopes of religion.

Blanche was thinking upon these things when she was aroused by a gentle tap at the door, almost immediately followed by the entrance of Eleanor Wentworth. This was the first day for nearly a week that they had met; and before, they had scarcely been together for more than a quarter of an hour at a time. Mrs. Wentworth's claims upon Eleanor's attention were incessant. No one else suited her; and her disposition, which perhaps in its original nature was exacting, as regarded those she loved, was now become so jealous and excitable, that it was painful to thwart her. It might have been from this cause that Eleanor was altered. Constant watchfulness and anxiety will work sad changes in a very short space of time, and Eleanor's face told a tale of great trial in her daily life. Or there might have been a deeper cause for the alteration—regret and self-reproach for the past, and forebodings of evil to come. The experience of one year, had brought memories which must last for life; and they had robbed her voice of its joyous tone, and had quenched the sparkle of her eye, and subdued the elasticity of her step: and when friends pitied her, and her father caressed her, Eleanor would often turn away in apparent coldness, but real wretchedness, because she knew that the griefs which excited their compassion were the consequences of her own misconduct.

It was only with Blanche that she was quite free. Blanche knew everything; all her resolutions and her failings, her temptations and her weakness. She could go back with her to their simple life at St. Ebbe's, and recal the serious devotedness of purpose with which they had knelt together at their confirmation; the earnestness and awe with which they had afterwards received their first Communion, and the energy with which they had entered upon the duties of life—armed by the same counsel, and animated by affection for the same friend. How widely since that time their paths had diverged Eleanor dreaded to think. Blanche, purified and strengthened by illness, was so far removed from herself that she seemed scarcely like a creature of the same sphere. Yet still she understood; still, even before Eleanor, could venture to enter upon the subject of her wanderings from the right path, Blanche seemed, by an intuitive perception, to comprehend them: and the few hours which they occasionally spent together, were seasons of salutary, though mournful, rest to poor Eleanor's wounded spirit; and were treasured in her recollection to be prized, she could not yet tell how dearly, when death should have parted them, and there should be no one left to whom she could say, "So we acted," or "so we thought and spoke, when we were children."

For it was not yet that she could fully understand the danger of Blanche's state. She came into the room that evening looking almost happy, merely because Lord Rutherford had told her that Blanche was much better than they could have expected, considering all she had gone through during the day. She had never been accustomed to the fluctuations of consumption; and she had heard of persons recovering who were much worse than she imagined Blanche to be; and, sanguine by nature, she could not divest herself of hope. Her spirits also had for the hour rallied as regarded her home-trials. Her mother seemed tolerably comfortable; and a penitent, affectionate—though melancholy—letter had been received from Charles, which had softened her father's feelings and melted his indignation into pity. It was this subject which first suggested itself when she found that Blanche was able to listen to her.

"I would have brought you the letter, dear Blanche," she said, as she took off her bonnet and sat down by the sofa; "but I was afraid you would be too busy and tired to attend to it. I don't know exactly why one should be pleased at what is evidently written very much out of spirits; but it is the tone which papa and I like. There is so much feeling for us, and so much thought for poor mamma."

"And Adelaide! Does she write too?" asked Blanche, always ready, even when weakened by illness, to throw herself into the interests of others.

"She sends her love in a postscript; but I am afraid that is only a matter of form. It is about her that Charles is worrying himself. She is just beginning to feel what the privations of a soldier's wife are, where there is no money; and I am afraid she reproaches him. She need not do that, though," added Eleanor, with some bitterness. "He has sacrificed as much for her as she has for him."

"They will be happier when they are abroad, I hope," said Blanche. "There will not be the same looking-back and longing for luxuries; and I think, after a time, my aunt and Sir Hugh will forgive them."

"It is not forgiveness which will make them happy," said Eleanor, with a heavy sigh. "Two people utterly unsuited must be miserable, if they had the wealth of Peru at command. That is the real wretchedness, and that is what I reproach myself for. I knew so well, from the very beginning, that they were no more fitted for each other than I am to be Queen of England. I believe, in fact, it was that which deluded me. I fancied that Charles never could be so blind as really to fall in love. But, Blanche, I want to talk of other things now, other people rather."

"Mrs. Howard and St. Ebbe's?" said Blanche, with a smile of interest.

Eleanor could not smile. She answered, sadly, "Yes, I want to talk of her, and to send a message; but I don't exactly know what. You must tell her—"

"Everything I can think of about you," said Blanche. "She will want to know everything."

"I could almost make up my mind to write to her by you," continued Eleanor; "but there is so much that I dread saying. She knows all the facts about me, those I have been forced to mention; but there are other things. Oh, Blanche! what would I not give to be you; to go back to her unchanged!"

Blanche stretched out her wasted hand, and said, "Not quite unchanged."

"No, not unchanged; you are right: but altered, advanced, beyond, far beyond whatever she would have imagined possible. Do you know, Blanche, there are times when it seems actually impossible that we could ever have been brought up together; and that my advantages were as great, even greater than yours. I cannot understand it, till I retrace it all, step by step, and see how I have gone back."

"You are always reproaching yourself, dearest," said Blanche; "I wish I could feel you were to have happier thoughts, now that I am going away."

"Happier when you are away!" exclaimed Eleanor, and tears filled her eyes: "that would be impossible; and then my mother—but we must not talk about her. I am obliged not to think more than I can help; for you know, Blanche, I cannot deceive myself; it has been in a great measure my doing; and that was what I wanted to say to Mrs. Howard. I should like her to know the worst; for she will feel for me, however she may blame me."

"And have you not written to her at all, lately?" asked Blanche, with some surprise.

"Yes, in a certain way; I have written facts—not the sort of letters she would wish to have, I know. But I could not bring myself to do it. You must tell her, Blanche. You must talk to her for me."

Blanche hesitated. "If I am able," she said; "but I am not going there directly; and I cannot tell how I may be when I get to St. Ebbe's."

Eleanor read what was in her mind, though for the moment the thought of her own griefs had absorbed her. "Blanche," she said, as she bent down and kissed her, "wherever you are, and however you may be, you will be happy." She waited eagerly for the answer, as if it would satisfy some rising doubt in her own mind.

A smile of inexpressible sweetness passed over Blanche's face, as she replied, "Yes, quite happy—quite. I had some fears—the dread of loneliness—of what, perhaps, I am to suffer at the last; but they are going. I do not wish to live."

"Papa does not think you worse," said Eleanor; "and Lord Rutherford says you are better."

Blanche smiled. "Yes, dearest; and I am not worse: perhaps even I am better. I may linger—I may return; but it is not probable—scarcely possible."

"And to part from you now, for ever; to live without you!" exclaimed Eleanor, bursting into a passionate flood of tears. "You are so young: they said you were so strong: there is no consumption in your family."

"I would rather see the truth," replied Blanche, quietly. "It is much better for me, for then I can prepare myself; and you must let me say to-night what I would, if I were quite sure of our never meeting again on earth."

"No, no," exclaimed Eleanor; "I cannot bear it; I cannot listen to it; and we shall meet again."

"Yes, indeed, in heaven. God grant it," said Blanche, solemnly, and Eleanor buried her face in her hands. Blanche waited for her to speak, but there was neither voice nor sound, save the ticking of the clock, which marked the minutes that were speeding towards Eternity. Then Blanche raised herself on the sofa, and said, as she joined her hands together and a flush tinged her ashy cheek, "We have often talked of this hour; we have thought what it would be to die. Eleanor, dearest, it is very awful—very real; more real far than anything in life, except prayer and communion with God."

"And that I have neglected," said Eleanor, without raising her head.

"Yes," continued Blanche, in the same earnest tone, "you have told me so; and I have thought about it when I have been lying here alone; and I hoped I might ask you—I might beg you—the wishes of the dying are sacred," she added, her voice changing into a touching gentleness of entreaty.

Eleanor rose from her seat, and, kneeling beside her, said, "Ask me what you will, if only I may be like you."

"I can see—I think I can," continued Blanche, what has been my own safety, in a measure, as far as I have been safe:—or rather," she added, correcting herself, "what has been permitted to help me. It was my rule—my order for every day; order in my prayers, I mean; not leaving them to chance or feeling, but being forced to go at fixed times. It was Mrs. Howard's wish that first made me feel that I was forced, and then it became necessary."

"Mrs. Howard gave me thc rule too," said Eleanor humbly, "but I did not keep it."

"But now, now, for my sake—in memory of me, when I am gone. Eleanor, it is my last wish, because I feel that in your case it involves all other duties. Only promise me that once in the day, not merely in the morning and at night, you will pray."

And Eleanor kissed her, and answered, "I will promise; but I shall never be like you."

Blanche sank back, with a smile, as if a weight had been taken from her mind, and after a moment's silence continued, "And one thing more I would say whilst time is granted me to speak. I would say it rather than write it, because I can speak it more earnestly, more truly, as it should be spoken. I told you I was happy. Eleanor, that does not express what I feel; it is all so strange and overpowering. But there is something beyond happiness—rest, peace, love." Her dark eyes were lighted up with the sparkling flash of intense feeling, as she added, "Love which is perfect, satisfying; the dream of my childhood, which now I have found." She became very exhausted, and Eleanor seeing that her presence was exciting, felt that she must go. But as she stood up to depart it seemed impossible. Blanche motioned to her to sit down again; Eleanor paused. She went to the table and took up a large morocco case, which she had laid upon it on her first entrance.

"Stay a few minutes longer," said Blanche; "I will not talk."

Eleanor approached her; the case was in her hand. "Hark!" she said, "it is six o'clock. My mother will be wanting me."

Blanche looked up with the impulse to send a message, but a blank, miserable recollection, checked her.

"She sent her love to you to-day," continued Eleanor, unable to restrain her tears, "and —" she held out the case.

Blanche stretched out her hand, but it was quite powerless; and she could only say in a feeble tone, "Open it."

"I will leave it with you," said Eleanor, "it is—"

"Yes, I know; open it—let me see it."

And Eleanor touched the spring, and revealed the bright, lovely features of the young Countess of Rutherford. The mother and the child;—how like! and yet how different! As Blanche motioned to Eleanor to place the picture near her, and Eleanor's eye wandered from one to the other, she could almost have supposed that the tale of each sweet face had been reversed; that the radiant beauty displayed by the artist was the image of Blanche just entering upon the world's enjoyments; and that the worn, sunk features of the gentle girl, were the signs of the life of sorrow about to find repose in death.

Blanche gazed at the picture long and silently. "Thank her," she said at length to Eleanor, in a trembling voice, "very much. Tell her—you know how I value it."

"It should have been yours before, dearest," said Eleanor.

"No, no; it is in time. It will do its work;" and turning away her head, she murmured, "he has made me happy, and she will forgive."

Eleanor drew near to say, good b'ye.

"God bless you, Eleanor, my own precious Eleanor; and keep you safe. Think of me when you pray—in Church—always;" and Eleanor could only answer by sobs, and the half-uttered, delusive hope, that they might meet again.

CHAPTER XXVI.

WHY should we linger so fondly over the last hours of the dying?—why should we delight to dwell upon the form and lineaments, and expression of that which is now so loved, and valued, but which soon must be hidden from our sight?—why should we treasure up each word and tone to be recalled in the hour of desolation, and pierce with a deeper anguish the heart that already is crushed to the dust? We are but adding to our grief: yet we would rather cherish it than part from it; for it is dearer than happiness, more precious than joy, since it is instinct with the hopes of immortality. It is a grief, however, which needs no description. We have but to ask our own hearts; and, even if the dread experience has as yet been spared us, we can tell all the outward forms which it must assume. That last departure from Rutherford, who cannot picture it? The momentary excitement—the struggle of conflicting feelings—of dying hope, and ever-present fear—the petty cares, and ordinary trials of a journey, and the never-ceasing anxiety and dread felt through all, lest the change should have been made too late.

The earl hoped, even then; though he thought he did not. If he had not hoped, he never would have taken Blanche away, for he saw at last how much it cost her. The pain of fatigue she could not hide, though the pain of regret she could. There is something in the very name of home inexpressibly dear to us when we are very ill; and Blanche's home, notwithstanding all her disappointments, had been a very happy one. But she left it without a word of complaint, or expression of sorrow; only with a few silent tears, as she looked for the last time on the window of her mother's chamber, and raised herself to smile a farewell to Eleanor, who, unable to leave Mrs. Wentworth as she had anticipated, was standing at the rectory gate to see her pass.

But that parting was over and the journey was borne with tolerable ease; and Blanche reached the place of her destination, and felt the freshness of the sea-breeze, and saw the sparkling of the bright waters beneath a brilliant noon-day sun; and, strengthened for a few days, seemed to enjoy her daily drive and the novelty of the view, and thought—yes, still she thought, and knew—that she was dying.

Yet days went by as before. Habits and customs, and old familiar ways and interests, crowd around us, even to the last; and in the spacious mansion, where provided with every luxury of refinement, guarded from every blast, shaded from every intruding glare, Blanche was learning to prepare herself for Heaven, there was a common life of vexing thoughts and worldly occupations pressing forward, eager, hopeful, save when it approached the sick chamber of her upon whose young brow was written the doom of all earthly beauty, "passing away."*

There all was stilled as in the presence of an angel visitant. For it grew, day by day, even hour by hour, the pure ethereal beauty of that heaven-born spirit which is the portion of God's elect. When

* From the stars of heaven and the flowers of earth,
From the pageant of power and the voice of mirth,
From the mists of morn on the mountain's brow,
From childhood's song and affection's vow—
From all, save that o'er which soul bears sway,
Breathes but one record—passing away.
MRS. HEMANS.

Blanche had put aside her few earthly cares, she was able to fix her thoughts steadily upon eternity. The world to which she was hastening became her home, and though her perceptions were dim, and her anticipations vague, she could still dwell upon some certainties, before which all earthly joys faded into nothingness.

She would be sinless there and at rest;—at rest in the presence of her Saviour; and the blessedness of that hope none can tell but they to whom every earthly affection is secondary. It was no dream to Blanche, that the love of God alone can satisfy the human heart; it was a fact, taught by each day's experience. The Being to whom she could turn in every trial, however slight; the Friend whose presence she always felt; the love which could never change, even with the changes of her own weak, unstable heart; were realities, beneath which her sinking spirit reposed as beneath "the shadow of a great rock in a weary land." When the terror of death overwhelmed her, she turned to them with an unutterable sense of safety and relief; whilst every trifling comfort and every moment of ease were regarded as the sure pledges of that untiring watchfulness which, if it guarded her so carefully in life, could never leave her lonely in death.

And it was not trust merely that Blanche felt. Trust is our faith in a Power; love is our devotion to a Person. She had trusted all her life, and she had loved too, more than she knew. Now she was beginning to comprehend her own heart, to understand its yearnings after perfection, its cravings for a fullness of affection which she had been told could be found on earth, but which she had often feared might, if it satisfied her, border upon idolatry. She could not envy others, even with the purest prospects of this world's happiness. She had found "the pearl of great price," and the wealth of the universe would have been worthless in its exchange.

Lord Rutherford saw that she was happy, and even in the midst of his anguish he could not be insensible to the comfort; yet the sight of "the peace which passeth understanding" was often goading to his self-reproach, since it seemed to widen the gulf that separated him and his child.

He was alone with Blanche, one evening, about a fortnight after their removal from Rutherford, and she was speaking to him of St. Ebbe's, and of her wish to go there soon, and saying that she was becoming anxious about it, for the distance was not very great;—she thought they might return if—she paused, and then finished her sentence firmly—if she should live.

He did not shrink from her words; but, as he fondly smoothed her hair, replied, that he did not see she was worse, but he was afraid she must be.

"Yes," she said, she knew that she was worse, for she was weaker; and she had spoken to Dr. Granville, and asked what he thought about her going to St. Ebbe's, and he had told her that if she really wished it so very much he could not say no, but he would not advise it. "I will not urge it, if you don't like it, dear papa," she added; "but Mrs. Howard could only come to me for one night, without great difficulty, and——"

The earl interrupted her, "Wish it, my child! my wishes against yours!"

"They ought to be against mine," said Blanche, "if you like it; but you have always been so kind; you have spoiled me, and now I am bent upon my own way." She spoke lightly and playfully, as she might have done months before. It was the voice more than the words which touched the weak chord of the earl's heart, and made the tears gather in his eyes.

"You have quite spoiled me," continued Blanche, in the same tone; but it changed the next moment, for her father was leaning his head against her pillow in silent wretchedness. "You must let me thank you," she said. "By-and-by, you will like to think of me as happy always—happy in my life with you, and very—very happy in my rest."

He raised his head and kissed her, and sank back into the same posture.

Blanche considered for a few moments, and then she continued. "Being ill has been a comfort to me in many ways; because we have been so much together, and we have been able to read the same books, and have liked the same things; and you will always like them now, dear papa; wont you, for my sake?"

Lord Rutherford could only press her hand; he had not words to answer.

"I have enjoyed so very much your reading to me every day," continued Blanche; "and it seems strange now, that I should ever have been afraid of asking you; but I know that, when I first came home, I should have felt quite frightened if I had been told to do it. Things have changed very much since then."

"Yes;" replied the earl, in a hollow voice; "they have indeed."

"And changed to make us happier too," said Blanche, with a little hesitation. "It would have been much worse to part then, than it is now."

"No, no," exclaimed the earl. "If I had never known you, Blanche—if you were only a child whom I had scarcely seen—"

"We might have loved each other less," said Blanche; "but we could never have thought of parting with the same peace."

"Peace!" repeated the earl bitterly. "Peace for me!" and then, as he again buried his face in his hands, he murmured, "There is no peace but for the innocent."

"Papa, my own dear papa," said Blanche, in a tone of gentle reproach, as she forced him to move his head, and look at her.

"I am right," he answered moodily. "Peace is for you, my child; and for you I can accept it, and be thankful."

"It would not be my peace," said Blanche; "if it was not yours too."

"Then it can belong to neither of us," exclaimed the earl: "unless a new power is given to mortals to blot out the past."

"It must be blotted out for us all," replied Blanche, "before we can find peace."

"I know what you would say," replied the earl. "I have heard all that divines can preach; and have read their books, and thought about them, too. But, Blanche, my child, let it be even as they say; let forgiveness be granted from heaven, let there be no reckoning of our offences before God;—still, still there is memory. Memory," he repeated to himself, "that mocking fiend! Blanche, when you are gone from me, who will give me peace?"

Blanche paused—presently she said, "Papa, if I could come back to you and tell you I was happy, would you not be so?"

The earl looked at her with a faint smile.

"If you could see me," continued Blanche, "and knew that I had no wish to return to earth, and that my home was brighter than even you could desire to make it; and that I was with mamma; and that she loved you dearly, and was longing for you to come to her; and if there was a place ready for you—a place in Paradise—in rest; would it not be peace then?" Lord Rutherford averted his head. "It is there," continued Blanche, her feeble tones becoming more earnest; "I see it in my dreams, when I am by myself alone in the twilight. It is a home for us all, and you will come to me; and mamma—"

He turned quickly, and caught her hand; and, in a voice convulsed with emotion, said, "Tell her I have repented; ask her to forgive me."

Blanche made no immediate reply; but drew towards her the case containing her mother's picture, which was laid on the sofa by her side, and touching the spring, showed the sunny smile, the beauty of youth, and joy, and hope, on which the shadow of harshness or reproach seemed as if it could not for a moment rest.

"Look! papa," she said, as she threw her arms around him. "You have made her child happy, and does not she forgive?"

Lord Rutherford took the picture from her. Blanche watched him anxiously. She saw the furrowed brow bent in anguish, and the mouth quiver and the dark eye become dim; and then, large, scalding drops fell slowly down the earl's cheeks, and pressing the picture to his lips, he exclaimed passionately, "God bless and keep you both for ever;" and left the room.

Blanche missed the picture from that evening, and she never asked for it again.

CHAPTER XXVII.

Once more it was towards the close of a summer's day in the quaint garden of the manor house of St. Ebbe's; and long shadows fell upon the lawn, and marked the hours on the dial-plate as they fleeted by; and the heavy tones of the great cathedral clock resounded solemnly from afar, and mingled with and subdued the cheerful voices of children at their play.

Once more! oh, many and many a time afterwards might the gladness of the day melt gently into the stillness of night; and the loveliness of nature's repose give rest to the weary heart; and the lightness of childish glee echo merrily amidst the old grey walls; but never again would Blanche Evelyn rejoice in the rush of early memories which thronged around her, as she looked from the window of her own chamber on the first evening of her arrival at St. Ebbe's.

She could indeed rejoice—most happy amongst the happy—most blessed amongst the blest. With her father to watch over her, and smile mournfully, yet with the sweetness of a hope better than that of life; and Mrs. Howard to sit by her, and talk to her; and Maude to busy herself in the arrangements which now were so necessary to her comfort; that first evening was one of quiet, full contentment to herself—what it was to others we need not raise the veil which hides the bitterness of mortal grief to describe.

The first meeting had been a great shock to Mrs.

Howard, much greater than she dared express. She was not at all prepared for Blanche's extreme weakness; for letters seldom really describe in detail, and it is only by details that those well practised in the sad scenes of illness, can tell the real state. Lord Rutherford had said she seemed rather better; Maude had written to make preparation, as if she would be able to sit up a great deal, and even to drive out; and Blanche, herself, had expressed the utmost delight at the prospect of her visit, though she said plainly that she felt it must be her last.

They were all then deluding themselves; looking forward to months! Mrs. Howard, when she saw her, could not hope for weeks. Yet she met Blanche calmly and cheerfully; congratulated Lord Rutherford on her having borne the journey so well; and suffered her to talk as long as she could about all that had passed; and then, when Blanche at length went to bed, quite worn out, Mrs. Howard retired to her own room, to find comfort in solitude for that heavy aching of the heart, which could not even obtain relief from tears.

This state of things continued for a few days; at least Lord Rutherford fancied that it did. He did not know every symptom of the complaint; and he had been so accustomed lately to its changes, that he was almost beginning to think little of them. Blanche was more feverish, he thought—but that he attributed to excitement—and he urged Mrs. Howard, to keep her more quiet; and Mrs. Howard, complying with his request, would take her work and sit in the room, and intend not to talk. But the intention could not easily be kept—there was so much to say and to hear; and Blanche felt so inexpressibly relieved when she could unburthen herself of the accumulated weight of anxieties which had grown up since they parted, and be assured that she had acted under them well and wisely. It was such a comfort, too, to speak of her father, and point out the indications of his change of mind, on which she so fondly dwelt; and to find that Mrs. Howard viewed them as she did herself. She tried to be quiet and unexcited, and for hours she would lie perfectly still from weakness; but some thought or recollection would then strike her, and conversation began, almost unawares, again. This was injurious to her; but it mattered little. Perfect repose, both of body and mind, could scarcely have retarded the progress of a disease, which, by trifling variations and imperceptible changes in its symptoms, too surely bore the mandate of approaching death.

No one saw it but Mrs. Howard. How she endured the certainty, without distressing others by her own convictions, she could never comprehend, except by referring her calmness to the support which is always sent when it is needed. Her love for Blanche was no common feeling: it had in it the strength of her long attachment to the Countess of Rutherford, and of the entire devotion of a mother to Blanche during her childhood; and the year which had parted them, though it had been full of incident and change to herself, had never separated them in thought. Still it had been her proud desire to see Blanche in her own home, shedding far around the light and charm of her goodness, and her beauty; and even when she said to herself that all was better as it was —that Blanche might have sank under the great temptations to which she was exposed; or, even if she had conquered them, might, eventually, have fallen a prey to the morbid depression of spirits which had so often shown itself in her mother's family—yet it was hard, really, to feel the truth of her own words. She knew it was best that Blanche should go—it was the appointment of Infinite Love; and it could not be other than merciful. Yet how was the parting to be endured?

They had been together about a week, and during that time Blanche had taken two drives, which seemed however to fatigue her; and Lord Rutherford therefore said, she had better wait till the weather was a little cooler. So she remained in the house, and tried to read a little, but her eyes were weak, and it was a trouble to her to hold a book in her hand. Lord Rutherford read to her occasionally, but she could not listen long; and for the last two days she had found it as much as she could bear to attend during the daily visits of the clergyman—the rector who had prepared her for confirmation. Her father was generally with her at these times, for she was not able to be left alone; and she liked him to kneel by her side, holding her hand in his, and repeating the prayers with her. He scarcely ever spoke more than was quite necessary, but he never seemed impatient or wearied; and Blanche could perceive a marked change in the tone in which he said the Confession. It was earnest and humble, as if it was a relief to him to join in it.

Blanche was quite sure that his feelings about religion were very different from what they had been; but she did not dare talk to him about them; and she could not ask him why he had altered so much since the day of their short conversation, when she had shown him the countess's picture. She fancied that perhaps he really felt now that her mother had forgiven him; and with that load of remorse and despair taken from his mind, she hoped he might shrink less from the thought of receiving the Holy Communion with her. She could scarcely realise the comfort that would be to them both; but she did not know how to approach the subject. It was difficult to tell whether she might or ought. He had neglected it she feared for so many years; though she knew that, as a very young man, he had been accustomed to receive it regularly; and once he had alluded to it and sighed, as if those were better and happier times than he could ever expect to return. She said something to Mrs. Howard about it, and hoped that through her it might be named to the rector; and that he would suggest what she might do. But one or two days slipped by, and there were some reasons for delay; and when the rector called again, Blanche was not able to see him. She was much later that morning than usual in waking, for she had scarcely slept at all during the early part of the night. Mrs. Howard thought she had better not leave her bed, but she was anxious to be dressed, for she thought she should be more comfortable; and they brought her into the sitting-room, in the afternoon, and laid her on the sofa, which was drawn in front of the window. Lord Rutherford was to have gone into the town in the afternoon; but she looked so ill, that he did not like to leave her, even for half an hour, and he sat in the room with her, writing; for she could not listen to reading. The house was kept very quiet, and Mrs. Howard and Maude were by themselves a great part of the time, for they were afraid to disturb her by having too many in the room. They did not go to her till it was growing late; and, when they opened the door, Lord Rutherford was reading one of the prayers from the Visitation Service; and they closed it again very softly and went away. Blanche had borne that so well that the earl thought he might venture to talk to her, and he kissed her, and said, it had been a bad day, but he hoped they should have a better one to-morrow.

Blanche smiled doubtfully. "Yes," she replied; it had been a bad day in many ways, but it had been very quiet, and she had not been suffering pain, except a little occasionally, and she was very glad to be able to be dressed and come into the sitting-room once more. "I don't think I shall come in to-morrow," she added.

The earl turned pale; "I am glad to see the sun set again," continued Blanche, "because I was always so fond of it—the sunset here especially. Papa, it was just at this very time in the evening, last year, that you came; do you recollect it?"

Poor Lord Rutherford! what would he not have given to have been able to forget?

"You will remember that sunset was my favourite time, wont you?" said Blanche; "and that it always seemed to me, when I was a child—and even sometimes it does now—as if it was part of Heaven, and as if all the forms of the clouds were real things, mountains and lakes. It is very bright and beautiful this evening," she added, gazing on it intently.

"We may hope to have many like it, at this time of the year," said the earl, in a tone which was fearfully calm.

"Yes, I hope you will have a great many," continued Blanche; "and you must not let them make you sad, dear papa; but you must think they are the pictures of my home—our home," she added, correcting herself.

The earl compressed his lips firmly together, and Blanche felt his hand tremble.

"You will take me back to Rutherford, I know," she said, after a pause, seeing that he could not trust himself to speak; "and, perhaps, by-and-by, you will be pleased to think that I am lying near you, when you are in church, as I used to think of mamma. And one thing, may I say it?—I cannot bear to pain you," and she kissed his forehead, and waited till he said "Go on."

"One thing I have a fancy about. I should not like anything grand to be put upon my coffin, only my name and the date, and a cross." She waited to take breath, for the exertion of much speaking was very trying.

"Anything else? tell me all," said the earl. He was summoning every effort to remain calm, for he knew now what these last wishes foreboded.

"I should be glad to feel that you would not go away from Rutherford," said Blanche; even then shrinking from that which might appear dictating to him. "I like to fancy that you will be near where I am resting; and I should feel that all the poor people whom I care about would be thought of; and that Dr. Wentworth would have some one to help him in what he wants to do in the parish. Perhaps by-and-by you would try and remember me to some of the old persons I used to visit, and to poor Susannah Dyer. I wrote their names down one day to give to you. Maude has the paper."

"Is that all?" said the earl.

"Yes, all; except the directions I gave before I left home, and"—she pointed to her Bible, from which the earl had been accustomed to read to her. "It was given to me by Mrs. Howard, on the day of my confirmation," she said; "will you keep it and love it? and——"

"Read it?" said the earl, earnestly; "Yes; that indeed I may promise."

"It is marked," continued Blanche. "I think you will understand the marks. I have put the date to some of the lessons which you have read to me; and there is my Prayer Book also; the Psalms I like best for prayers are marked in that." She feebly turned the pages, till the book was opened at the office for the Holy Communion. It was headed by a date of the preceding year. "The day of my first

Communion," she said, pointing to it; and as the earl bent down to look nearer, or, possibly, to hide the feelings which were visible in his face, she added, "Will you mark it with the date of the last? to-morrow, if it may be."

"To-morrow! Blanche, my precious, precious child; I cannot part with you. God forgive me! Oh grant that I may bear it!"

Blanche would not let him give way. She said, he must not; it would be wrong now when they had such infinite comfort; when they were one—one whatever might happen. The next Communion might not be the last; but she thought it would; and she was going to ask him to write to the rector, and fix it decidedly. It had been left a little uncertain on the preceding day. The earl seized some note-paper, and began to write. Blanche put out her hand to stop him. Her look was so anxious, so pleading, that he threw aside his pen, and knelt beside her. "Together," said Blanche, and in her agitation, she gasped for breath; "for the first and last time together." And as the earl bent his head upon her hand his answer was, "Pray for me, that I may not be rejected."

Blanche was taken early to her bed that evening, for she was very much weakened, and in some pain; and her breathing was very short. Lord Rutherford sat up with her, and Mrs. Howard. Till this sudden change it had been sufficient to have a servant sleeping in her room. The earl looked ill and worn, but no one thought of advising him to go to rest.

Blanche was very restless all the night, and they could not quiet her in any way; though sometimes Mrs. Howard said a verse of a Psalm to her, and she appeared to like it. She scarcely spoke, except to ask for a little tea; but she was quite sensible, and smiled at her father when he came up to her, and followed him with her eye when he turned away; and, at last, after he had been trying to settle her more comfortably, she laid her head on the pillow, resting on his arm, and fell asleep with her hand clasped in his.

She slept in this way for about an hour and a half, and woke as if startled. Lord Rutherford was in the room with her alone. There was a change; he saw that directly, and rang the bell.

Blanche looked up eagerly, and tried to say something, and the earl bent down to catch the words: "Will he come? Will there be time, do you think?" she asked.

The earl hesitated for an instant. Then he answered with perfect composure: "We can send, and he will come at any moment;" and Blanche joined her thin hands, and said, "Thank God," and sank quietly back on the pillow.

It was but half an hour from that time, and the Service for the Communion of the Sick was celebrated in Blanche's dying chamber. Mrs. Howard, Maude, and Lord Rutherford kneeling by her bed.

And it was over—and Lord Rutherford knelt still; and Blanche's eyes closed, and her lips moved in prayer. A few minutes passed of peace unutterable; and then Blanche faintly smiled upon Mrs. Howard and Maude; and tried to press her father's hand, and whispered: "Papa, good b'ye." The earl raised his head, but she never spoke again.

Long, long, he remained listening to the faint, scarcely perceptible breathing, until at length there was a gentle sigh,—and the stillness of death rested upon the features of his darling child.

They laid her to rest by her mother's side, in the vault beneath the chapel of the Evelyns, in the old church of Rutherford. There, not many years afterwards, reposed the mortal remains of one who, if a deep repentance can avail to obtain mercy, most surely carried with him to his grave, the pardon of God, as well as the blessing of man.

Lord Rutherford never left his home for more than a few months, when he returned to it after Blanche's death. If ambition, or indolence, or the love of pleasure had charms for him, they were sacrificed in the service of the Master, to whom, though late, he had devoted himself.

His memory is still cherished amongst his people. They talk of his truth and uprightness, his thoughtfulness and liberality, his piety and consistency; and if they say that he was cold in manner, and solitary in his habits, they know that he lived in spirit with the dead, and they marvel not that he had few affections left to devote to the living. Even now, when his castle is the possession of another, they point out the terrace where he used to walk,—sometimes with Maude, the only person who was ever known to visit him in his retirement, but oftener alone—watching the golden sunset intently, as if it was a reality of heaven rather than a dream of earth; and when they point to the escutcheon of his earthly glory, and sigh over the honours of a race extinct, there are many to pray that, like the last Earl of Rutherford, they may one day rest in the "sure and certain hope" of "those who sleep in Jesus."

END OF VOL. II.

Stevens and Co., Printers, Bell Yard, Temple Bar.

www.ingramcontent.com/pod-product-compliance
Lightning Source LLC
LaVergne TN
LVHW020913110826
845150LV00004B/663

* 9 7 8 1 4 2 5 5 5 5 9 1 7 *